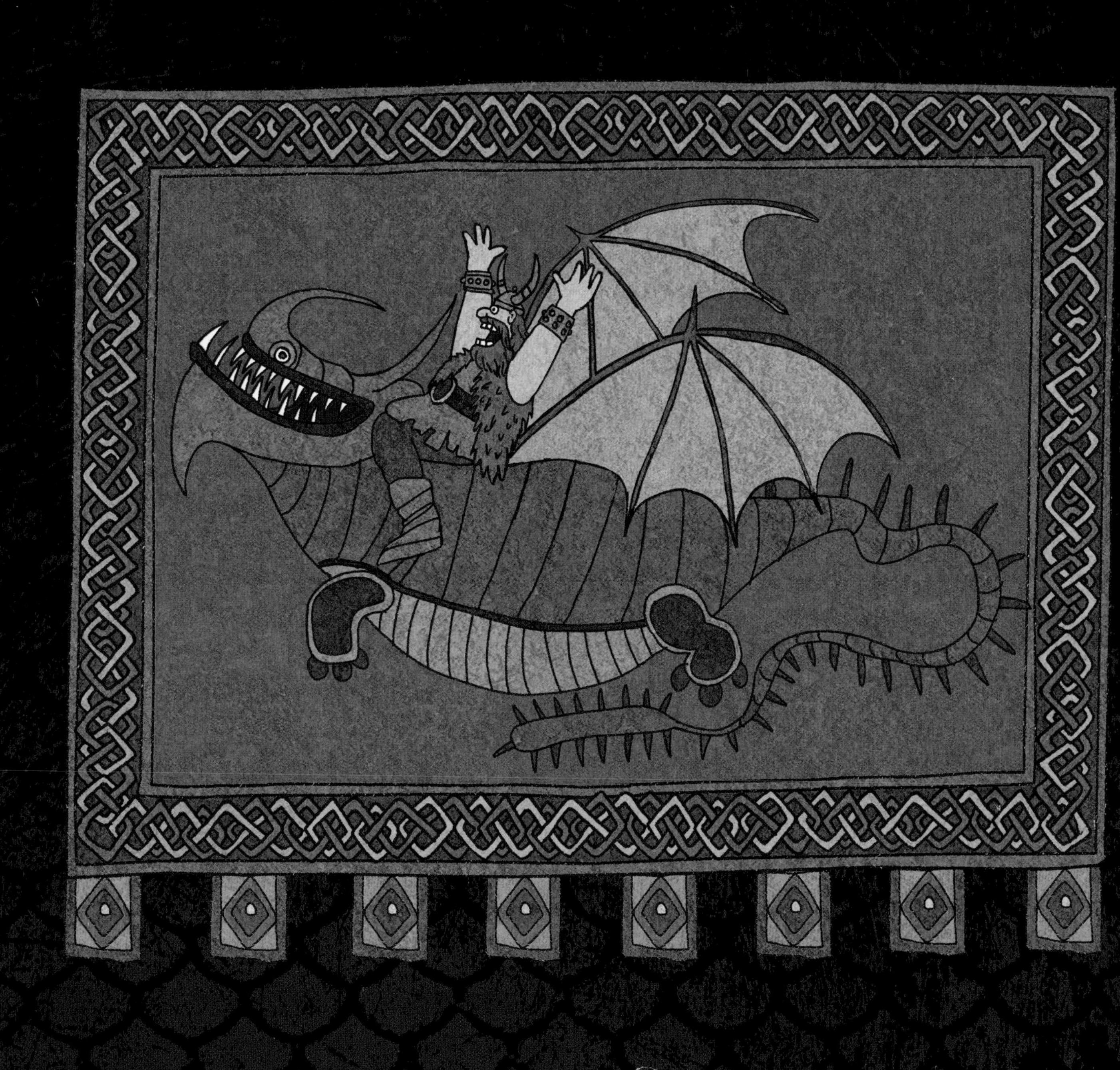

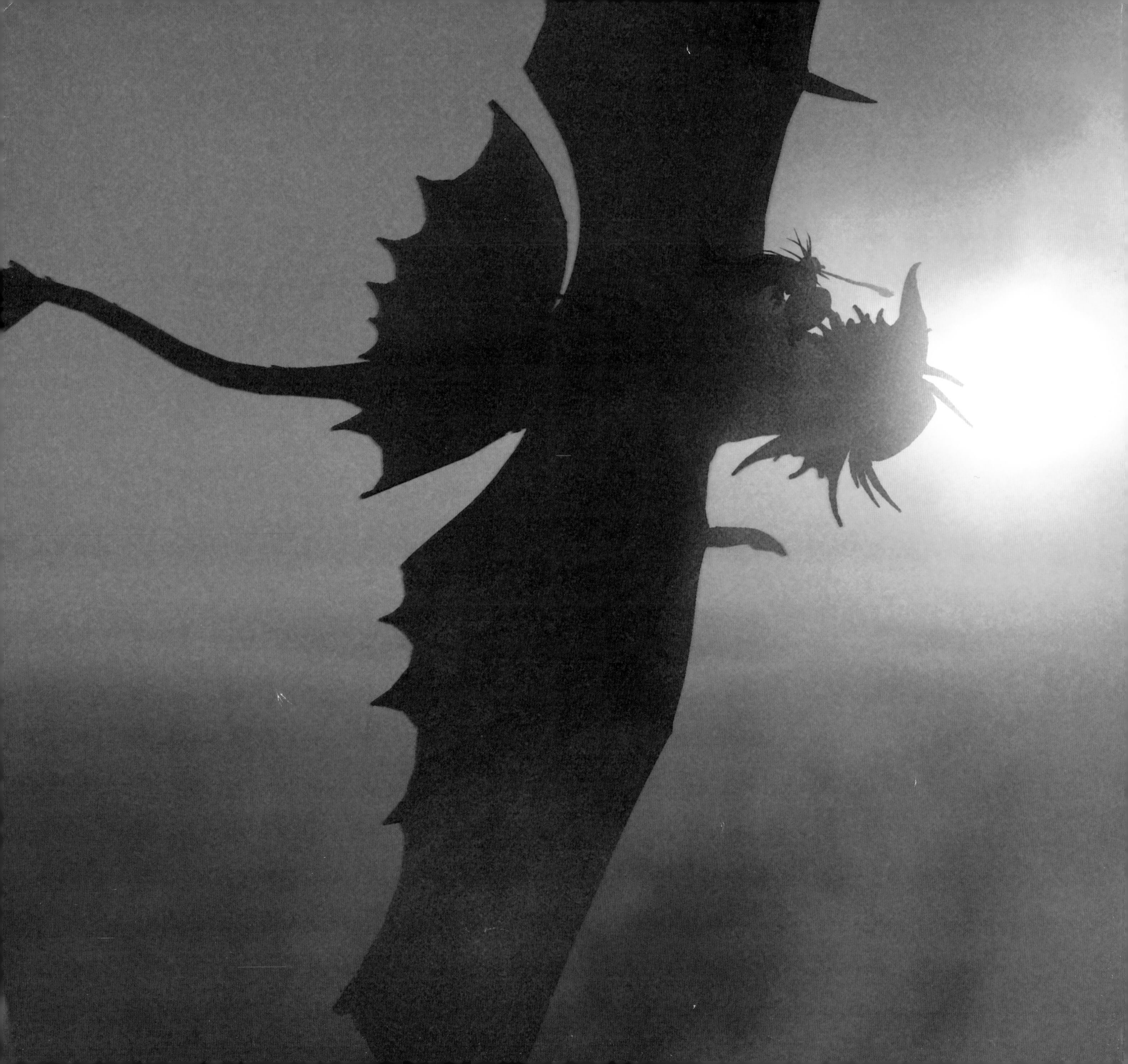

*Foreword by*
Gerard Butler
*Introduction by*
Dean DeBlois
*Text by*
Linda Sunshine

The Art of

DreamWorks

# How to Train Your Dragon 2

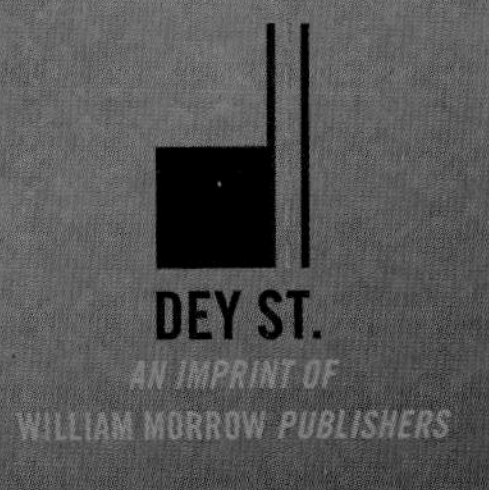

 For information address HarperCollins Publishers, 10 East 53rd Street, New York, NY 10022.

HarperCollins books may be purchased for educational, business, or sales promotional use. For information please e-mail the Special Markets Department at SPsales@harpercollins.com.

FIRST EDITION

Designed by Iain R. Morris

Library of Congress Cataloging-in-Publication Data has been applied for.

ISBN: 978-0-06-232335-4

19 ID6/IG 10 9 8 7 6 5

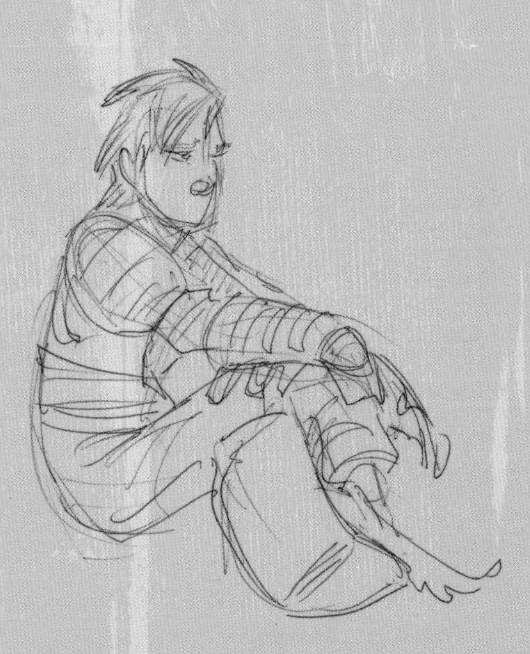

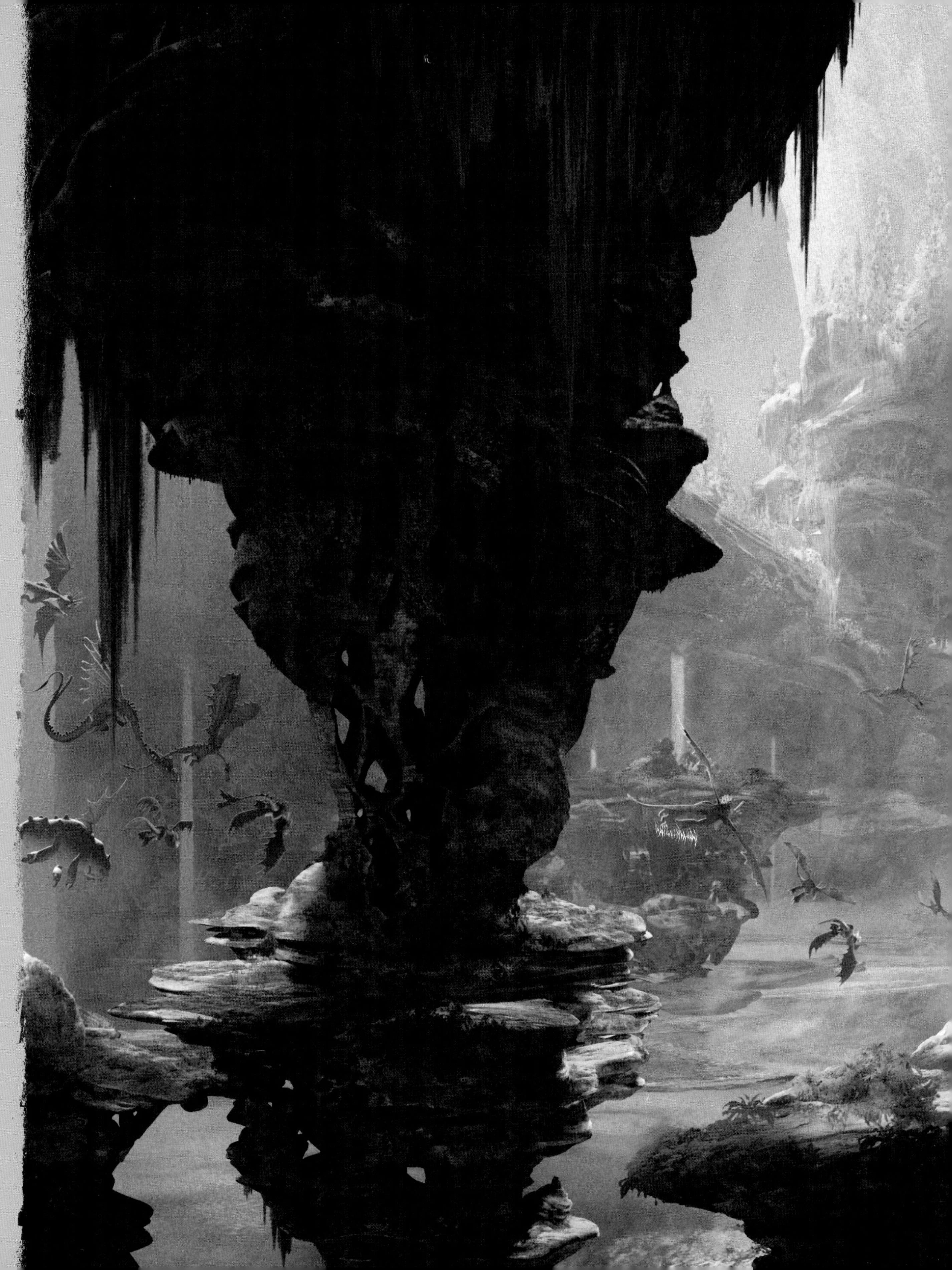

PAGE 1: Berk Banner ✦ *Kirsten Kawamura*
PREVIOUS PAGES: Hiccup Meets the Dragon Warrior ✦ *Pierre-Olivier Vincent*
ABOVE: Hiccup Sketch ✦ *Dean DeBlois* ✦ *pencil*
RIGHT & OPPOSITE PAGES: Oasis ✦ *Pierre-Olivier Vincent*
FOLLOWING PAGES: Northern Cliffs ✦ *Pierre-Olivier Vincent*

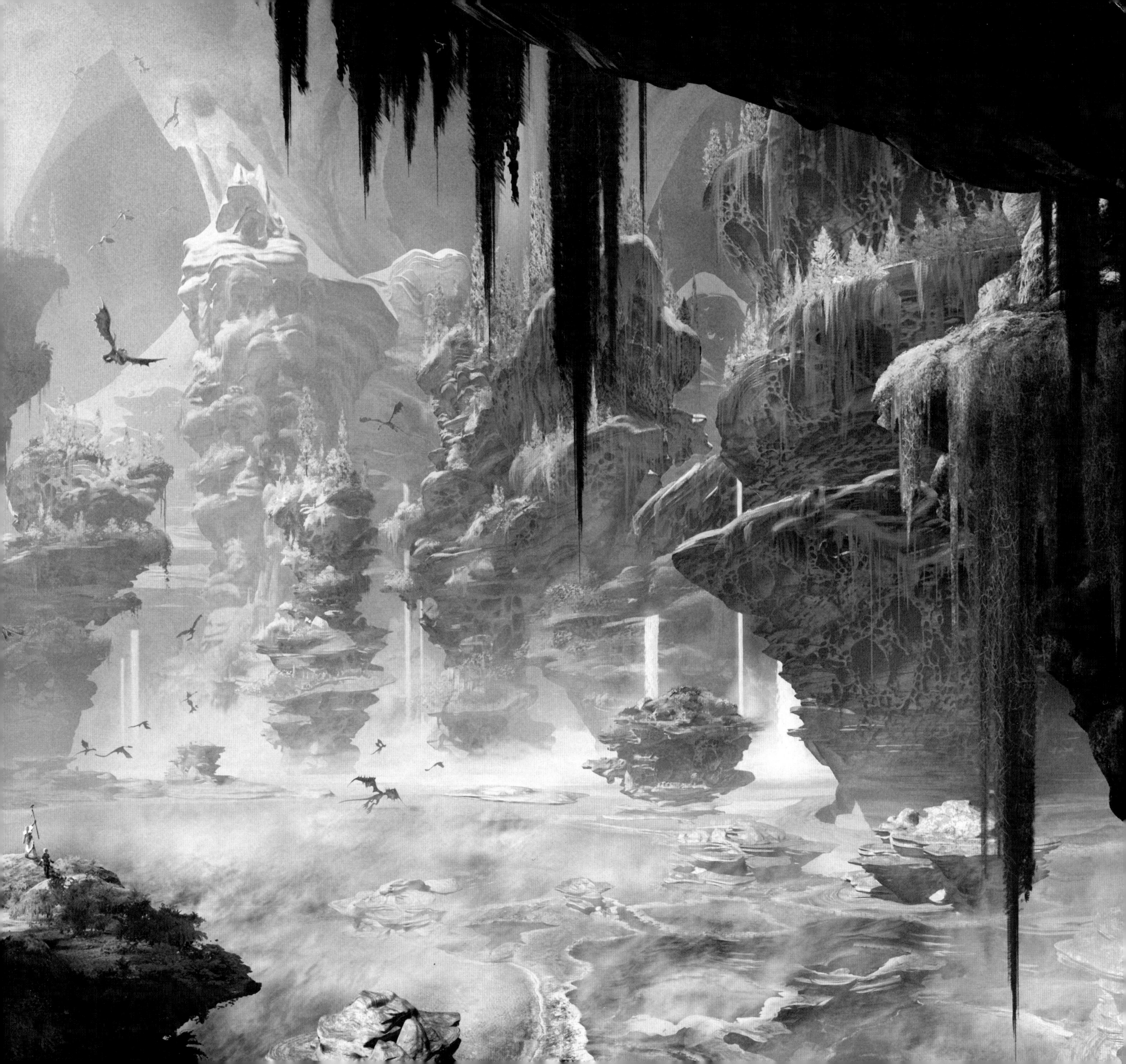

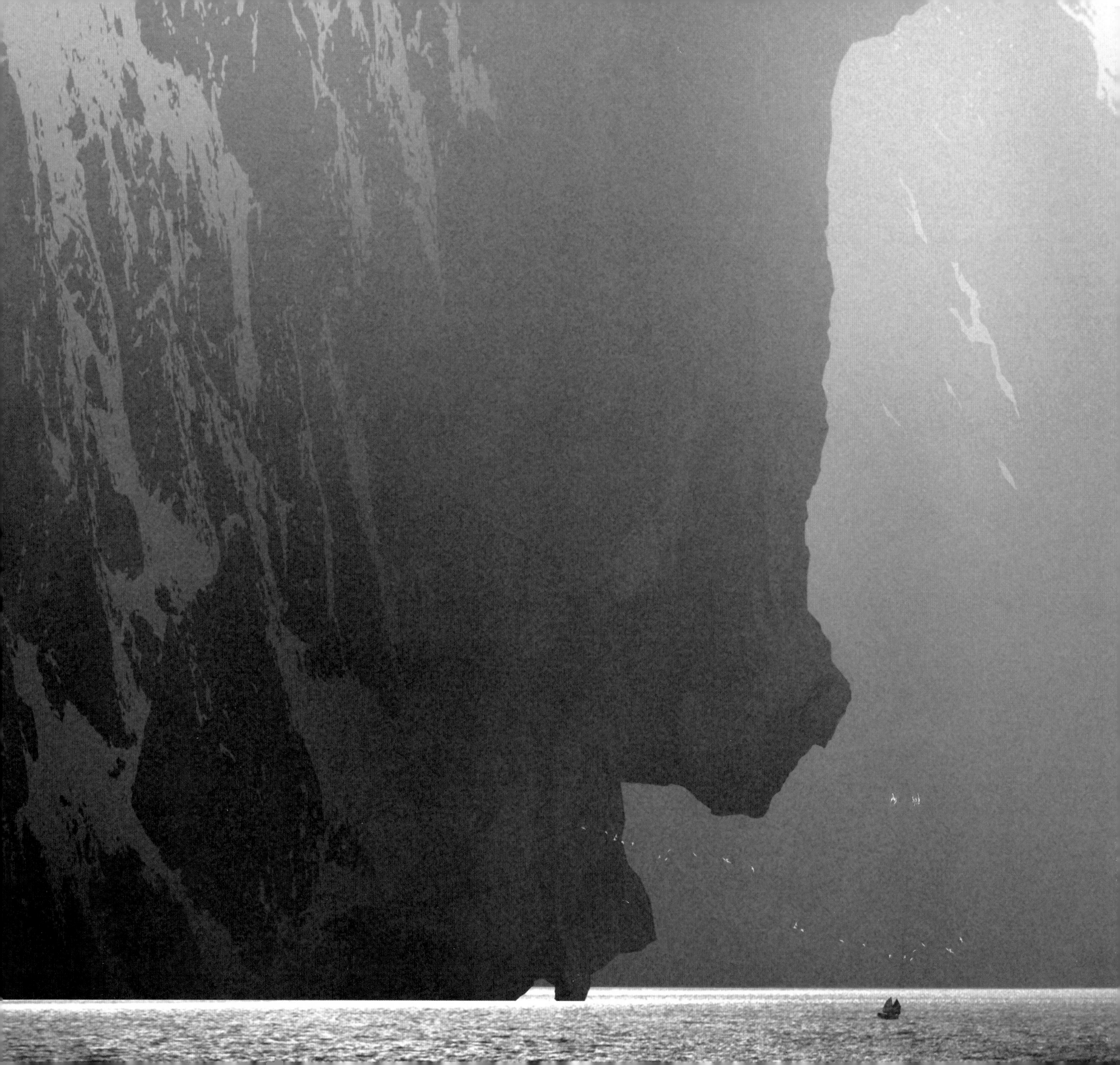

# CONTENTS

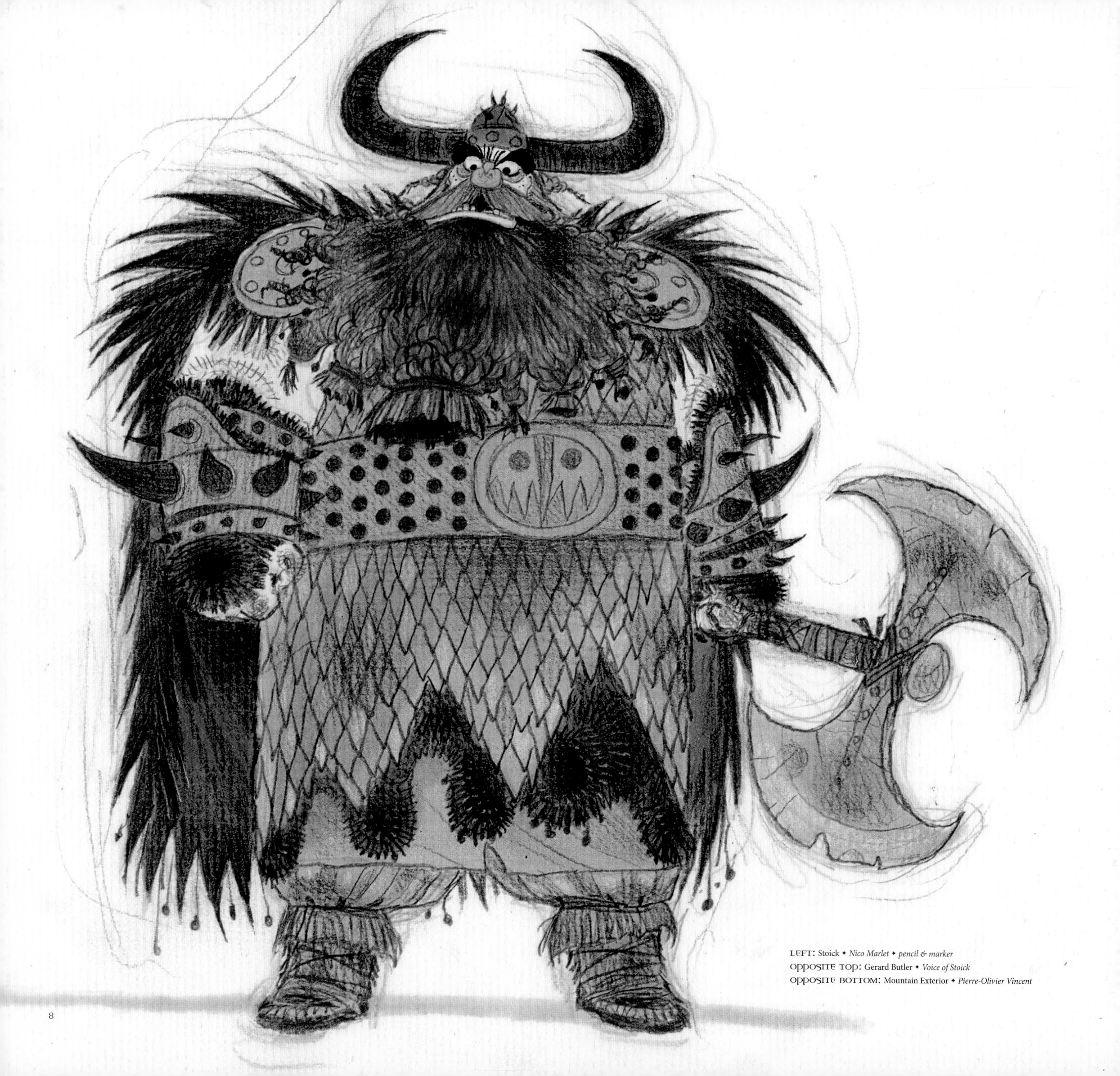

LEFT: Stoick ✦ *Nico Marlet* ✦ *pencil & marker*
OPPOSITE TOP: Gerard Butler ✦ *Voice of Stoick*
OPPOSITE BOTTOM: Mountain Exterior ✦ *Pierre-Olivier Vincent*

# Foreword
## *by Gerard Butler*

I have always loved fantasy worlds. In fact, when I was young I had this dream about being in a faraway land of wizards with magical powers, and it was so powerful that it changed my life. Because of that dream, I decided that I wanted to be an actor so that I could spend all my time exploring fantasy worlds. Diving into the world of *How to Train Your Dragon* reminded me of exactly why I wanted to be an actor in the first place. Not only was it a thrill to work with DreamWorks Animation but when I heard that the movie was about Vikings and dragons, I was even more excited. This movie could not be more perfect for a Celt and a Scot like myself. I believe I have a lot of Viking blood in me.

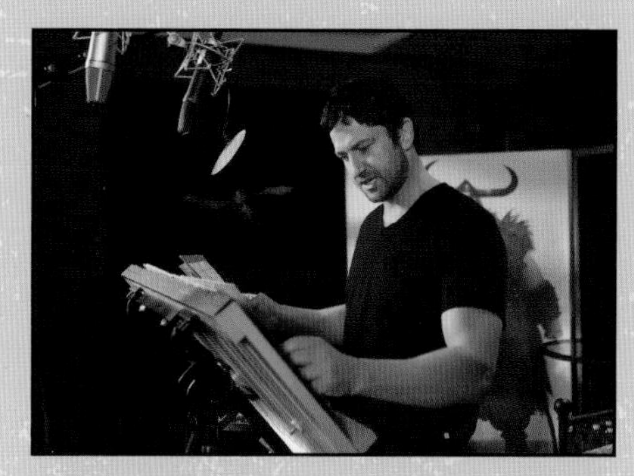

I had a fantastic experience making the first movie and was really delighted when Dean [DeBlois, the director] told me we'd be doing a sequel and working together again. (Dean and I share a love of Viking culture, the northern hemisphere, and an Icelandic band called Sigur Rós.) Working on the sequel was another wonderful opportunity to experience the joy of this world and delve deeper into the character of Stoick. Here was yet another huge Christmas present from DreamWorks Animation!

Playing a warrior like Stoick was very much in my wheelhouse and somewhat typical of many parts I've played in movies. I felt very involved because Dean always wants to know my ideas about how to play the character, which makes me feel that I am very much a part of bringing Stoick to life. I also loved the opportunity to use my own Scottish accent for Stoick. To me, this was a completely appropriate creative choice for the character. The voice of the Scotsman is the voice of war. It's the voice of *Braveheart* and *Rob Roy*. I used this accent in *300* because there is strength and fierceness to the Scottish growl.

We worked hard to bring a sense of humor and insightfulness to Stoick. It was important to show the power and fire of a character who is the leader of his tribe, but there are also some hilarious, awkward, and poignant moments when Stoick is dealing with his son, Hiccup. Those scenes were so much fun to capture. The best moments in making this film were always about Dean's enthusiasm and passion when an idea really worked. If I get goose bumps during a session, that's my litmus test and then I know that the scene is working. I had many, many of those moments on this movie.

A truly defining moment in my life was when I saw the finished movie for the first time and realized how much hard work and creative genius had gone into making the film. The final animation—combined with the story, the editing, and the phenomenal music—just took my breath away. *How to Train Your Dragon* was so much more than I could have hoped for or even imagined; it left me feeling awestruck and inspired. The filmmakers did a phenomenal job taking us into this magical, mysterious, dangerous fantasy world and giving us this incredible tale of courage and tolerance, and of the strength and power of family, friendship, and loyalty. I can't wait to see the completed version of *Dragon 2*, which I know has so many more surprises and thrilling moments.

I've always loved the movies and, like a lot people, many of my fondest childhood memories are from the films I saw when I was growing up. Since it is rare for me to get a chance to work on a family film, it is doubly rewarding when I am introduced as the voice of Stoick and I see that look of wonder in a child's eyes. That really gives me goose bumps.

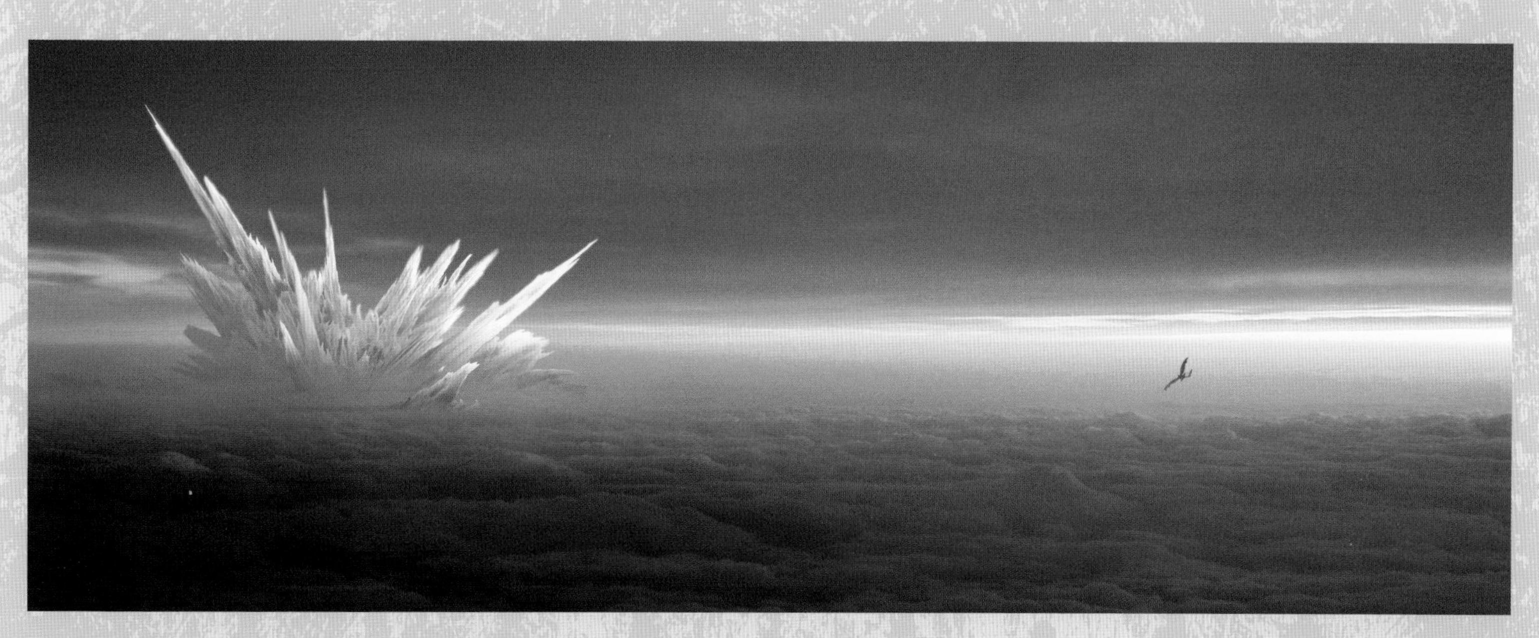

# Introduction
## *by Dean DeBlois*

One of my favorite things about animation is that the boundaries are as limitless as our imaginations. Entire worlds can be conceived and brought to life without any of the physical restrictions that other filmmakers often encounter. If we can dream it, we can make it. And if we do it well, audiences will believe wholeheartedly.

As with any storytelling medium, the chance to create a unique world is often the best part. The more we explore it, the more dimensional and real that world becomes, until it feels as though other stories already exist within its folds, just waiting to be discovered. The world of *How to Train Your Dragon*, with its brazen Vikings, larger-than-life settings, and endless varieties of dragons, is one such playground rich with possibilities. So when I was asked to come up with ideas for a sequel, I jumped at the chance to explore those uncharted recesses, to see what I could dig up. Like Hiccup expanding his map into mysterious new lands, the idea of leaving the familiar comforts of Berk in search of adventure seemed like a lot of fun. And surrounded by a top-notch team of visionary artists, I knew it would be breathtaking at every turn.

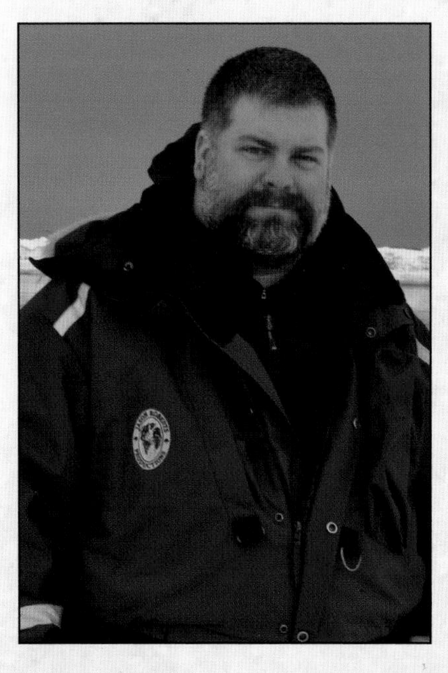

My only stipulation, if you could call it that, was that I wanted this sequel to be part of a trilogy, so that it would serve as a kind of second act in a larger three-act story. Too often, sequels feel recycled, disconnected, or unnecessary, but here was a chance to tell a story that would evolve as organically as its hero did, charting Hiccup's coming of age while expanding upon story threads that were set up in the first film, and planting seeds that would flourish in its third and final chapter. My pitch for a trilogy was well received by the studio heads (Jeffrey Katzenberg, Ann Daly and Bill Damaschke) so in the early months of 2010, I began to map out the tantalizing possibilities.

It was early February, and on a picnic table overlooking a baseball field at Skywalker Ranch, I scribbled down the first outline for what would become the sequel, while nearby, our sound team finessed the final mix for *How to Train Your Dragon*. It would go on to be released the following month to rave reviews and box-office success, thereby assuring that we had a green light for the second installment.

The first movie had departed significantly from the narrative of Cressida Cowell's books, so that left the possibilities wide open going forward. I knew that I wanted to bring more sophistication and scope to the story, so one of the fundamental ideas was to set the story five years after the first, so that Hiccup and his friends were now twenty-year-olds on the cusp of adulthood and dealing with a whole new set of problems. I loved the idea of telling an epic adventure story about a search for identity, against the backdrop of domineering parents.

Yes, that's right, parents. The idea of Hiccup's mother reentering the story after being presumed dead for twenty years was one of the first twists that I pitched. Everyone seemed to respond with enthusiasm—it felt like a strong hook, one that promised intrigue and emotion. The idea of a dragon-saving recluse living deep in the arctic and cut off from human interaction was very compelling to me. Valka was always meant to be a complicated character, flawed and interesting. On one hand, she was designed to represent what Hiccup yearned for—a wild, exciting, dragon-centric life filled with purpose—the opposite of what awaited him back at home. But she was also conceived to challenge Hiccup's belief in the coexistence of dragons and humans, by representing segregation in order to keep dragons safe.

Drago Bludvist, the film's main villain, enters the story quite late, which is unconventional, but also interesting for that very reason. It allows for a chance to build up an anticipation and mythology surrounding Drago by first hearing accounts of him and seeing the impact on others who have crossed his path. Any man who could cause Stoick to ground all dragons and lock down Berk *must* be a force to reckon with. Drago brings an element of scope to the story—an ambition from the start. His mysterious, exotic origins and multi-cultural army suggest distant lands yet to be explored and a world that goes on and on.

One of the elements that I was most proud of in the first film was its daring quality. Elements like Hiccup losing his leg were admittedly risky, but they felt right, and the fact that we were able to stay true to the integrity of the story gave me great courage going forward. The lasting hallmark of *How to Train Your Dragon* is its wonder and its heart, and they've been my guiding principle ever since. I hope that this story will feel uncompromising in its emotion, and daring in its twists and turns. We have lots of comedy and adventure in store, but more important, we have moments that are hopefully touching and magical. They make it all worth the effort.

It's such an inspiring and humbling experience to work alongside the amazing artists that we assembled for this film. We all have our specialties and areas of focus, but when a whole crew believes in a project so passionately, it seems that everyone contributes on every level. We hold ourselves to a high standard and challenge one another to do the unexpected. The results are fun, surprising, and breathtaking. These pages show just a sample of the heaps of whimsical, gorgeous work that my colleagues have created for *How to Train Your Dragon 2*. I am blown away every day by their incredible talent. I hope their art inspires future generations to come.

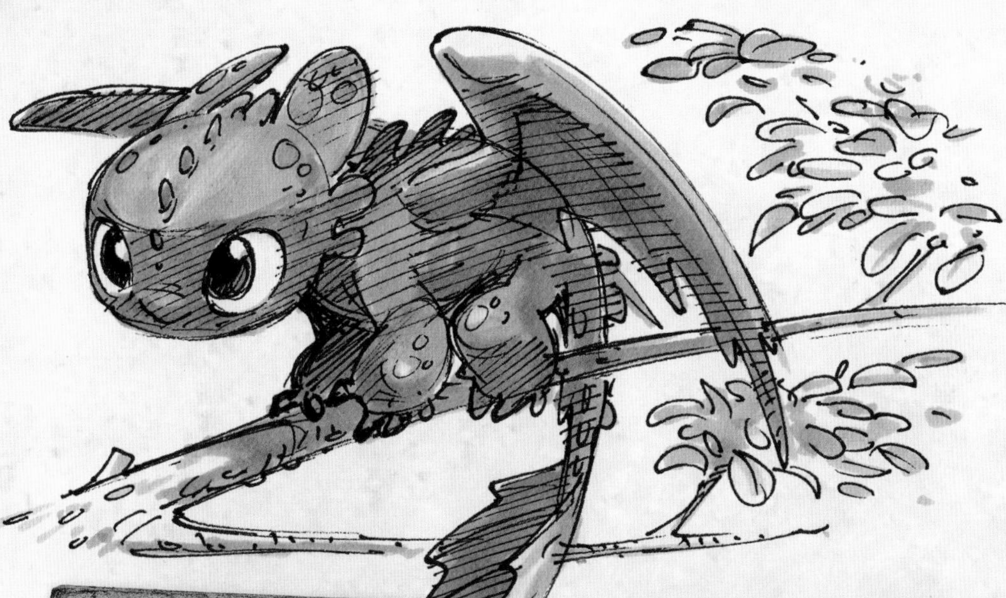

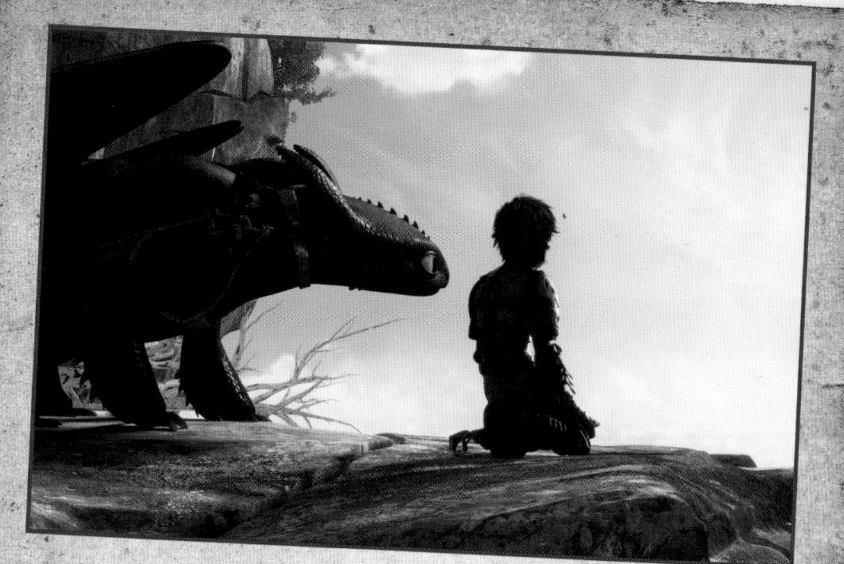

We all knew that the first movie could be something quite special, but it wasn't until the first preview that we all began to realize just how big of a hit we had. From that first preview, you could just feel the reaction from the audience. The response has grown tremendously since the first film was released, so going into the sequel, we all feel a responsibility to these beloved characters. We felt that given the scope of their world, we had to choose big ideas for our two lead characters, Hiccup and Toothless. Their world is changing radically, but the movie is about how nothing can come between their bond. I think people can see their own relationships in that bond.

*—Bill Damaschke, chief creative officer, DreamWorks Animation*

After the first movie was so successful and we decided to do another film, Dean came in and said he didn't want to do a film about the further adventures of Hiccup and Toothless. He saw the story in a much bigger framework and wanted to create a trilogy, which meant signing up for two new movies.

Dean pitched the idea that the characters would be five years older, the mother would come back, and we would bring in another nemesis so that Hiccup gets drawn into this confrontation. The battle would be between a dragon vigilante and a dragon killer and it just so happens that one of these people is his mother.

*—Bonnie Arnold, producer*

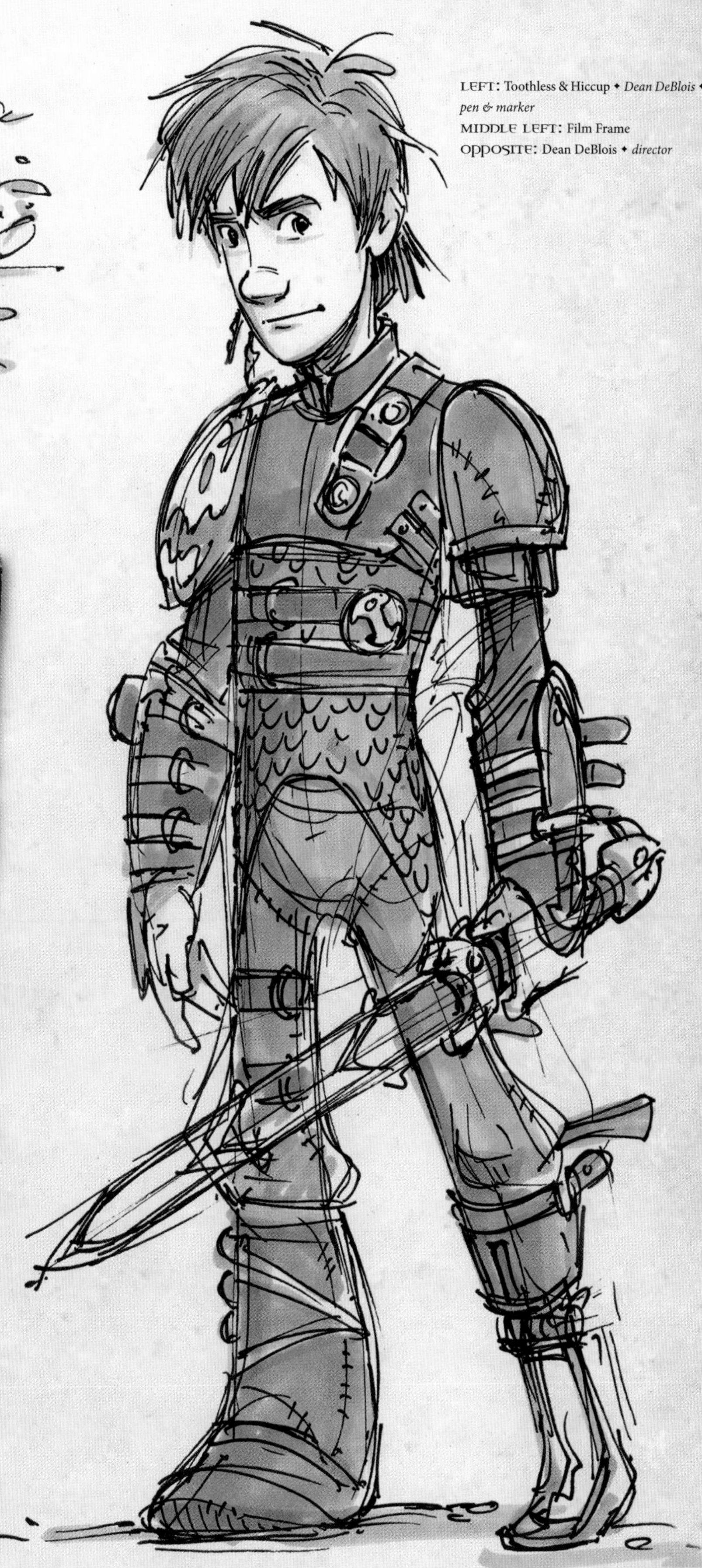

LEFT: Toothless & Hiccup ✦ *Dean DeBlois* ✦ *pen & marker*
MIDDLE LEFT: Film Frame
OPPOSITE: Dean DeBlois ✦ *director*

# Destination Norway
## *by Bonnie Arnold, Producer*

For any live action film, we always do a location scout. We look at the places where we will shoot both for research and for inspiration for the creative team.

As we segued from the first film into the second (and the third) movie, it became clear that Dean's scripts would be exploring new lands. The fantasy location of the first movie was the general area of the North Sea. Berk is not a real location, of course, but it does have origins in the Viking lands. So we started talking about what we could do for visual development to generate new ideas. Of course, you can go online for ideas but as a team-bonding experience we wanted to explore where Hiccup might go and what he might encounter once he started his exploration of new lands.

We decided to take the team to Norway. In the process of planning the trip, I reached out to Norway's film commission. What if we were actually filming in and around Norway? Where in the country did the Vikings live?

The film commissioner in Oslo put me in touch with Jason Roberts, an Australian who lives in Svalbard, an archipelago in the Arctic Ocean and the northernmost part of Norway. Jason has worked on all kinds of spectacular live-action nature movies like *Walking with Dinosaurs*. He spends half his time on the North Pole and the other half on the South Pole, so he was a tremendous resource for us. No one knows more about that part of the world than Jason! With his help, we focused our itinerary.

We started in Oslo because of the amazing museums like the Norwegian Folk Museum, which features traditional handicraft items, folk costumes, and artifacts of the Viking culture. We also planned a trip to the Viking Ship Museum, where we saw ships dating as far back as the ninth century. We took a beautiful train ride to Bergen, on the coast, and a boat trip in the fjords. The landscapes were absolutely spectacular and inspirational.

A small group of our team (Dean DeBlois, Gregg Taylor, and Roger Deakins) went up to Svalbard for a few days to see the glaciers. They took snowmobiles in polar bear country, saw ice floes, and stayed overnight in a ship that was completely icebound. It was that location that influenced the creation of Valka's fortress.

Even though we all work in the same place, traveling together is a different experience and the trip really helped cement our working relationships. The conversations about the movie and what the movie would be both visually and in terms of storytelling really bubbled up just by spending time together and seeing such interesting sights. We were in Norway for just over a week but a lot of the inspiration for the movie came out of that trip.

Below from left: Mike Necci, Simon Otto, Hans Otto "Nicco" Nicolayssen (Norway's film commissioner), Dean DeBlois, Bonnie Arnold, John Carr, Pierre-Olivier Vincent, James Deakins, Gregg Taylor, Kendra Haaland, Gil Zimmerman, ZhaoPing Wei, Roger Deakins.

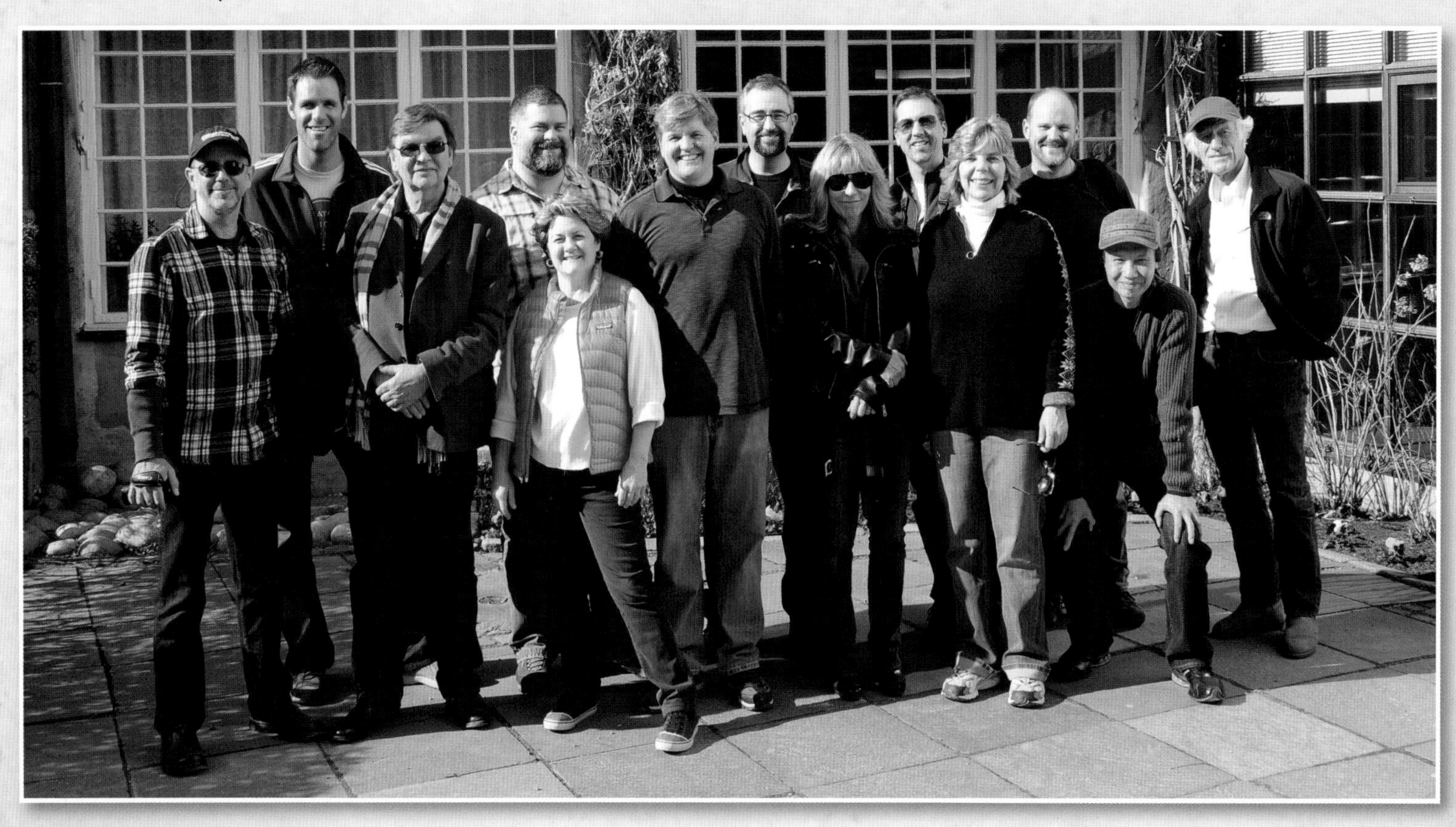

After the first movie did so well, we wanted to do something very, very special for the team. Since the second film was so much about exploration and expanding Hiccup's world of dragons, we decided to take the team on an exploration to expand their own horizons about that part of the world.

I met up with the team in Norway and we spent a lot of time talking about story and character. We visited some amazing landscapes and fjords. In a way, we went on our version of what we thought the early Vikings had done when they were out exploring.

*—Bill Damaschke, chief creative officer, DreamWorks Animation*

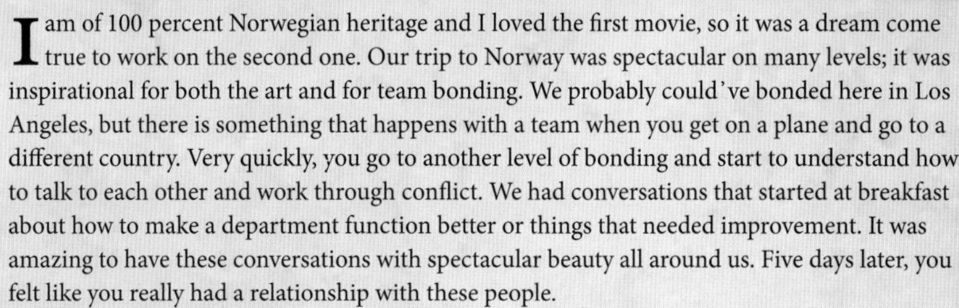

The scale of the landscapes, the fjords, and the mountains that we saw was as close as we could get to pretending to be actual Vikings.

*—Pierre-Olivier Vincent, production designer*

Had we not gone to Norway, it would have been impossible for us to imagine the kind of world in which the Vikings lived. At the museums we visited, we could reference materials like the kinds of furs they wore and the tools they used. Every piece of history allowed us to create an authentic world for the film because, even though our movie is about dragons, we wanted to stay true to the world of the Vikings.

*—ZhaoPing Wei, art director*

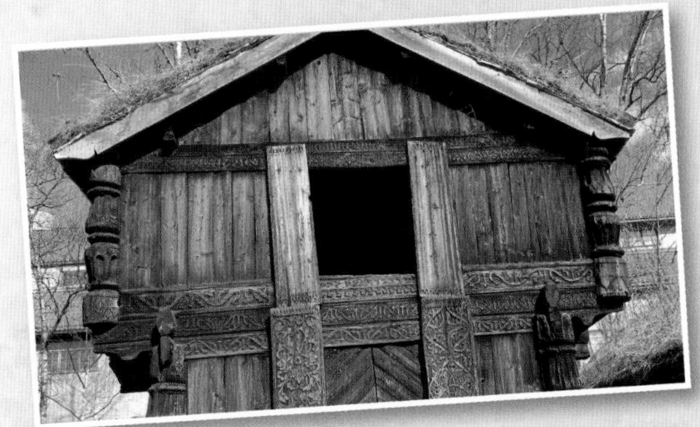

The trip was mainly a leadership bonding experience where you start building relationships and talking about ideas inspired by the world around you. From a production design world, you want to be inspired by these landscapes, but you don't want to be limited by your research. For me, it was mostly about visiting the museums and getting the flavor of the Nordic culture. The trip was successful more in terms of the time we got to spend with each other talking about the characters and being away from studio life.

*—Simon Otto, head of character animation*

The experience of being in a fjord was the single most impactful thing to help me understand how large our world is. There is just innate drama in the mountains and the water. It gave me a visceral sense of the Vikings and what hardy people they must've been.

*—Gil Zimmerman, head of layout*

From a team-building perspective, the trip to Norway allowed us to get to know each other in a very short amount of time. We would meet daily for good chunks of time while observing sights in Norway that were applicable to our film. I think the look of the fjords, the scale and the scope of them, was a real inspiration. The fjords rise up immensely high on either side of you. It was part of what we wanted to capture in this movie, that sense of the vastness of the land compared to the size of the humans.

*—Mike Necci, digital supervisor, environments*

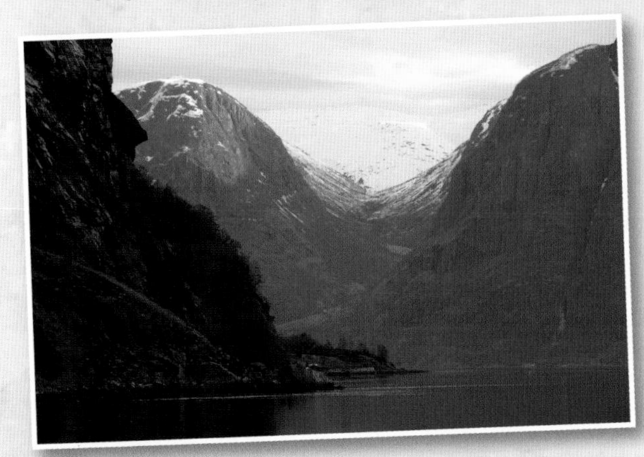

I am of 100 percent Norwegian heritage and I loved the first movie, so it was a dream come true to work on the second one. Our trip to Norway was spectacular on many levels; it was inspirational for both the art and for team bonding. We probably could've bonded here in Los Angeles, but there is something that happens with a team when you get on a plane and go to a different country. Very quickly, you go to another level of bonding and start to understand how to talk to each other and work through conflict. We had conversations that started at breakfast about how to make a department function better or things that needed improvement. It was amazing to have these conversations with spectacular beauty all around us. Five days later, you felt like you really had a relationship with these people.

*—Kendra Haaland, co-producer*

For myself, I am not a big photographer. I've never been one to take pictures, but we had six people with us in Norway who brought along massive cameras, including Roger Deakins. Actually, Roger had the most compact camera but I noticed that Roger would take pictures very discretely while the others seemed to always be shooting. As time went by, whenever Roger would take out his camera, the other photographers would gravitate to where he was shooting. Whatever Roger was shooting, everyone wanted to shoot.

*—Bill Damaschke, chief creative officer, DreamWorks Animation*

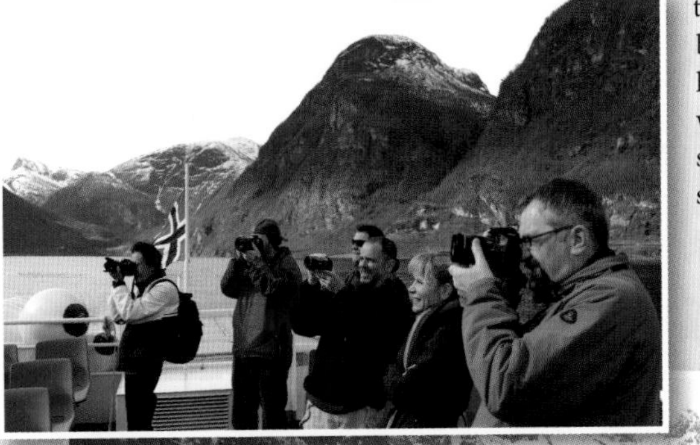

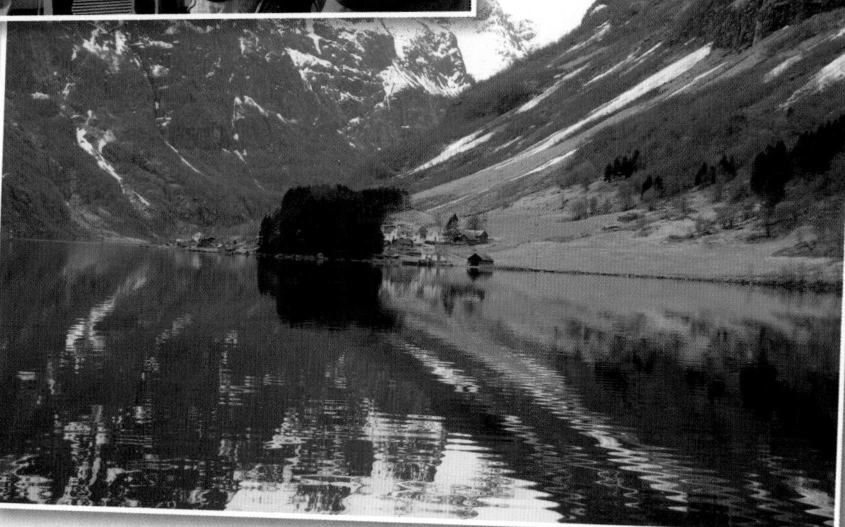

# 5,000 Polar Bears

One of the things I discovered back on *Lilo and Stitch* is that if you set an animated film in a place you want to visit, there's a chance you might get to go there.

Previous to making this movie, I had spent quite a bit of time in Iceland. I first arrived there to direct a film for an Icelandic band called Sigur Rós and I loved it so much that I kept going back. Aside from New Zealand, Iceland might be the most beautiful spot on earth. I love the raw nature of the landscape, the diversity of the people, the music, and all the talented people I encountered there.

During one trip, I met a couple of backpackers who talked about Svalbard in the deep Arctic, north of Norway. It got me interested, so I found a couple of travel books and the more I read, the more obsessed I became with going there one day.

When the idea came up of doing a sequel to *How to Train Your Dragon*, we were planning a research trip to Norway and I knew this was my chance to see Svalbard, which fit into some of the ideas I was considering for the second film. I had this notion of another dragon rider and a remote nest set deep in the frozen Arctic, so it was thrilling to have the chance to see the actual landscape.

When we arrived in Svalbard, we discovered that there were 2,000 people living in a small settlement called Longyearbyen and, beyond that, there was no one.

Four of us then departed on a five-day snowmobile safari with armed tour guides. They were armed because of the polar bears. While there are only 2,000 people in Svalbard, there are 5,000 polar bears that do not hesitate to eat whatever moves. The danger is eerily real and ever-present. It is a very strange feeling to know that you are prey.

It wasn't like the bears were jumping out from behind every chunk of ice. We didn't see many of them, which was unnerving, because our guides pointed out that the bears knew we were there. In the end, we only saw one mother with her two cubs resting on the shoreline. They had clearly just eaten because the mother bear was too lazy to even lift her head.

We also saw an abandoned Russian mining settlement, ancient trappers' cabins, sprawling glaciers, and magnificent frozen fjords. Even though the only things keeping you alive are the gas in your snowmobile and the guide with a rifle, the trip was unbelievable. There is nothing quite like the sensation of knowing that every step is probably the first step ever taken on that land by a human being.

I've never seen anything quite like that place. It was incredible and inspiring in so many ways—and the light, the skies, the expanses of untouched arctic wilderness, and the way color filters through at those northern latitudes definitely found its way into the movie.

It was the most amazing trip I've ever taken and my mind drifts back there whenever I feel a little overwhelmed.

*—Dean DeBlois, director*

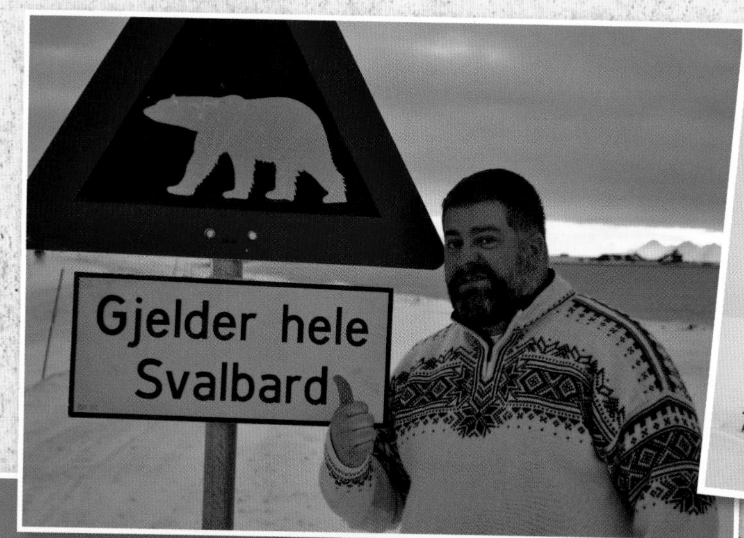


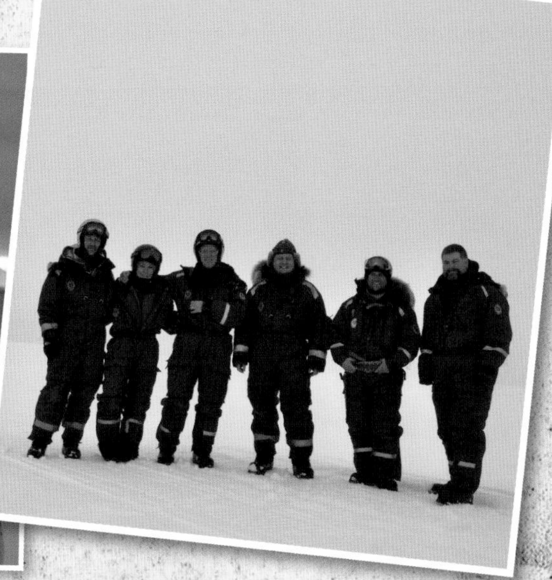

The trip to Norway really influenced the look of the movie. Our photographs were a good reference. In the movie we used that feeling of low light on the horizon and the kind of shifting of color between the sun, the blue of the ice, and the blue of the sky. We tried to bring variation of colors into it because most of the time in Svalbard, when we were traveling across the snow on our skimobiles, it just looked white and bright—blue sky and bright white ice. However, we tried to bring into the film all the details of the colors that we observed.

In the far east of Svalbard, we went to this glacier, which constantly changes and so was new for us. We traveled out on the frozen ocean until we came to a 100-foot wall of ice, which broke off the glacier. We went into ice caves that are a kind of blue I've never seen before; it is almost unreal because it's so vivid. The edges of the glaciers have picked up some dirt so there's kind of a brown in there, along with greens and blues, all sorts of colors. In the film, we tried to bring those splashes of color into something that would otherwise look monotonously white.

*—Roger Deakins, visual consultant*

FOLLOWING PAGES: Color Key • *Woonyoung Jung & ZhaoPing Wei*

Our research trip to Svalbard was a life-altering experience. We were in the Arctic Circle in the northernmost settlement on the planet; it was an amazing sensation to be at the top of the world. Svalbard is an intimidating, harsh place yet it is breathtakingly beautiful. Between the threat of polar bears and the severe weather, venturing out of town is an extreme adventure. Everyone carries a gun to defend themselves against polar bears. Seeing a woman pushing a baby stroller through the snow with a shotgun strapped across her back is not a sight you see every day.

The greatest memory for me was the snowmobile trip I took with Dean DeBlois and Roger Deakins. It made it easy to imagine what the expeditions must've been like on the *Endurance* or *The Fram*. The only way to get to the boat, our base camp, was by snowmobile, cross-country skis, or dogsled. When I watch the movie, I certainly see the inspiration from our trip especially in the production design, color choices, and Roger's spectacular lighting.

*—Gregg Taylor, head of feature development, DreamWorks Animation*

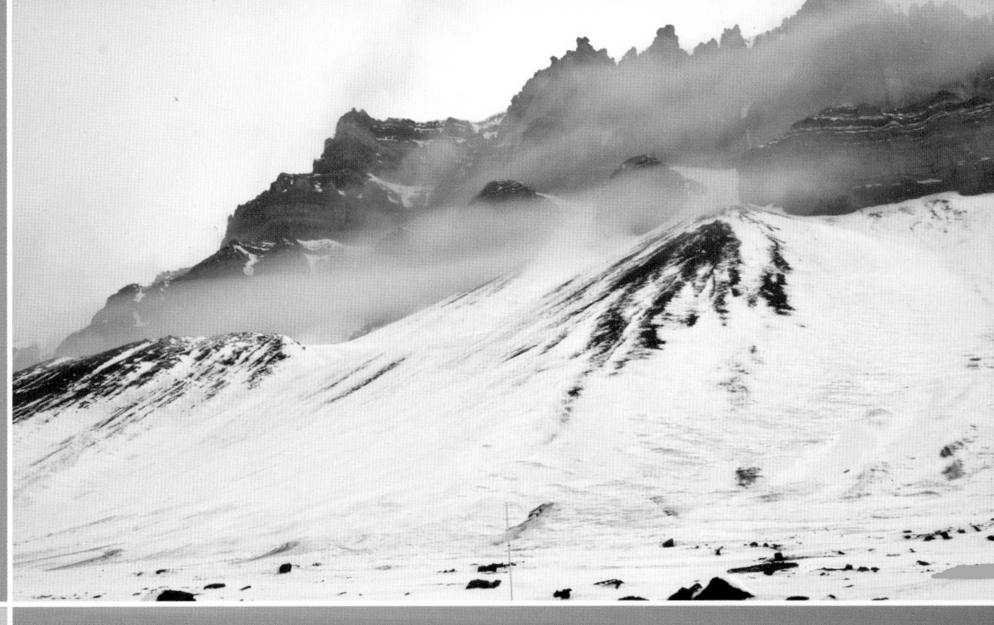

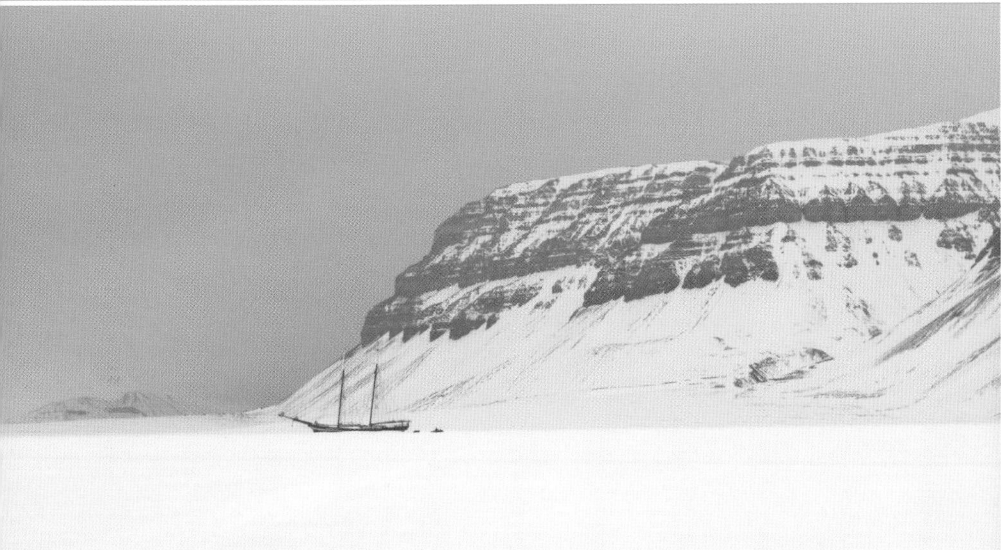

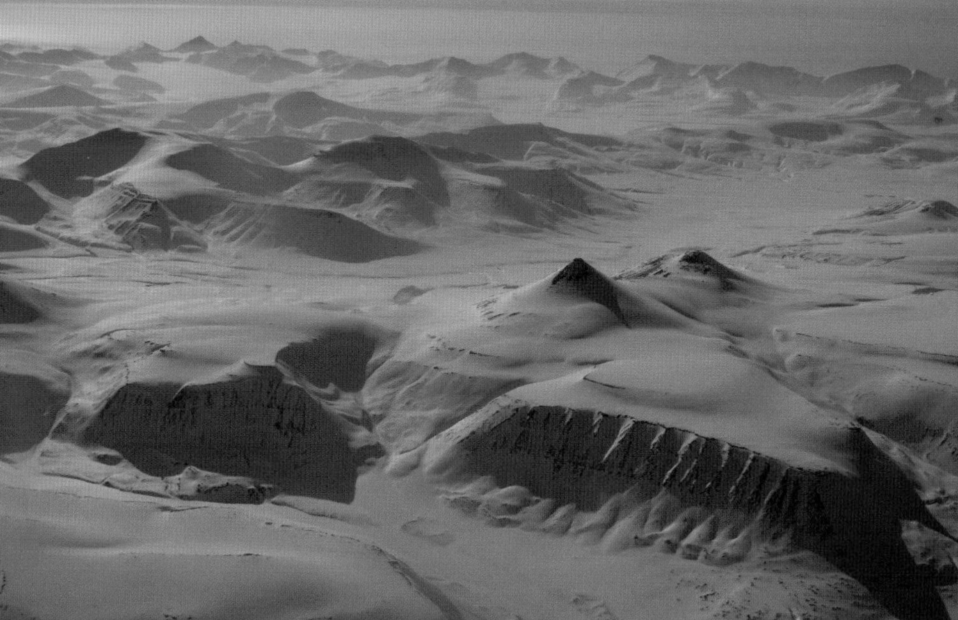

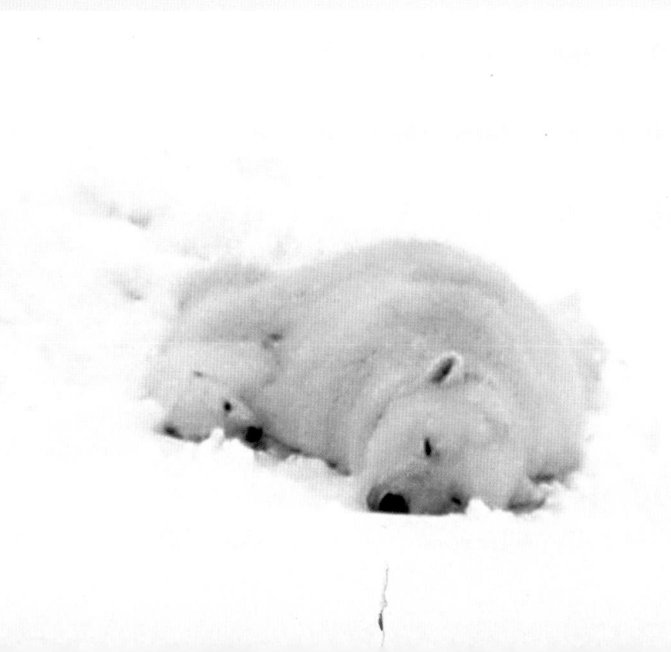

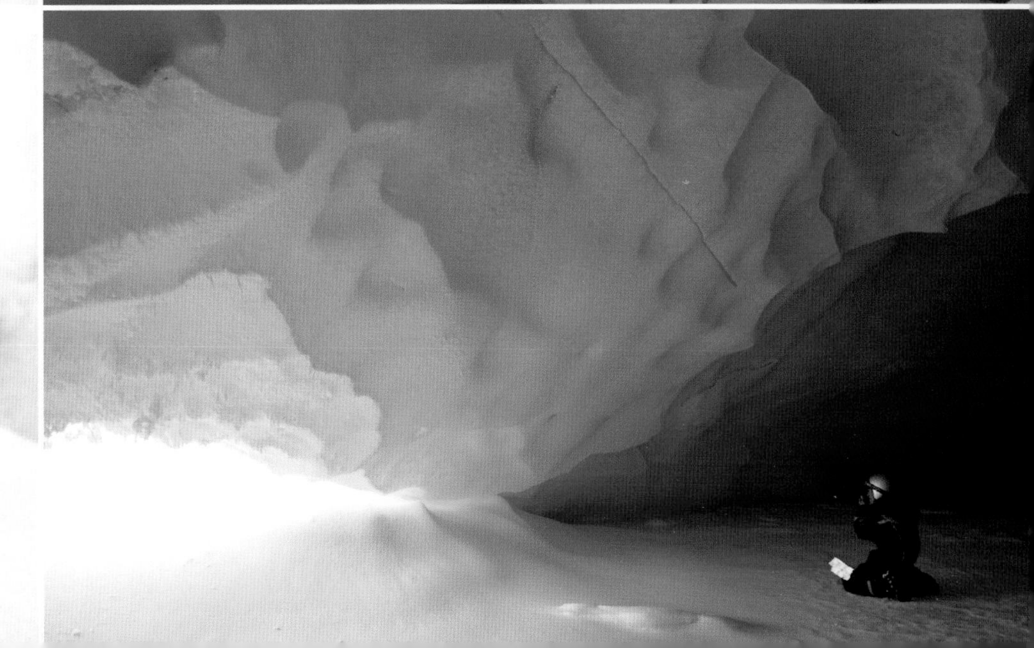

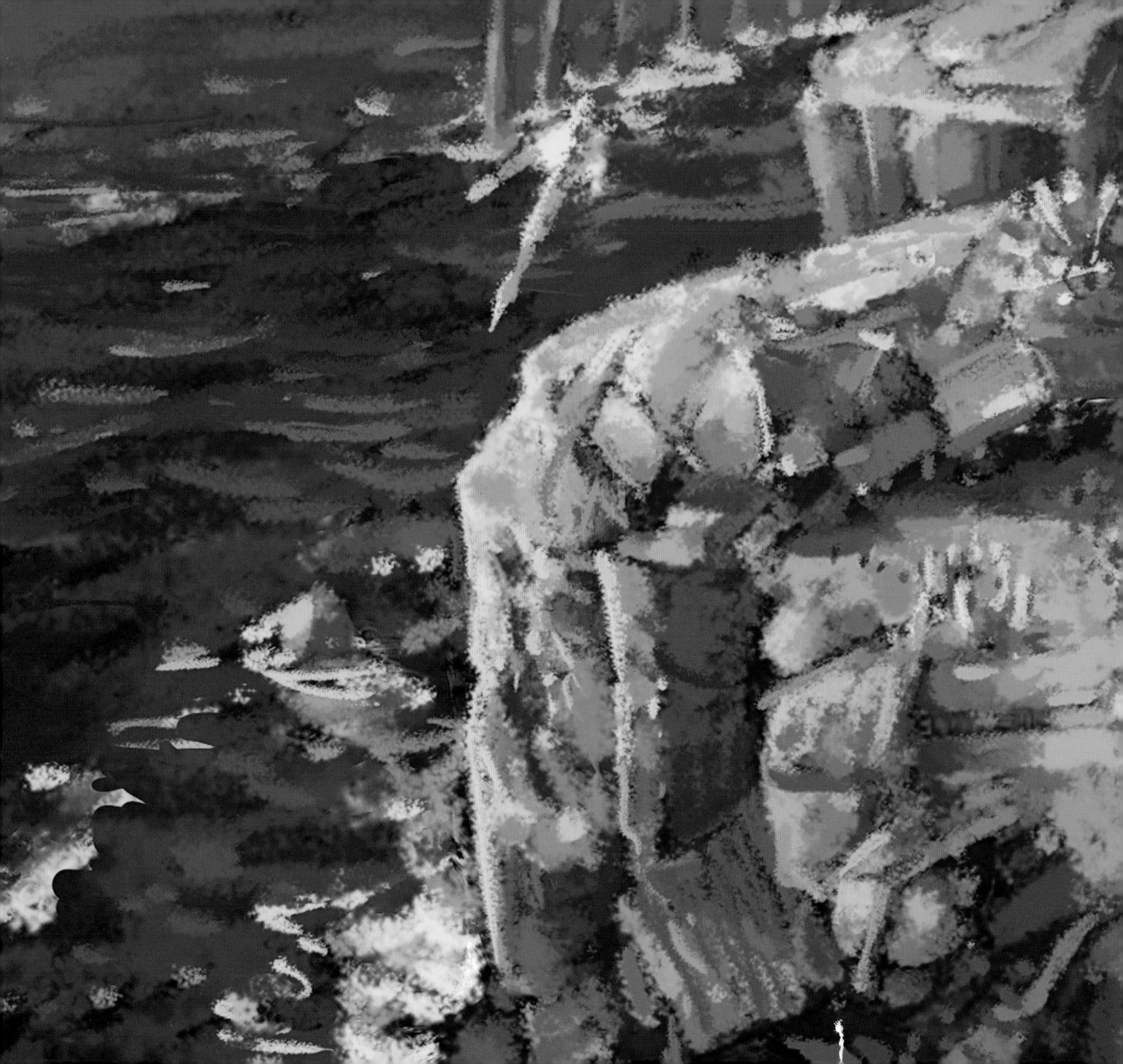

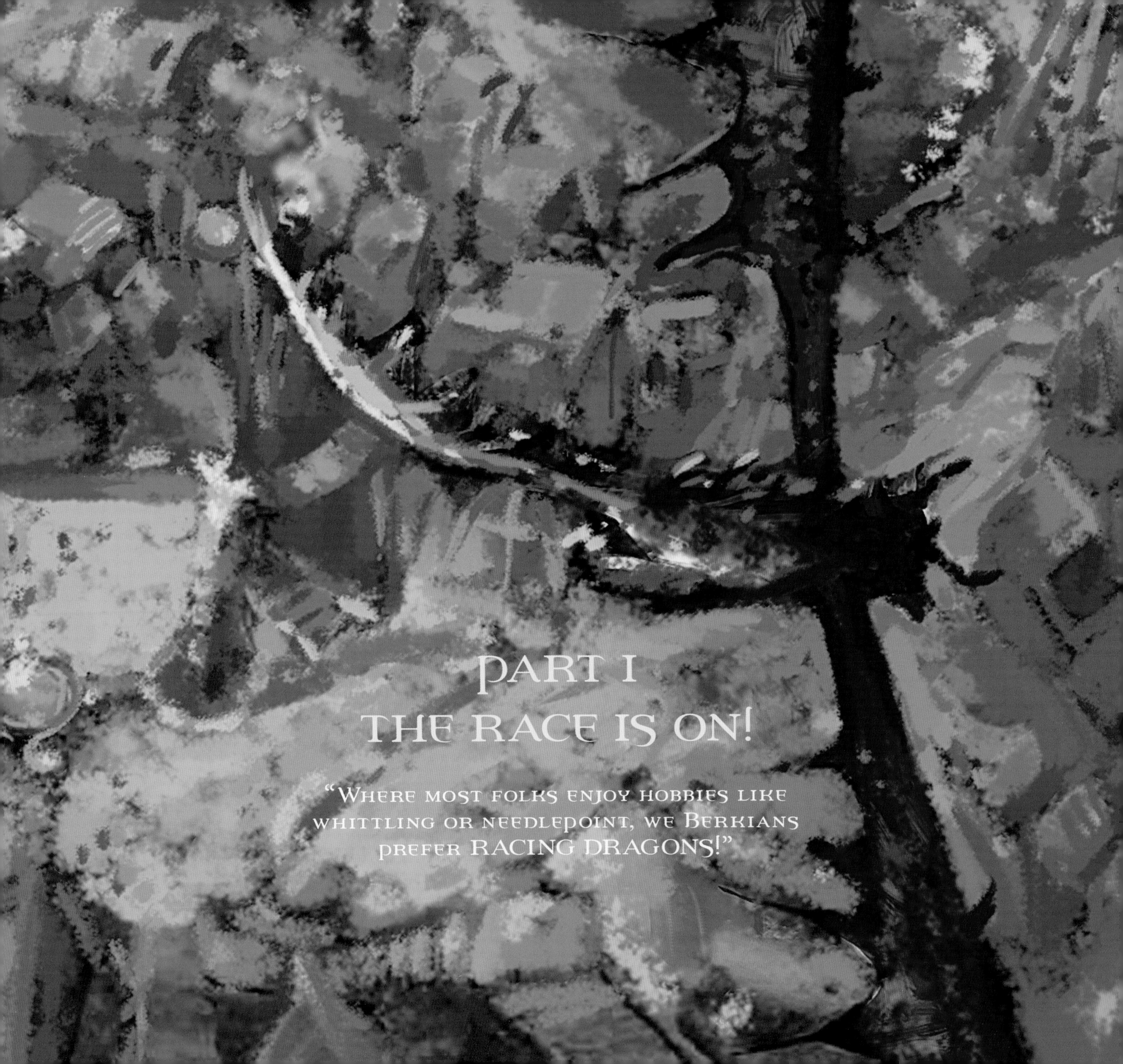

# PART I
# THE RACE IS ON!

"Where most folks enjoy hobbies like whittling or needlepoint, we Berkians prefer RACING DRAGONS!"

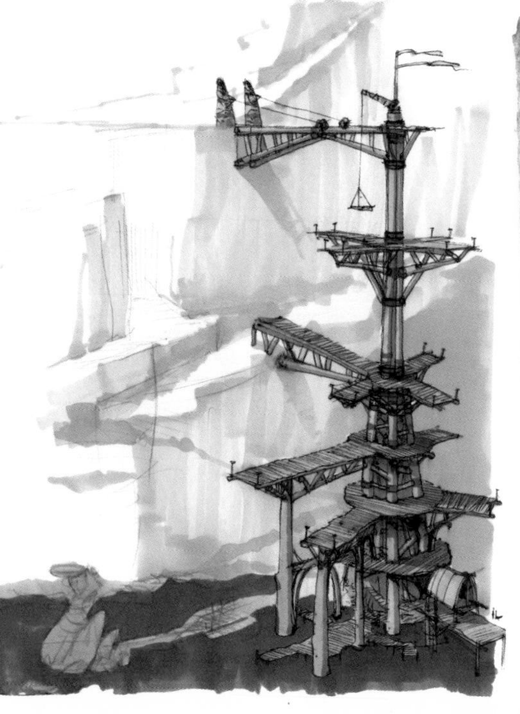

ABOVE: Berk Docks ✦ *Iuri Lioi* ✦ *pencil & marker*
RIGHT: Weathervane & Watchtower Horn ✦ *Nicolas Weis*
BELOW: House Dragon Perch Ideas ✦ *Iuri Lioi* ✦ *pencil & marker*

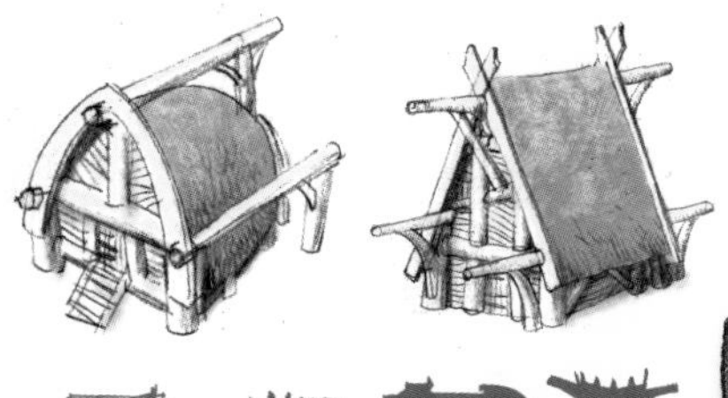

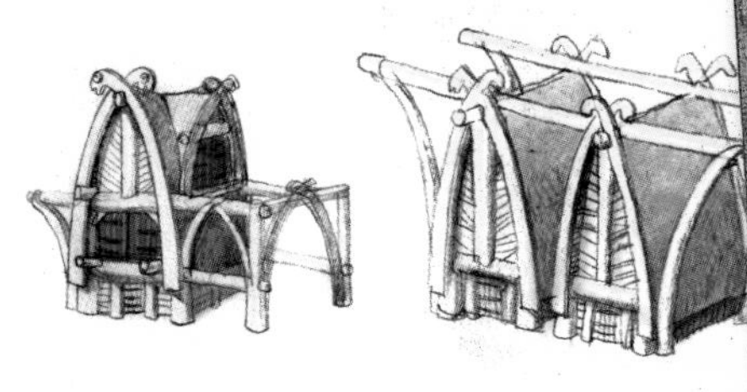

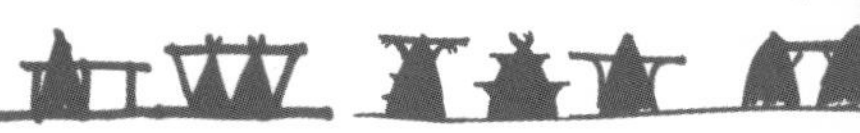

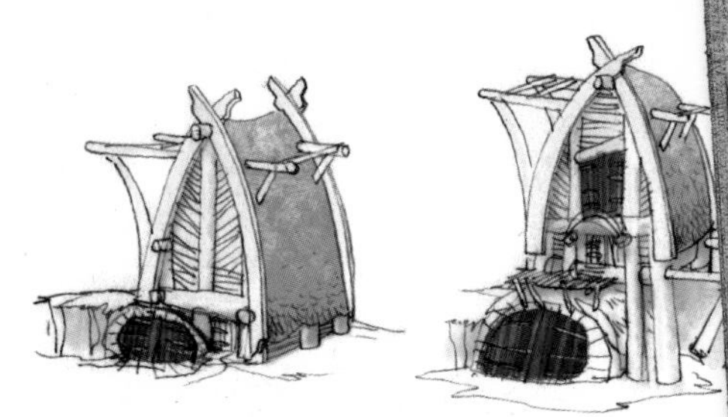

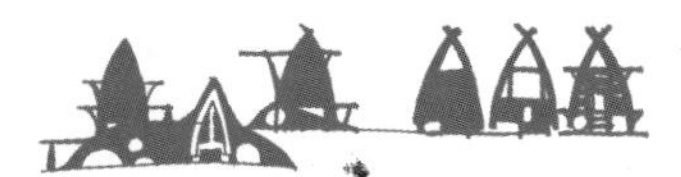

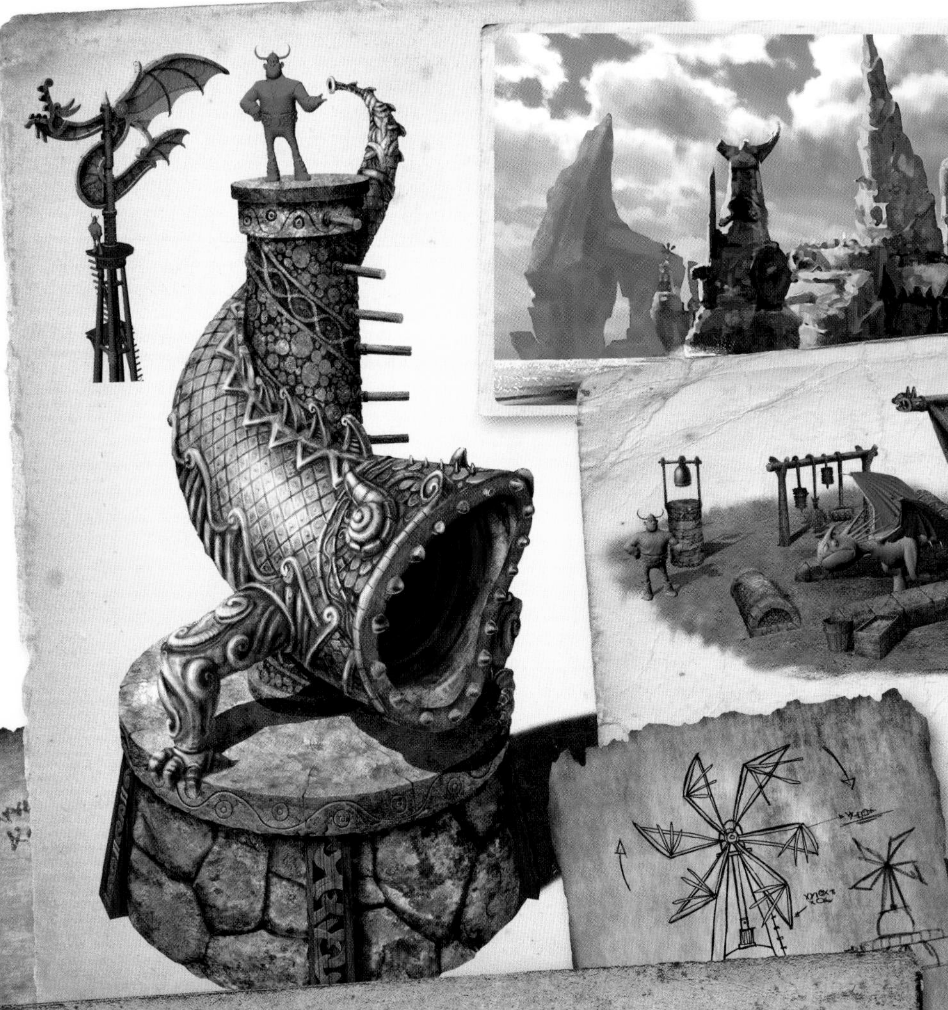

TOP: Color Key ✦ *Woonyoung Jung & Ron Lukas*
ABOVE: Berk Grooming Station ✦ *Nicolas Weis*
LEFT & BELOW: Hiccup Drawings: Windmill, Weathervane & Water Tower ✦ *Kirsten Kawamura*
BOTTOM: Rune ✦ *Kirsten Kawamura*

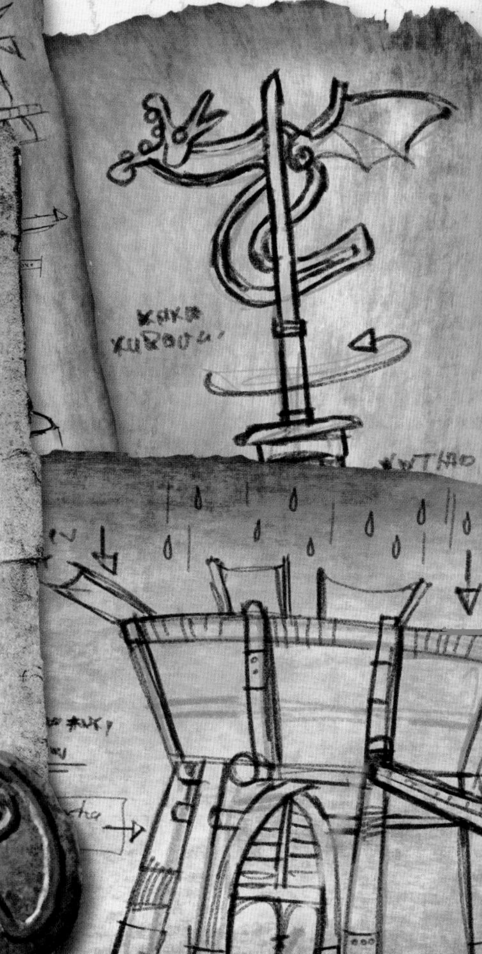

## Welcome to a Dragon-Friendly Utopia by Hiccup

This is Berk—just not the Berk you remember. These past five years have called for some necessary updates to the way we do things around here. That's because dragons, who used to be bit of a nuisance in these parts, have all since moved in. Every one gets along now, which is great. We don't have to rebuild our houses quite as often, but living with giant inflammatory constituents and their insatiable appetites comes with its fair share of challenges. We've had to invent ways to keep life with them fun and a little less dangerous.

The first order of business was figuring out where to put them. Luckily, our village is built above a sprawling cavern that runs deep beneath the island. We converted it into a giant dragon hangar, boasting cool custom stables and enclosures to fit every dragon type and temperament. There's enough space to accommodate every one of Berk's hundreds of new residents, including newbies that I find and bring back here every day.

The main entrance features a massive covered runway with automated storm doors and a water delivery system to keep things squeaky clean. The rear exit looks more like a giant birdhouse, if you ask me, built to pacify the fussy types who require a little more sun.

Aboveground, we've added feeding and grooming stations to keep the dragon population well-fed and significantly less smelly. After eating their fill, our contented winged friends can take a hot coal bath and scrub off dead scales to maintain a bouncy healthy shine. A happy dragon is an exfoliated dragon.

As I am sure you can imagine, our dragons eat a lot—almost as much as our Vikings—so we've really had to up our food production on every level. In place of the old wartime catapults and trebuchets, our defense towers now house a new dragon-winged windmill, water tower, and rainwater reservoir.

Living with the fire breather's requires top-of-the-line fire prevention, so we've also incorporated a network of aqueducts to douse flames wherever they might pop up.

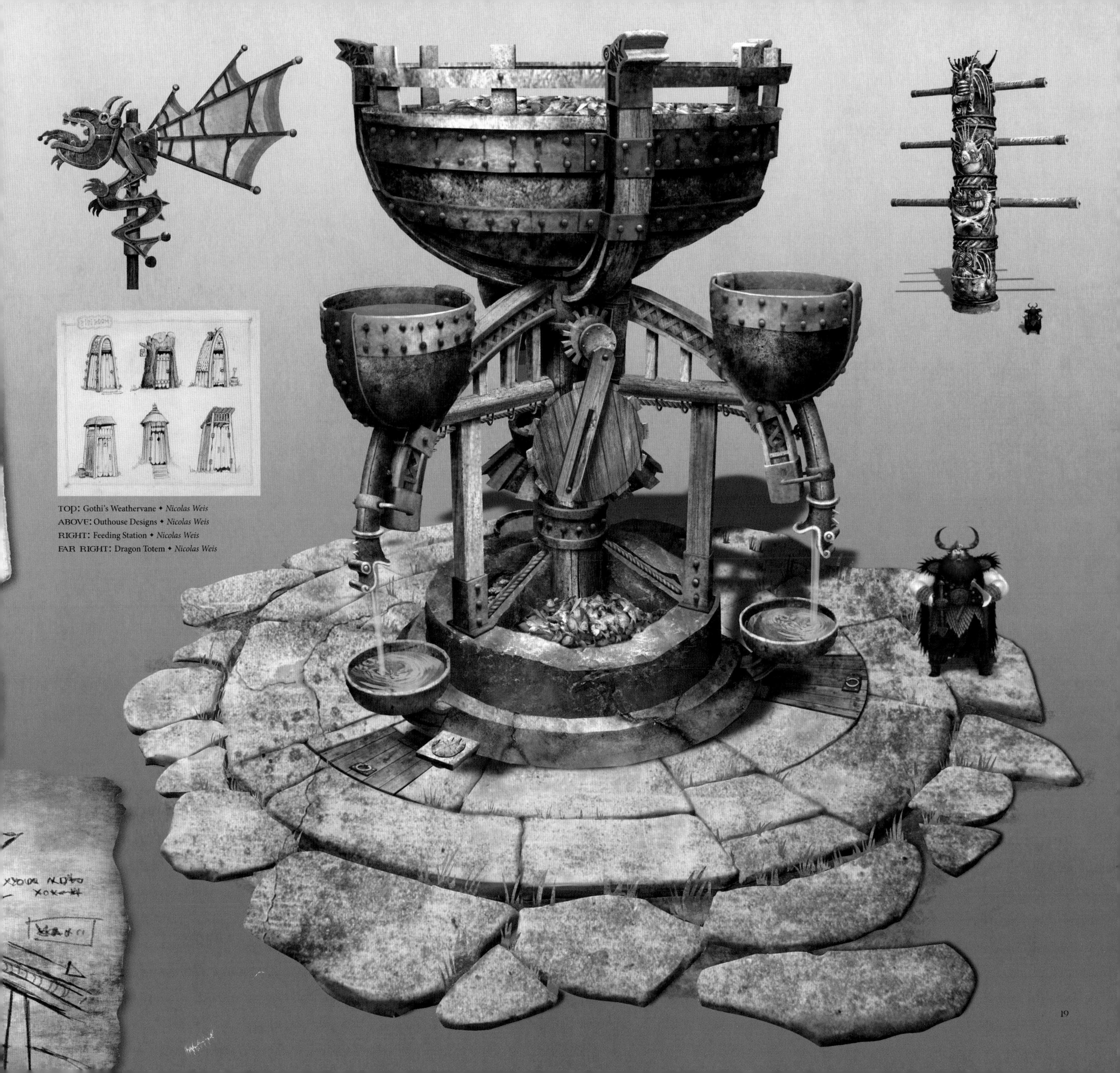

TOP: Gothi's Weathervane ✦ *Nicolas Weis*
ABOVE: Outhouse Designs ✦ *Nicolas Weis*
RIGHT: Feeding Station ✦ *Nicolas Weis*
FAR RIGHT: Dragon Totem ✦ *Nicolas Weis*

But the true headquarters for all things dragon-related on Berk is the Dragon Armory. Five years ago, it was just Gobber's sad little blacksmith stall, but since then, we expanded it into an amazing one-stop dragon service center. Here, Gobber and I build customized saddles, make fire-proof riding gear, and treat all sorts of dragon maladies from sprained wings to chewing problems. We even do dragon dentistry. A windmill out back powers all sorts of automated workshop tools that I designed specifically for building my dragon-friendly creations. Call it the nerve center of New Berk.

And that's just a quick gander at the major overhaul we underwent to usher in this era of a dragon-friendly utopia. It hasn't been easy, but we're getting the hang of it. Turns out peace is actually hard work, but, you know—we Vikings wouldn't have it any other way.

—Written by HICCUP
and TOOTHLESS
helped too!

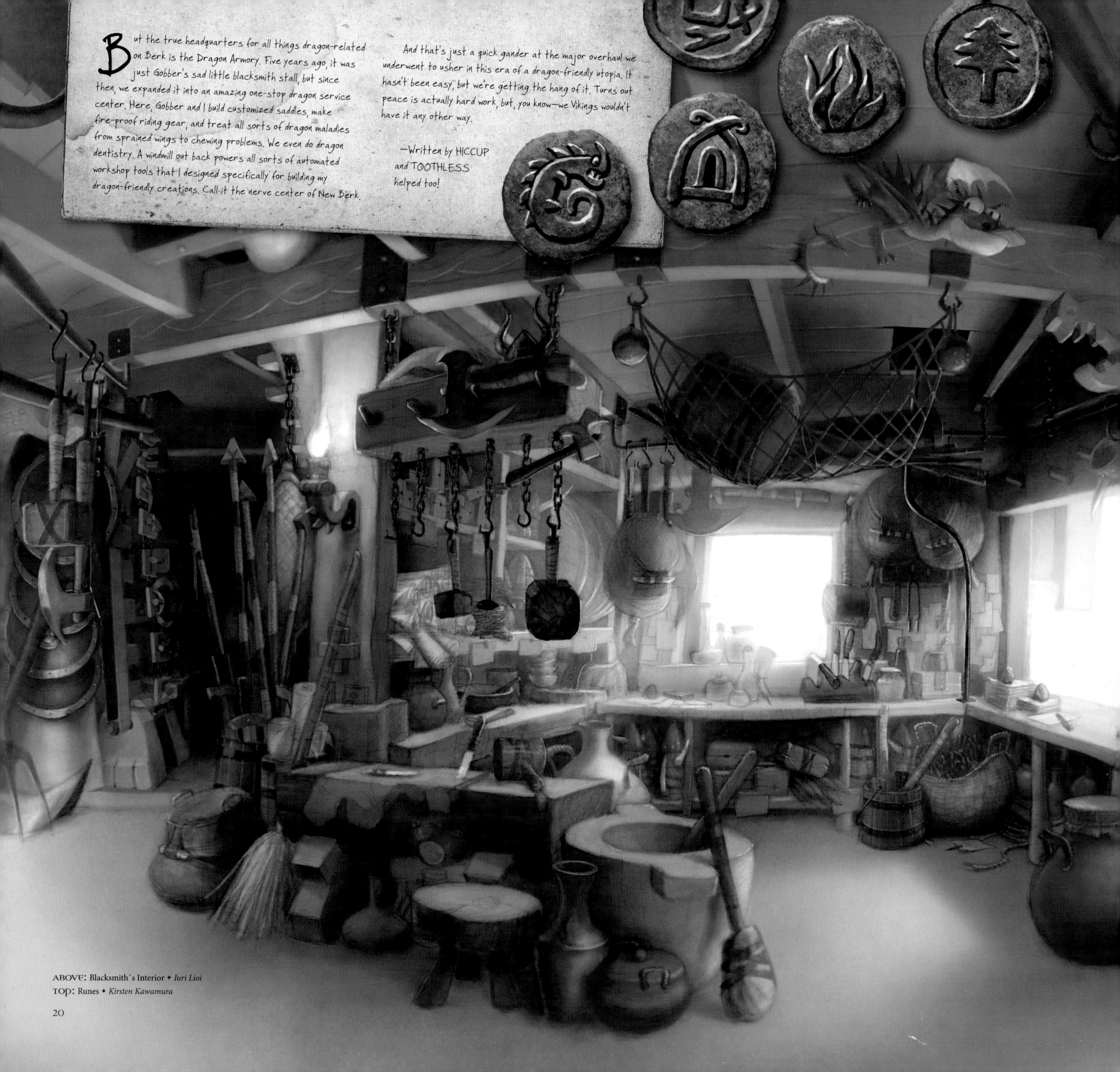

ABOVE: Blacksmith's Interior • *Iuri Lioi*
TOP: Runes • *Kirsten Kawamura*

LEFT: Armory Saddle Forms ✦ *Iuri Lioi*
BELOW: Gobber's Worktable ✦ *Iuri Lioi*
BOTTOM: Berk Cutaway Map ✦ *Iuri Lioi*

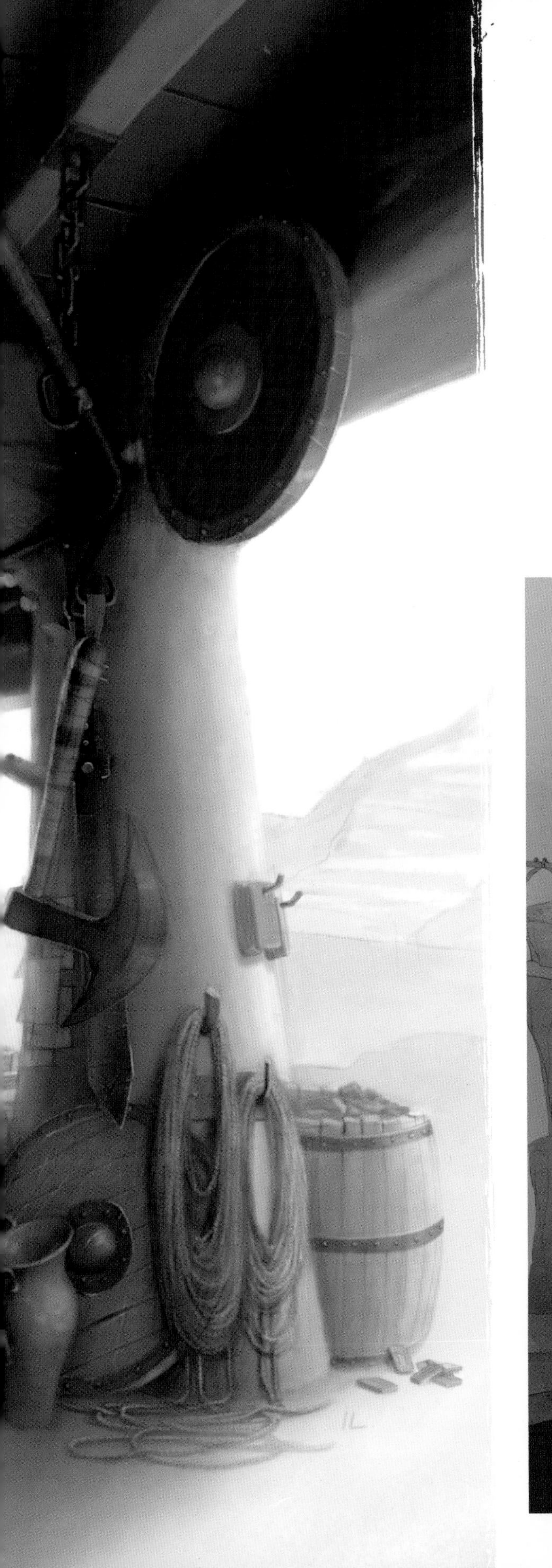

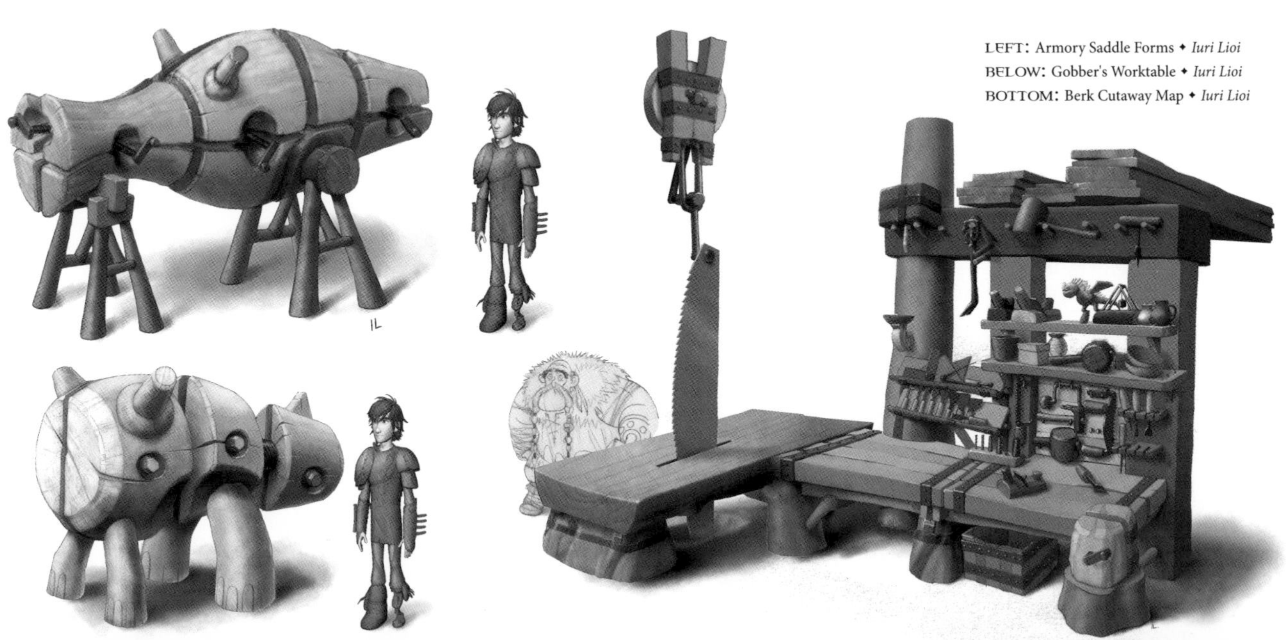

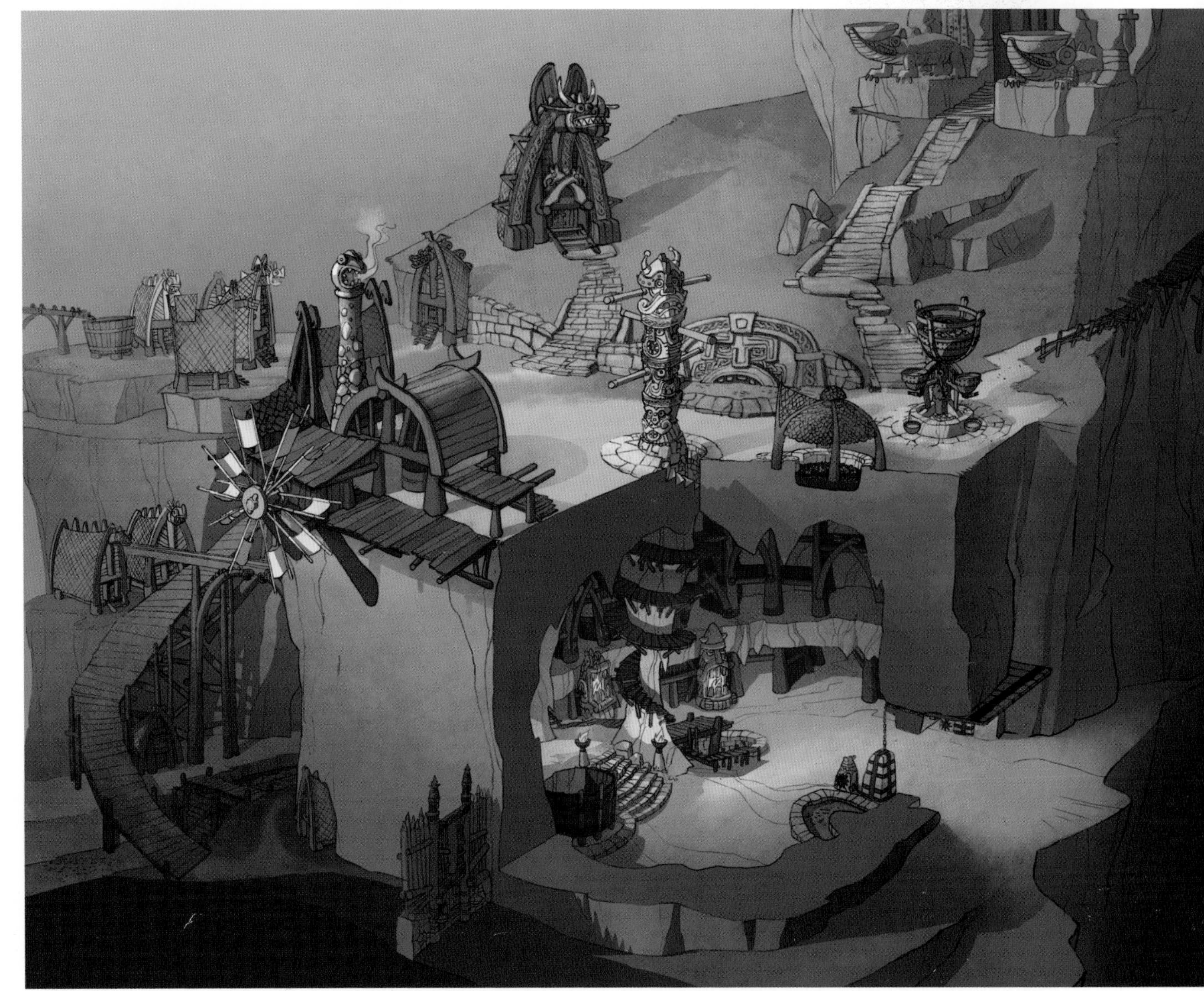

# Berk at Peace

Right from the first conversations about making a sequel, we knew that we had a few big opportunities. Instead of creating a world from scratch we now had the chance to refine our characters and set pieces, as well as expand the universe we had created. There was this hope of being able to do something that had never been done in animation. We now had the freedom to intensify and dramatize the movie not just tonally but visually. Our concept for the sequel was that we would create a dragon utopia. Now we could build all the things that would be needed in this new world, which in itself was a designer's dream.

*—Simon Otto, head of character animation*

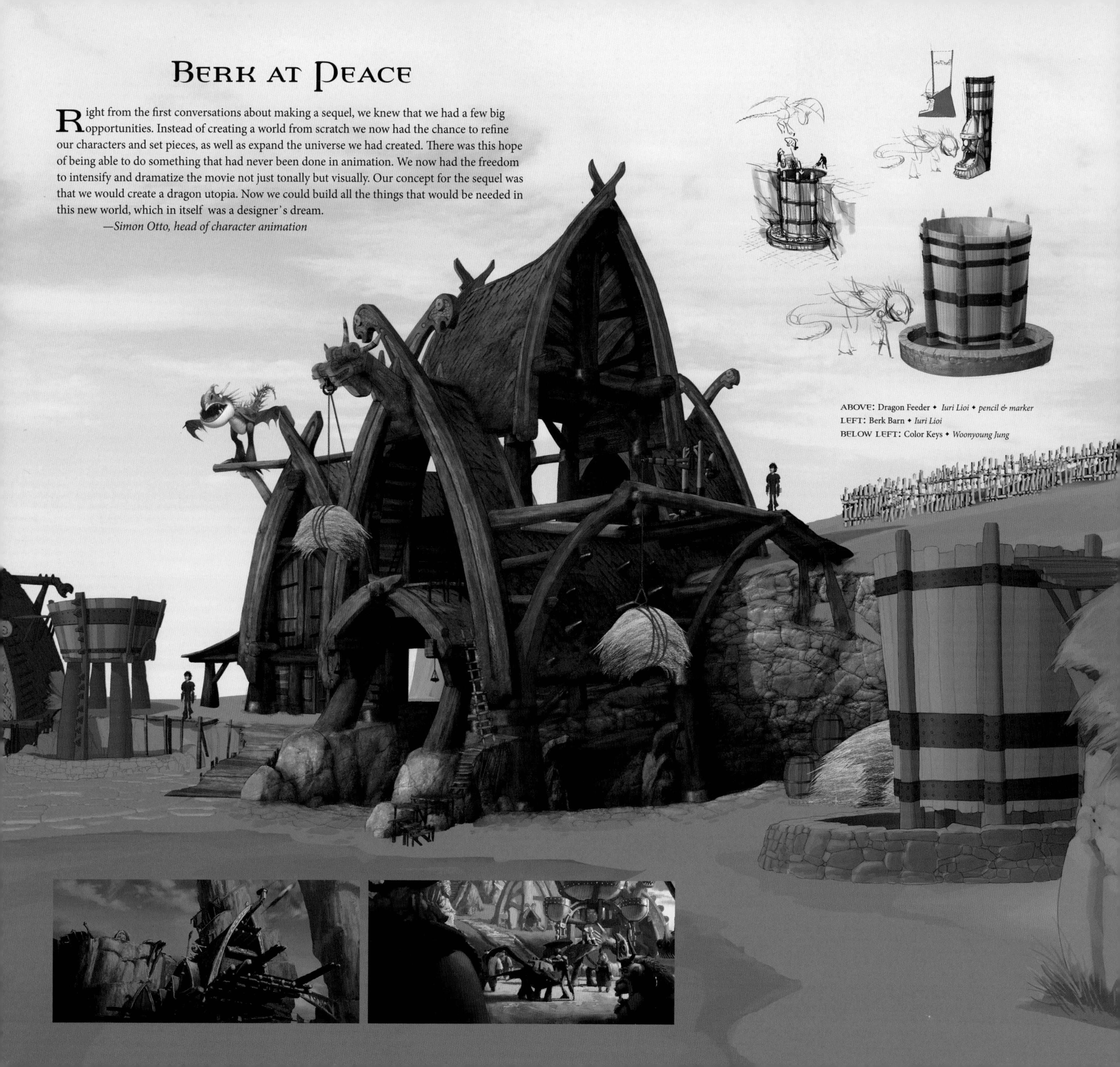

ABOVE: Dragon Feeder ✦ *Iuri Lioi* ✦ *pencil & marker*
LEFT: Berk Barn ✦ *Iuri Lioi*
BELOW LEFT: Color Keys ✦ *Woonyoung Jung*

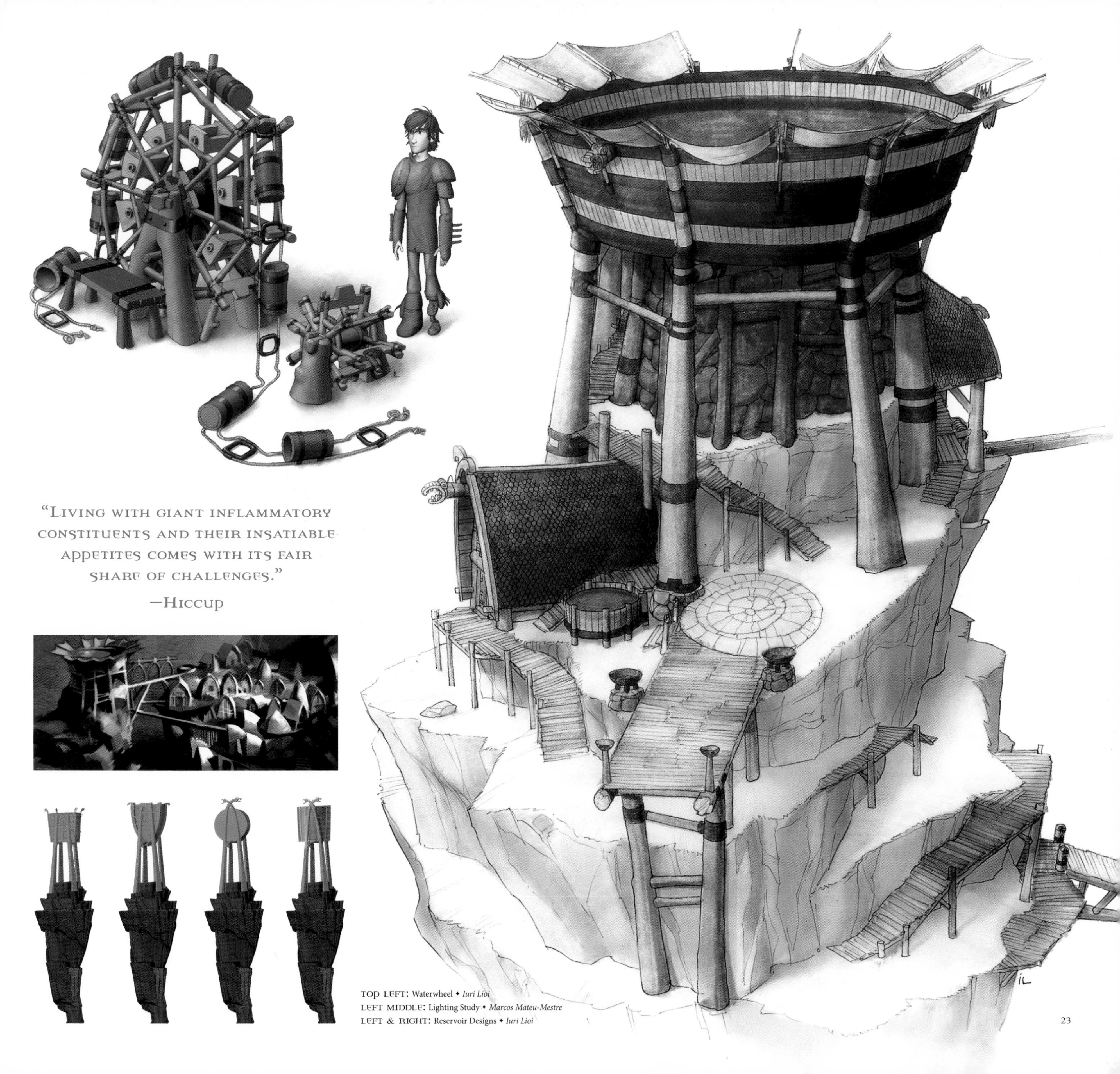

"Living with giant inflammatory constituents and their insatiable appetites comes with its fair share of challenges."

—Hiccup

Top Left: Waterwheel ✦ *Iuri Lioi*
Left Middle: Lighting Study ✦ *Marcos Mateu-Mestre*
Left & Right: Reservoir Designs ✦ *Iuri Lioi*

TOP & MIDDLE RIGHT: Dragon Stables
✦ *Iuri Lioi* ✦ *pencil & marker*
BOTTOM RIGHT: Dragon Stables ✦ *Iuri Lioi*
BELOW: Saddle Racks ✦ *Iuri Lioi* ✦ *pencil*
BELOW RIGHT: Saddle Rack ✦ *Iuri Lioi*
BOTTOM LEFT: Dragon Stables
✦ *Kirsten Kawamura*

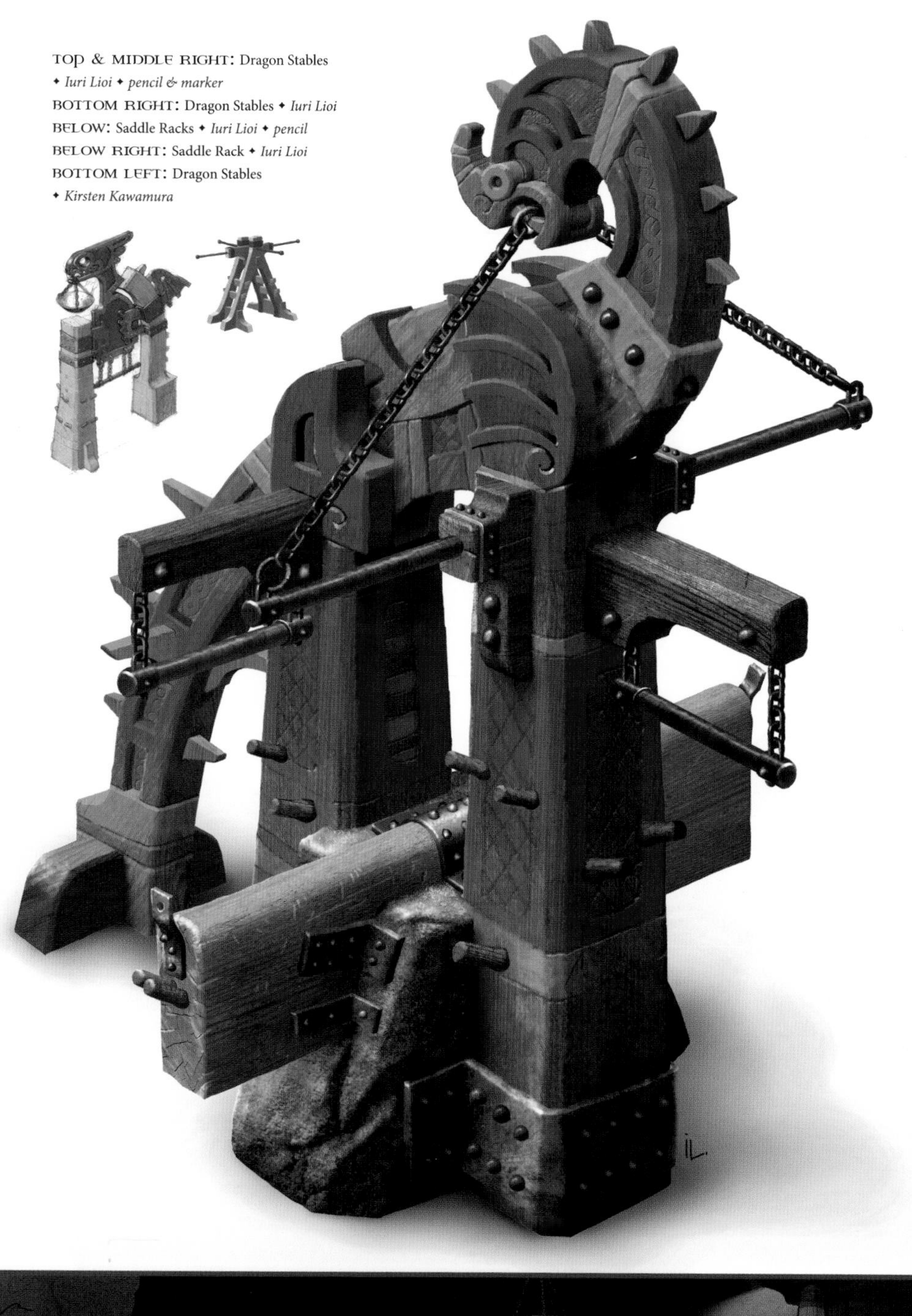

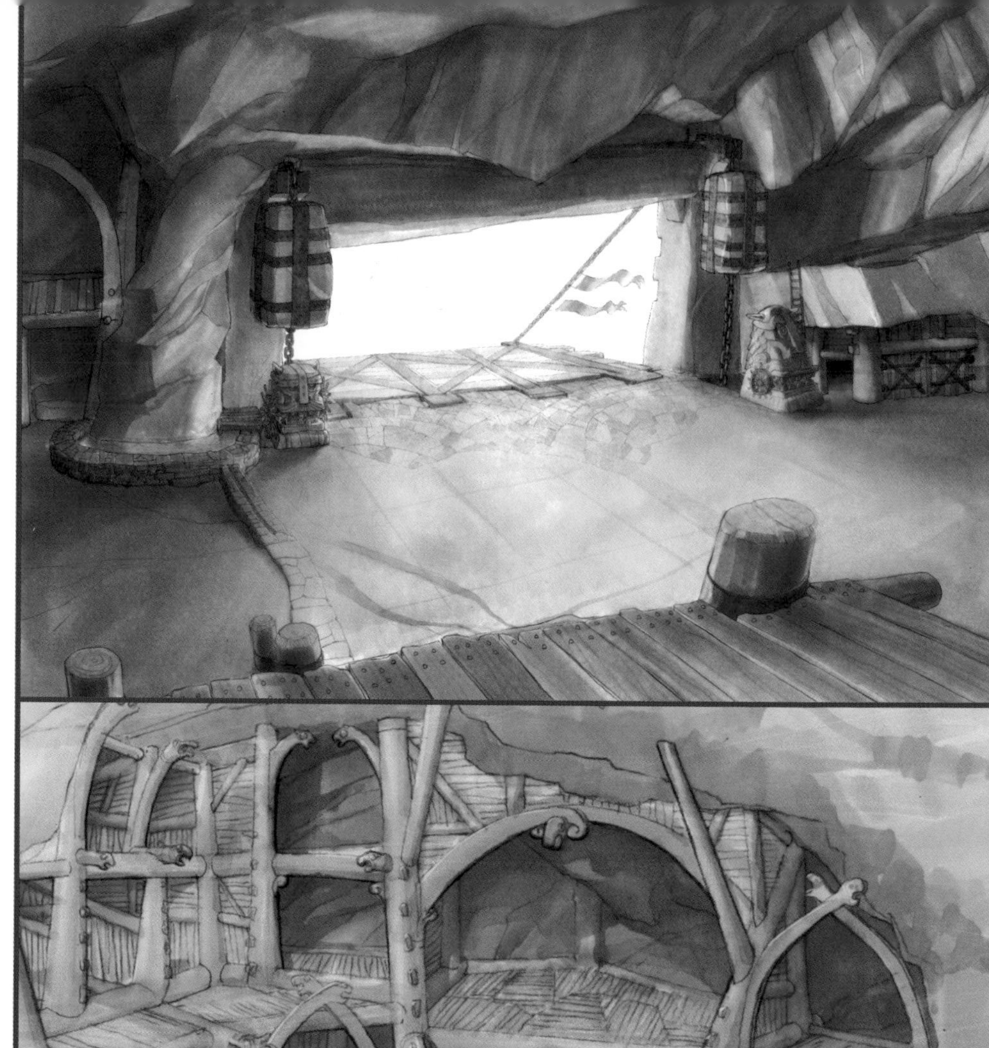

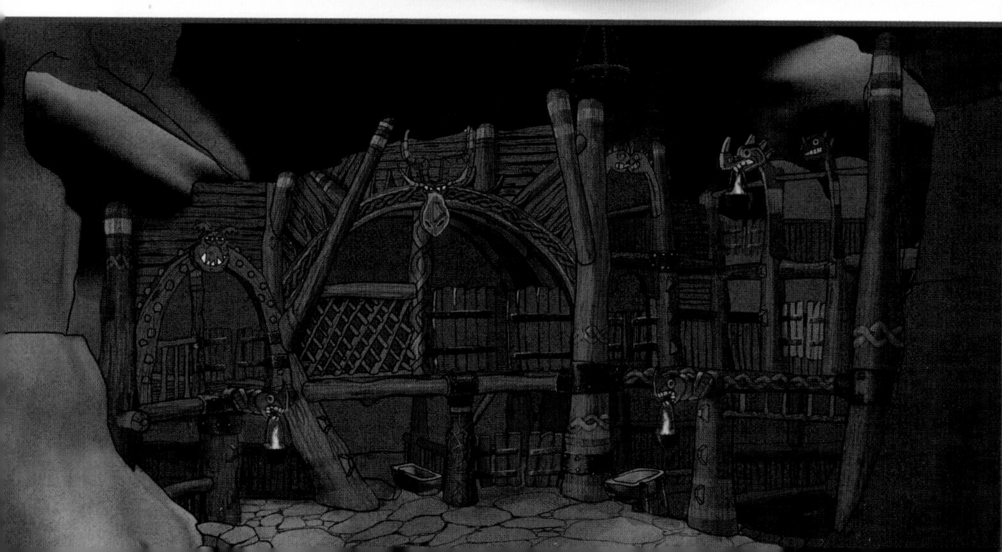

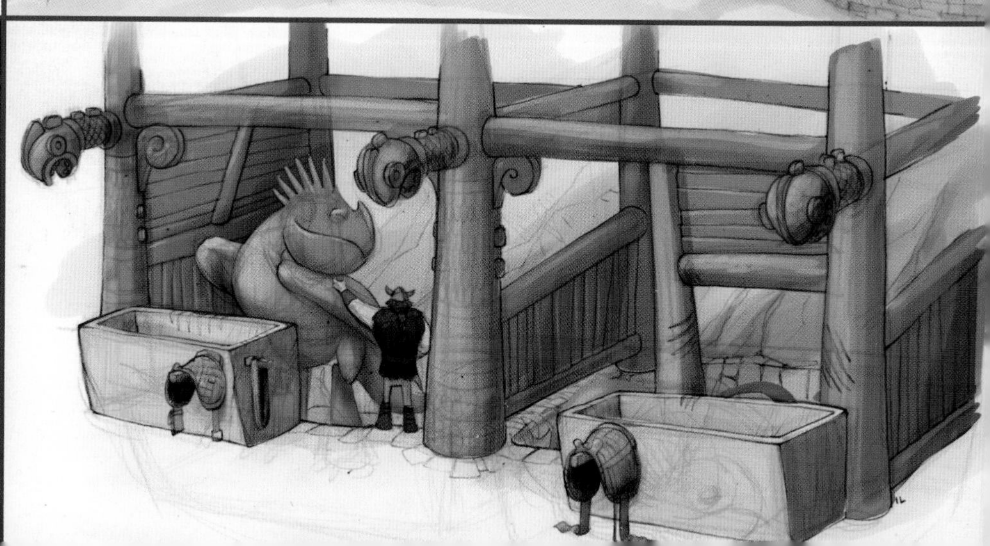

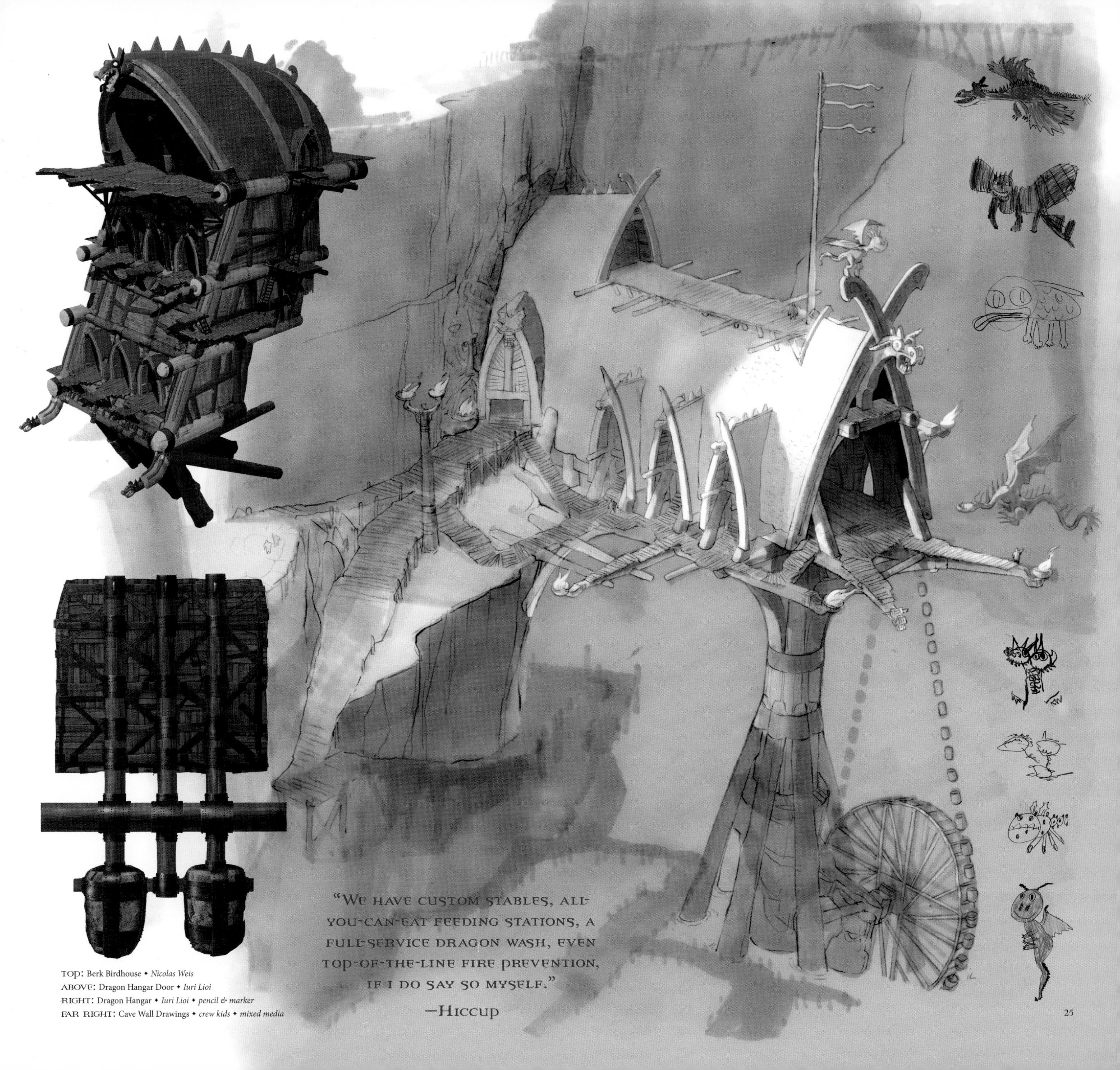

"We have custom stables, all-you-can-eat feeding stations, a full-service dragon wash, even top-of-the-line fire prevention, if I do say so myself."

—Hiccup

TOP: Berk Birdhouse ✦ *Nicolas Weis*
ABOVE: Dragon Hangar Door ✦ *Iuri Lioi*
RIGHT: Dragon Hangar ✦ *Iuri Lioi* ✦ *pencil & marker*
FAR RIGHT: Cave Wall Drawings ✦ *crew kids* ✦ *mixed media*

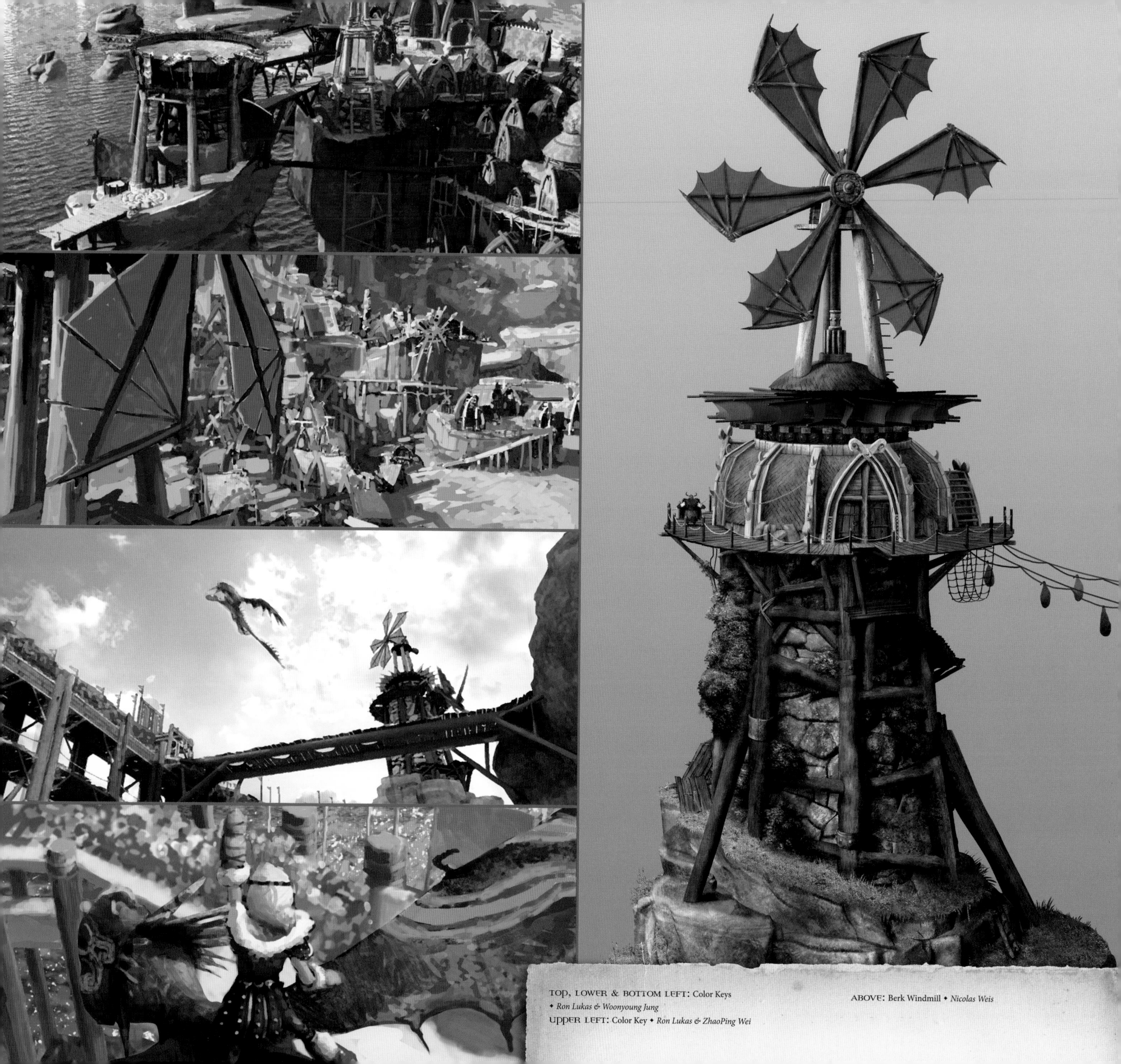

TOP, LOWER & BOTTOM LEFT: Color Keys
◆ *Ron Lukas & Woonyoung Jung*
UPPER LEFT: Color Key ◆ *Ron Lukas & ZhaoPing Wei*

ABOVE: Berk Windmill ◆ *Nicolas Weis*

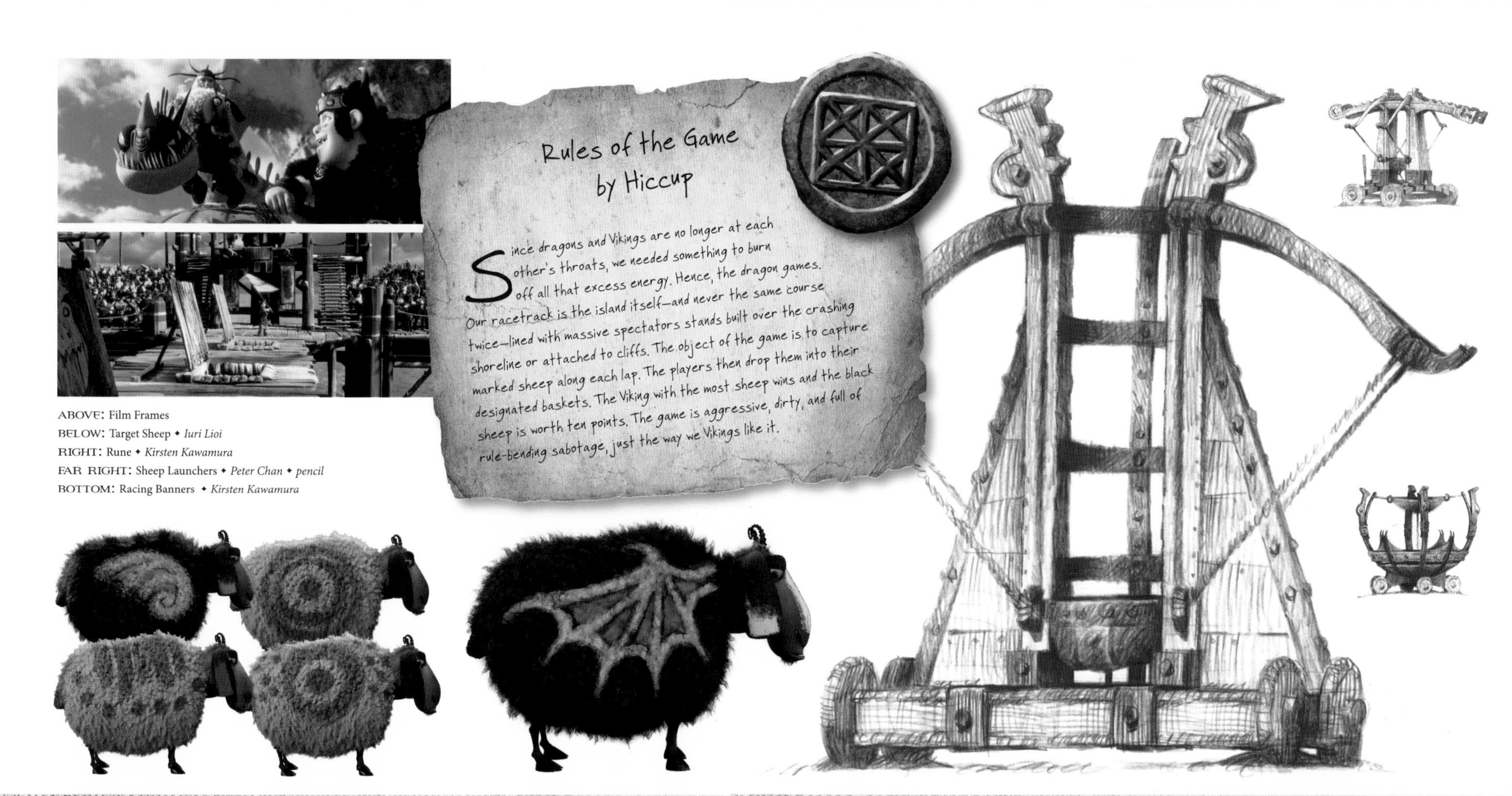

## Rules of the Game
### by Hiccup

Since dragons and Vikings are no longer at each other's throats, we needed something to burn off all that excess energy. Hence, the dragon games. Our racetrack is the island itself—and never the same course twice—lined with massive spectators stands built over the crashing shoreline or attached to cliffs. The object of the game is to capture marked sheep along each lap. The players then drop them into their designated baskets. The Viking with the most sheep wins and the black sheep is worth ten points. The game is aggressive, dirty, and full of rule-bending sabotage, just the way we Vikings like it.

ABOVE: Film Frames
BELOW: Target Sheep ✦ *Iuri Lioi*
RIGHT: Rune ✦ *Kirsten Kawamura*
FAR RIGHT: Sheep Launchers ✦ *Peter Chan* ✦ *pencil*
BOTTOM: Racing Banners ✦ *Kirsten Kawamura*

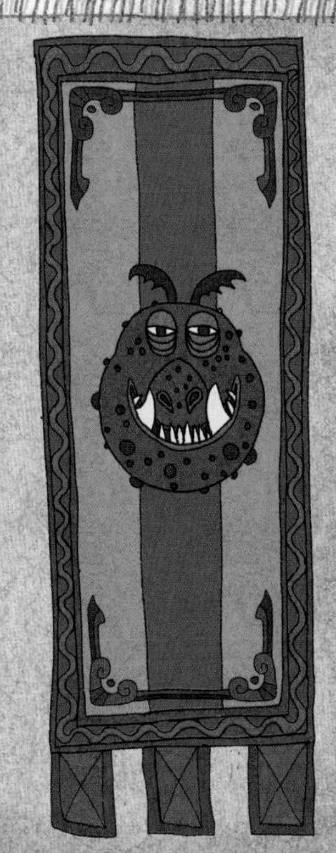
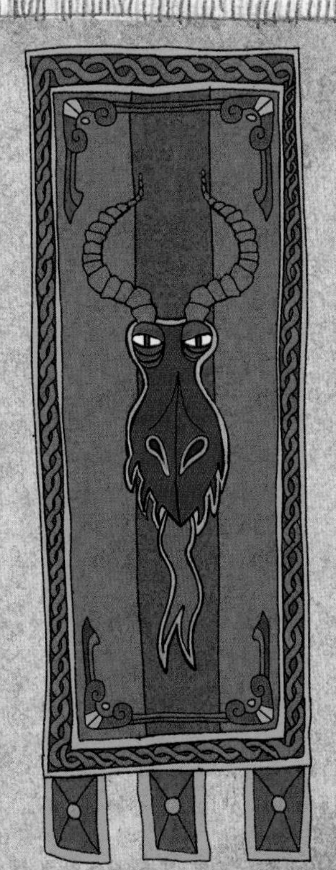
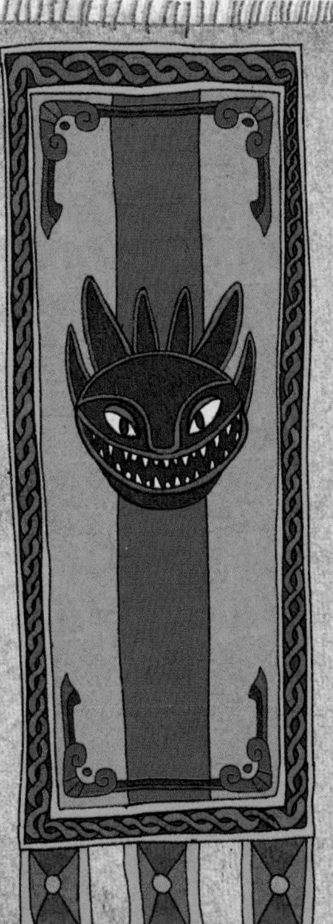
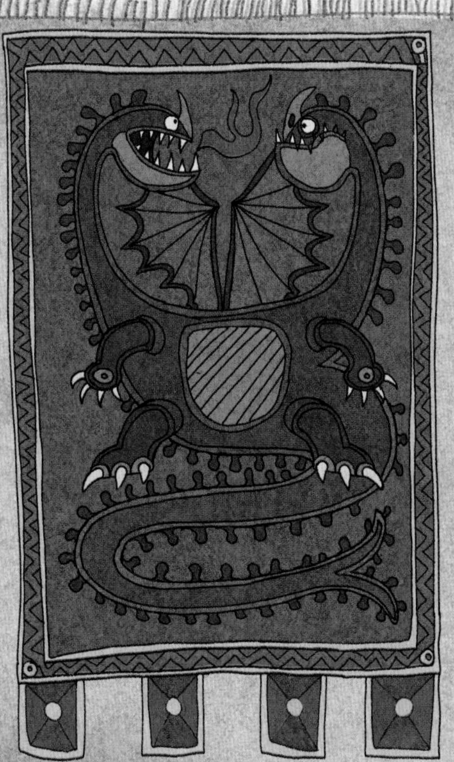
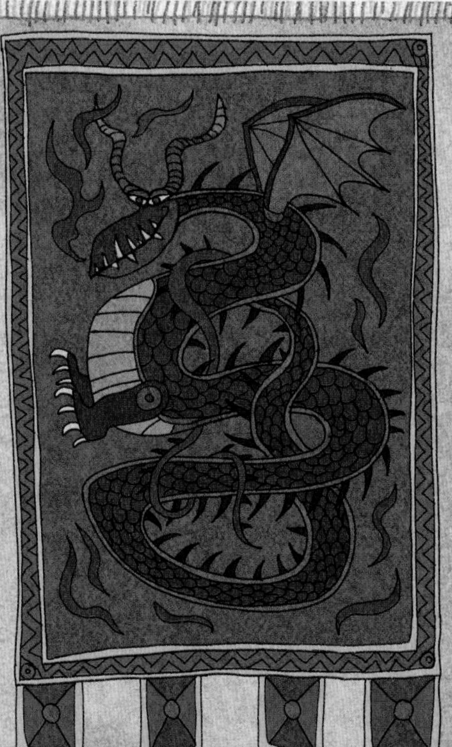

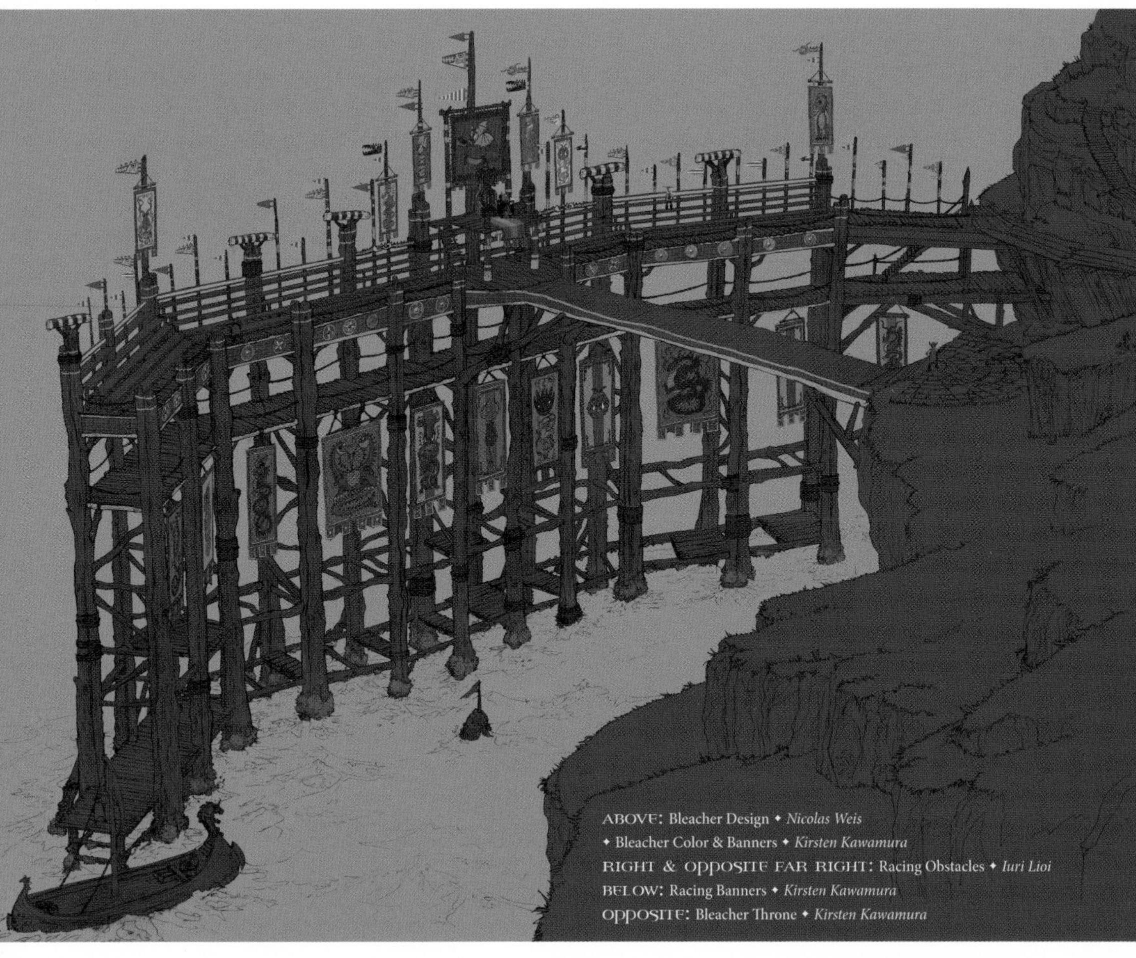

ABOVE: Bleacher Design ✦ *Nicolas Weis*
✦ Bleacher Color & Banners ✦ *Kirsten Kawamura*
RIGHT & OPPOSITE FAR RIGHT: Racing Obstacles ✦ *Iuri Lioi*
BELOW: Racing Banners ✦ *Kirsten Kawamura*
OPPOSITE: Bleacher Throne ✦ *Kirsten Kawamura*

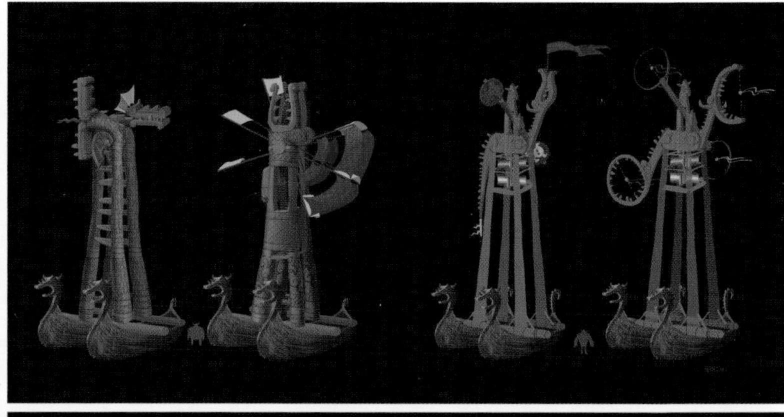

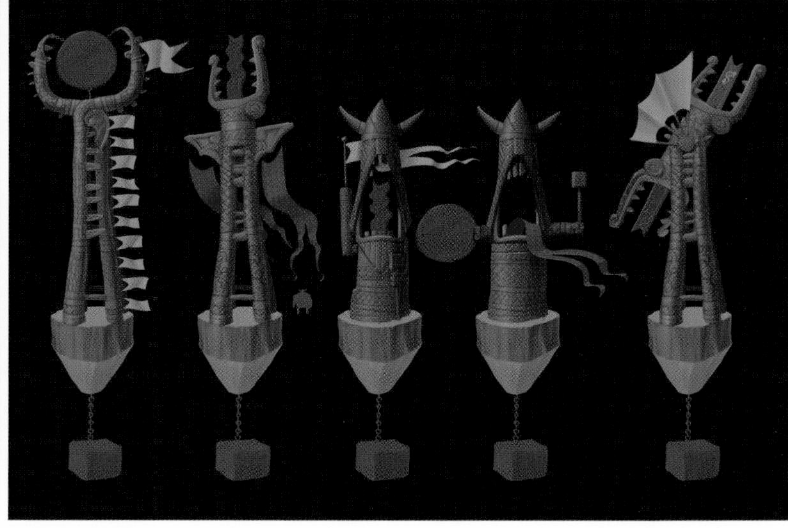

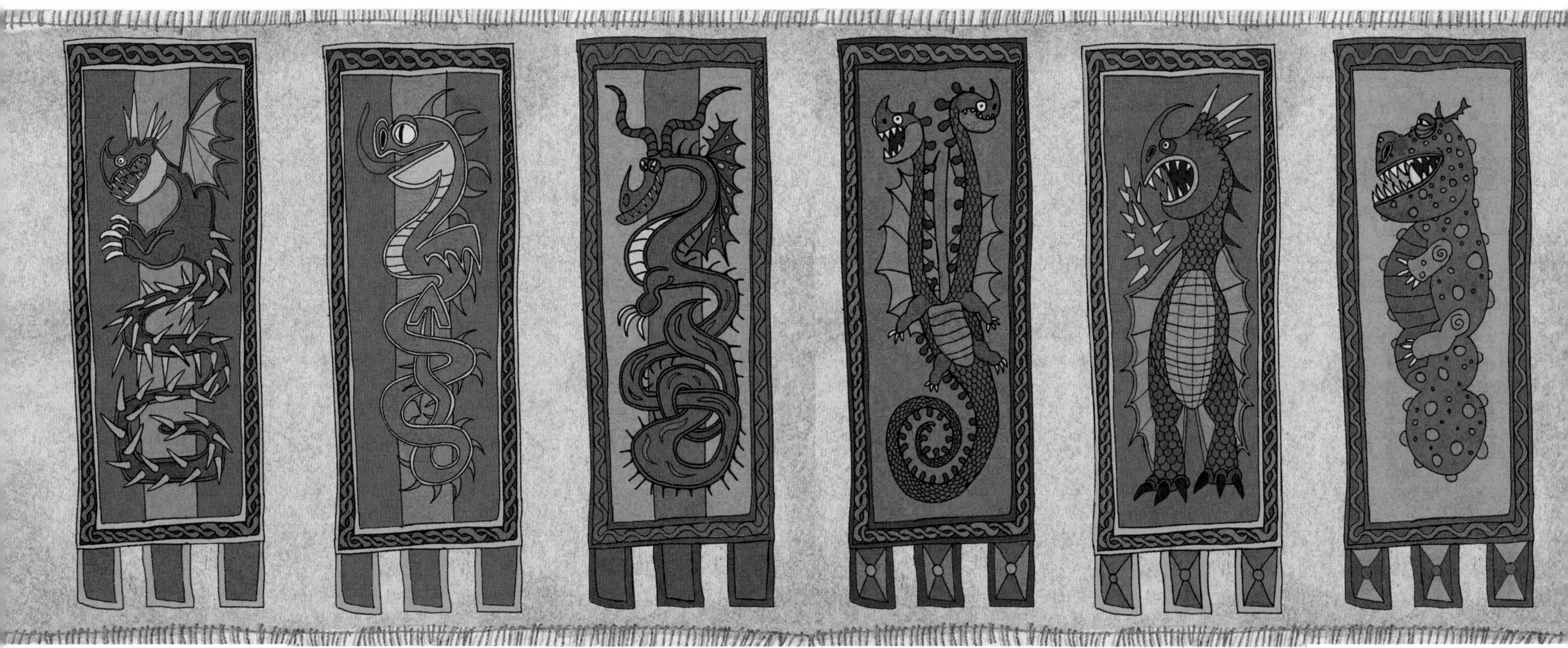
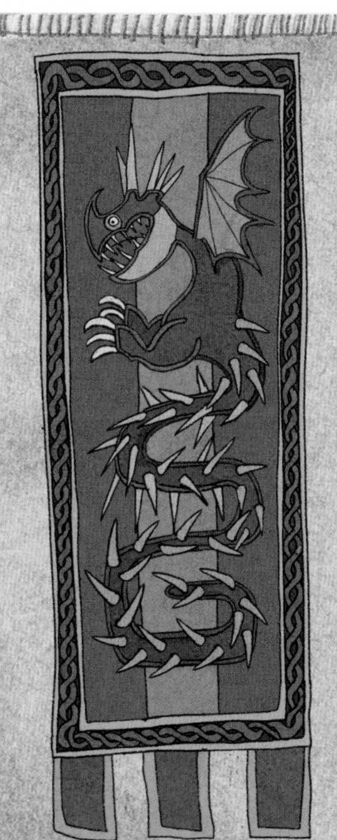
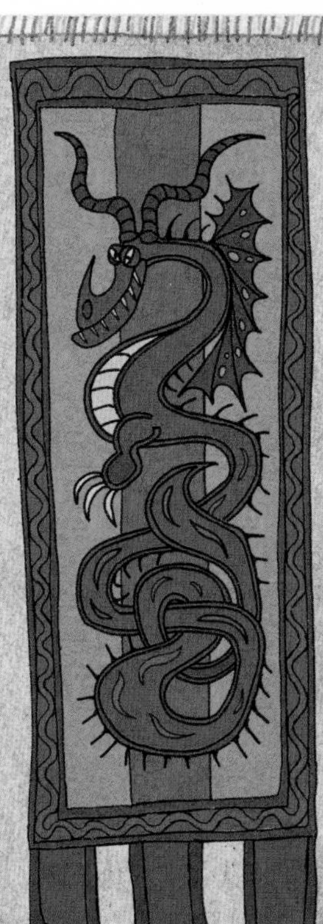
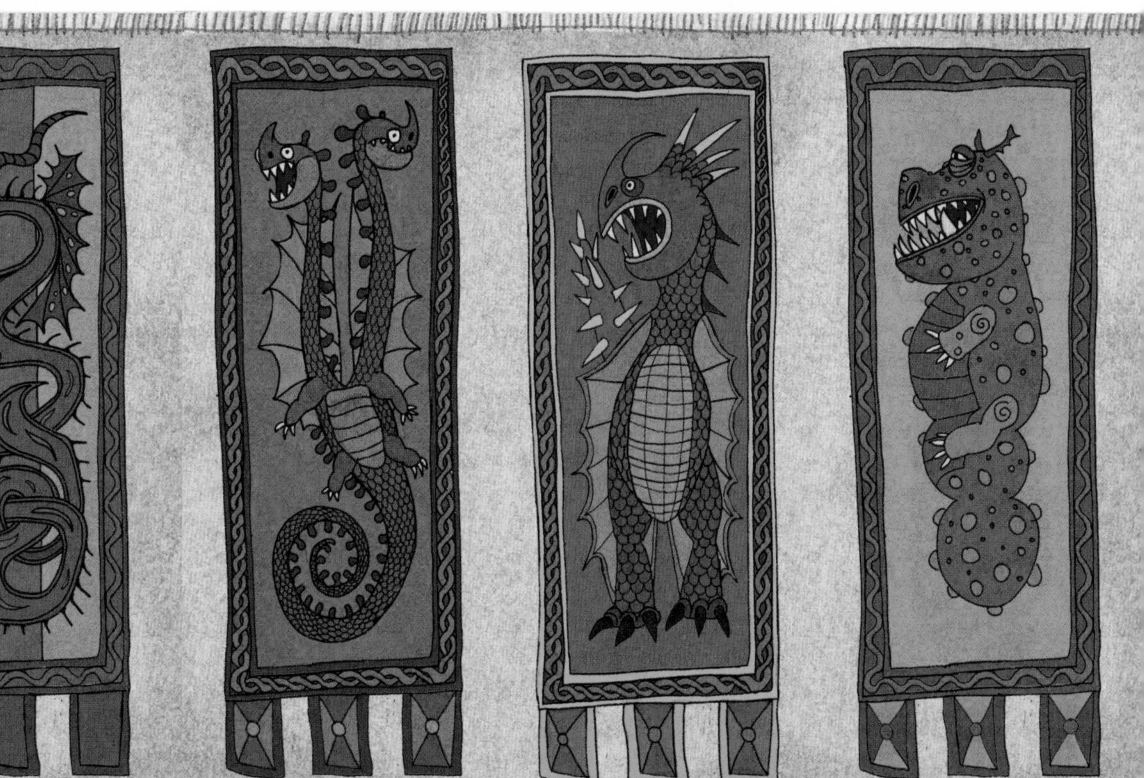
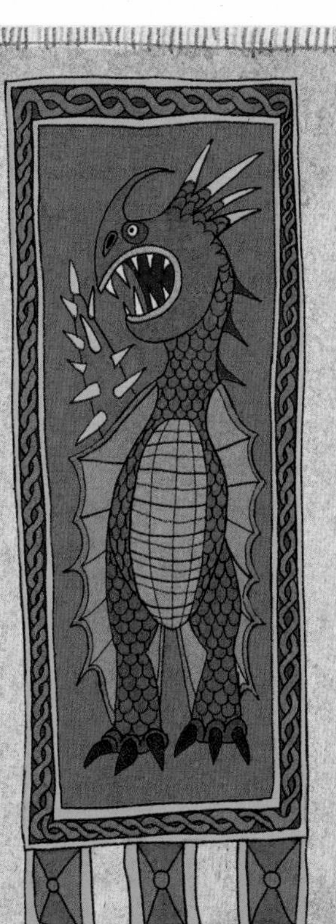
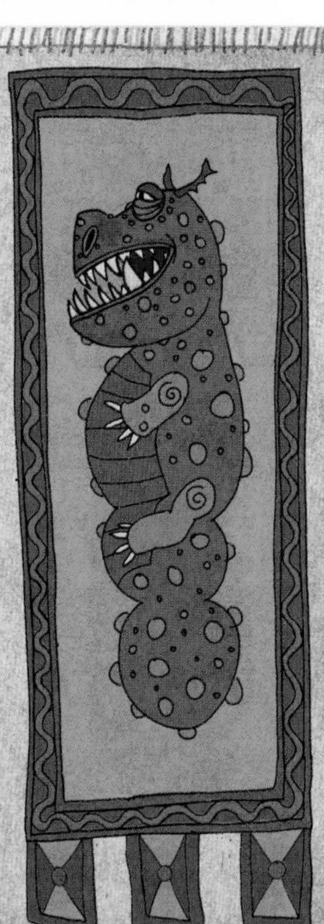

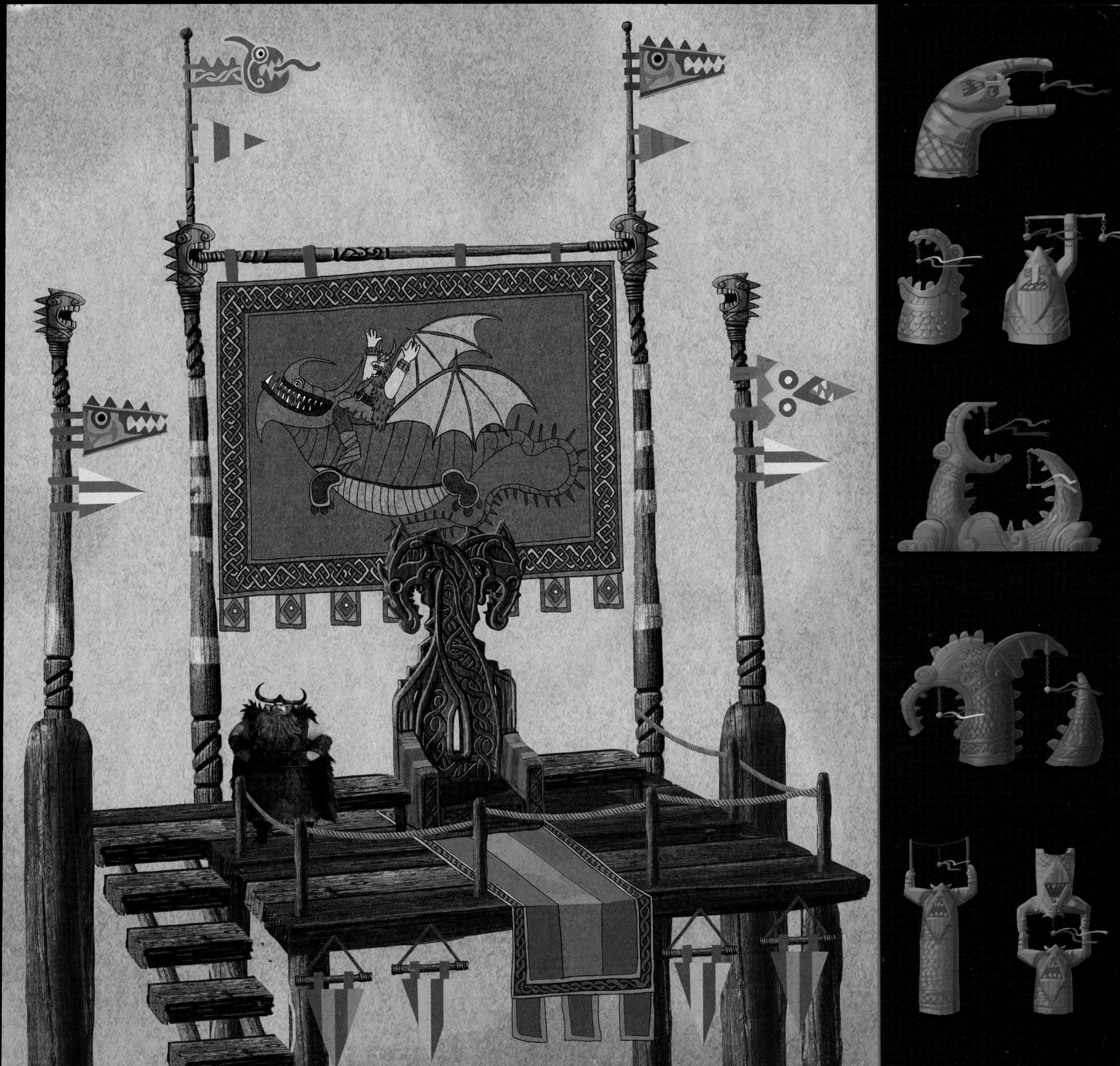

# PART II
# VIKINGS OF NEW BERK

"No task is too small when it comes to serving your people."

# Up, Up & Away

Sequence 300 started out as a short sequence meant to reintroduce the characters of Hiccup and Toothless five years later. It picked up where the first movie left off, showing Hiccup and Toothless flying together. The storyboards were beautifully drawn, and the entire flight was about a minute long. After layout delivered their 3-D footage to editorial, we cut it together and immediately noticed this was more than just a reintroduction to Hiccup flying a dragon. After watching it, we all felt there was something magical here, and we wanted to see more.

We needed the audience to be immersed in the experience, and feel the sensation of what it would be like to soar in the clouds with Toothless. We spent more time with this sequence and ultimately, it turned out to be twice as long as its original length, but infinitely better.

*—John Carr, editor*

One of our challenges in the lighting department is that our movie takes place in the northern part of the hemisphere where the sun doesn't set. This creates a unique light quality that doesn't occur anywhere else on the planet. We've been trying to capture that in certain places and it's difficult because if you take a picture of this particular light, the photo doesn't really tell the story. It's more of a feeling than something you can see in a photo. It might be 3:00 in the morning when the picture was taken but the light looks like it was shot at 5:00 in the afternoon.

We want our lighting to convey that you don't quite know what time of day it is. We avoid the midday sun because it is out of place here. But even in the opening sequences when we are flying around Berk, there is the feeling that a storm just passed. It's early in the morning and it feels like the sun just came out, but it does feel a little wet and cold.

*—Pablo Valle, head of lighting*

LEFT: Color Key ✦ *Woonyoung Jung*
OPPOSITE TOP: Color Keys ✦ *Woonyoung Jung*
OPPOSITE MIDDLE: Film Frames
OPPOSITE BOTTOM & PREVIOUS PAGES: Hiccup Explores ✦ *Pierre-Olivier Vincent*

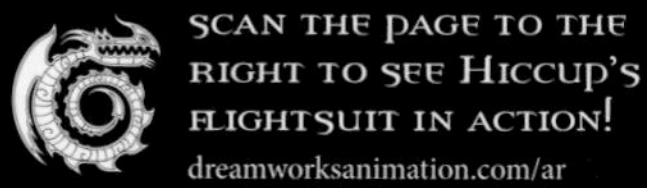

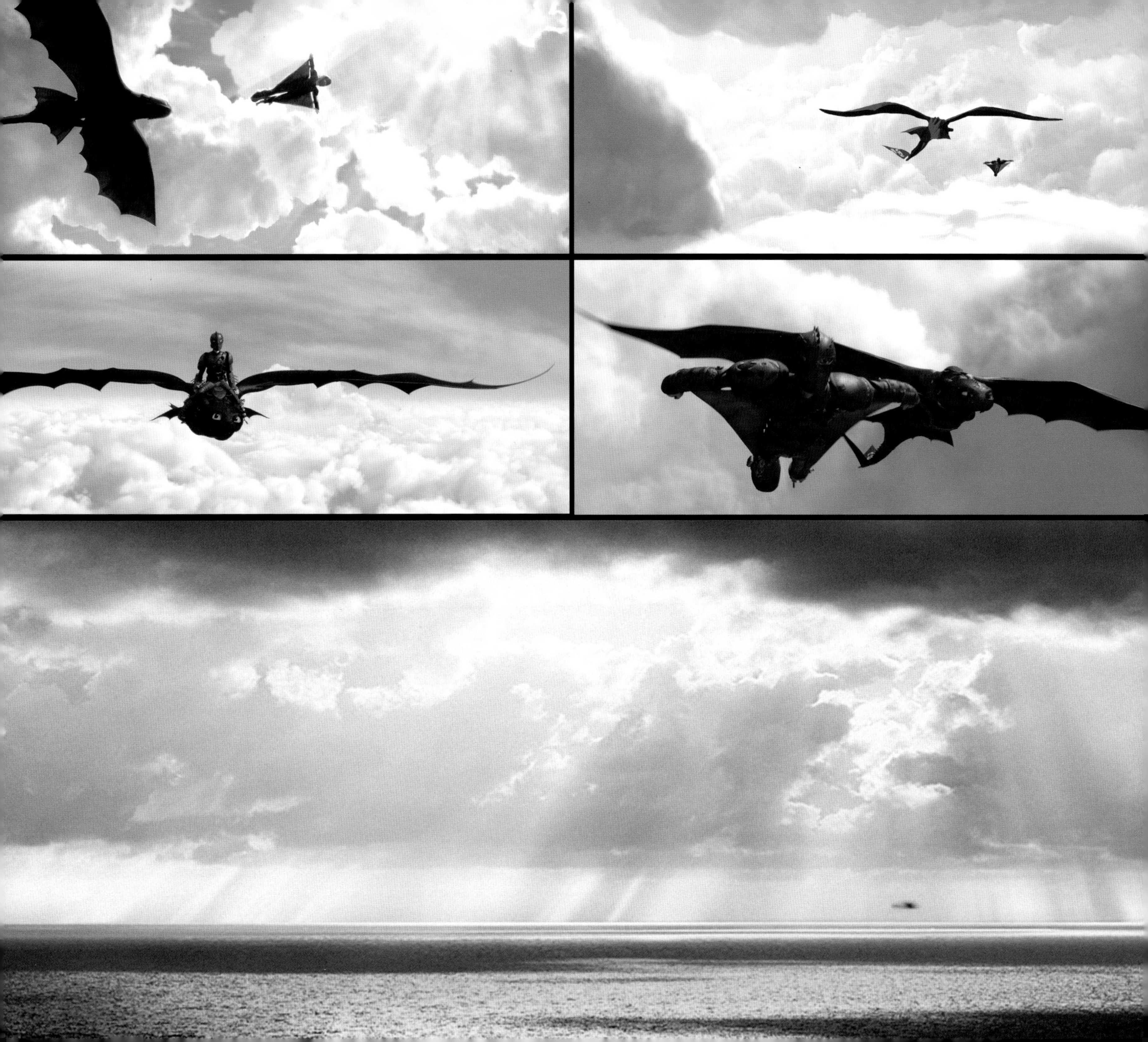

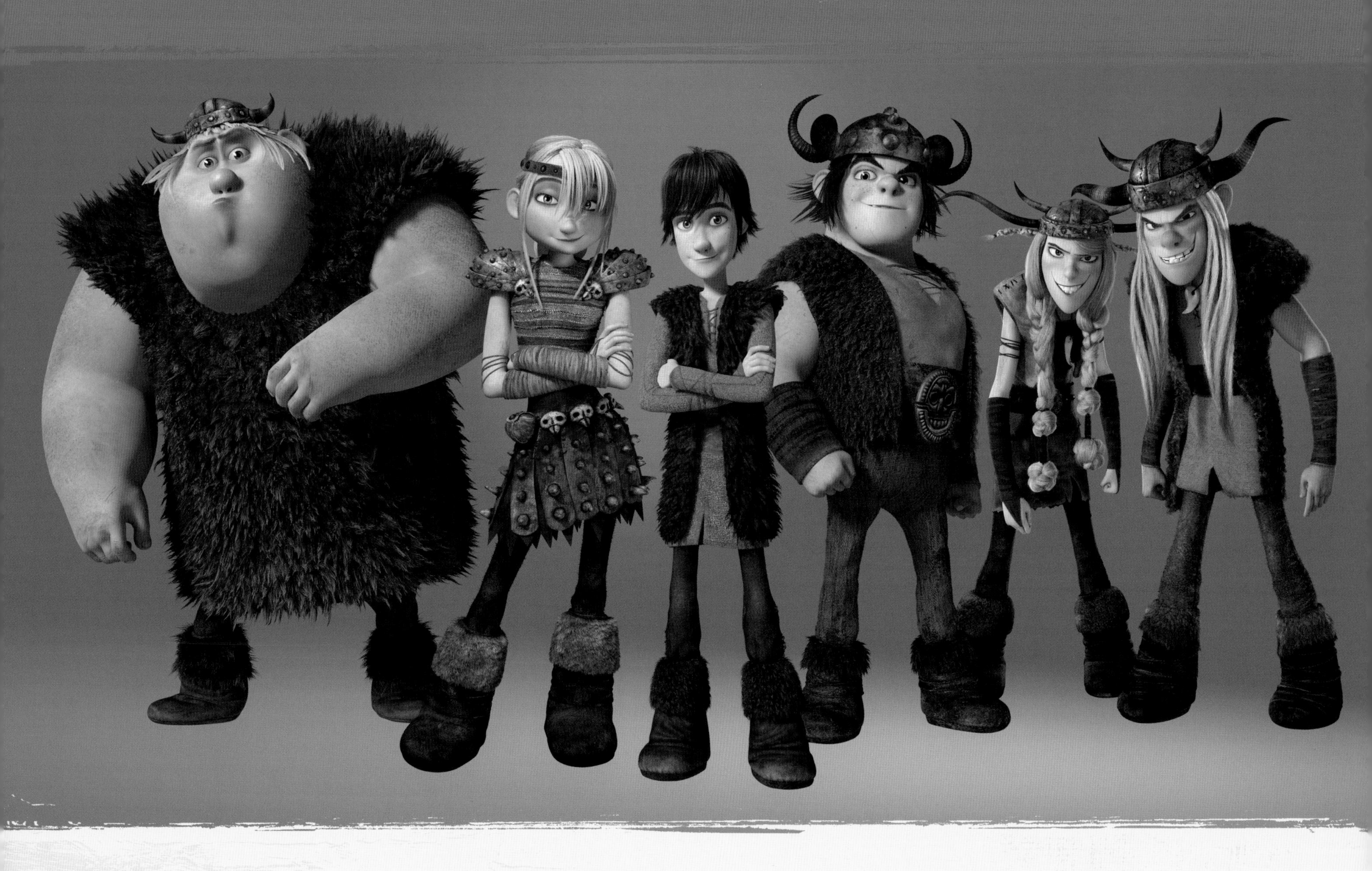

# Aging Up the Characters

Aging up characters is rarely done in animation, so it was a fun challenge to revisit Hiccup and his friends with an eye toward making them older. It was an opportunity to inject more of the character traits that we had discovered in the first movie, channeling them into the revamped designs. Of course, we wanted to retain the recognizable stamp of each character, so the real challenge lay in subtle shifts—and lots of trial and error. Hiccup, in particular, was a tricky redesign because he's not only the main character, but he's also the most realistic looking of the cast.

In coming up with his new look, we had to factor Hiccup's story line into our thinking. After all, Hiccup is now a town hero. He's no longer pining for the acceptance and respect that he once longed for. He has transcended his status of Berk's nuisance underdog, so that has to affect his confidence and the way he carries himself. At the same time, most of Hiccup's charm comes from his gangly awkwardness, so we wanted to keep that too. He is tenacious and witty and often self-deprecating. So we approached his design as that of a thrill-seeking adventurer—restless and on the cusp of adulthood, but also vulnerable in that he isn't sure of who he is to become. He still isn't the burly Viking that his father had hoped for, but he has grown up and come into his own regardless. He's cool, but in an unkempt, nerdy sort of way. His flight suit, designed to be the equivalent of Viking biker leather, was conceived to look like an evolution of Hiccup's own design sense—functional and aerodynamic, but also a bit geeky and over-the-top from his girlfriend's perspective.

*—Dean DeBlois, director*

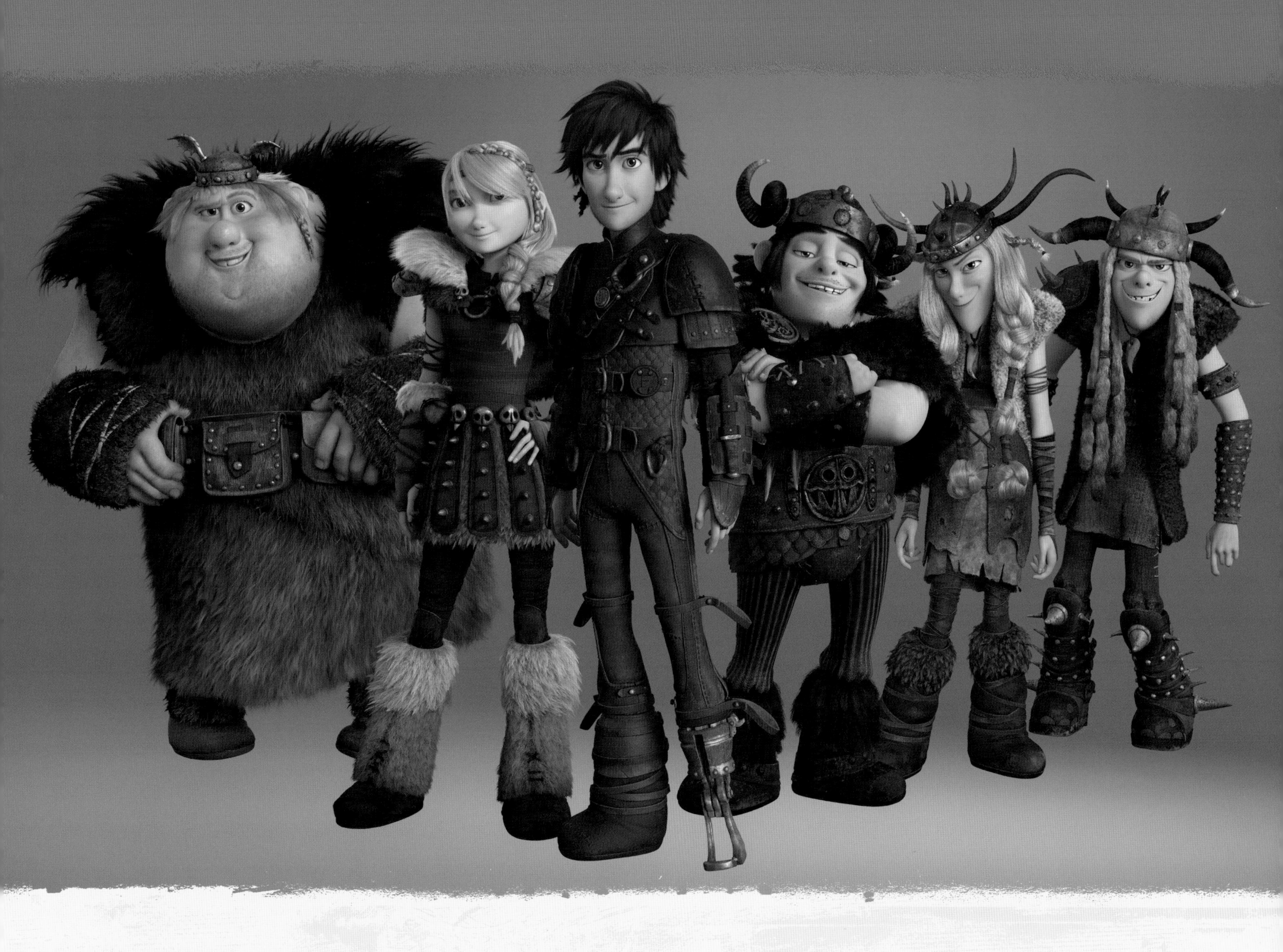

Dean's gutsy decision to age up the characters was an exciting opportunity for the storytelling as well as a challenge for our art department. The narrative became more than just the further adventures of Hiccup and Toothless. The audience will actually get to see how all the things that happened to our two heroes in the first film plays out five years later. Just for the record, I was the one who had to tell the guys that Astrid needed a bit more of a bustline.

*—Bonnie Arnold, producer*

We wanted to show that years had passed in their lives and they have new responsibilities in their village while, at the same time, keeping true to their characters. We also wanted to show the maturity that some of the characters developed. Many of the boys looked older when we added facial hair.

Colors played an intricate role in helping develop an older look. For example, the leather on their costumes was made to look more worn and used. Overall, the characters no longer gave off a "cute" look; everyone looked more mature, more like adults.

*—ZhaoPing Wei, art director*

OPPOSITE PAGE: Character Designs ✦ *How to Train Your Dragon*
ABOVE: Character Designs ✦ *How to Train Your Dragon 2*

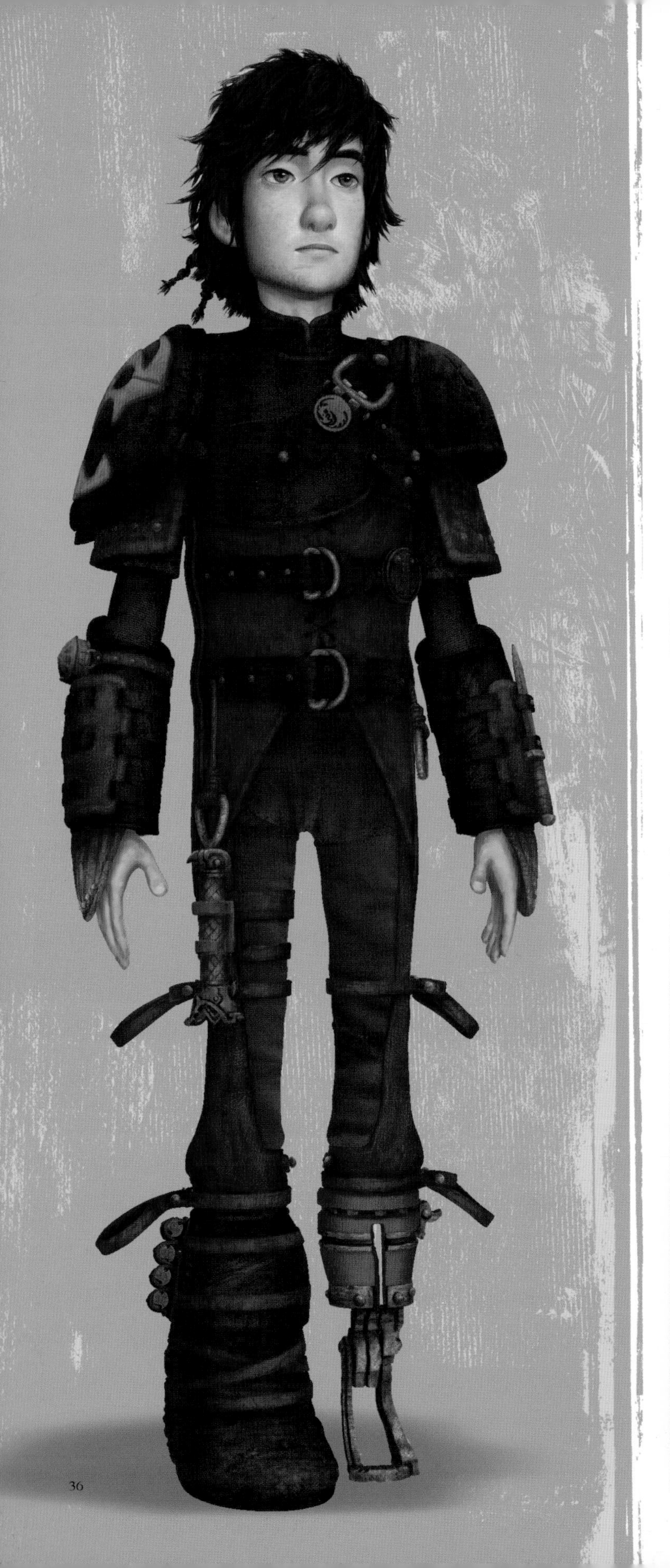



# Hiccup

*How to Train Your Dragon* was really a departure from anything that DreamWorks had ever done before. Hiccup has an entertaining point of view about the world, but he doesn't tell jokes or take pratfalls. In a way, this film is more like a character-driven, live-action comedy, only with fire-breathing flying dragons along for the ride.

—*Bill Damaschke, chief creative officer, DreamWorks Animation*

Hiccup was fifteen years old in the first film and now he is twenty. Like all the characters in the film, we wanted him to stay true to his original design but we had to age him. Our design plan was to emphasize the Viking/Leonardo DaVinci aspect of his character. By now, Hiccup has established himself as the creator of this new Viking society. He is more sophisticated, more aware of who he is, what he does, and what he is good at doing. We made him taller and slightly better looking than he was in the first film.

—*Pierre-Olivier Vincent, production designer*

We wanted Hiccup to have the same appeal that made him so popular in the first movie, only he had to be older. We changed his haircut and made it a bit more scruffy. We altered the proportions of his face but it was so subtle that most of the work was done on the 3-D model.

—*Nico Marlet, character designer*

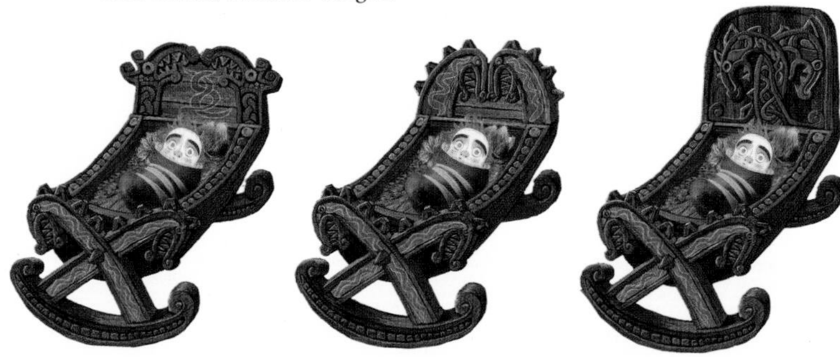

LEFT: Hiccup Painting • *ZhaoPing Wei* • Model • *Jaewon Lee*
ABOVE LEFT: Baby Hiccup Painting • *Ron Lukas* • Model • *Matt Paulson & Kull Shin*

ABOVE RIGHT: Cradle Variations • *Kirsten Kawamura*
BELOW LEFT & RIGHT: Toothless's Racing Stripes Concept • *Kirsten Kawamura* • Model • *Matt Paulson & Jaewon Lee* • Surfacing • *Greg Hettinger & Carson James McKay*

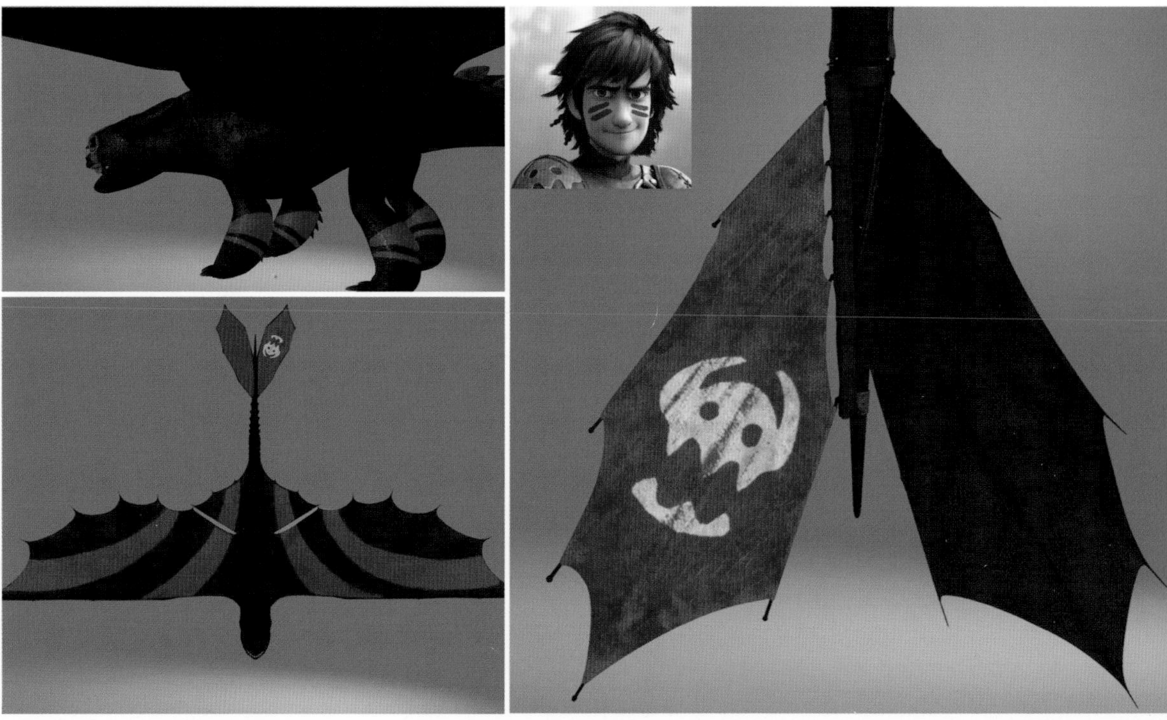

## Life Issues

*How to Train Your Dragon* has taken the age-old story of a teenage boy sorting through his fundamental life issues—fit in, figure out self, get the girl, don't disappoint Dad—set it in ancient Viking times and still managed to give it a thoroughly modern spin. A millennium later and this kid would head an Internet start-up or have a reality show on cable. . . . Hiccup is slight of build in a clan of hearty folk; an out-of-the-box thinker before boxes were invented. By making Hiccup sincere as well as clever rather than the overused and vastly overrated irritatingly precocious, it's easier to care about his journey.

—*Betsy Sharkey,* Los Angeles Times, *March 26, 2010*

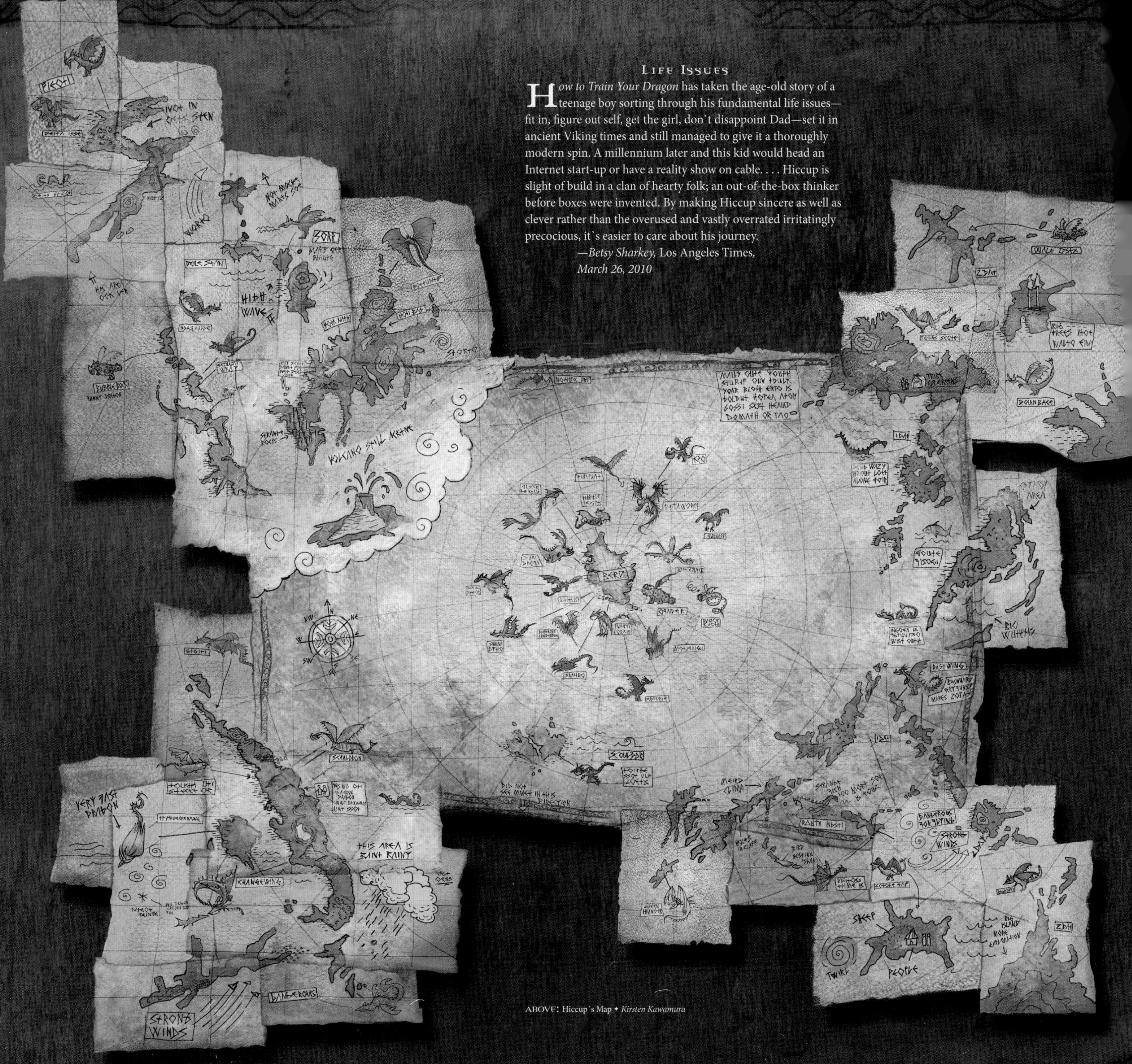

ABOVE: Hiccup's Map ✦ *Kirsten Kawamura*

"He's just twenty. And a Viking. I mean, could there be a worse combination?"

—Gobber

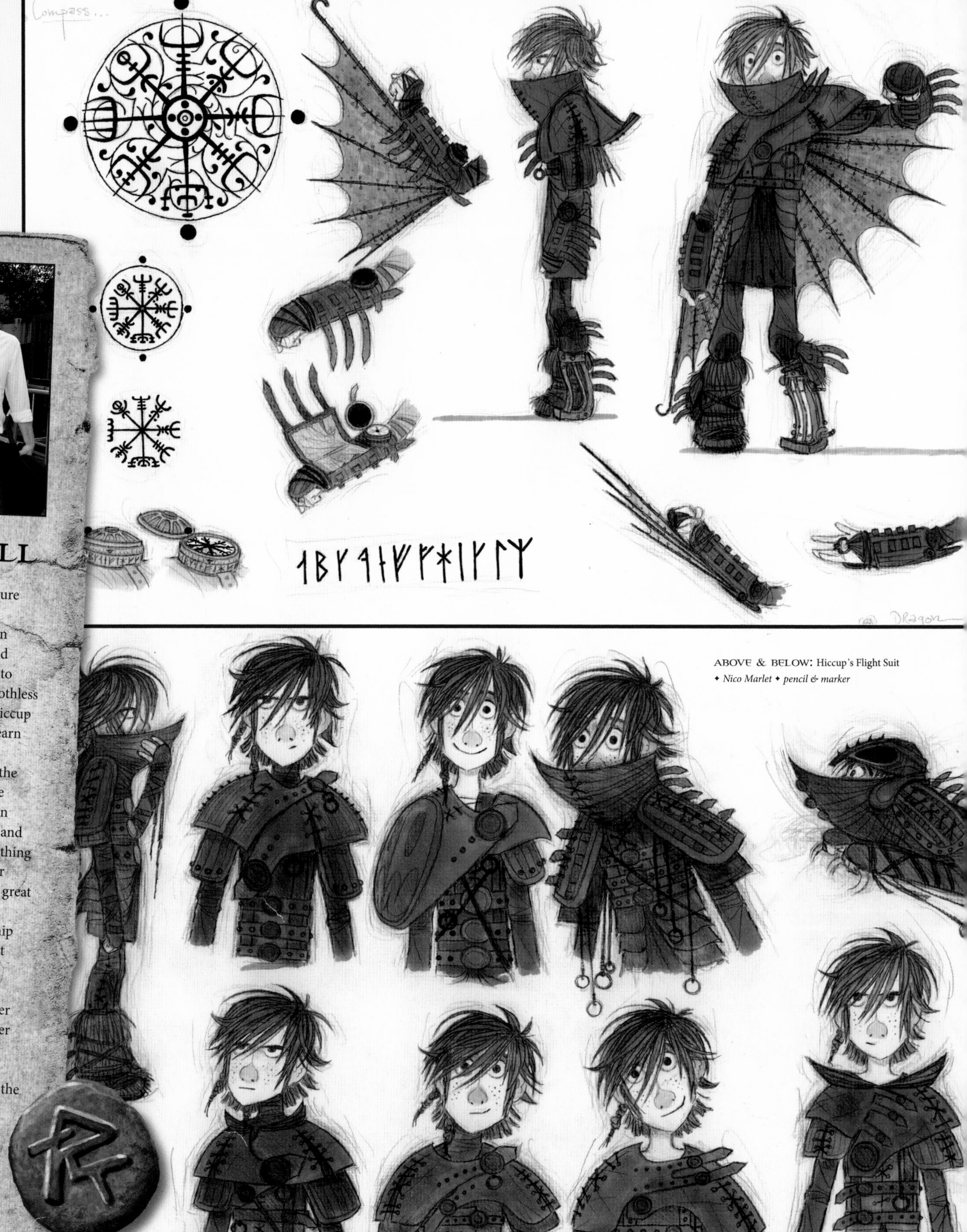


ABOVE & BELOW: Hiccup's Flight Suit
✦ *Nico Marlet* ✦ *pencil & marker*

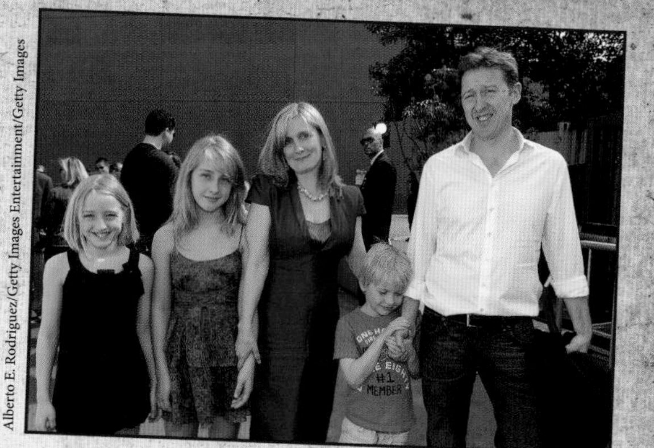


# Cressida Cowell

In the first movie, we had to make a major departure from the original book by Cressida Cowell.

Some books you read and you can see the movie in your head, but this one just wasn't like that. Dean and Chris (Sanders) made crucial story changes in order to make it more cinematic. In the book, Hiccup and Toothless were both runts. Toothless was the tough runt and Hiccup was the klutzy runt that didn't fit in. Hiccup has to learn from Toothless. One of the biggest changes we made was that, in the opening of our movie, Toothless and the dragons are the enemies of the village. In the book the dragons were more like the Flintstones, they worked in the fields and they were pets. In our movie, Toothless and Hiccup first meet as enemies so that Hiccup has something to overcome; it upped the stakes and made for a bigger story. We did however try to keep the essence of these great characters that Cressida created.

It was very important to me to establish a relationship with Cressida. We all wanted her to like this movie that was made from the creations of her imagination. Her books have a huge following and I give her credit for coming to terms with the way we changed her story. Her books still have their loyal fans and our movie is another interpretation of her ideas.

At first, Cressida was unsure about the movie's new story line. She flew to Los Angeles to see a screening of the film and brought along her three children. They loved the new version of the story and assured Cressida that it would be a big hit. She was so supportive of the finished film. It gives the movie more credibility to have the original author's endorsement.

*—Bonnie Arnold, producer*

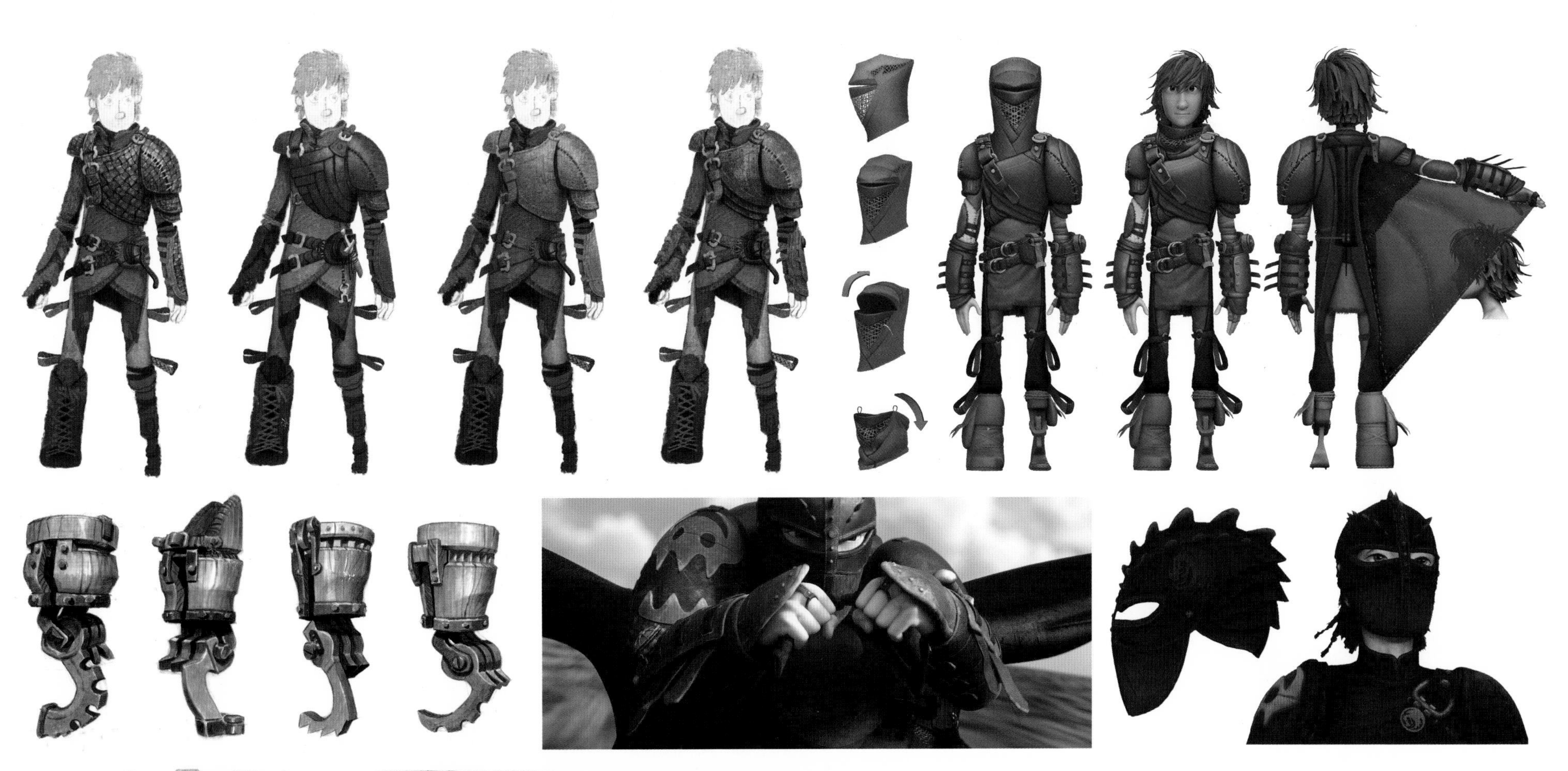

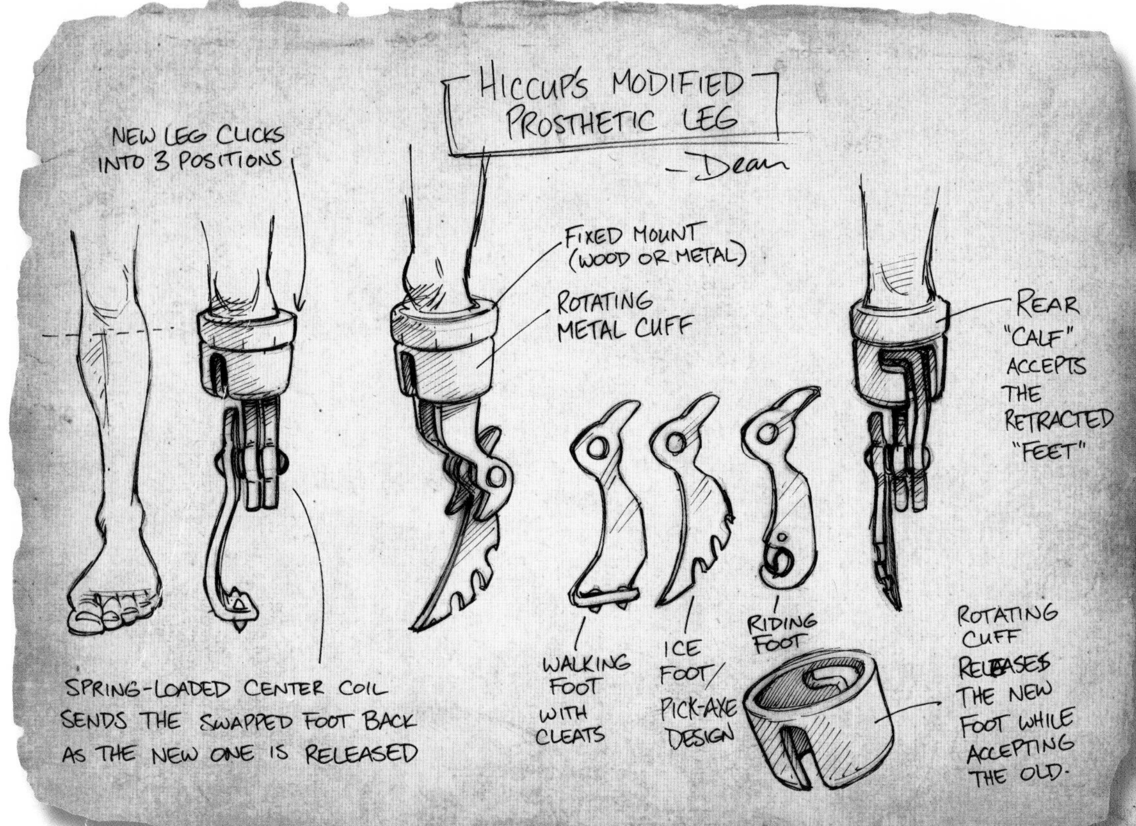


TOP: Flight Suit ✦ *Peter Chan*
ABOVE LEFT: Hiccup's Prosthetic Leg ✦ *Peter Chan*
ABOVE: Film Frame
BOTTOM LEFT: Modified Prosthetic Leg ✦ *Dean DeBlois*
ABOVE RIGHT: Helmet Painting ✦ *ZhaoPing Wei* ✦ Model ✦ *Jaewon Lee*
RIGHT: Rune ✦ *Kirsten Kawamura*

# The Flight Suit

New technology is a gigantic factor in making an animated film and the new software we used went hand-in-hand with making this sequel a bigger movie and growing it up in tone. We knew we were the first show taking advantage of the next generation of software. When we set out to make this film, we had some ambitious goals and Premo, our new animation tool, allowed us to add a lot more detail. Now when I am animating, I can see everything about the geometry because our hardware and software can carry so much more information. We can work in hi-res at any given moment.

If you compare Hiccup from the first movie to the sequel, you can see how his design got much more detailed in terms of his facial structure, his neck, and also his outfit. We had the freedom to build Hiccup's flight suit in great detail. We didn't have to compromise to compensate for any limitations of how much geometry the computer can handle, which opened up the world for us.

—*Simon Otto, head of character animation*

For the sequel, the first thing Dean said was that he wanted Hiccup to have a flight suit and that we needed to change his helmet. We put a lot of detail into his new suit.

—*Nico Marlet, character designer*

# The Dragon Blade

As intrepid explorers, flying deep into uncharted lands, Hiccup and Toothless sometimes encounter aggressive new dragons. To command their respect and help dragons see him as one of their own, Hiccup invented a device to mimic dragon fire. One end has a telescoping blade that coats itself in flammable Monstrous Nightmare saliva. The other expels explosive Hideous Zippleback gas. A built-in lighter ignites both ends, forcing testy dragons to keep their distance. With this device, Hiccup can train any dragon, and defend himself if necessary.

—*Dean DeBlois, director*

In this world of barbarians, Hiccup is the most evolved and he believes in peace. He is the thinker of the future, a teaching kind of hero. Hiccup brings everyone along with him because all the other characters have to change to keep up with him. He is like the King Arthur of his time.

—*Bonnie Arnold, producer*

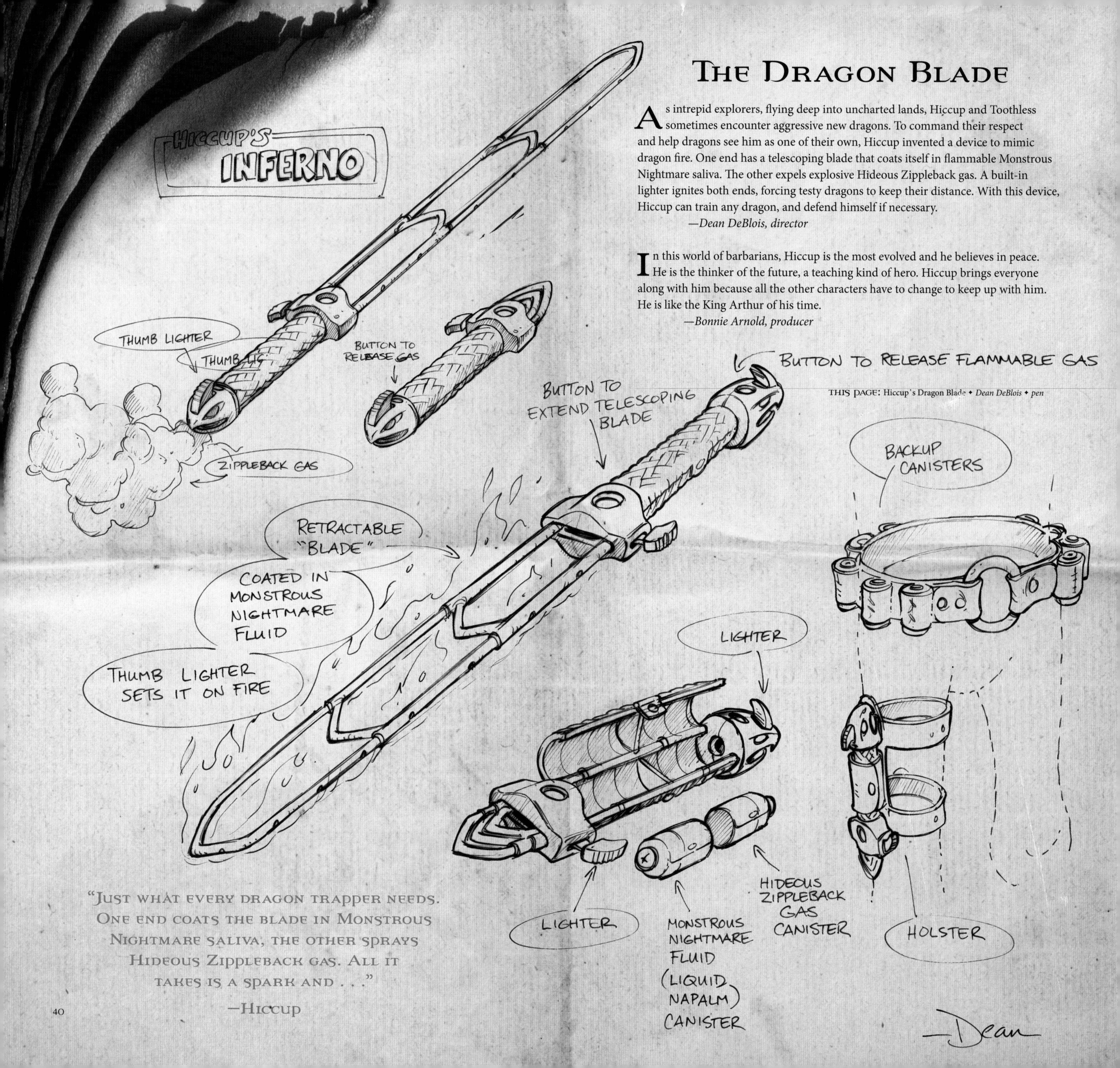


THIS PAGE: Hiccup's Dragon Blade ✦ *Dean DeBlois* ✦ *pen*

"Just what every dragon trapper needs. One end coats the blade in Monstrous Nightmare saliva, the other sprays Hideous Zippleback gas. All it takes is a spark and . . ."

—Hiccup

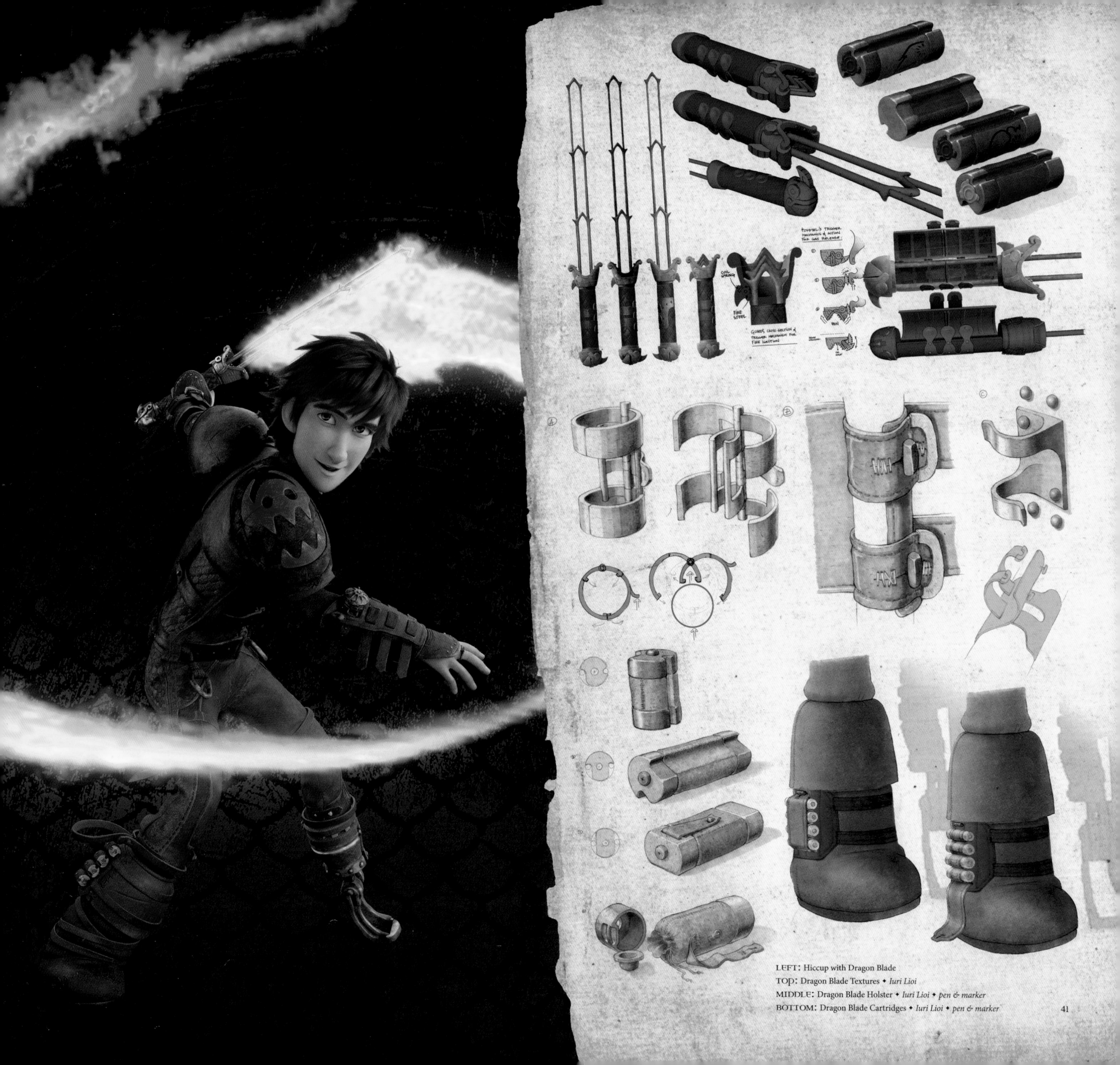


LEFT: Hiccup with Dragon Blade
TOP: Dragon Blade Textures • *Iuri Lioi*
MIDDLE: Dragon Blade Holster • *Iuri Lioi* • *pen & marker*
BOTTOM: Dragon Blade Cartridges • *Iuri Lioi* • *pen & marker*

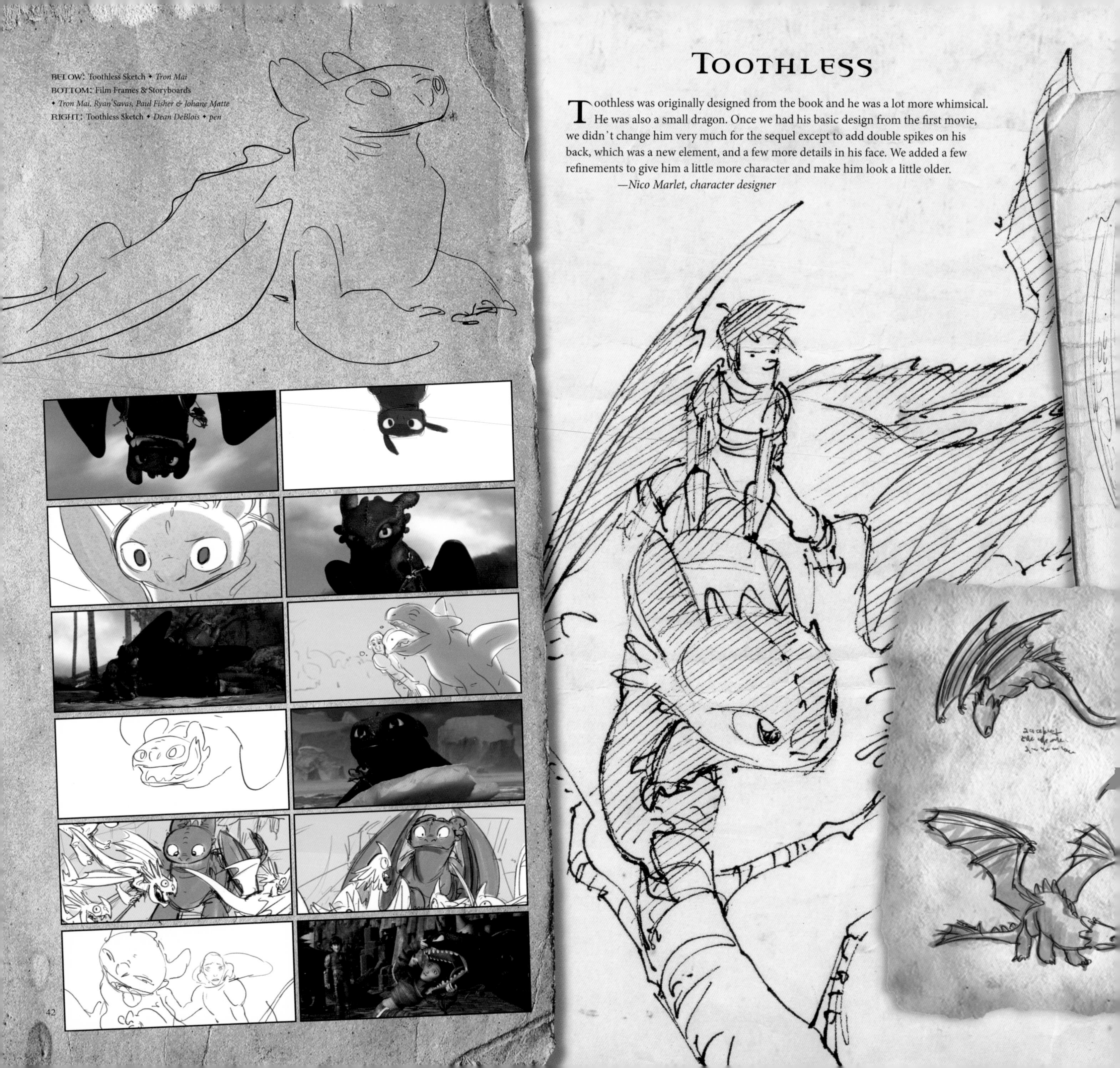

BELOW: Toothless Sketch ✦ *Tron Mai*
BOTTOM: Film Frames & Storyboards
✦ *Tron Mai, Ryan Savas, Paul Fisher & Johane Matte*
RIGHT: Toothless Sketch ✦ *Dean DeBlois* ✦ *pen*

# Toothless

Toothless was originally designed from the book and he was a lot more whimsical. He was also a small dragon. Once we had his basic design from the first movie, we didn't change him very much for the sequel except to add double spikes on his back, which was a new element, and a few more details in his face. We added a few refinements to give him a little more character and make him look a little older.

—*Nico Marlet, character designer*

BELOW & RIGHT: Toothless & Hiccup Sketches ✦ *Dean DeBlois* ✦ *pen*
BOTTOM LEFT: Toothless Studies ✦ *Mel Zwyer*
BOTTOM RIGHT: Toothless & Hiccup ✦ *Dean DeBlois* ✦ *pencil & watercolor*

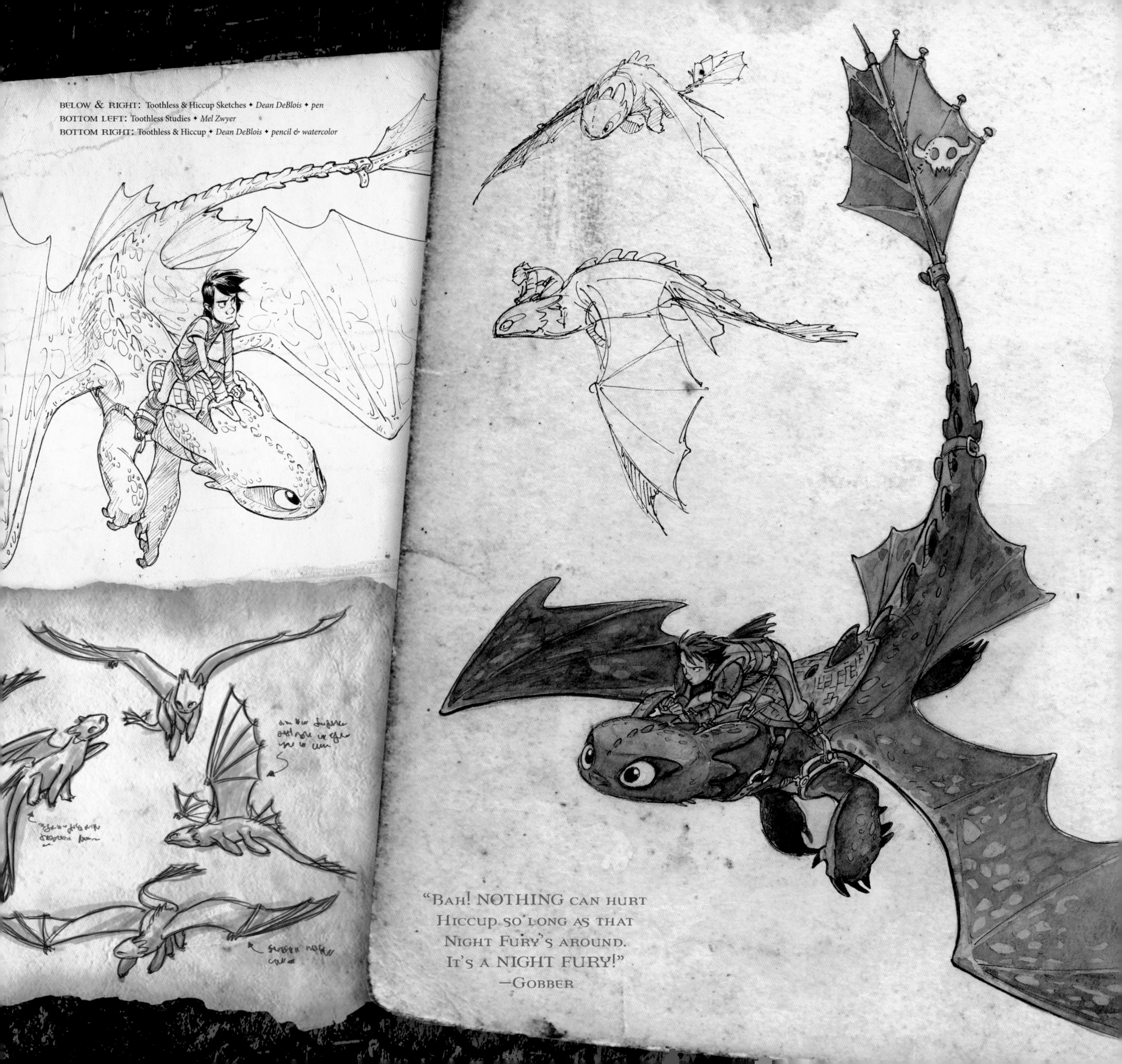

"Bah! NOTHING can hurt Hiccup so long as that Night Fury's around. It's a NIGHT FURY!"
—Gobber

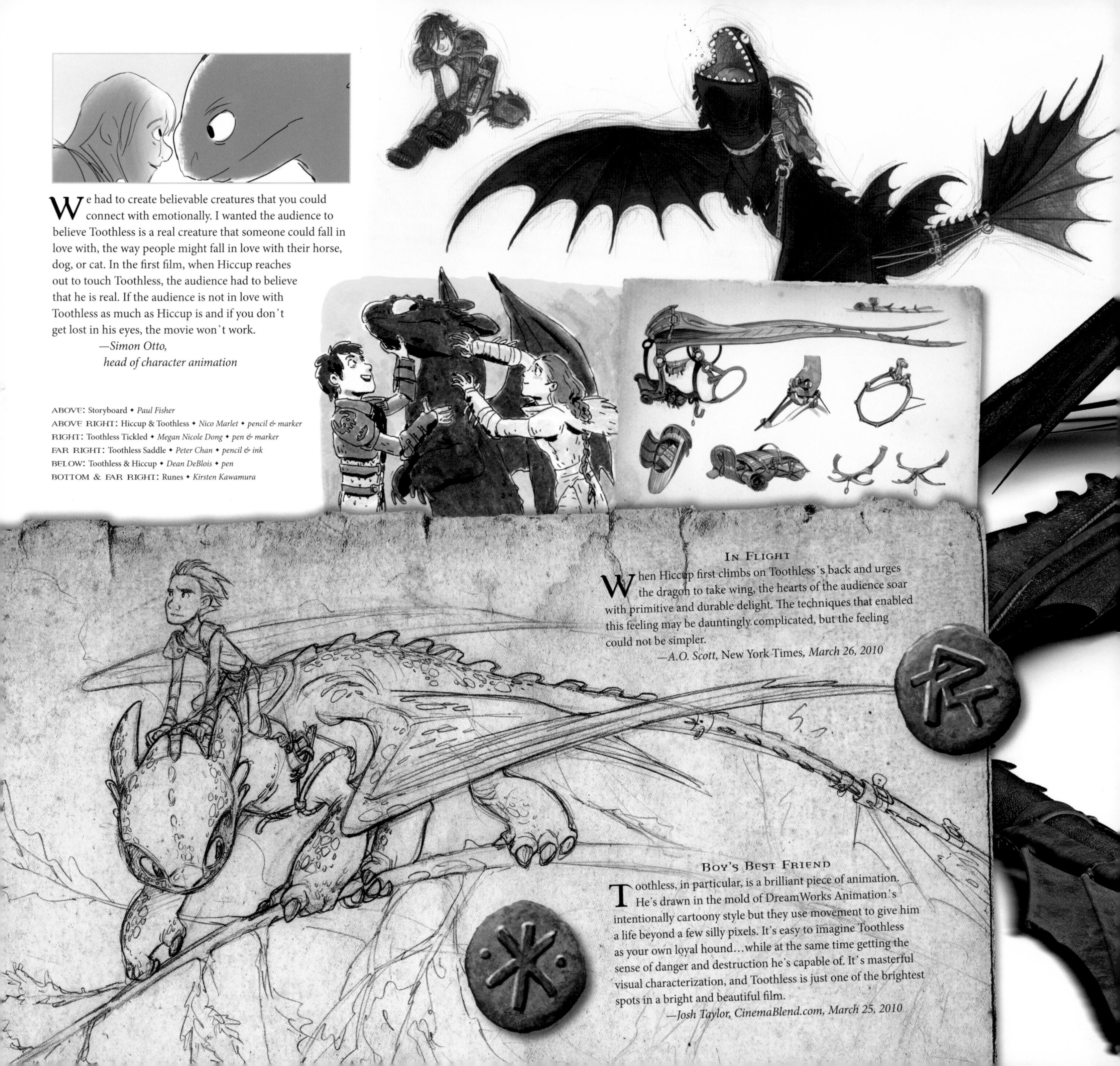

We had to create believable creatures that you could connect with emotionally. I wanted the audience to believe Toothless is a real creature that someone could fall in love with, the way people might fall in love with their horse, dog, or cat. In the first film, when Hiccup reaches out to touch Toothless, the audience had to believe that he is real. If the audience is not in love with Toothless as much as Hiccup is and if you don't get lost in his eyes, the movie won't work.

—*Simon Otto, head of character animation*

ABOVE: Storyboard ✦ *Paul Fisher*
ABOVE RIGHT: Hiccup & Toothless ✦ *Nico Marlet* ✦ *pencil & marker*
RIGHT: Toothless Tickled ✦ *Megan Nicole Dong* ✦ *pen & marker*
FAR RIGHT: Toothless Saddle ✦ *Peter Chan* ✦ *pencil & ink*
BELOW: Toothless & Hiccup ✦ *Dean DeBlois* ✦ *pen*
BOTTOM & FAR RIGHT: Runes ✦ *Kirsten Kawamura*

### In Flight

When Hiccup first climbs on Toothless's back and urges the dragon to take wing, the hearts of the audience soar with primitive and durable delight. The techniques that enabled this feeling may be dauntingly complicated, but the feeling could not be simpler.

—*A.O. Scott,* New York Times, *March 26, 2010*

### Boy's Best Friend

Toothless, in particular, is a brilliant piece of animation. He's drawn in the mold of DreamWorks Animation's intentionally cartoony style but they use movement to give him a life beyond a few silly pixels. It's easy to imagine Toothless as your own loyal hound…while at the same time getting the sense of danger and destruction he's capable of. It's masterful visual characterization, and Toothless is just one of the brightest spots in a bright and beautiful film.

—*Josh Taylor, CinemaBlend.com, March 25, 2010*

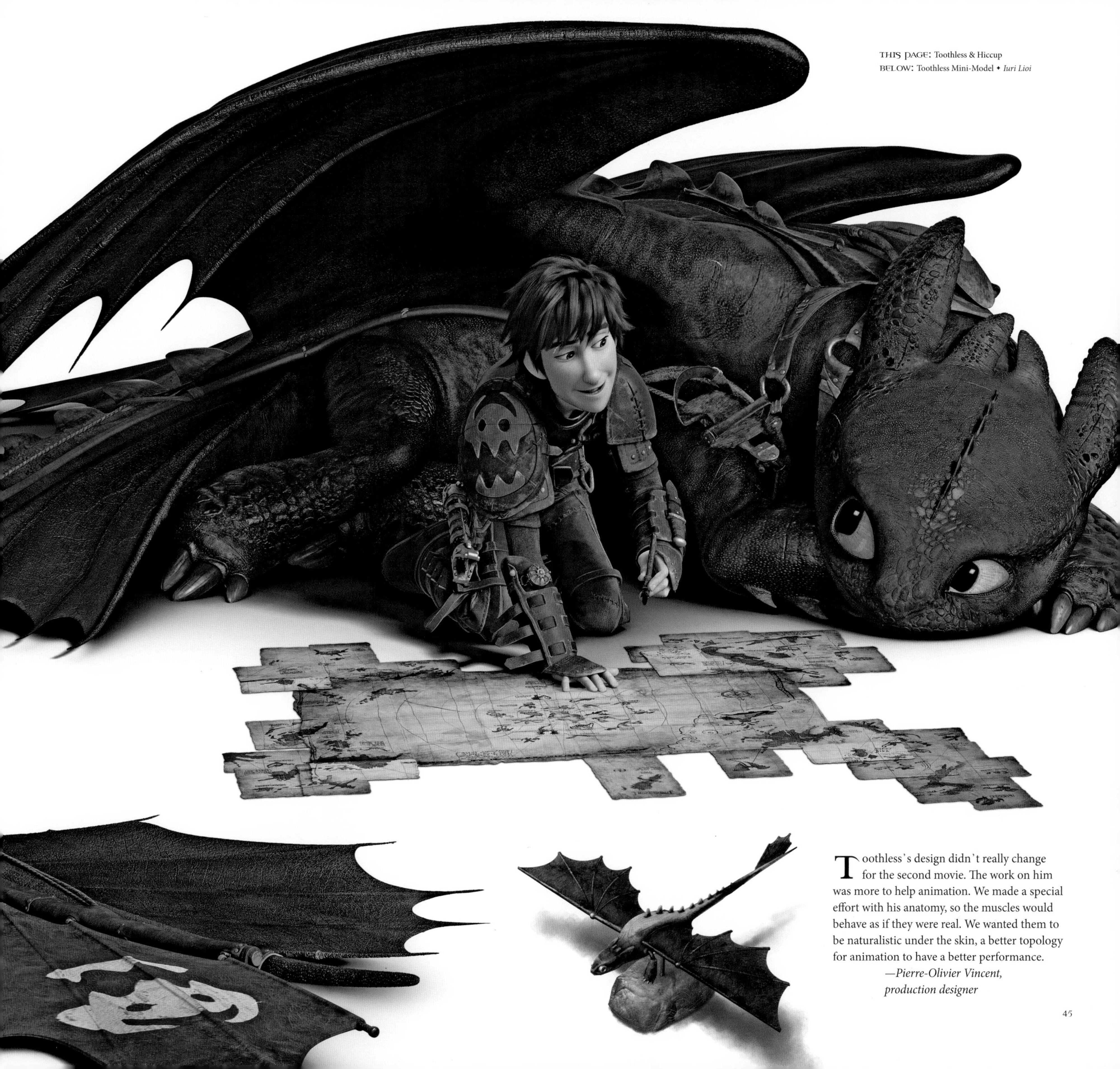

THIS PAGE: Toothless & Hiccup
BELOW: Toothless Mini-Model ◆ *Iuri Lioi*

Toothless's design didn't really change for the second movie. The work on him was more to help animation. We made a special effort with his anatomy, so the muscles would behave as if they were real. We wanted them to be naturalistic under the skin, a better topology for animation to have a better performance.

*—Pierre-Olivier Vincent, production designer*

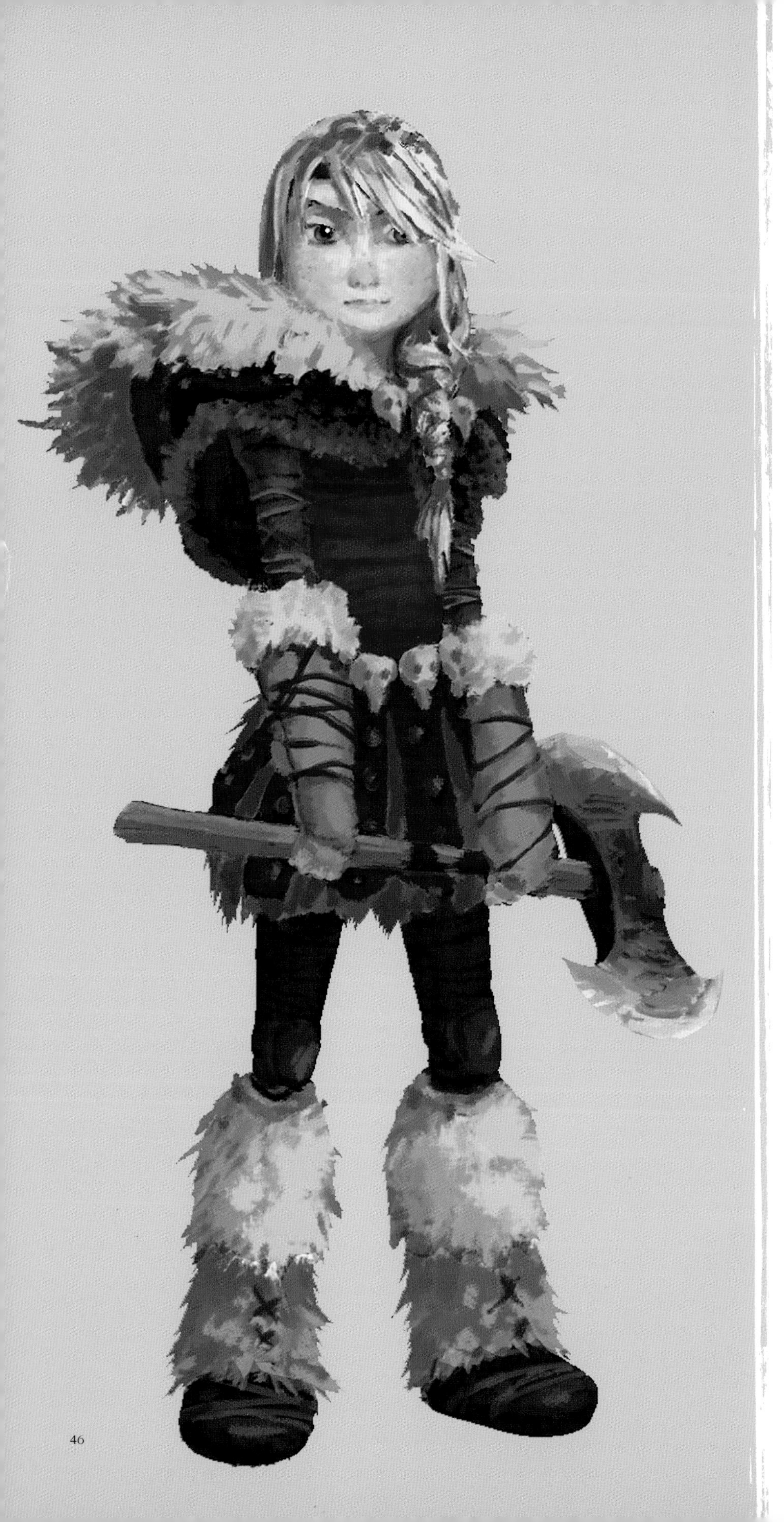



# Astrid

Astrid is still a strong feminine character. But she is a little less tomboy and a little more glamorous. Her relationship with Hiccup has evolved. They are somewhat like Prince William and Kate Middleton, only Viking style.

*—Pierre-Olivier Vincent, production designer*

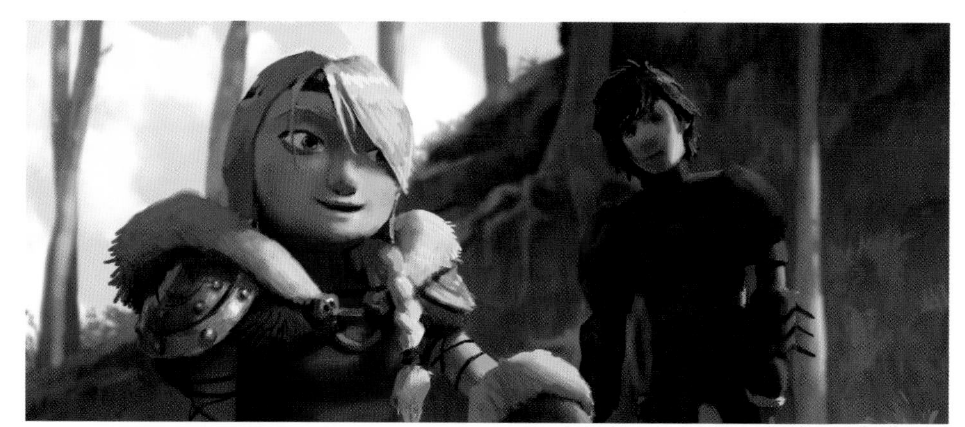

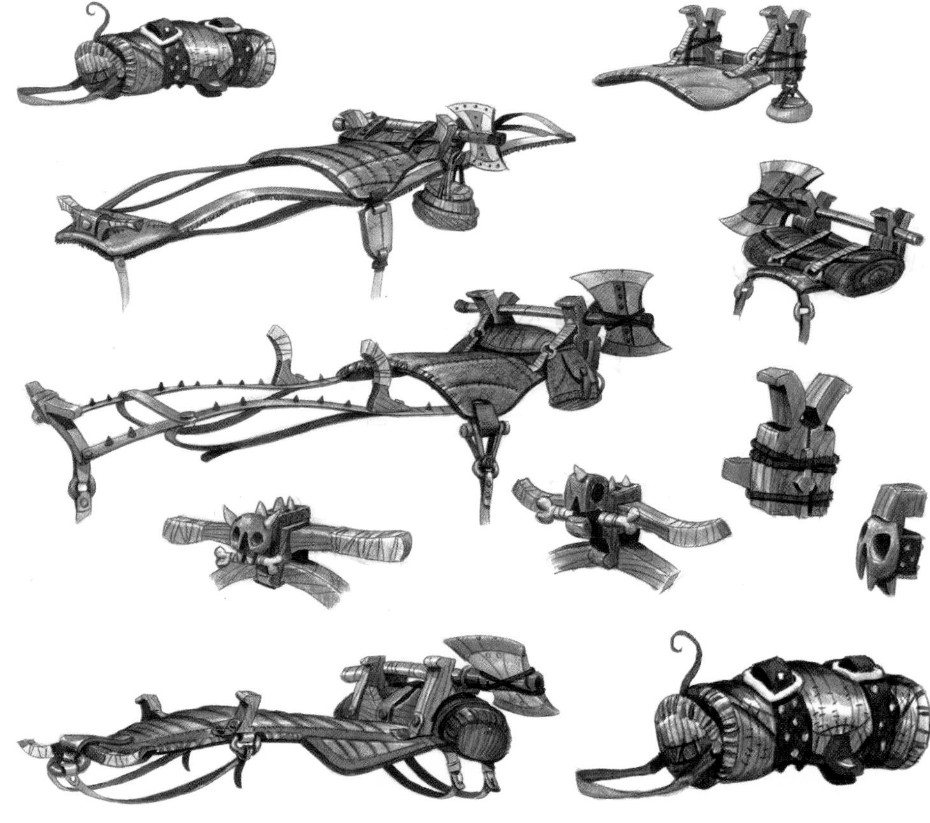

LEFT: Astrid Painting ✦ *ZhaoPing Wei* ✦ Model ✦ *Kull Shin*
TOP: Color Key ✦ *Woonyoung Jung*
ABOVE: Nadder Saddle ✦ *Peter Chan* ✦ *pencil & ink*
OPPOSITE: Astrid Outfits ✦ *Megan Nicole Dong*
OPPOSITE BOTTOM LEFT: Stormfly & Astrid Racing Stripe Concepts ✦ *Kirsten Kawamura* ✦ Model ✦ *Jaewon Lee & Kull Shin* ✦ Surfacing ✦ *James Martin & Robbin Huntingdale*
OPPOSITE BOTTOM RIGHT: Nadder Racing Logos ✦ *Kirsten Kawamura*

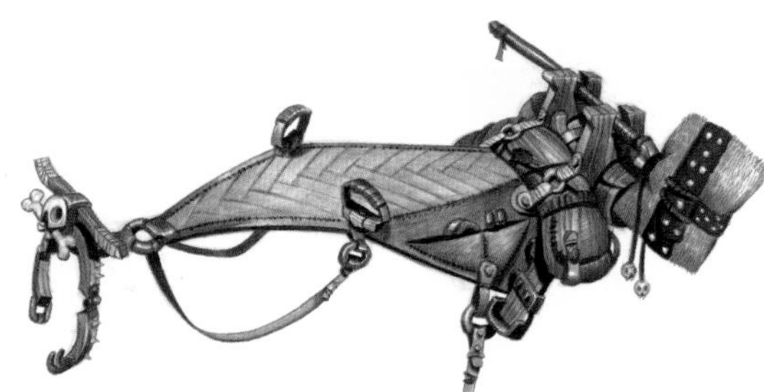

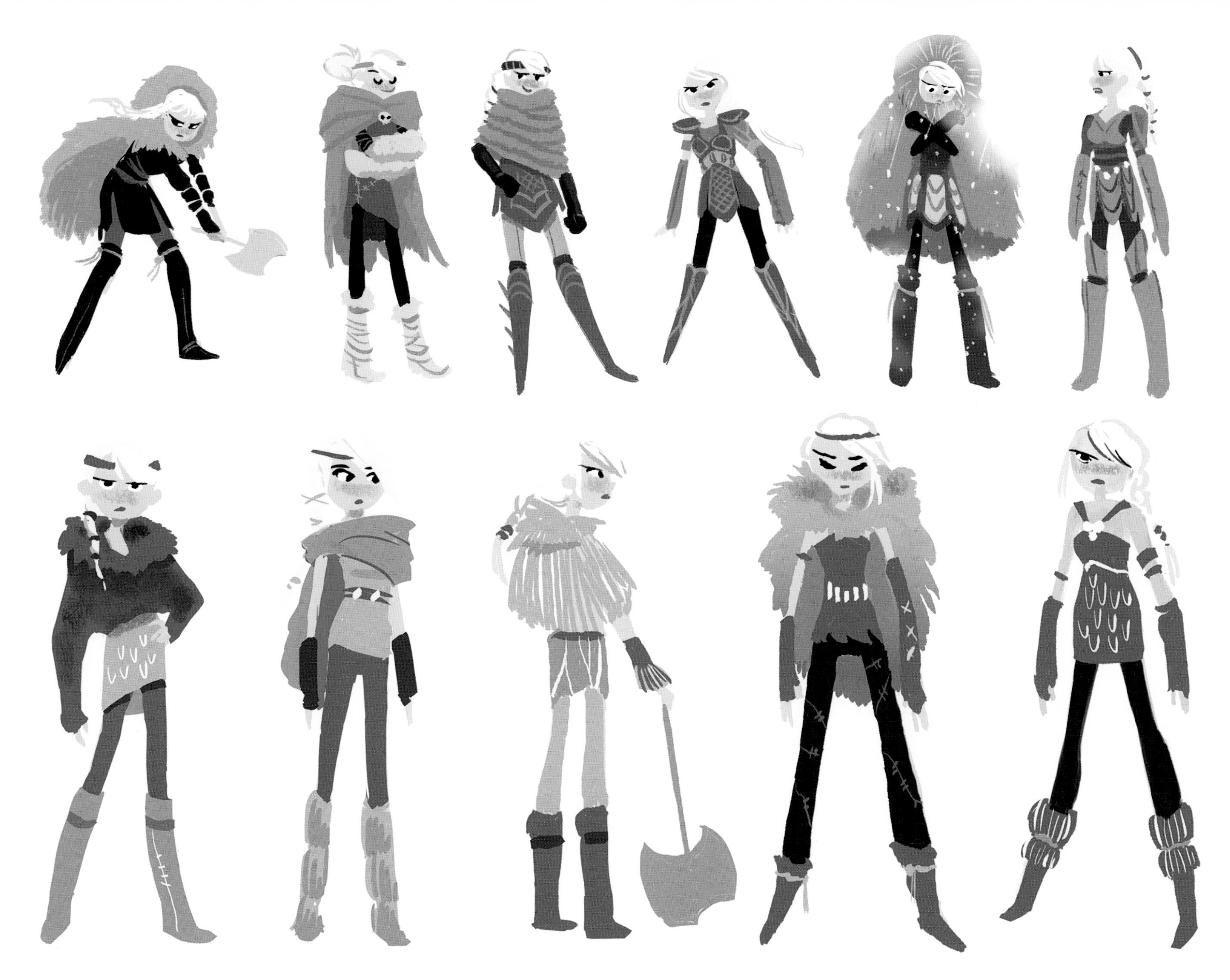

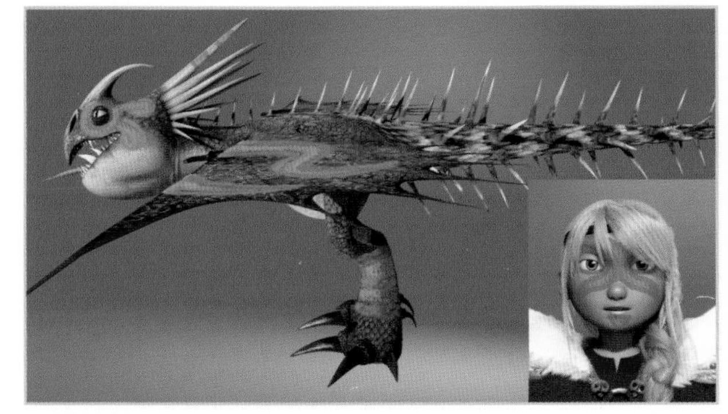

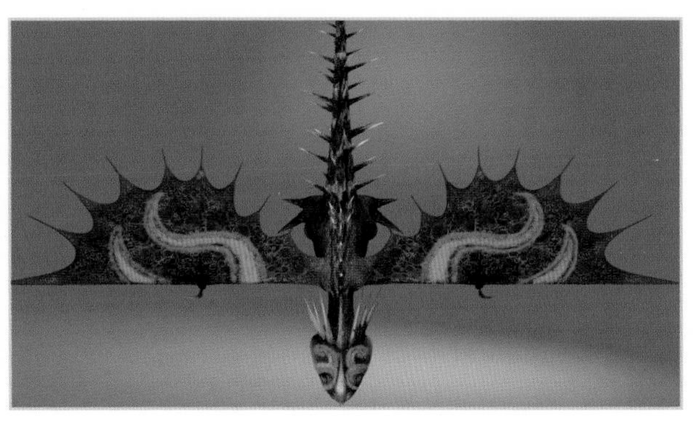

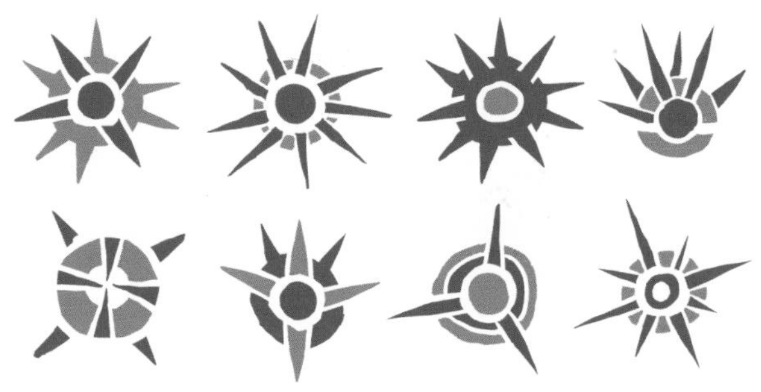

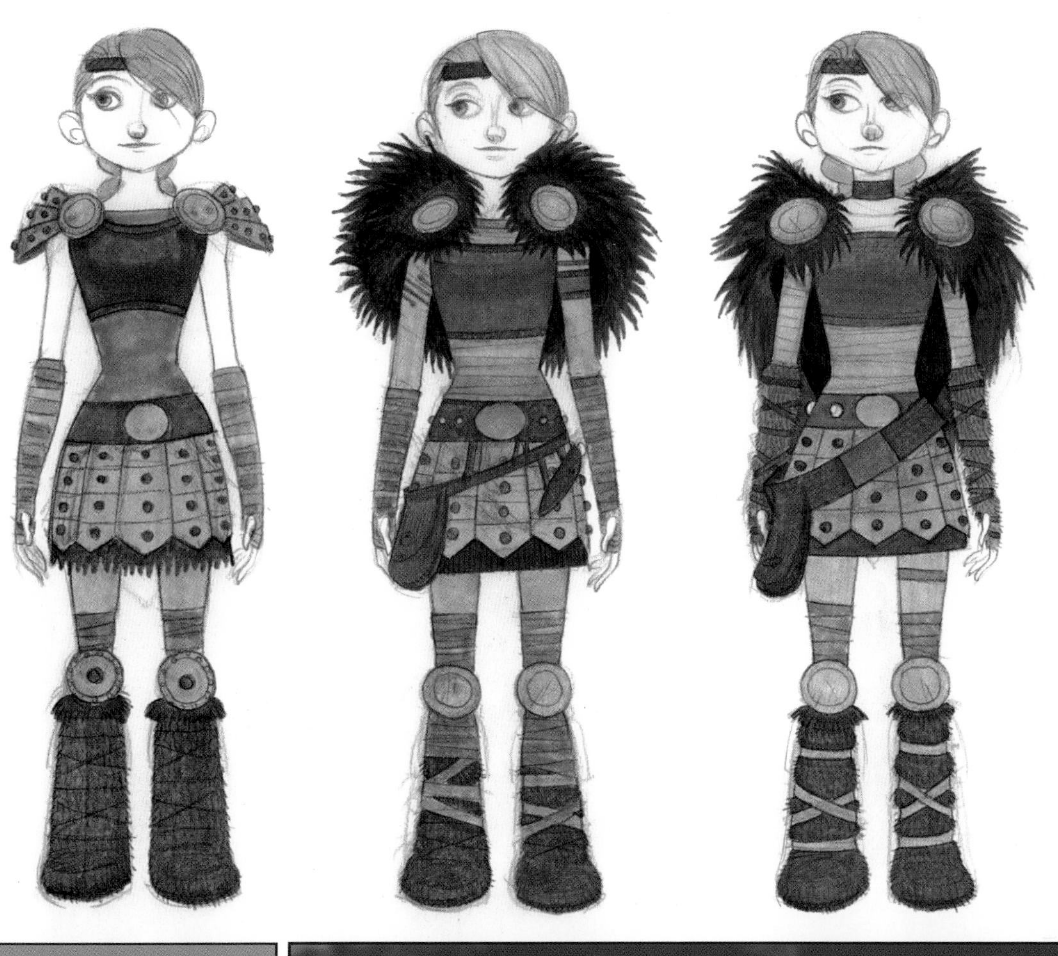

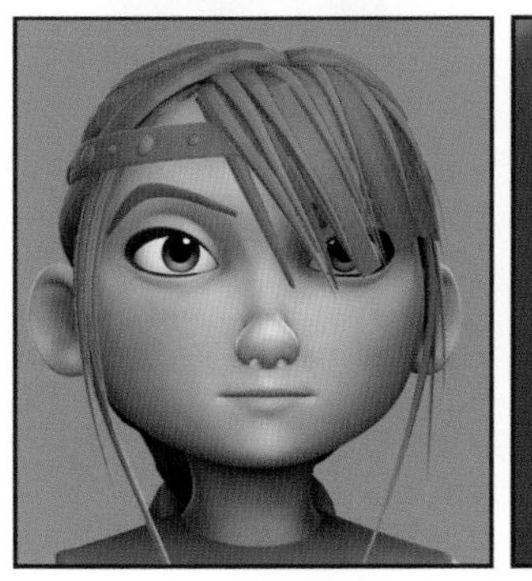

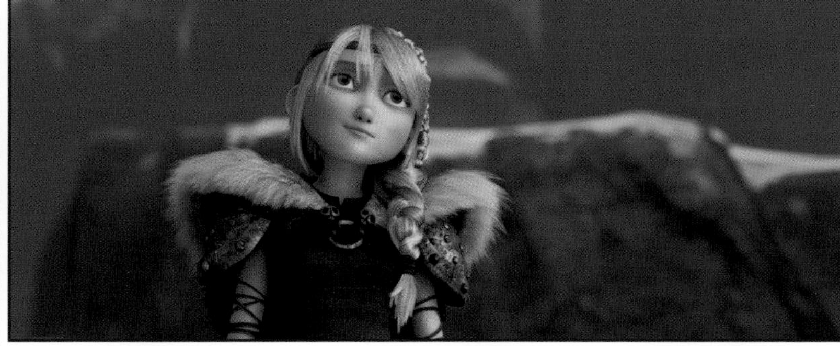

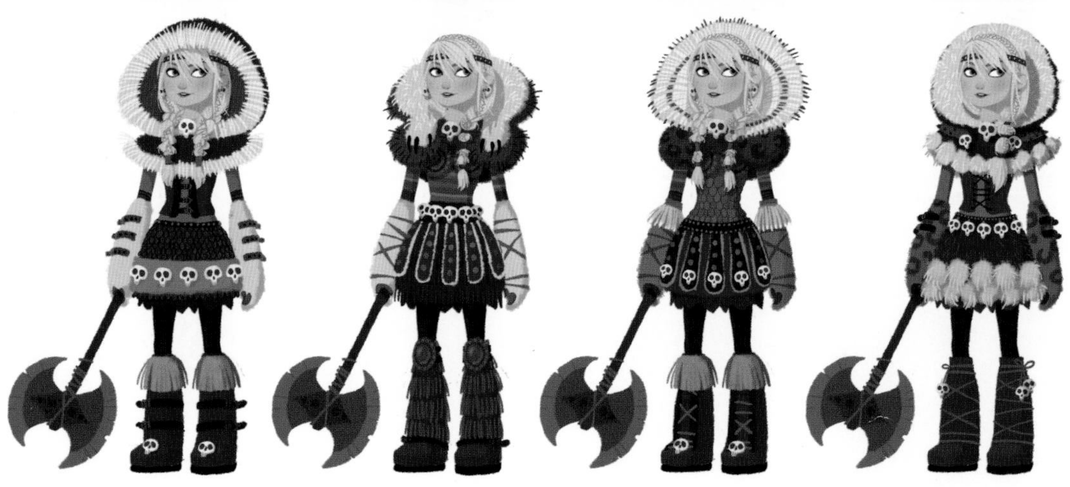

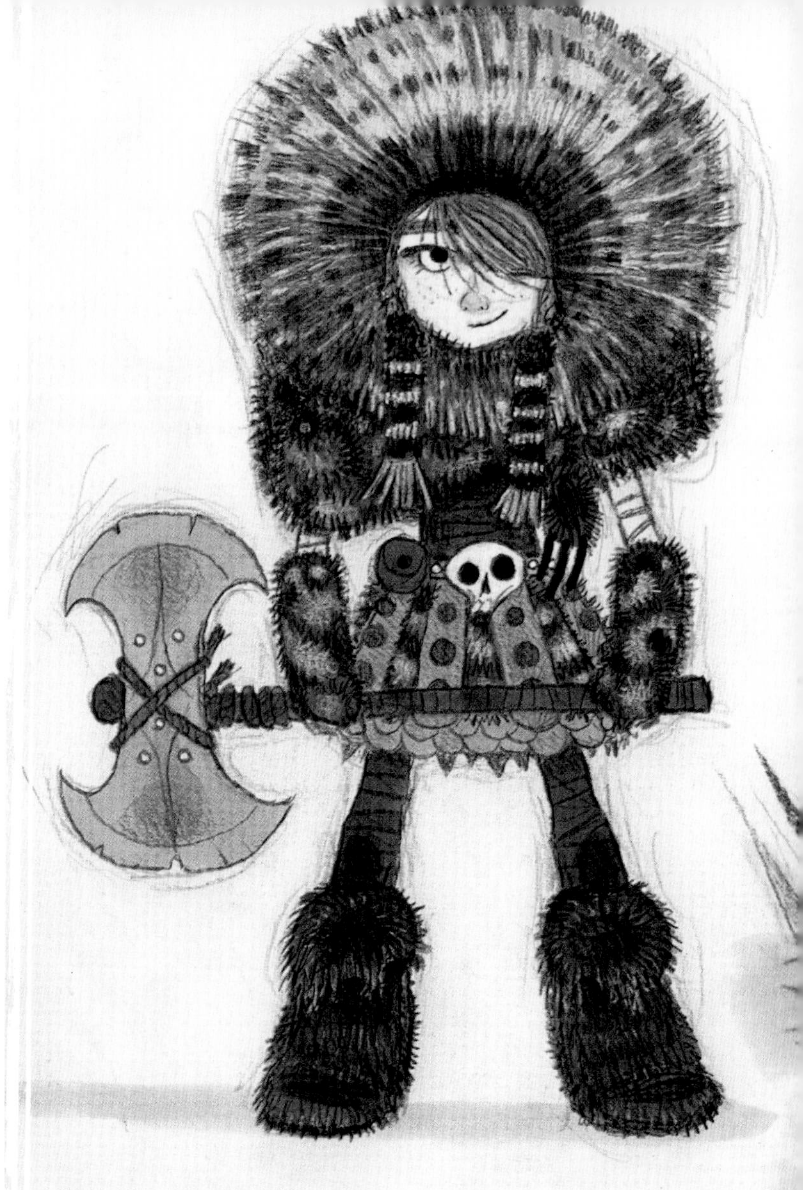

TOP LEFT: Astrid Outfits ◆ *Iuri Lioi* ◆ *pencil & marker*
LEFT: Film Frame
FAR LEFT: Astrid Portrait ◆ *Leo Sanchez*
BOTTOM LEFT: Astrid Costumes ◆ *Griselda Sastrawinata-Lemay*
RIGHT & OPPOSITE: Astrid ◆ *Nico Marlet* ◆ *pencil & marker*

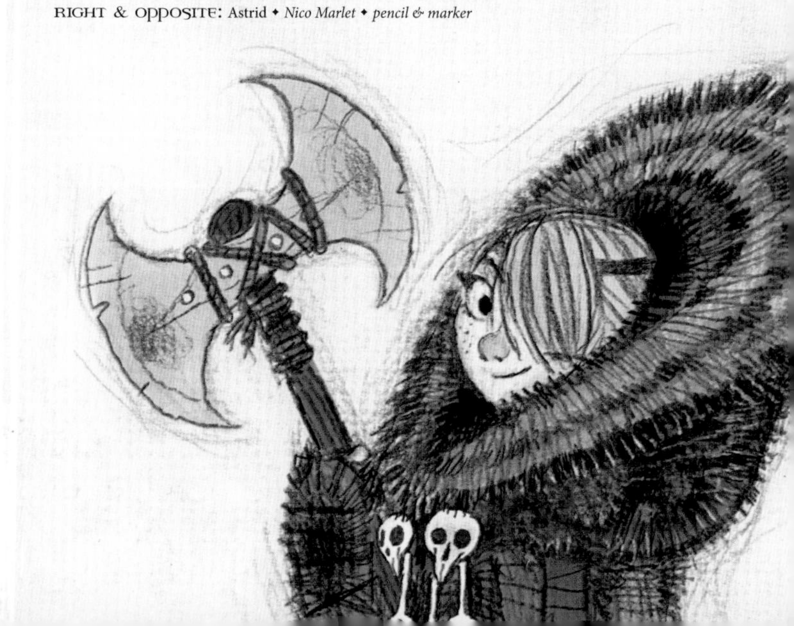

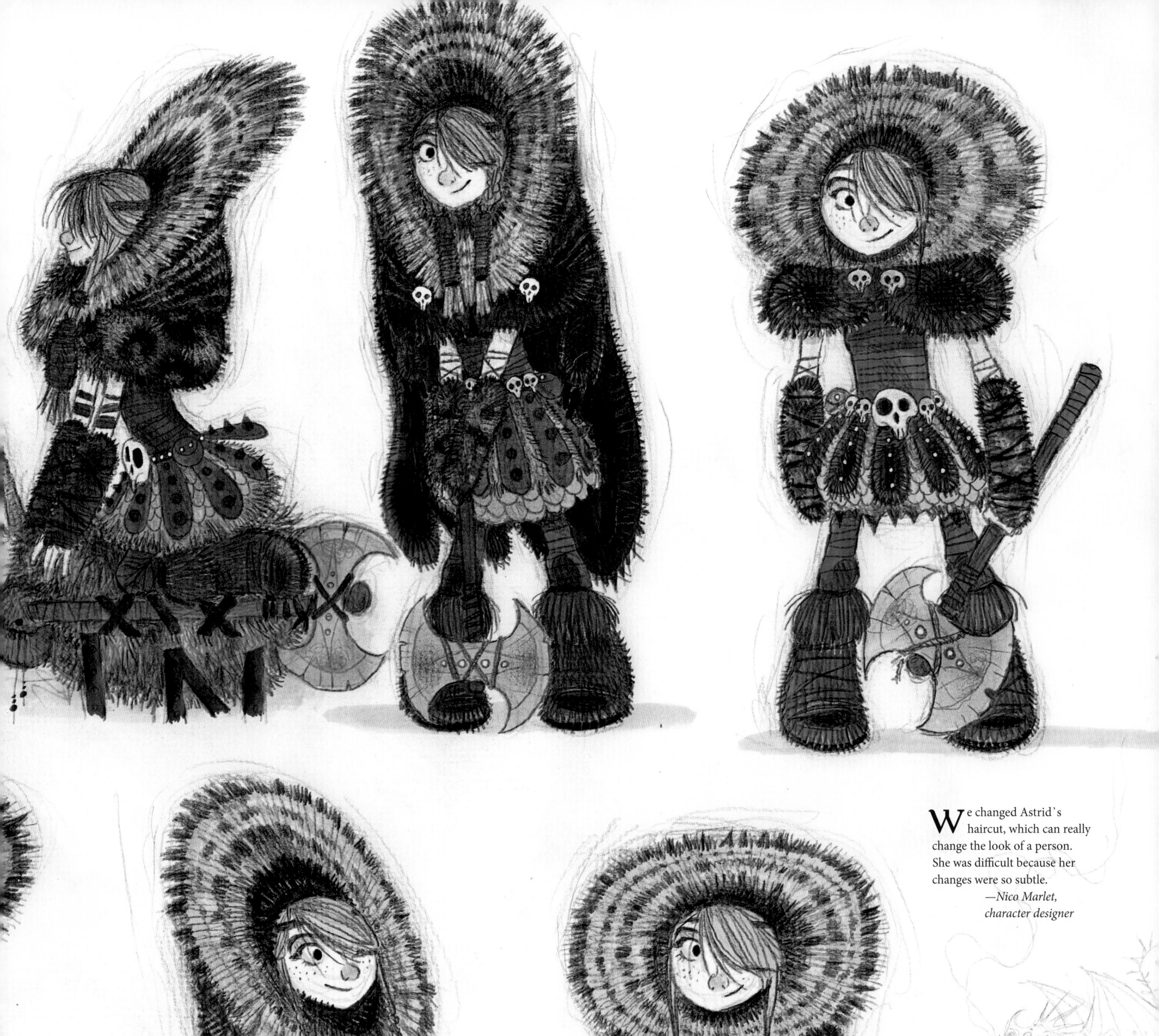

We changed Astrid's haircut, which can really change the look of a person. She was difficult because her changes were so subtle.

*—Nico Marlet, character designer*

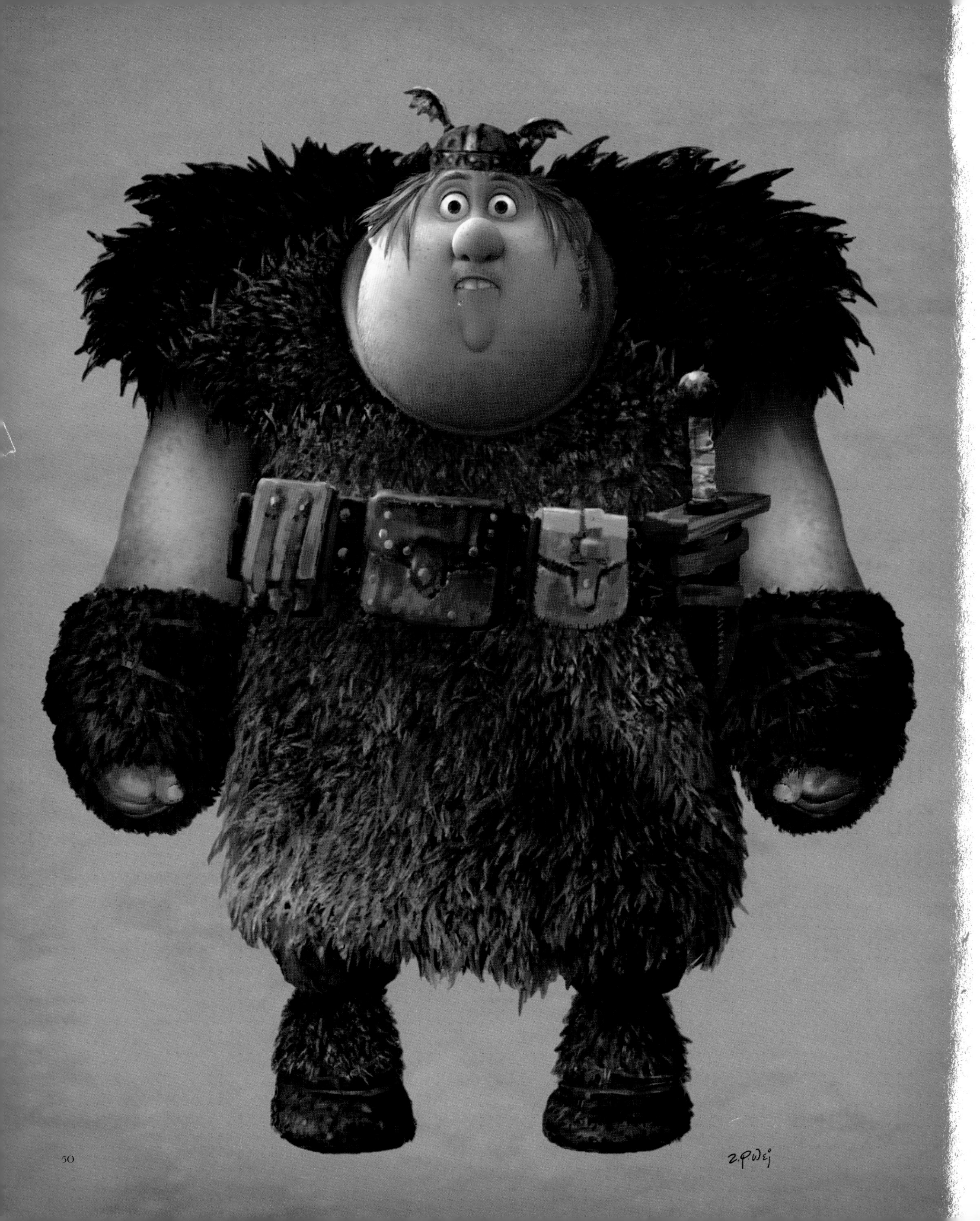

# Fishlegs

Fishlegs is a nervous, geeky kind of guy who likes plucking at his hair. He overacts a lot and speaks with a very staggered, slightly panicked pace. Our graphic idea was that he was like a square blob, with his homemade outfit creating that furry outline. He always keeps his arms close to his body. He sits on his heels with slightly bent knees; his head never leaves that silhouette.

He has his dragon cards in his pockets and he is always looking at them for reference, like baseball cards. He is always quoting dragon stats. Even if we don't show some of these collected ideas in the final film, it is how we build a character, how we find and understand the essence of the character, much like an actor finds his character in a live-action film.

*—Simon Otto,*
*head of character animation*

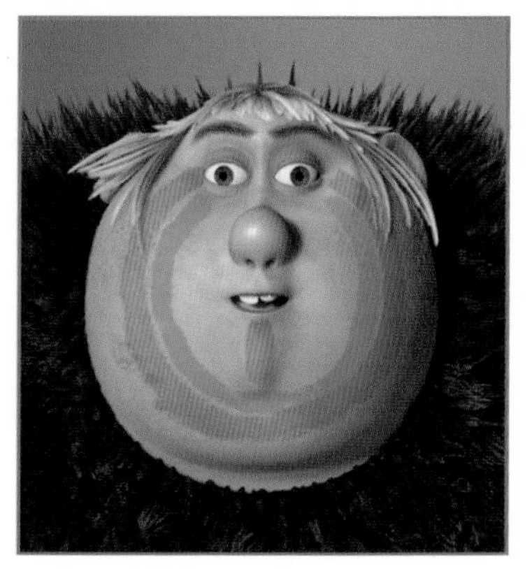

LEFT: Fishlegs Painting ✦ *ZhaoPing Wei* ✦ Model ✦ *Matt Paulson*
ABOVE: Fishleg's Racing Stripes Concept ✦ *Kirsten Kawamura* ✦ Model ✦ *Matt Paulson* ✦ Surfacing ✦ *Gentaro Yamamoto*
OPPOSITE TOP: Face Concept Models ✦ *Leo Sanchez*
OPPOSITE MIDDLE: Facial Hair Options ✦ *ZhaoPing Wei*
OPPOSITE BOTTOM: Meatlug Racing Stripe Concept ✦ *Kirsten Kawamura* ✦ Model ✦ *Matt Paulson* ✦ Surfacing ✦ *Tomijann Nabors*
OPPOSITE BOTTOM CENTER: Racing Logos ✦ *Kirsten Kawamura*

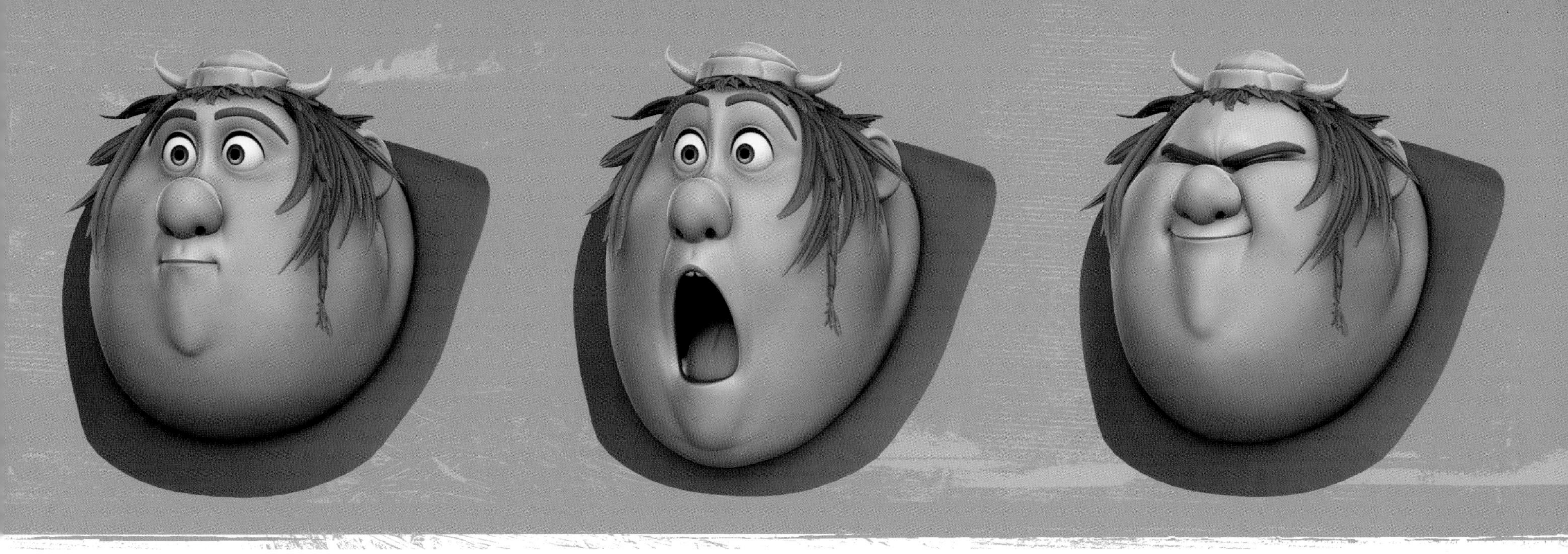

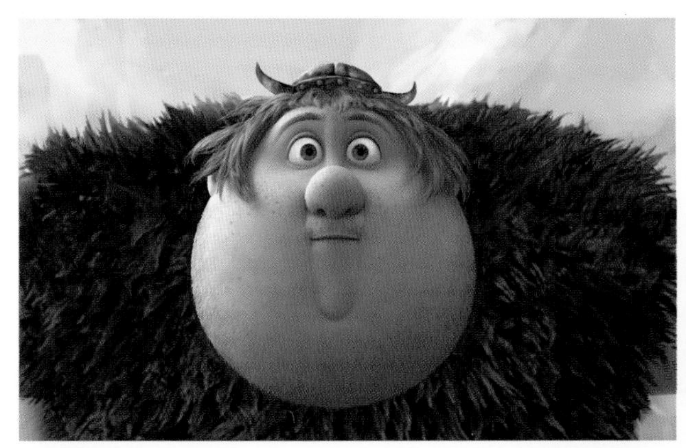

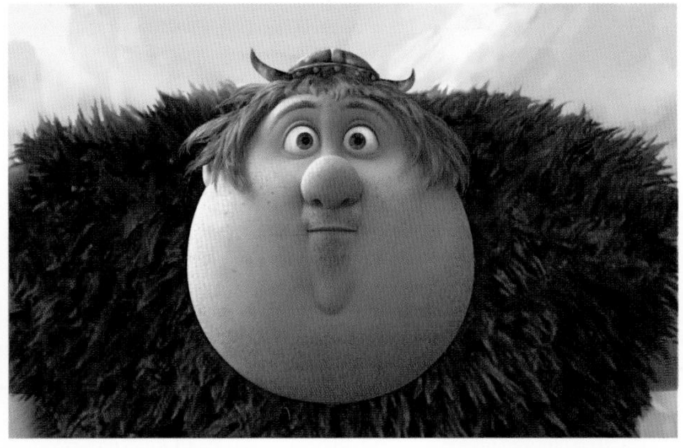

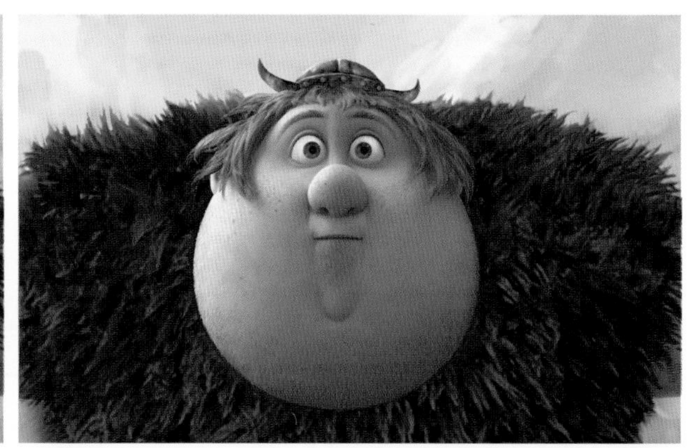

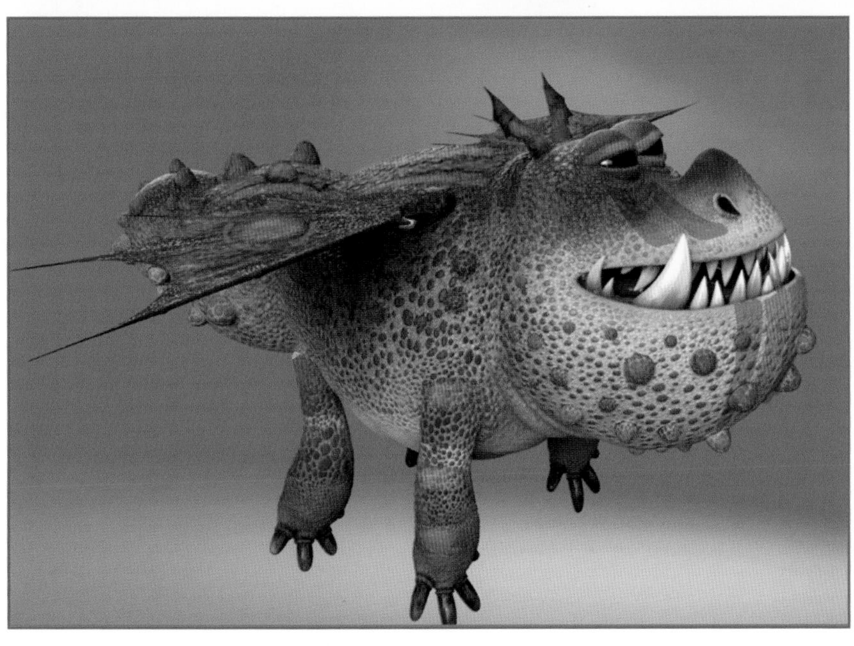

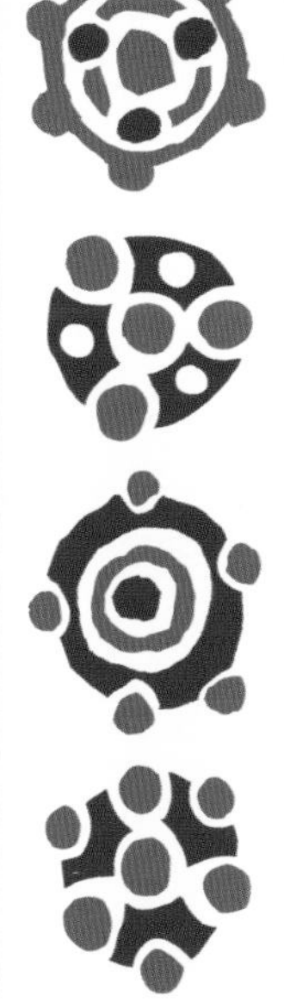

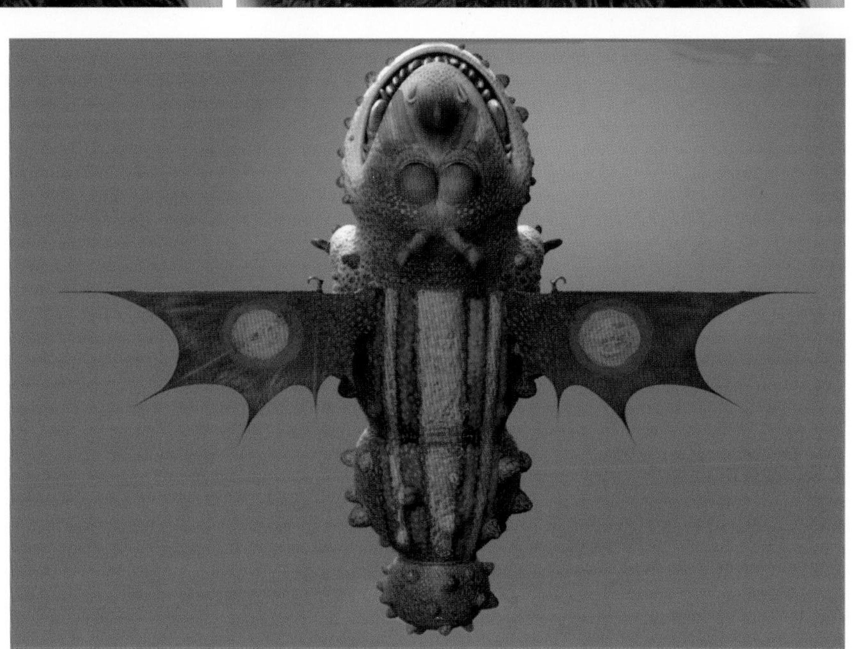

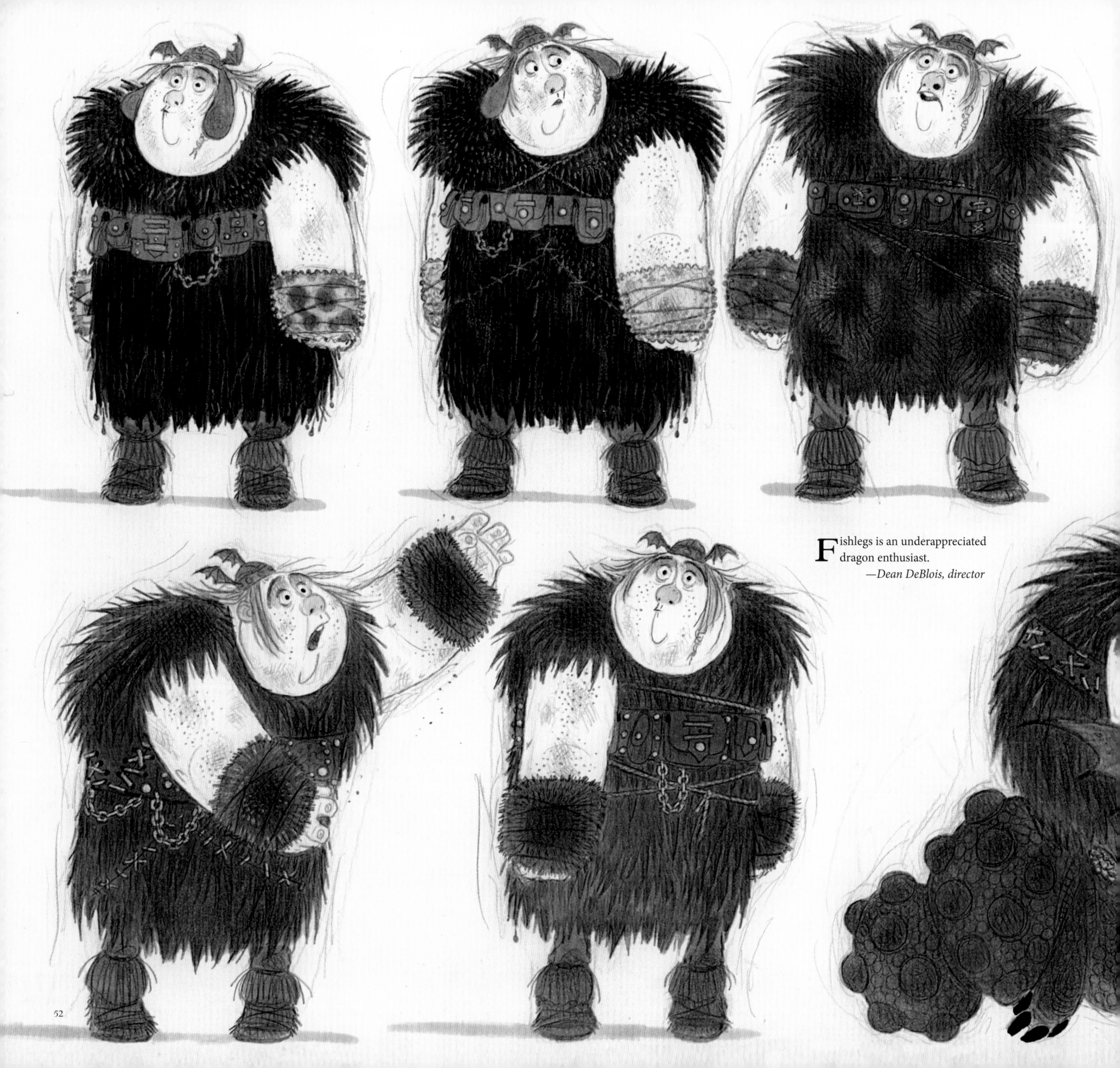

Fishlegs is an underappreciated dragon enthusiast.
*—Dean DeBlois, director*

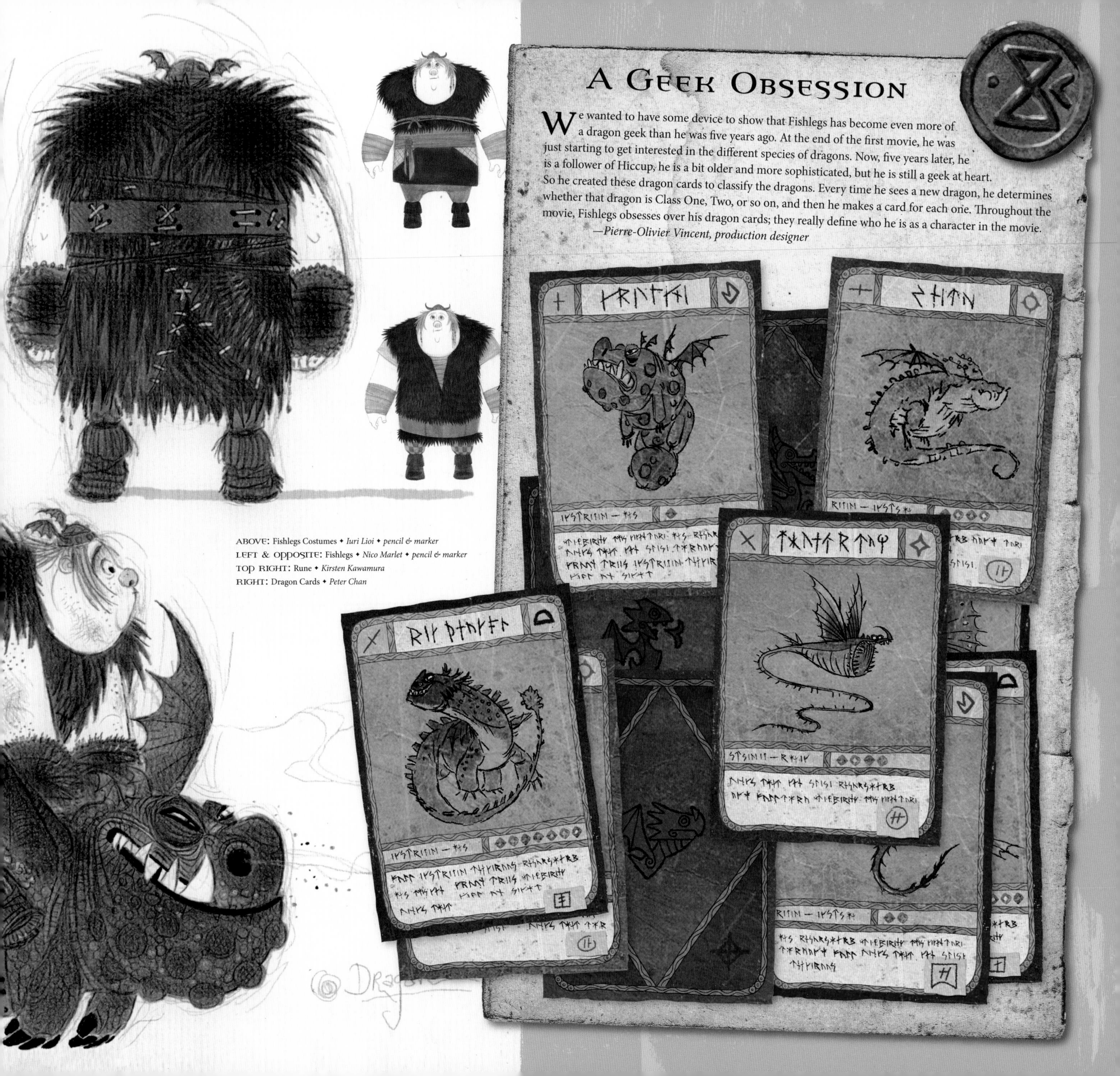

# A Geek Obsession

We wanted to have some device to show that Fishlegs has become even more of a dragon geek than he was five years ago. At the end of the first movie, he was just starting to get interested in the different species of dragons. Now, five years later, he is a follower of Hiccup, he is a bit older and more sophisticated, but he is still a geek at heart. So he created these dragon cards to classify the dragons. Every time he sees a new dragon, he determines whether that dragon is Class One, Two, or so on, and then he makes a card for each one. Throughout the movie, Fishlegs obsesses over his dragon cards; they really define who he is as a character in the movie.

—*Pierre-Olivier Vincent, production designer*

ABOVE: Fishlegs Costumes ✦ *Iuri Lioi* ✦ *pencil & marker*
LEFT & OPPOSITE: Fishlegs ✦ *Nico Marlet* ✦ *pencil & marker*
TOP RIGHT: Rune ✦ *Kirsten Kawamura*
RIGHT: Dragon Cards ✦ *Peter Chan*

# Snotlout

One of the key style aspects of our film is that we wanted to have a whimsical world with exaggerated shapes and size contrast and push the extremes, but we wanted to surface and texture it in a way that is naturalistic and truthful. For me, in terms of animation, that was the stepping-stone for how I approached the animation style. It is a very believable, credible world where the emotions of the characters are based on truthful experience, but at the same time, we want to have fun with it and be broad and stylized when we can. We are presenting a world that is larger than life but real and feels like you could live in this world. It's not an alternate universe where everything is so stylized that you are looking at it more like an observer of a piece of art. We wanted to bring the audience into this world and have them feel like they are part of it.

*—Simon Otto, head of character animation*

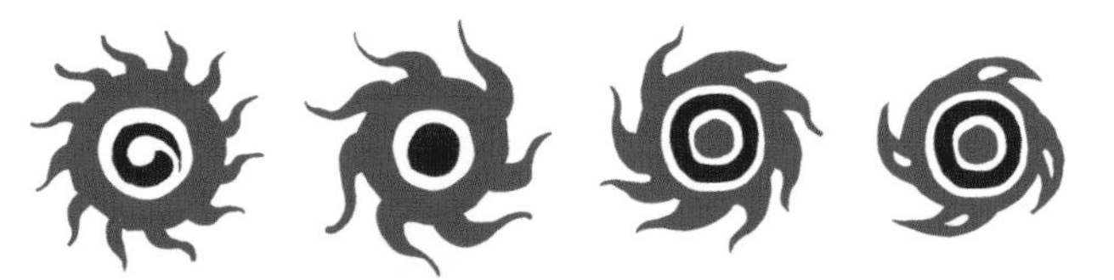

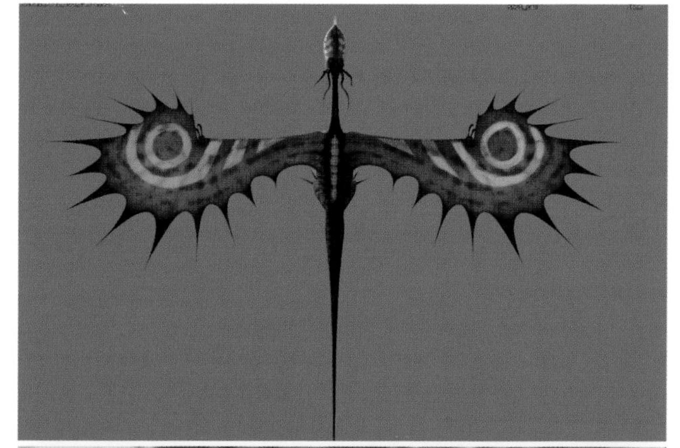

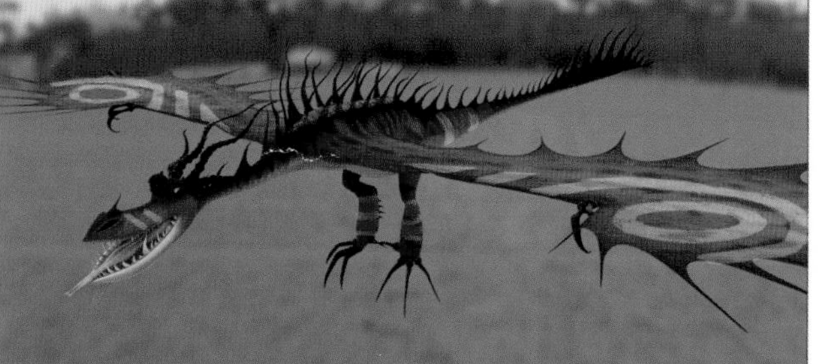

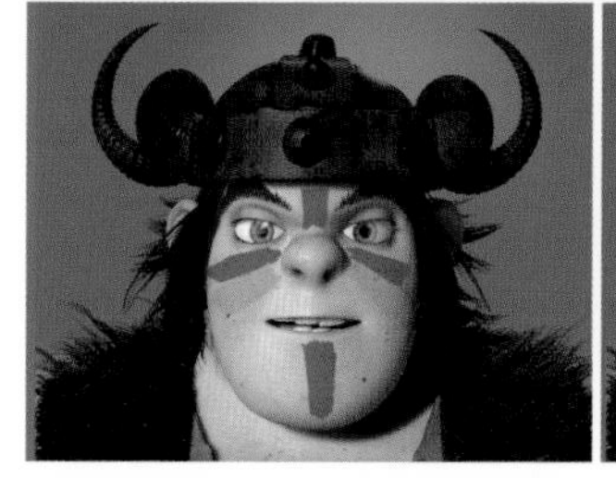

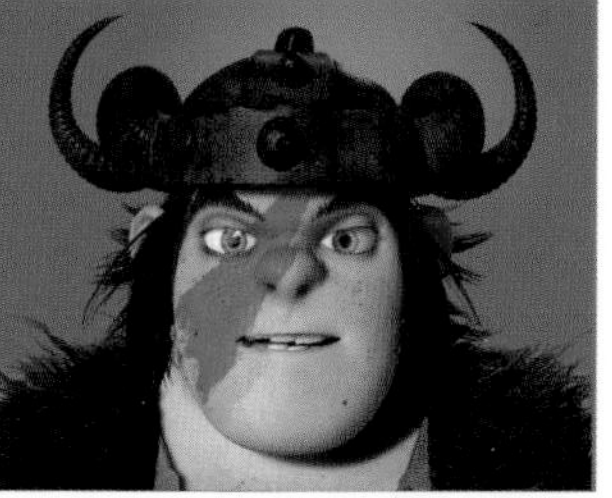

LEFT: Snotlout Painting ✦ *ZhaoPing Wei* ✦ Model ✦ *Charles Ellison*
RIGHT: Hookfang & Snotlout Racing Stripes Concept ✦ *Kirsten Kawamura* ✦ Model ✦ *Abraham Meneu Oset & Charles Ellison* ✦ Surfacing ✦ *Ted Davis & Cara Khan*
TOP RIGHT: Nightmare Racing Logos ✦ *Kirsten Kawamura*

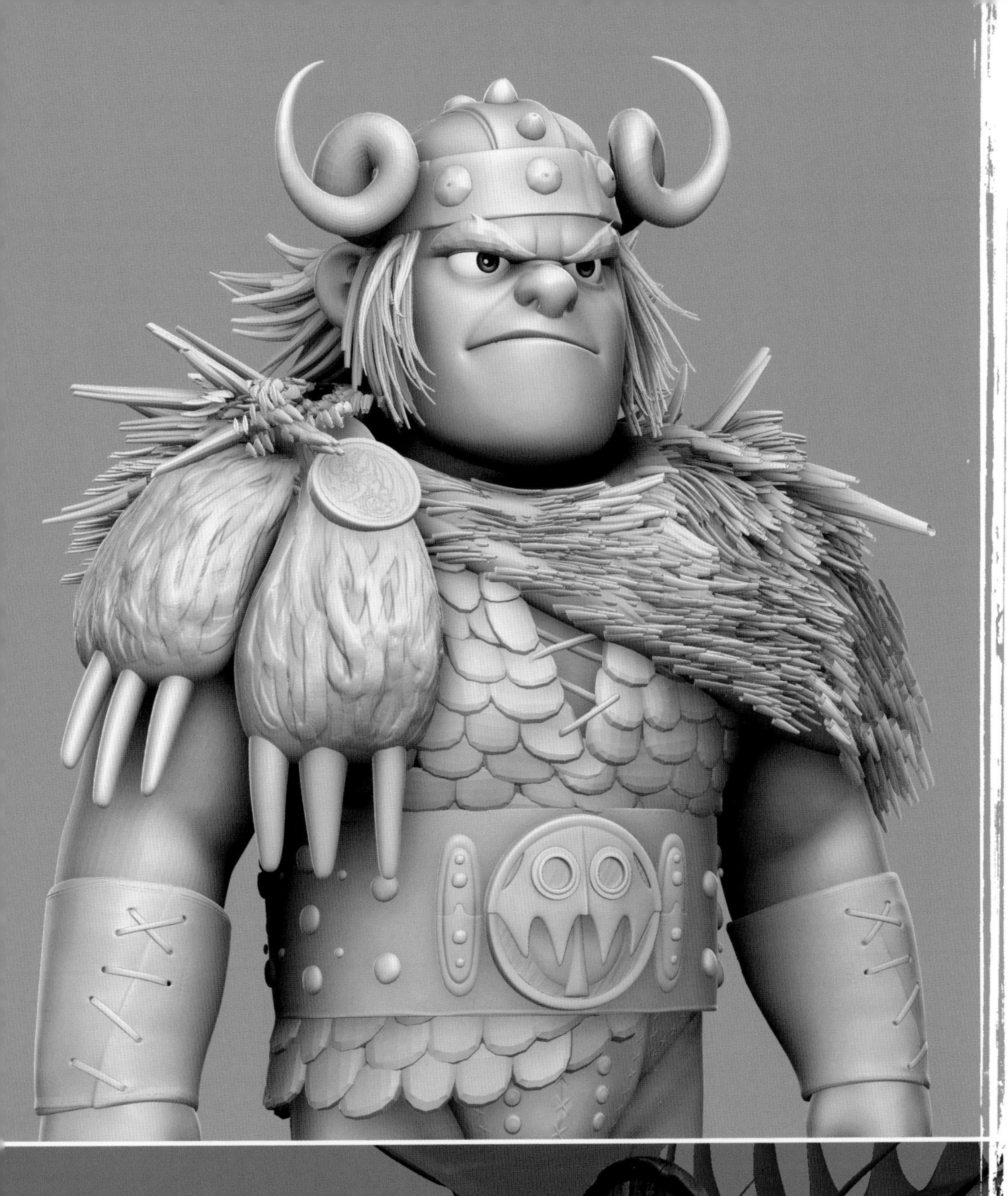

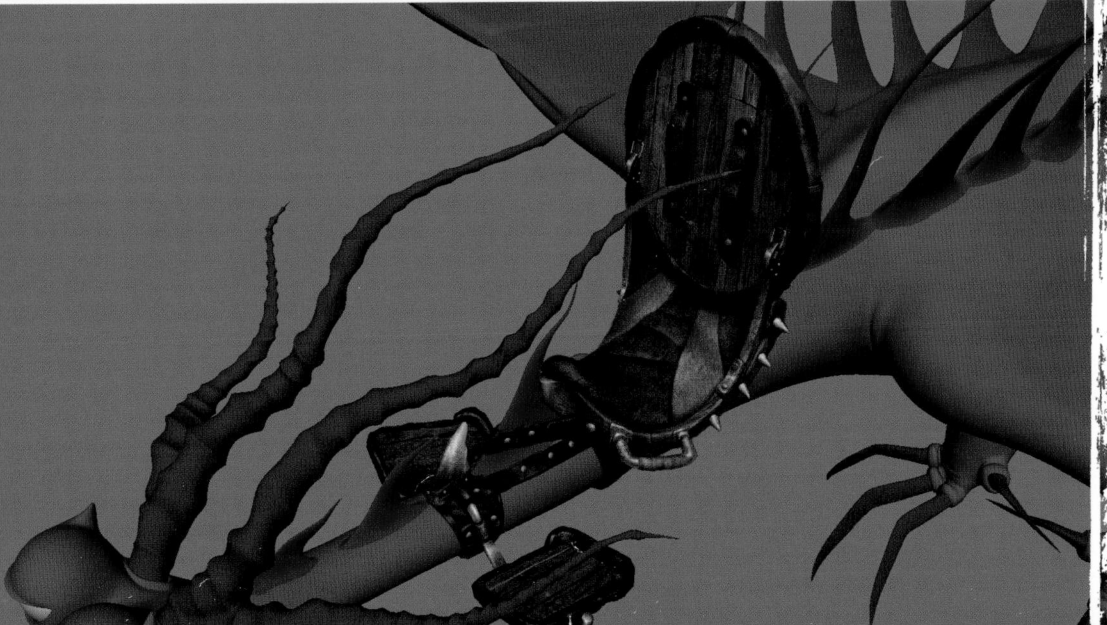

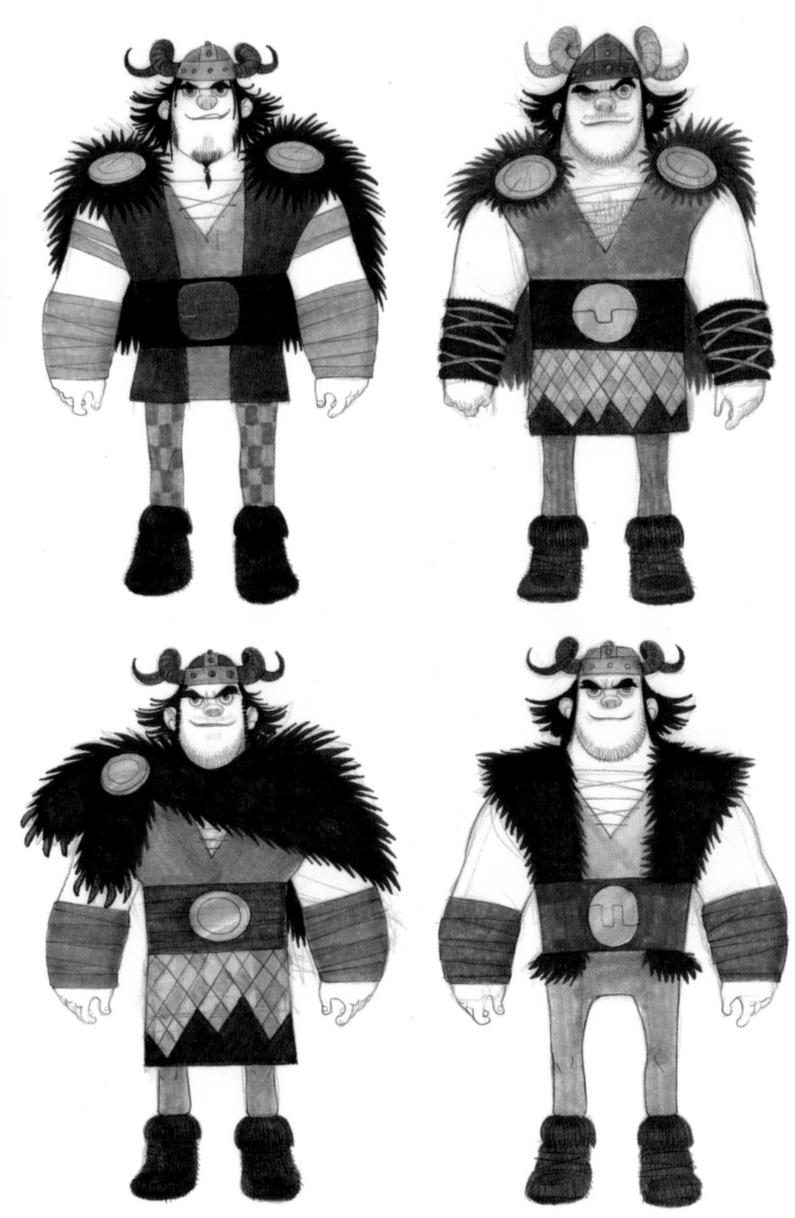

Snotlout is even more cocky and outrageous than he was in the first movie.
*—Pierre-Olivier Vincent, production designer*

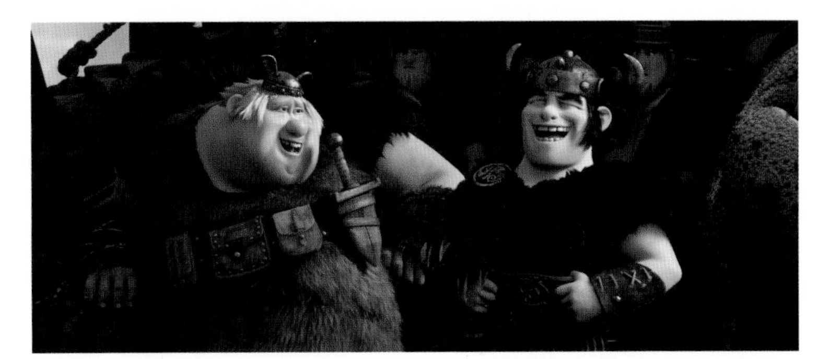

TOP LEFT: Snotlout Concept Model ◆ *Leo Sanchez*
LEFT: Hookfang Saddle Painting ◆ *Peter Chan* ◆ Model ◆ *Charles Ellison*

TOP: Snotlout Costumes ◆ *Iuri Lioi*
ABOVE: Film Frame

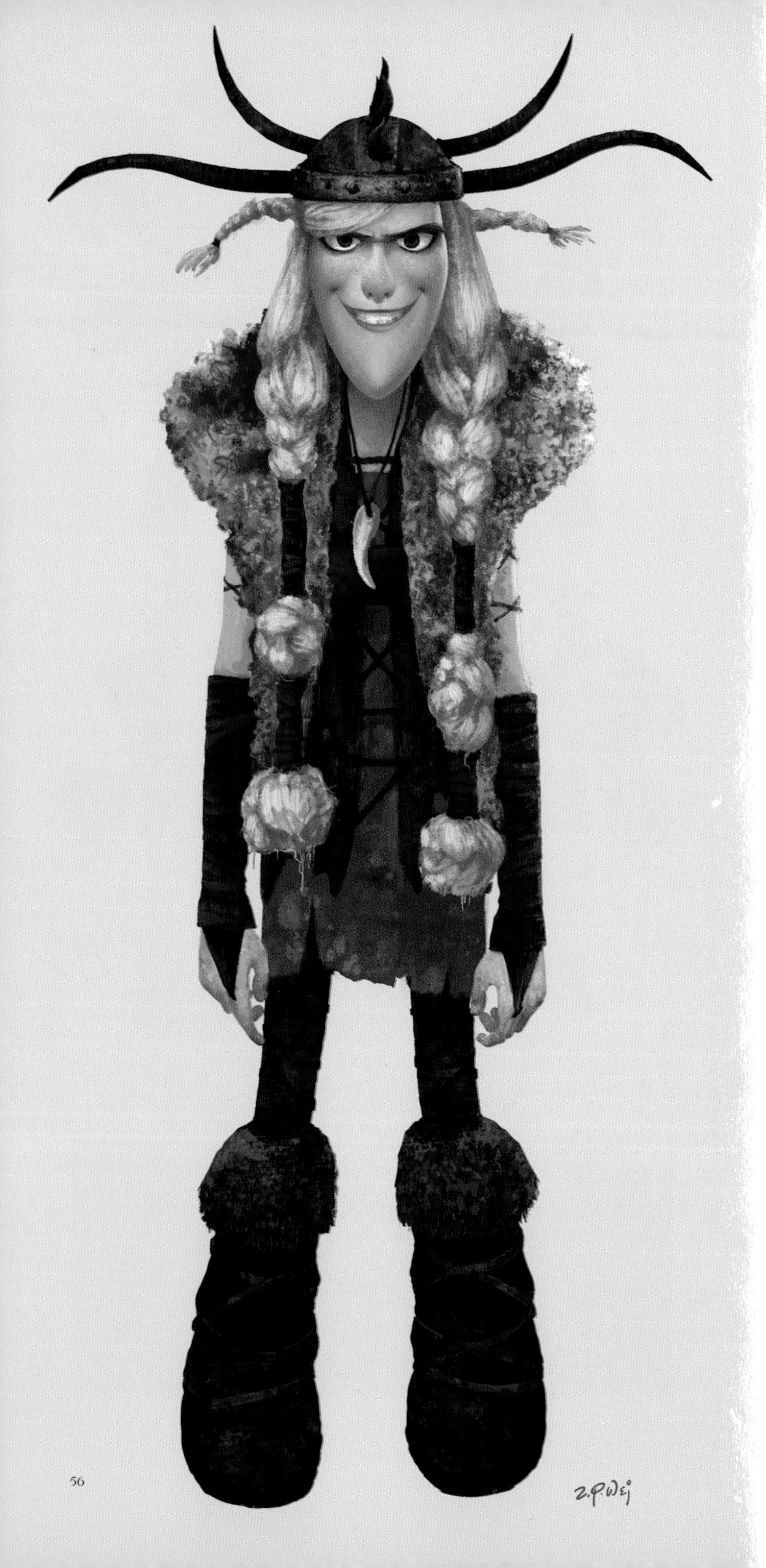

# Ruffnut & Tuffnut

Ruffnut and Tuffnut, the comic duo, are more of what they were in the first movie. There is also a new running gag in the movie about Ruffnut's attraction to Eret.

It was a very difficult task to take these characters from the first movie and make them look five years older. The transition, especially for adolescents entering adulthood, is very subtle. We wanted to stay true to our original characters so we basically kept all their specifics in terms of design and acting. Then we made those elements a little more extreme with more detailing on their surfacing to make them look a little more sophisticated. Even though they look older, we wanted to keep the charm they had in the first film. They were like bratty kids in the first movie and now they are like bratty young adults.

*—Pierre-Olivier Vincent, production designer*

LEFT: Ruffnut Painting ✦ *ZhaoPing Wei* ✦ Model ✦ *Abraham Meneu Oset*
BELOW & RIGHT: Ruffnut Concept Model ✦ *Leo Sanchez*

BELOW LEFT: Barf & Belch and Tuffnut & Ruffnut Racing Stripes Concept ✦ *Kirsten Kawamura* ✦ Models ✦ *Matt Paulson, Abraham Meneu Oset & Robert Vignone* ✦ Surfacing ✦ *Ted Davis, Carson James McKay, & Gentaro Yamamoto*

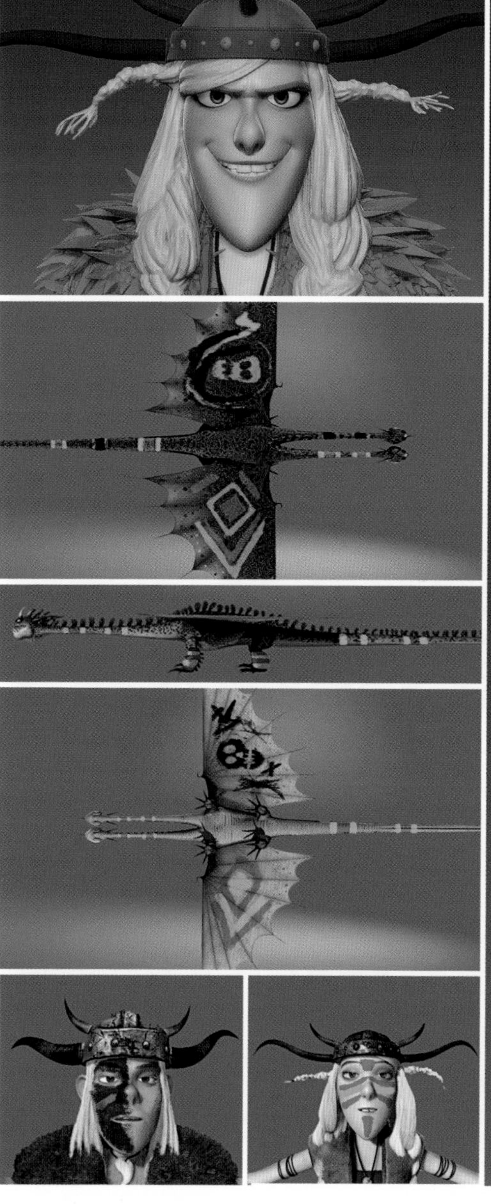

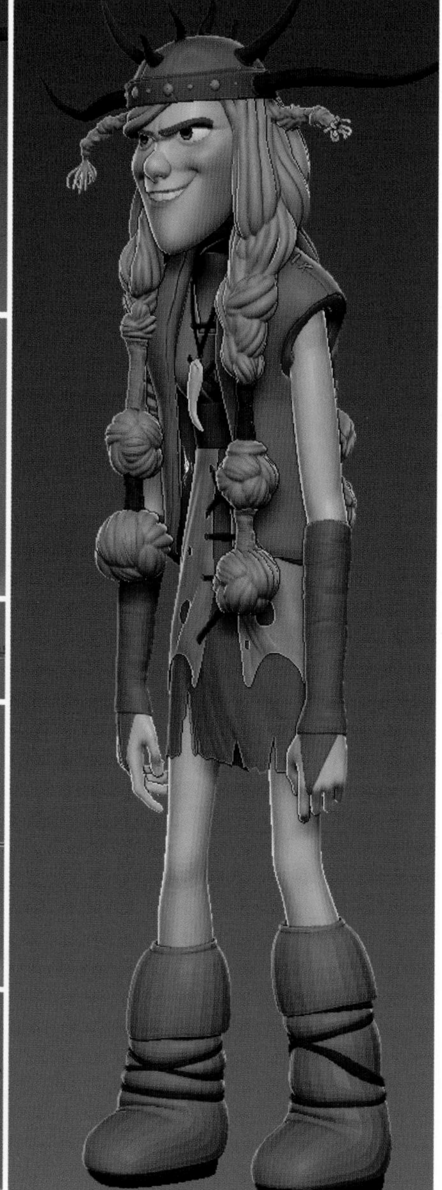

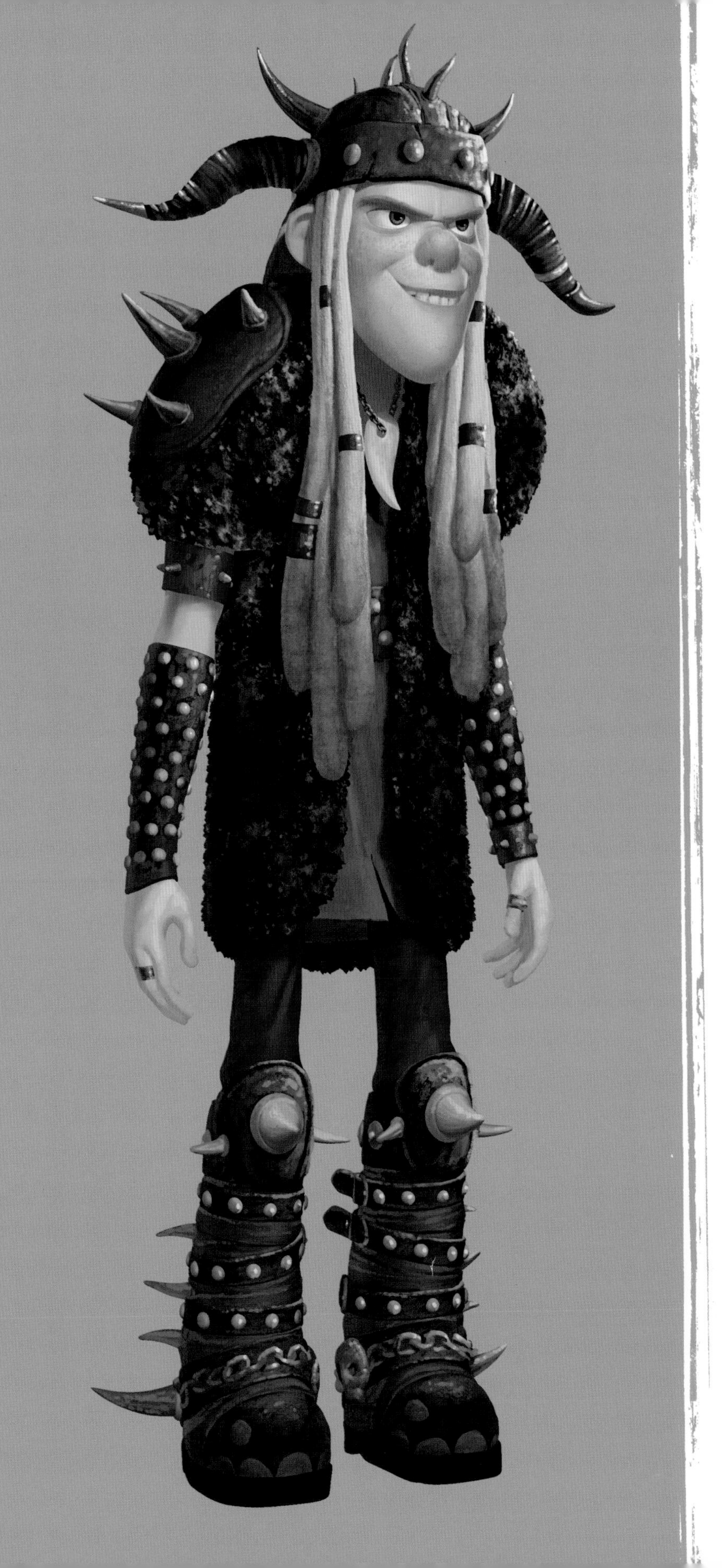

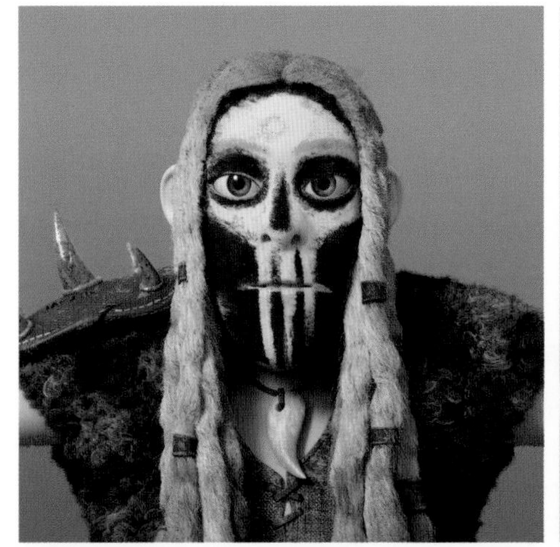

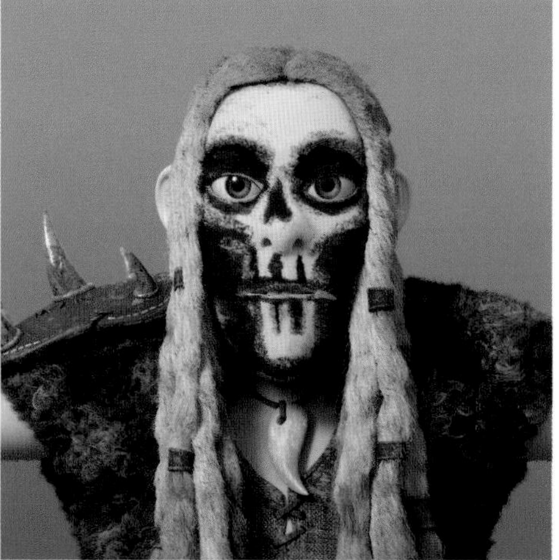

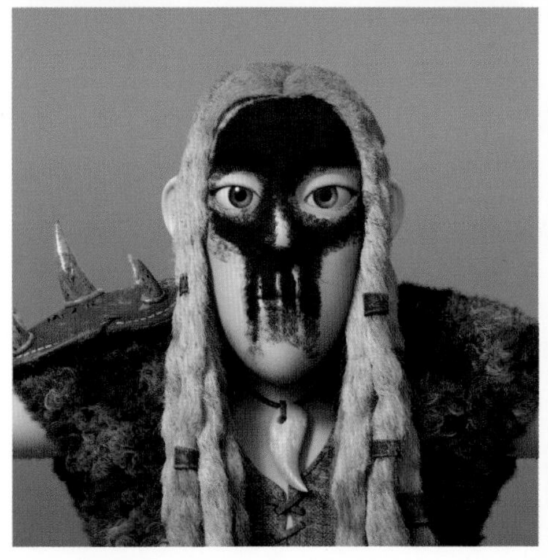

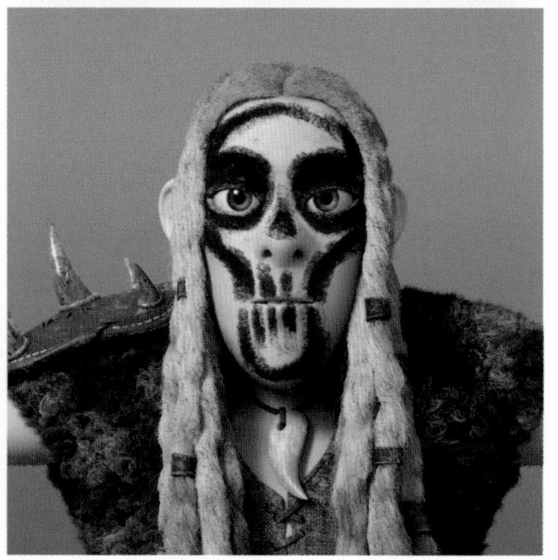

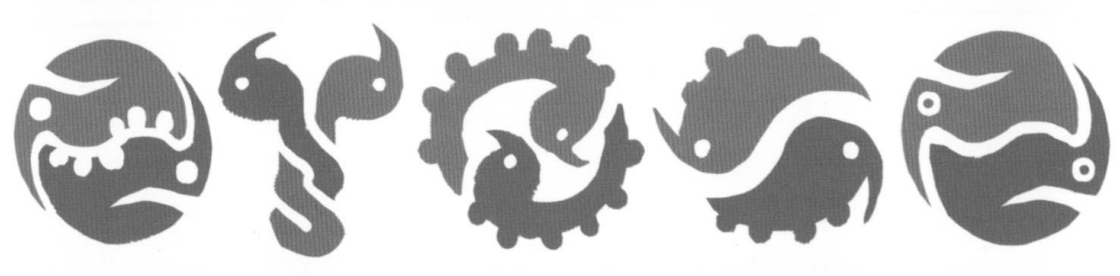

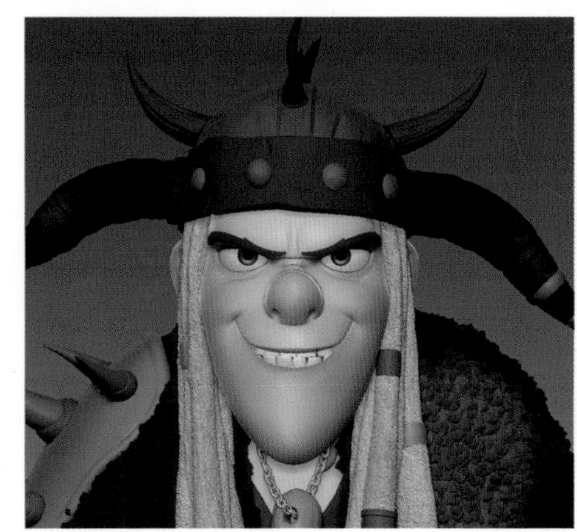

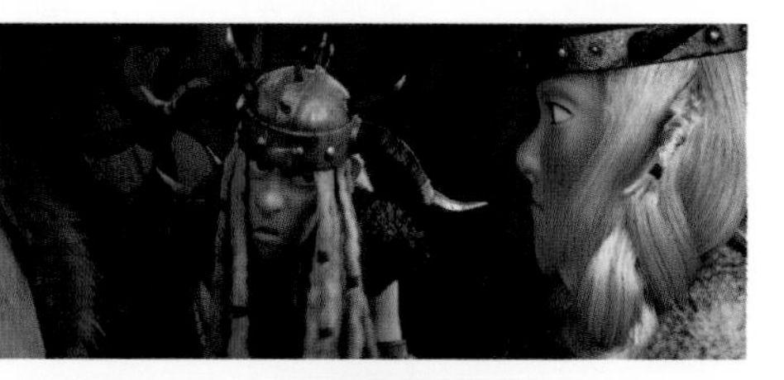

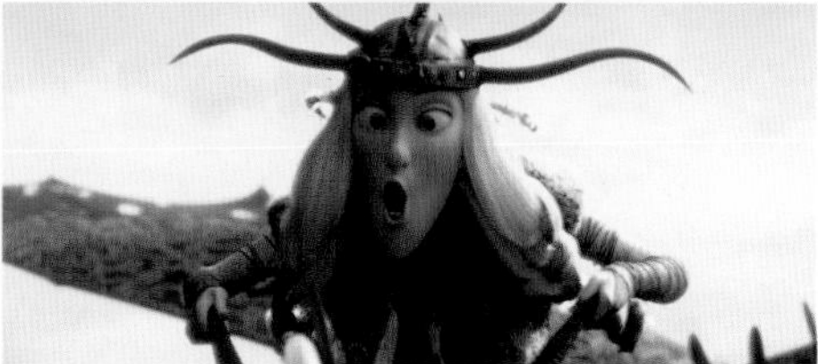

LEFT: Tuffnut Painting ✦ *ZhaoPing Wei* ✦ Model ✦ *Robert Vignone*
TOP: Tuffnut Facepaint Variations ✦ *Iuri Lioi*
ABOVE MIDDLE: Zippleback Racing Logos ✦ *Kirsten Kawamura*
ABOVE LEFT: Tuffnut Concept Model ✦ *Leo Sanchez*
ABOVE RIGHT: Film Frames

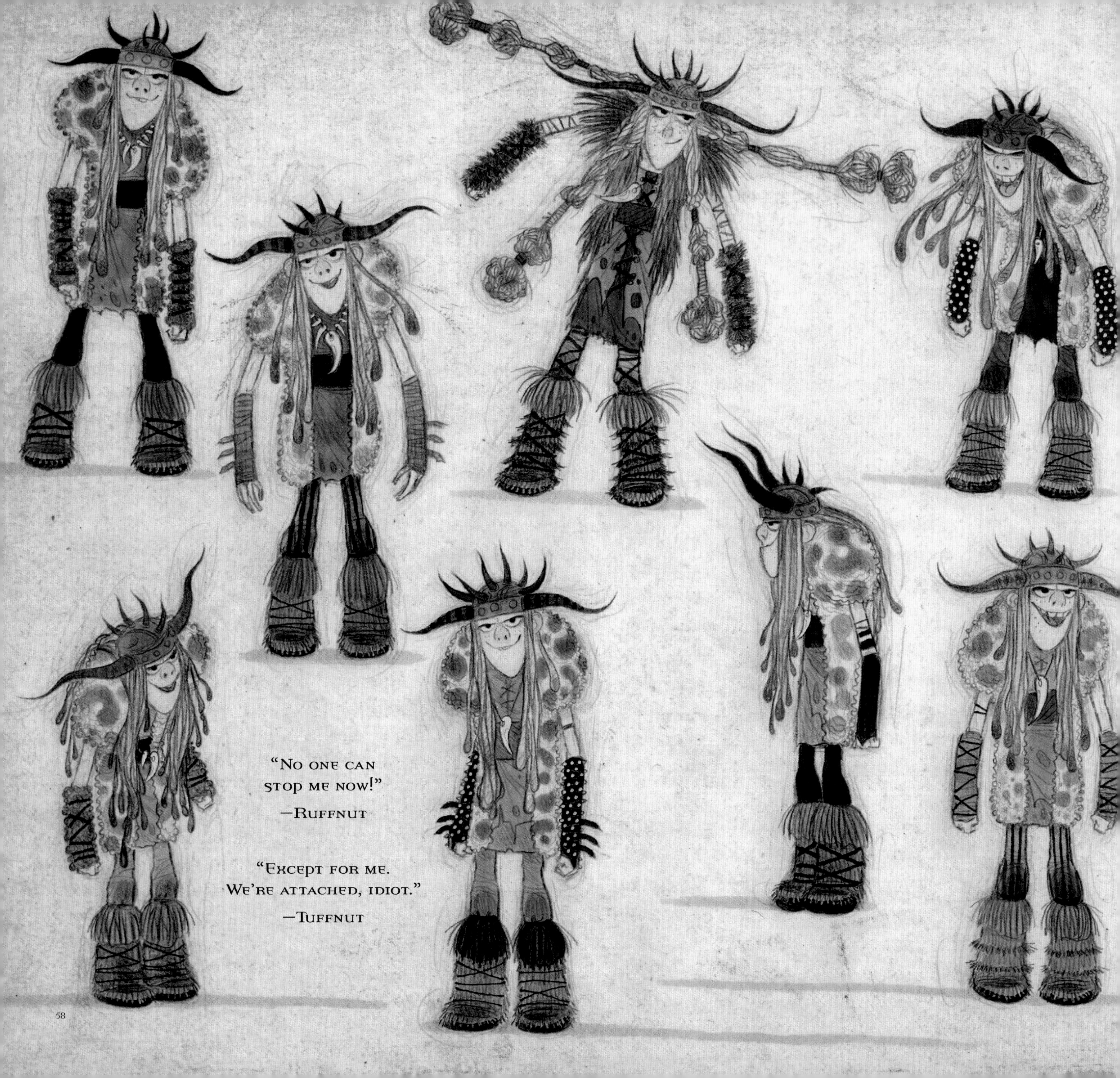

"No one can stop me now!"
—Ruffnut

"Except for me. We're attached, idiot."
—Tuffnut

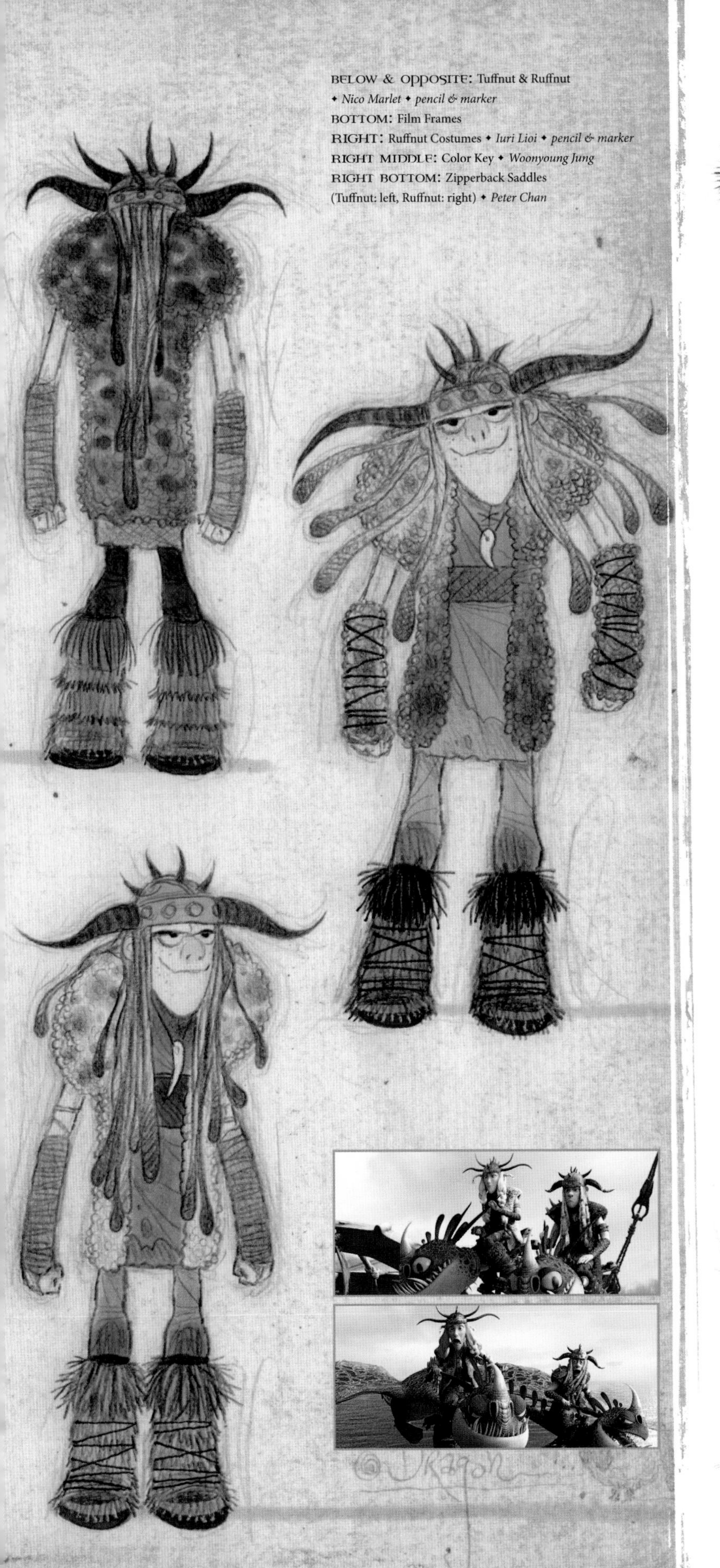

BELOW & OPPOSITE: Tuffnut & Ruffnut
✦ *Nico Marlet* ✦ *pencil & marker*
BOTTOM: Film Frames
RIGHT: Ruffnut Costumes ✦ *Iuri Lioi* ✦ *pencil & marker*
RIGHT MIDDLE: Color Key ✦ *Woonyoung Jung*
RIGHT BOTTOM: Zipperback Saddles
(Tuffnut: left, Ruffnut: right) ✦ *Peter Chan*

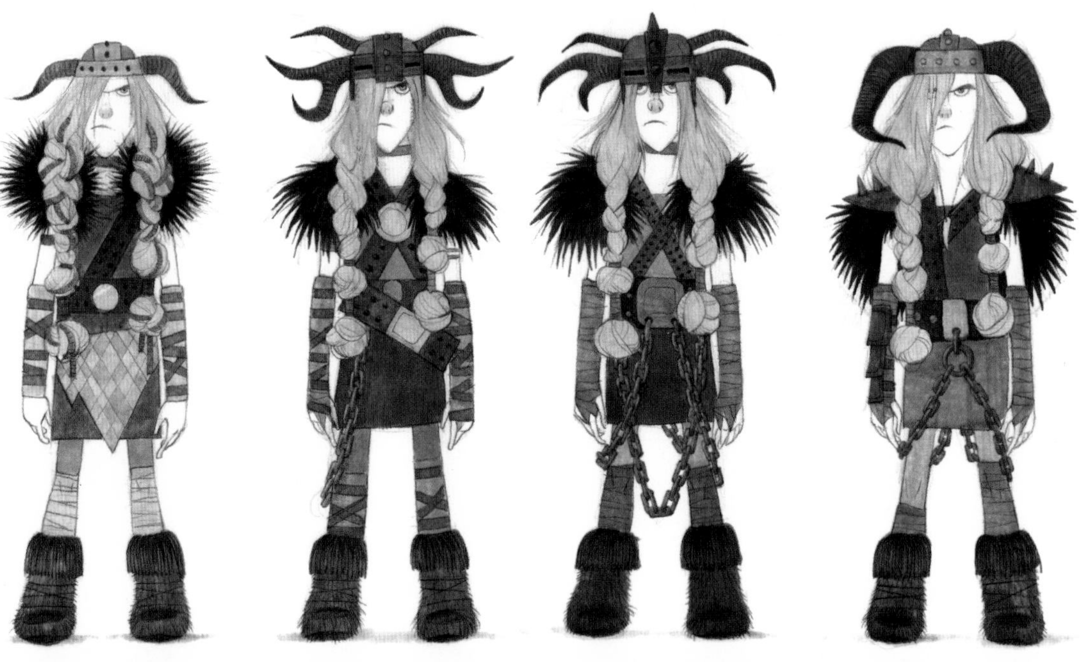

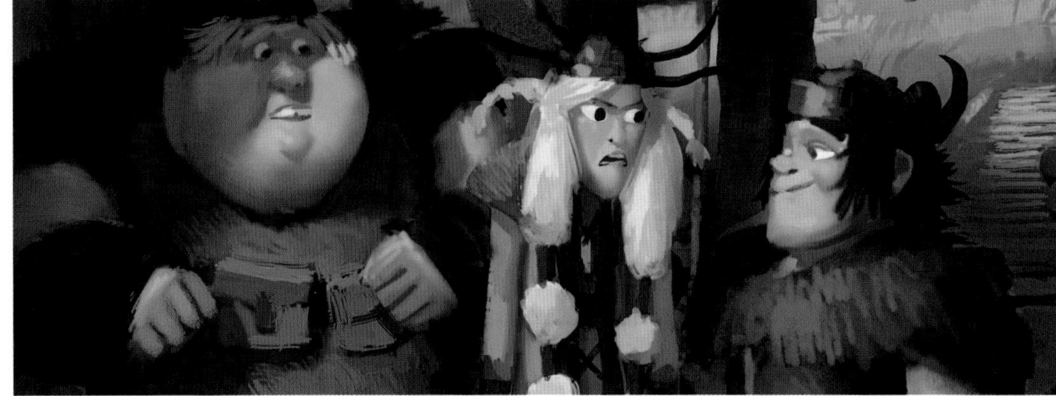

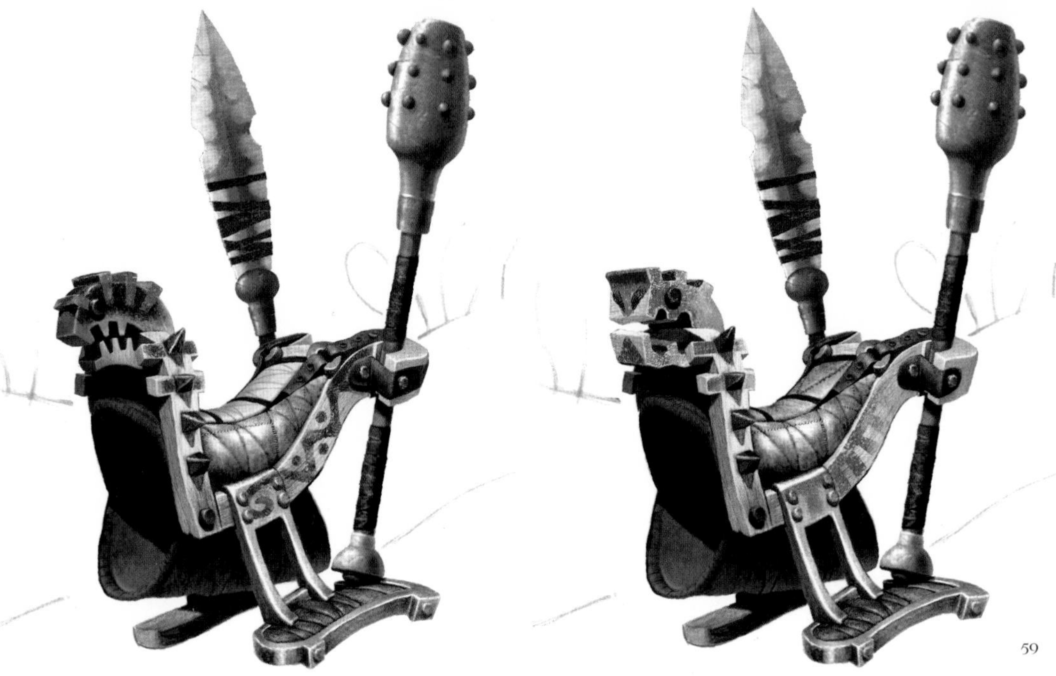

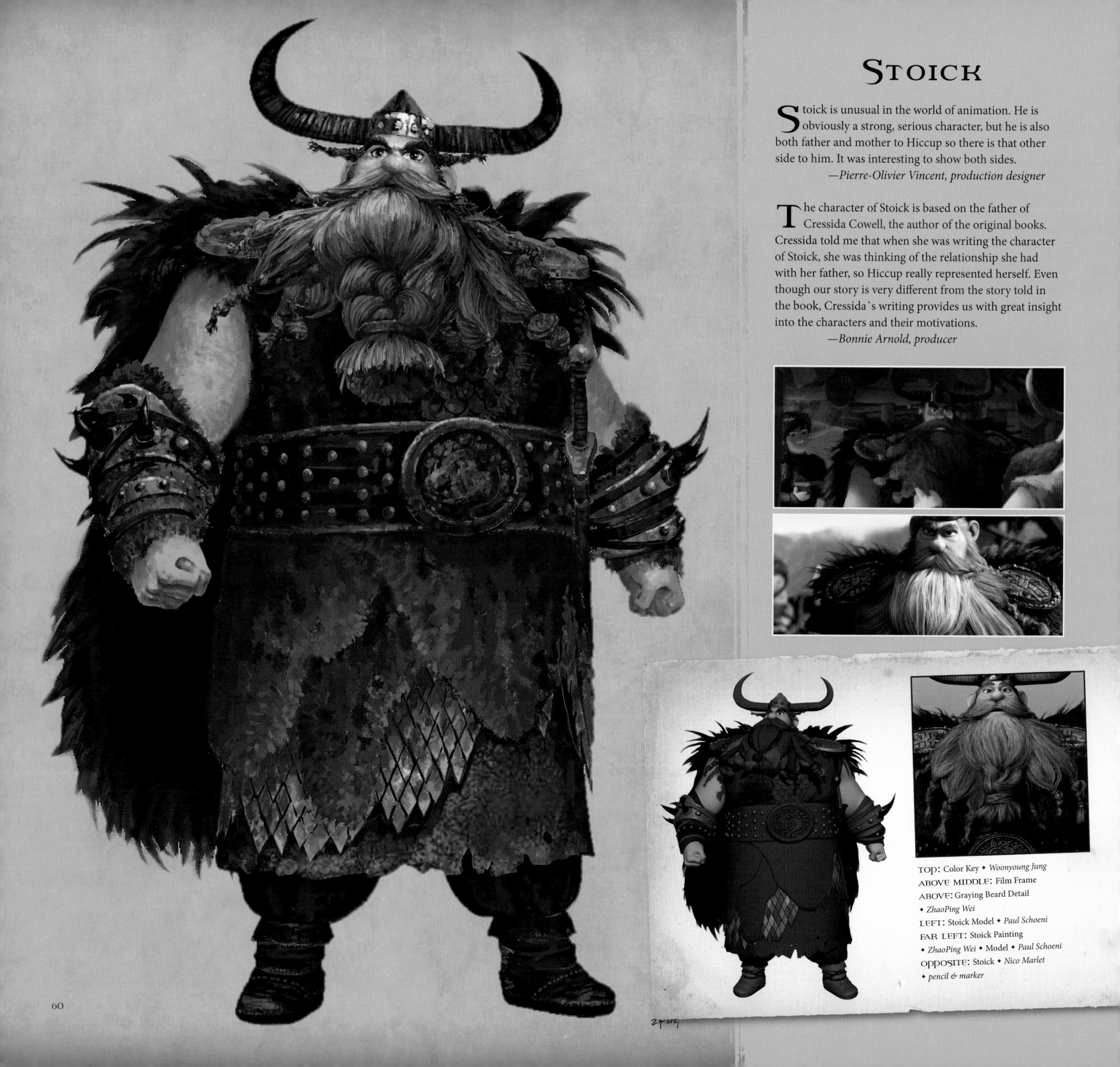

# Stoick

Stoick is unusual in the world of animation. He is obviously a strong, serious character, but he is also both father and mother to Hiccup so there is that other side to him. It was interesting to show both sides.

*—Pierre-Olivier Vincent, production designer*

The character of Stoick is based on the father of Cressida Cowell, the author of the original books. Cressida told me that when she was writing the character of Stoick, she was thinking of the relationship she had with her father, so Hiccup really represented herself. Even though our story is very different from the story told in the book, Cressida's writing provides us with great insight into the characters and their motivations.

*—Bonnie Arnold, producer*

TOP: Color Key ✦ *Woonyoung Jung*
ABOVE MIDDLE: Film Frame
ABOVE: Graying Beard Detail ✦ *ZhaoPing Wei*
LEFT: Stoick Model ✦ *Paul Schoeni*
FAR LEFT: Stoick Painting ✦ *ZhaoPing Wei* ✦ Model ✦ *Paul Schoeni*
OPPOSITE: Stoick ✦ *Nico Marlet* ✦ *pencil & marker*

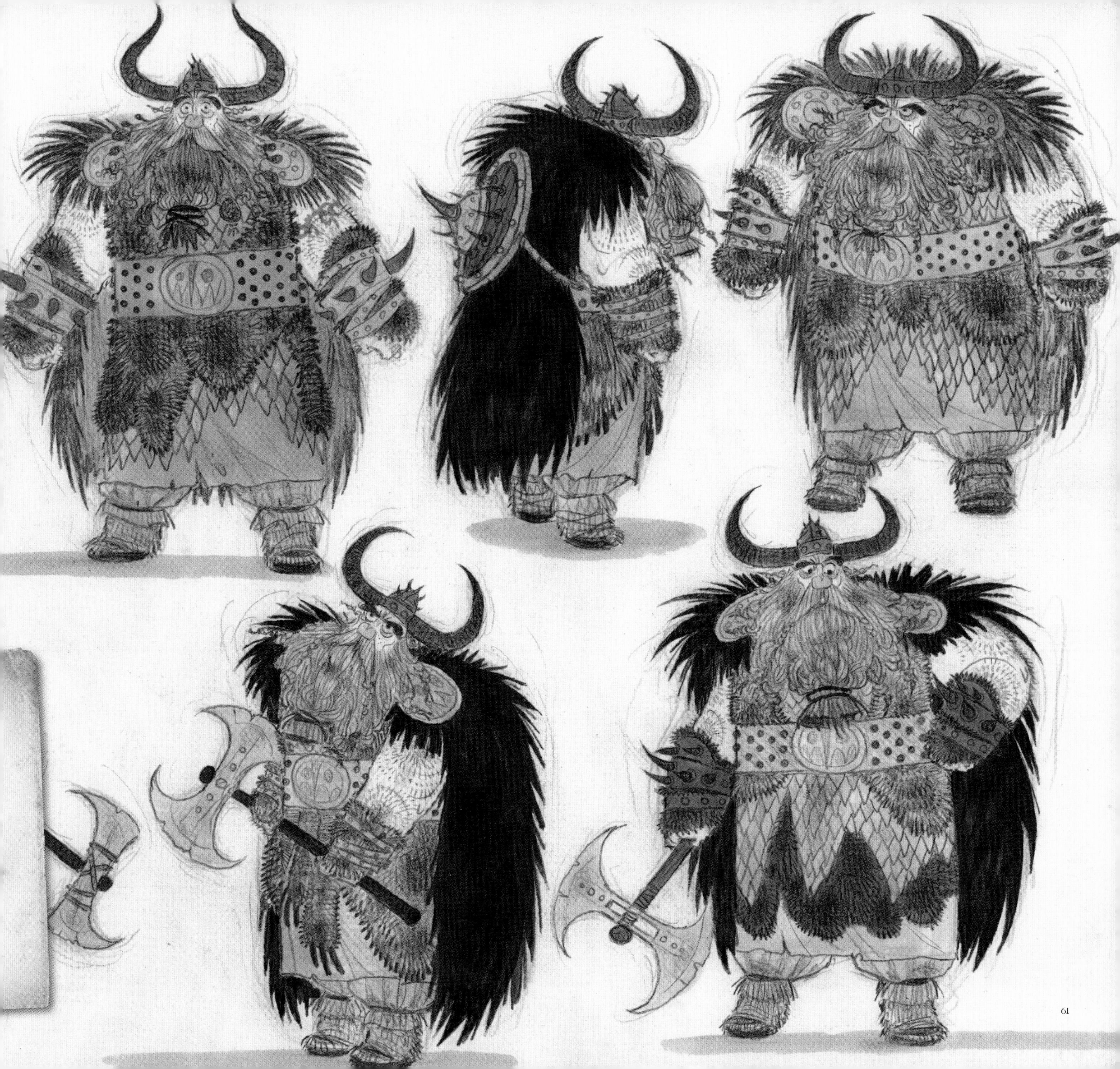

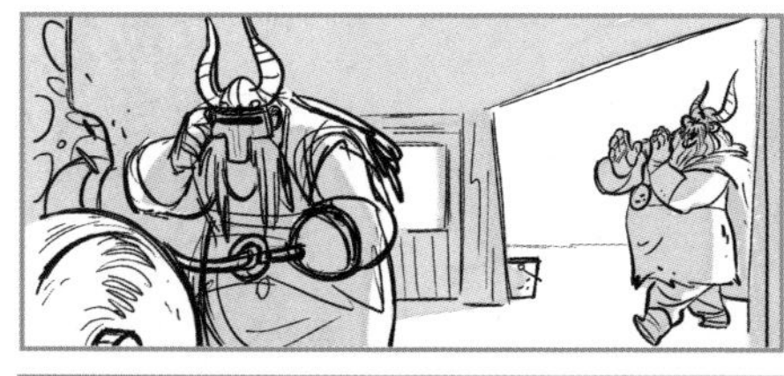

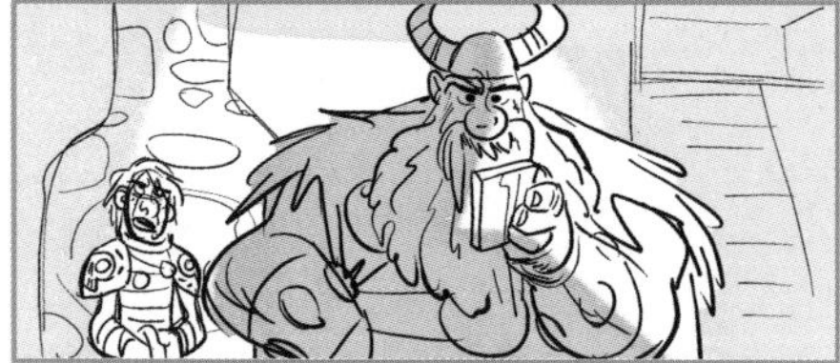

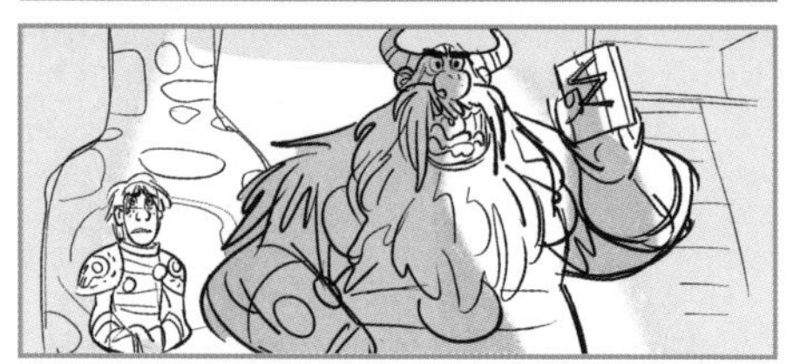

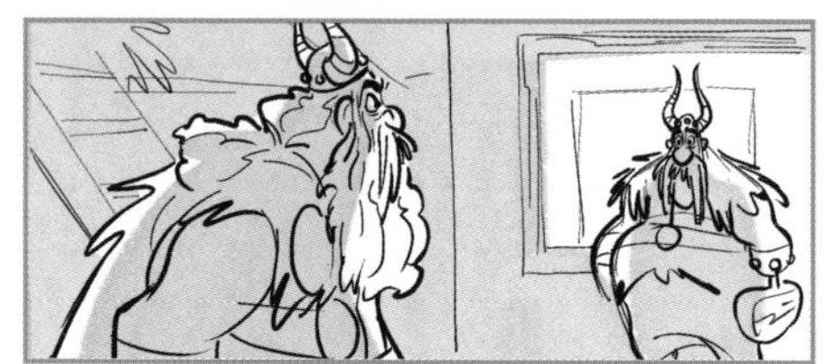

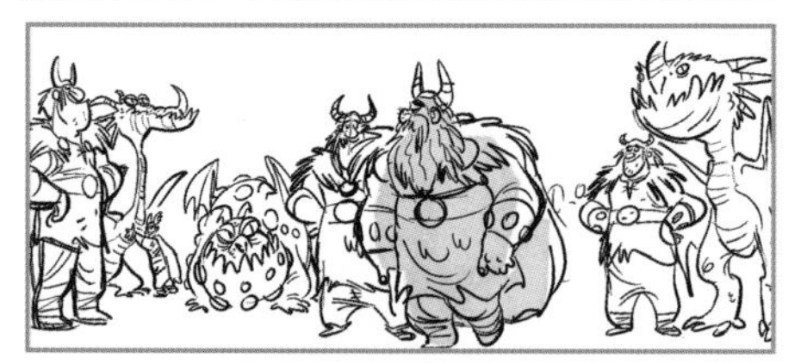

Stoick's story line is fraught with surprises in this second installment. At every turn, he has crashing new realities to deal with, from his son going rogue to the resurgence of an old enemy and the shocking return of a long lost love. We put him through the wringer, taking him from jovial dad to no-nonsense warrior and back again. His legacy is rich with fatherly love, humility, and pride. He represents a perfect, if sometimes overbearing, role model for Hiccup. Even though his is a story of a reluctant heir, Hiccup is very much cut from the same cloth as his father.

*—Dean DeBlois, director*

It was very appropriate for me to use my Scottish accent for Stoick because the Vikings and the Scots have a very close connection. You have to remember that the Vikings are very much made up of Celtic blood. The Vikings migrated down to Scotland and many of them settled there. They took our best women! At least 25 percent of Icelandic blood is made from Celtic DNA. I also like that the accents in the movie are used as a generational tool. The kids have American accents and sound more modern than the adults. I appreciate those kinds of artistic and creative choices.

*—Gerard Butler, actor and voice of Stoick*

Stoick has come a long way from the first movie where he hated dragons and was a little ashamed of Hiccup—always wanting him to man up. Now Stoick loves dragons, embraces the culture, and is deeply proud of his son. A lot of what happens with Stoick in the second movie centers around his improved relationship with Hiccup even though he is being a little pushy. He wants Hiccup to assume the responsibility of being chief and is trying to usher his son into the next phase of his life. Hiccup is pushing back a little and wants to maintain some semblance of freedom to go out exploring. Also, it's not in Hiccup's nature to want to lead, though it falls into his lap anyway. In this movie, Stoick's motivation is clearly that he thinks the world of Hiccup and looks forward to showing him what he can do.

*—Tom Owens, head of story*

ABOVE & RIGHT: Storyboards ✦ *Tom Owens*
FAR RIGHT: Skullcrusher Saddle Views ✦ *Peter Chan*
BELOW: Stoick ✦ *Nico Marlet* ✦ *pencil & marker*

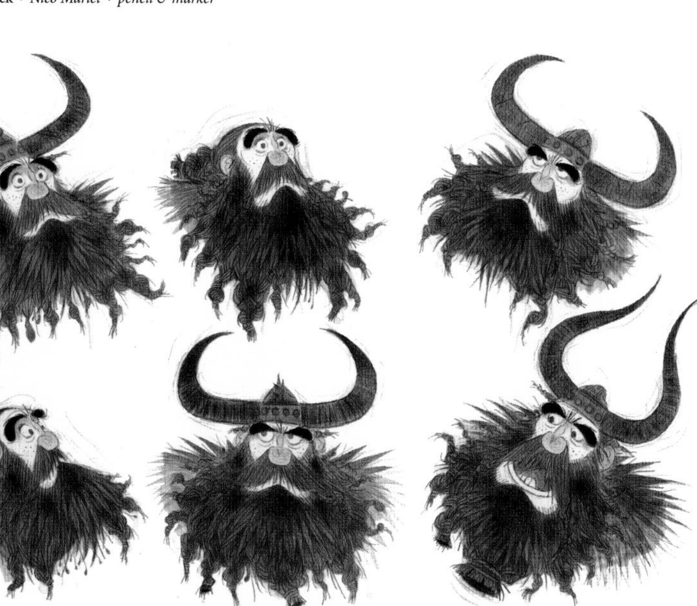

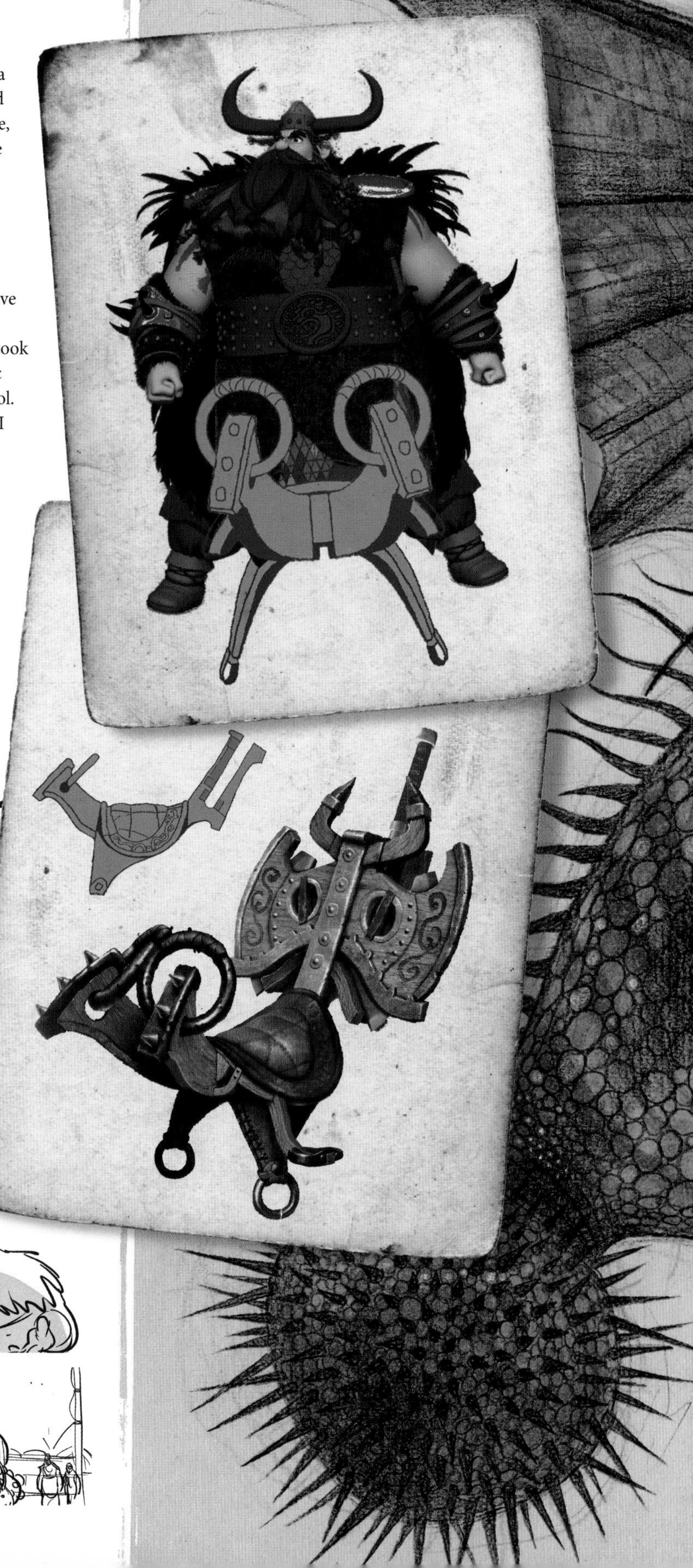

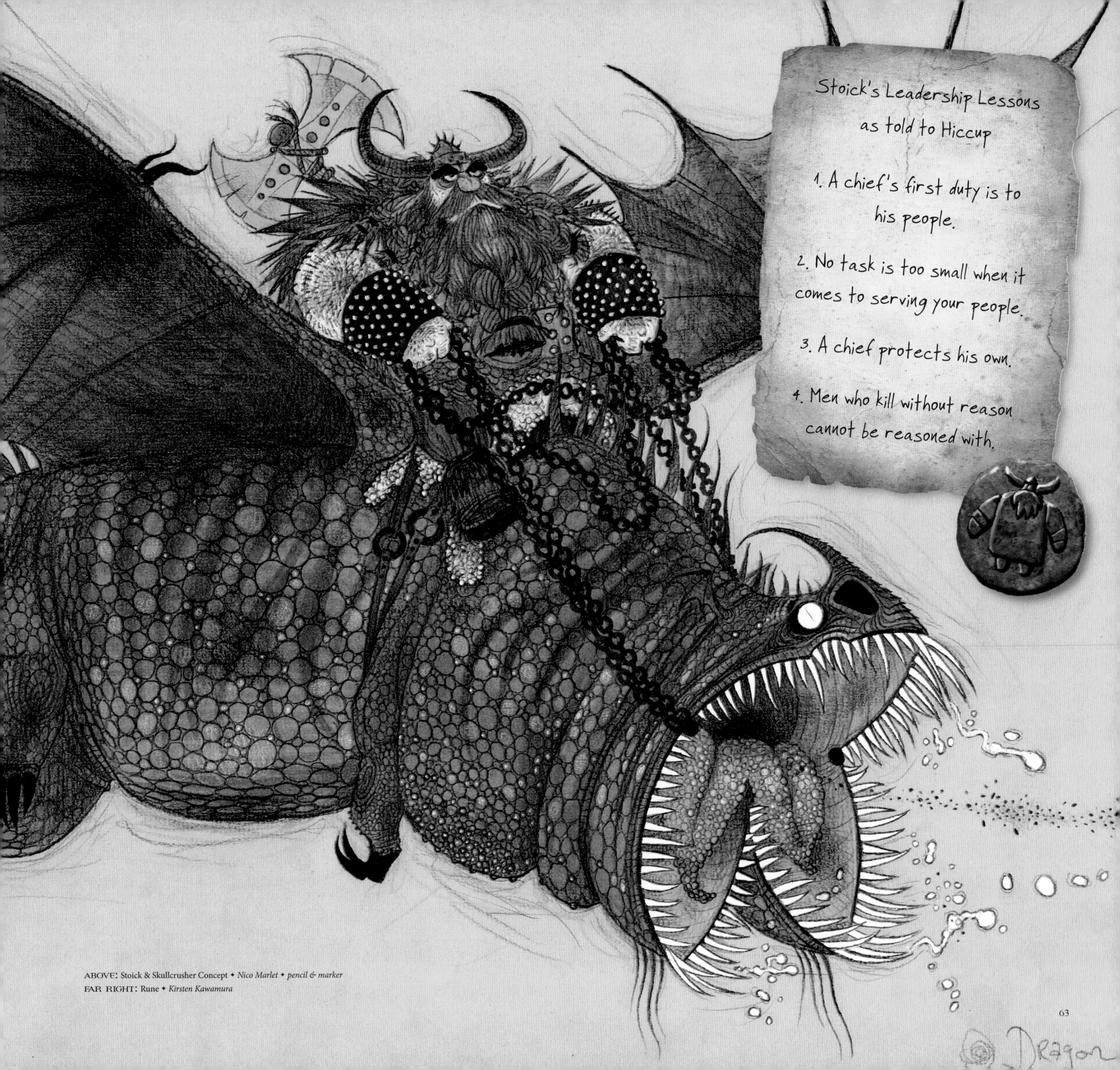


ABOVE: Stoick & Skullcrusher Concept ✦ *Nico Marlet* ✦ *pencil & marker*
FAR RIGHT: Rune ✦ *Kirsten Kawamura*

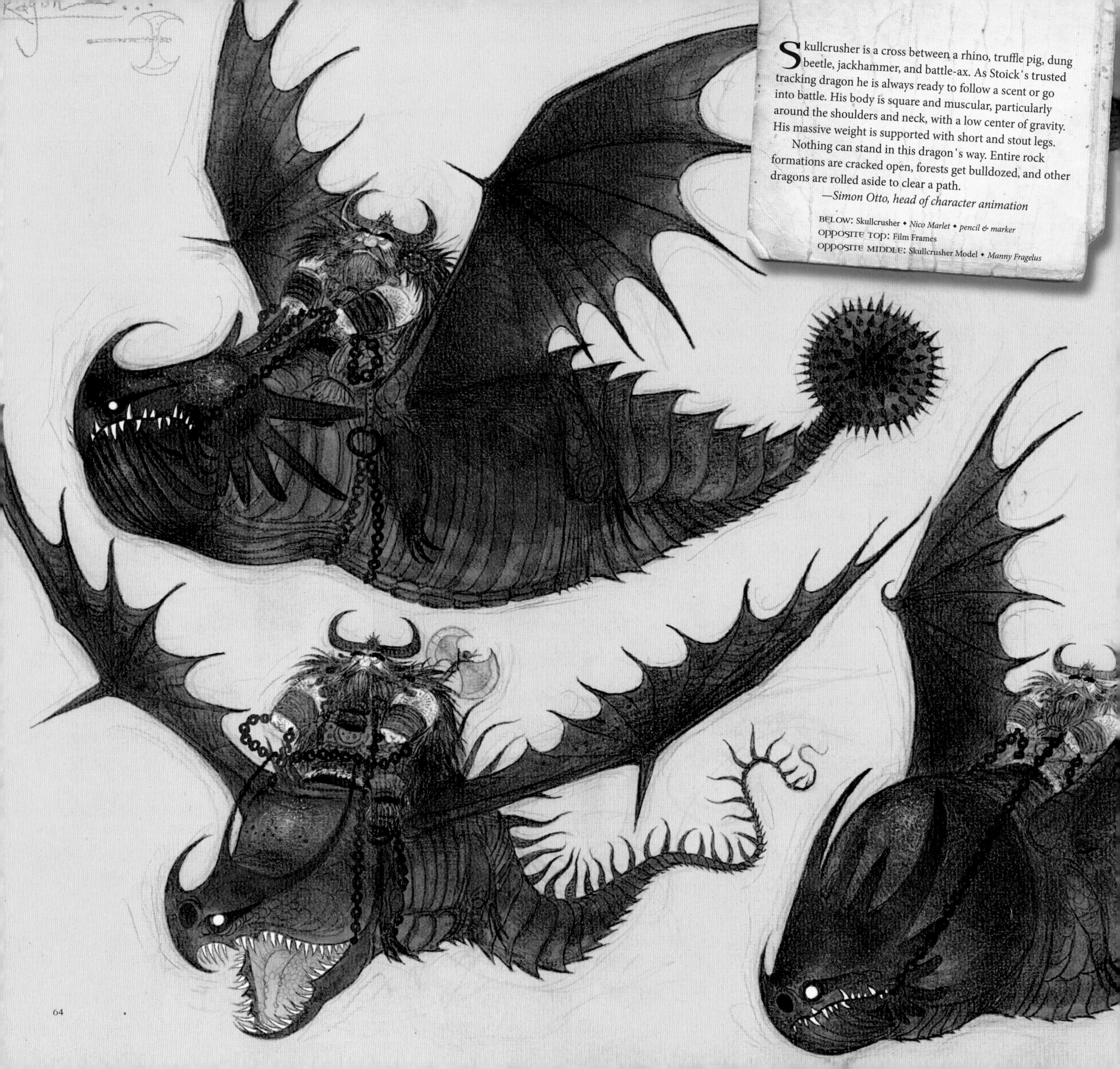

Skullcrusher is a cross between a rhino, truffle pig, dung beetle, jackhammer, and battle-ax. As Stoick's trusted tracking dragon he is always ready to follow a scent or go into battle. His body is square and muscular, particularly around the shoulders and neck, with a low center of gravity. His massive weight is supported with short and stout legs.

Nothing can stand in this dragon's way. Entire rock formations are cracked open, forests get bulldozed, and other dragons are rolled aside to clear a path.

*—Simon Otto, head of character animation*

BELOW: Skullcrusher ✦ *Nico Marlet* ✦ *pencil & marker*
OPPOSITE TOP: Film Frames
OPPOSITE MIDDLE: Skullcrusher Model ✦ *Manny Fragelus*

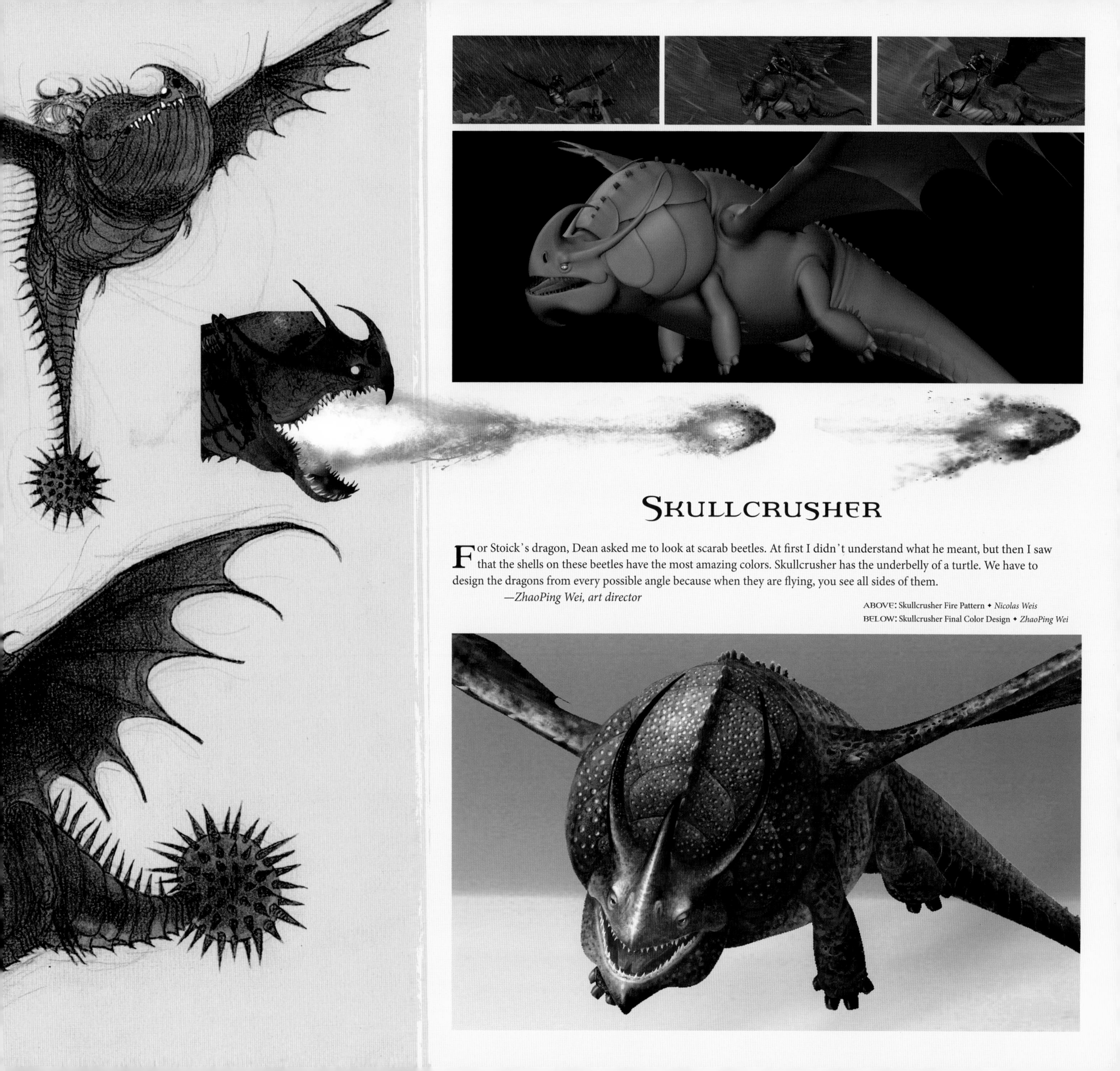

# Skullcrusher

For Stoick's dragon, Dean asked me to look at scarab beetles. At first I didn't understand what he meant, but then I saw that the shells on these beetles have the most amazing colors. Skullcrusher has the underbelly of a turtle. We have to design the dragons from every possible angle because when they are flying, you see all sides of them.

*—ZhaoPing Wei, art director*

ABOVE: Skullcrusher Fire Pattern ✦ *Nicolas Weis*
BELOW: Skullcrusher Final Color Design ✦ *ZhaoPing Wei*

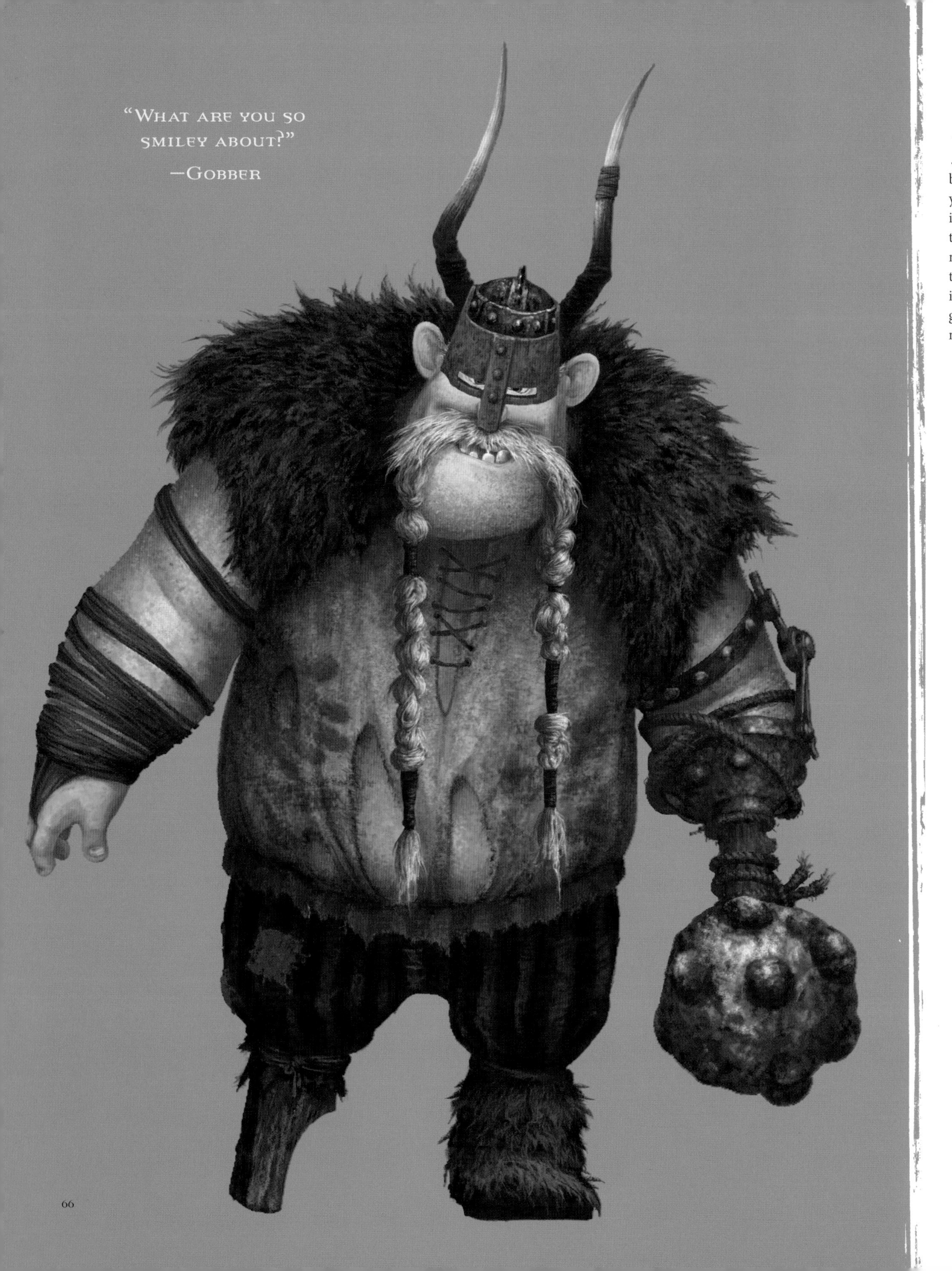

"What are you so smiley about?"
—Gobber



# Gobber

Most of the voice-over sessions were done alone in the booth and that was interesting because you don't have to worry about anyone else; you can throw out any wacky, crazy idea that comes into your head. But then I had a couple of sessions together with Jay Bucharel and Craig, which were so much fun that we wanted to do all of our sessions together. Craig Ferguson is an old friend of mine and, if you ask me, he steals the show as Gobber. He is just genuis! I was half expecting Craig to get an Oscar nomination, even though he's an animated Viking.

*—Gerard Butler, actor and voice of Stoick*

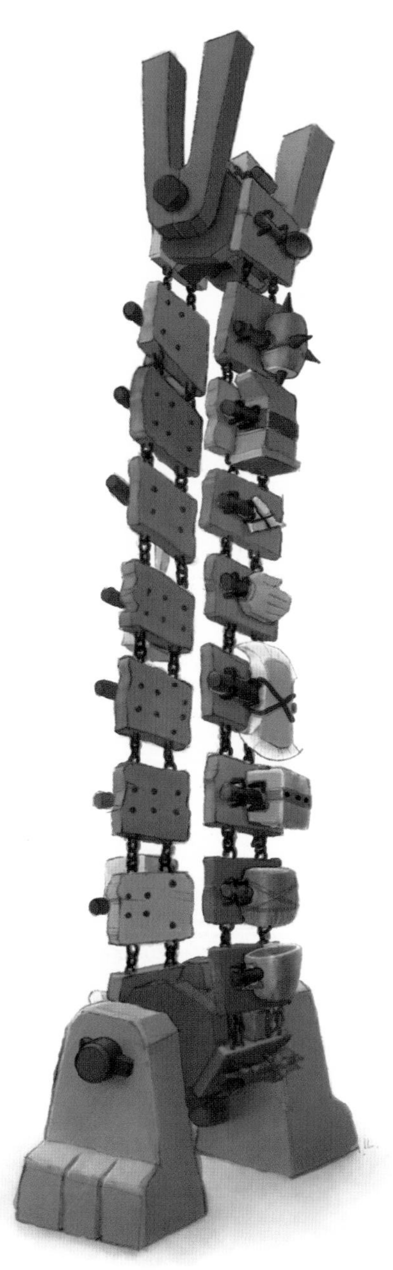

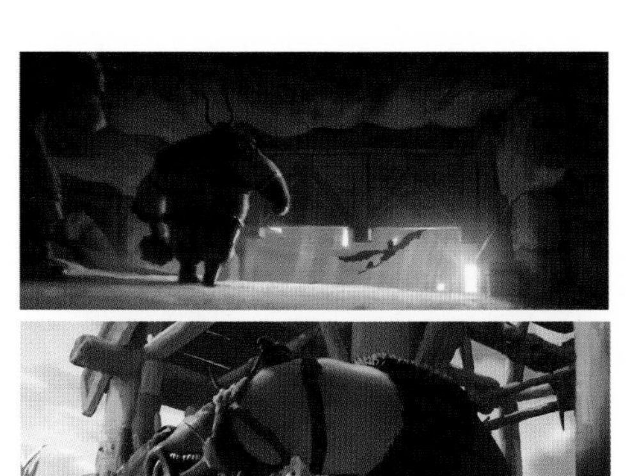

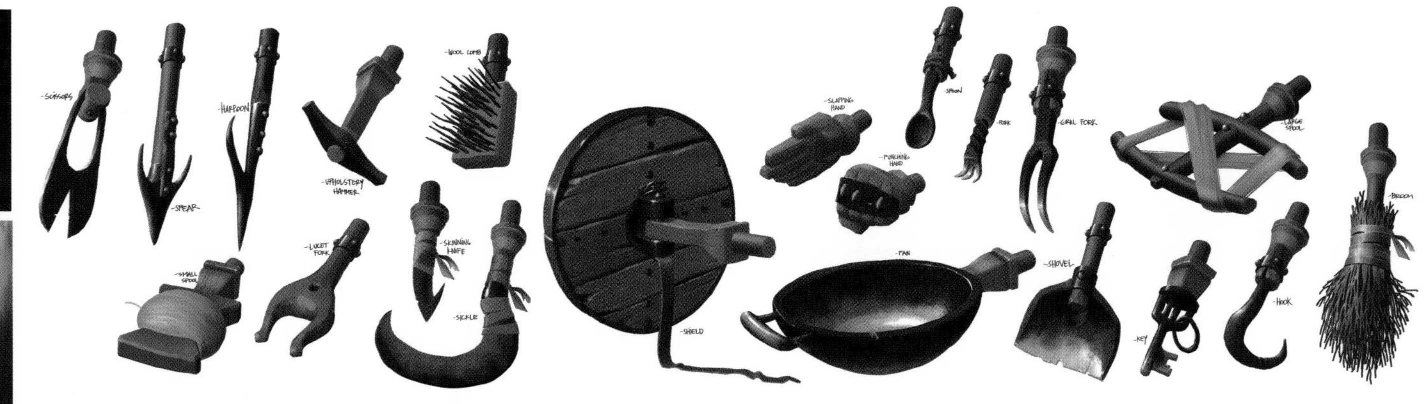


ABOVE: Color Keys ✦ *Woonyoung Jung*
ABOVE RIGHT: Arm Attachments ✦ *Iuri Lioi*
BELOW: Gobber & Arm Attachments ✦ *Nico Marlet* ✦ *pencil & marker*
OPPOSITE LEFT: Gobber Painting ✦ *ZhaoPing Wei*
✦ Model ✦ *Matt Paulson*
OPPOSITE RIGHT: Arm Attachments Rack ✦ *Iuri Lioi*

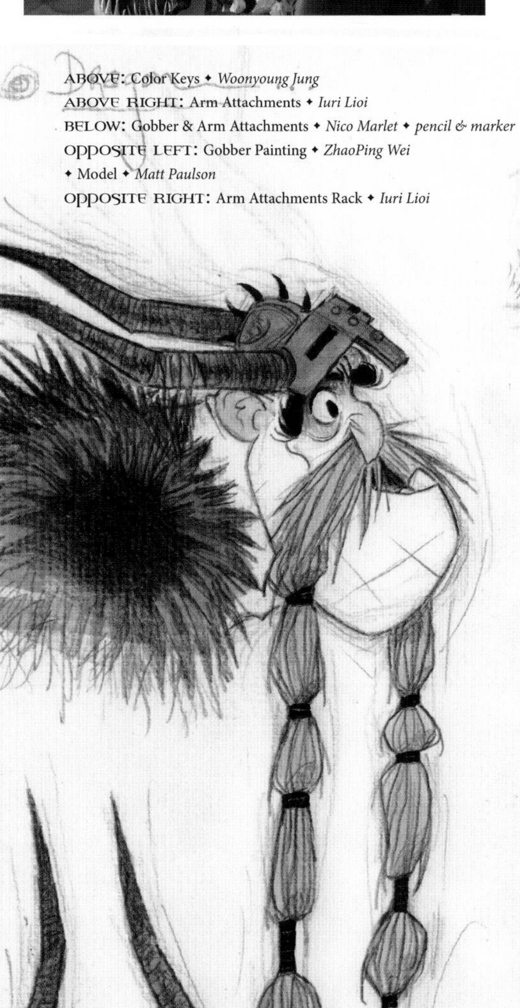

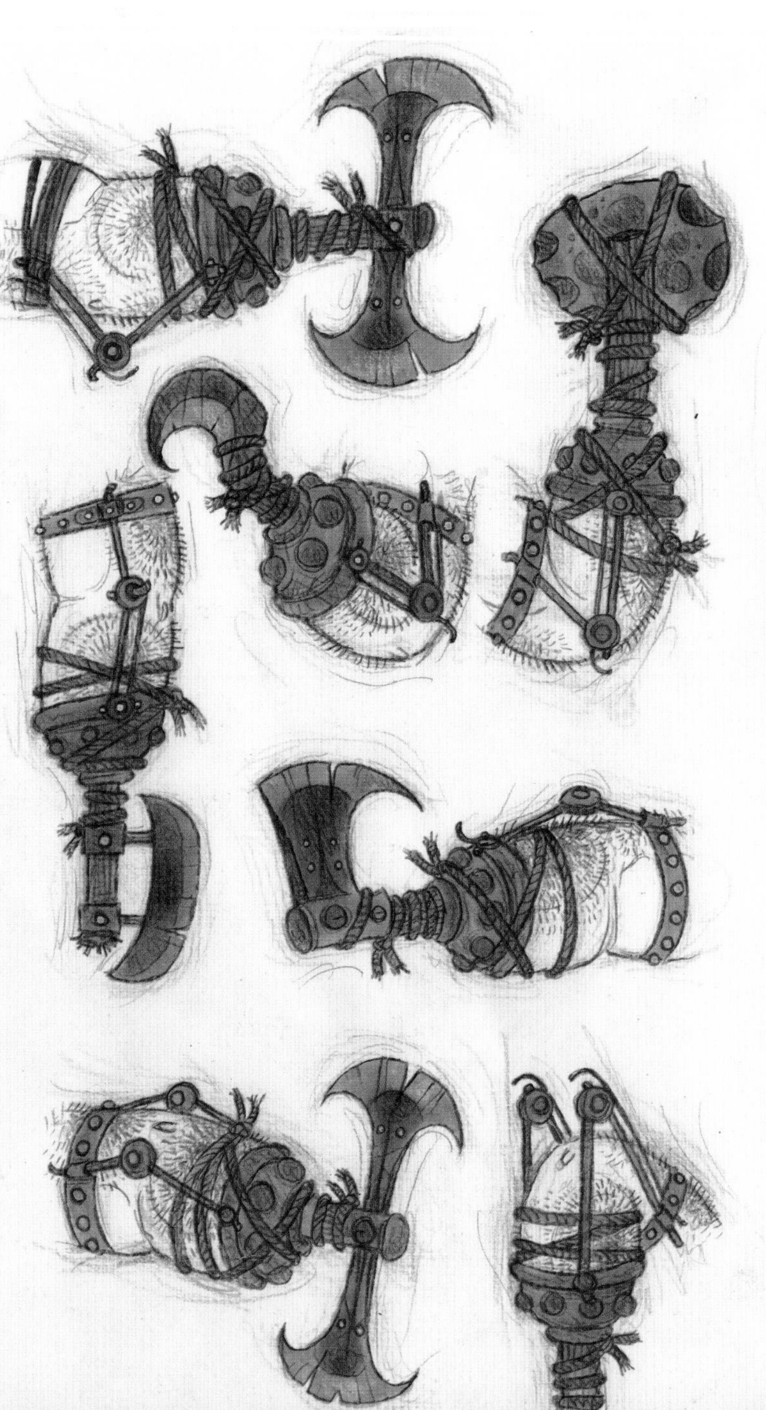

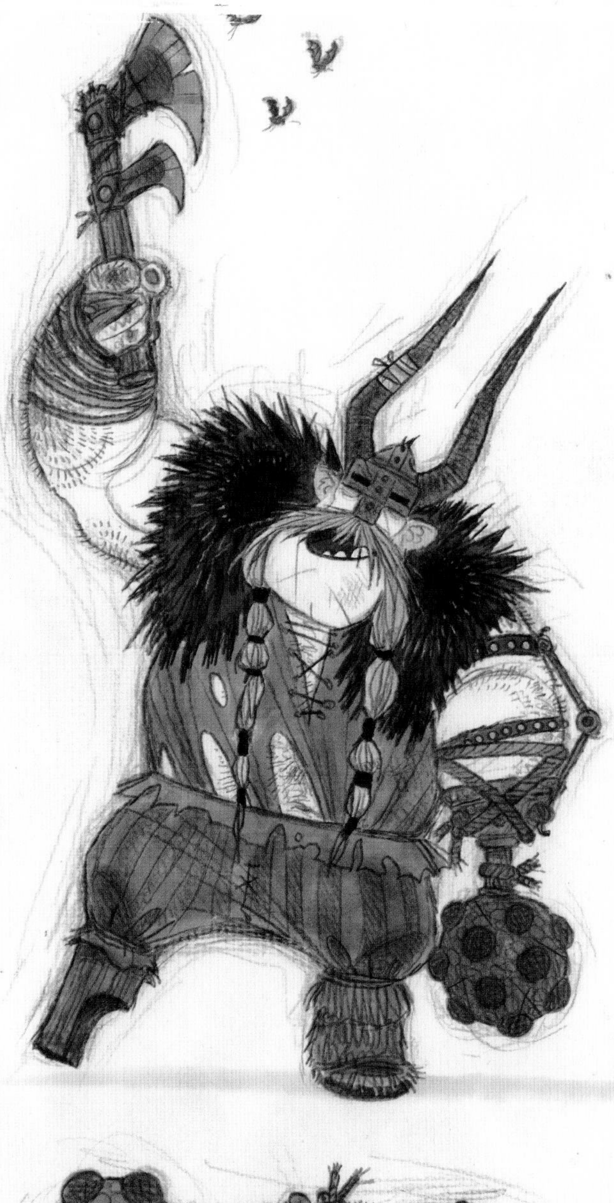

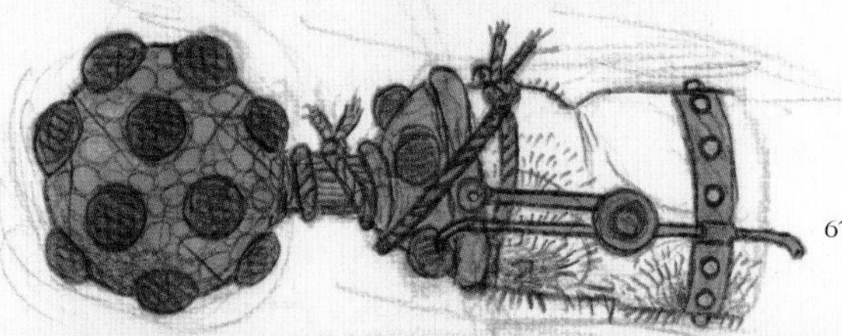

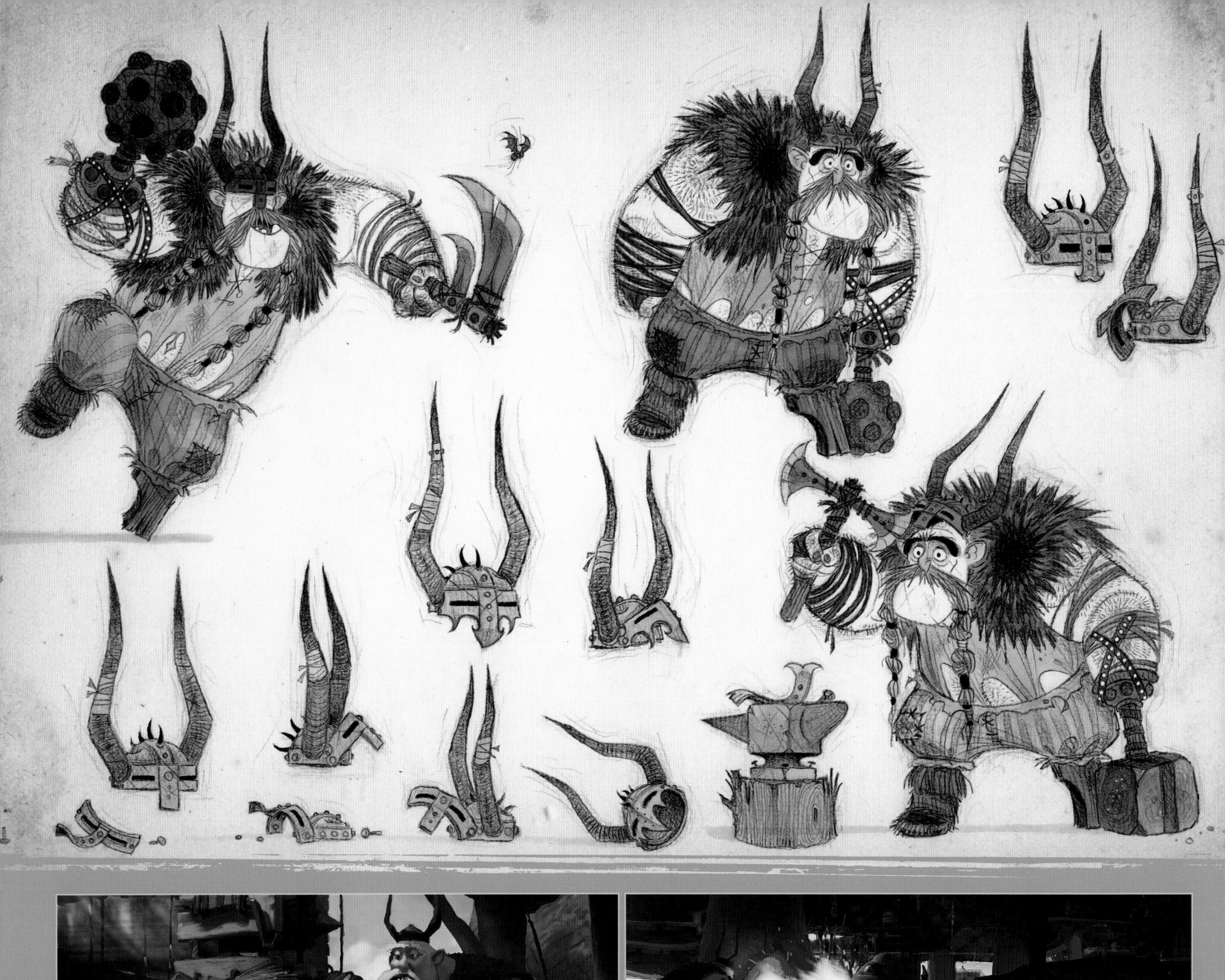
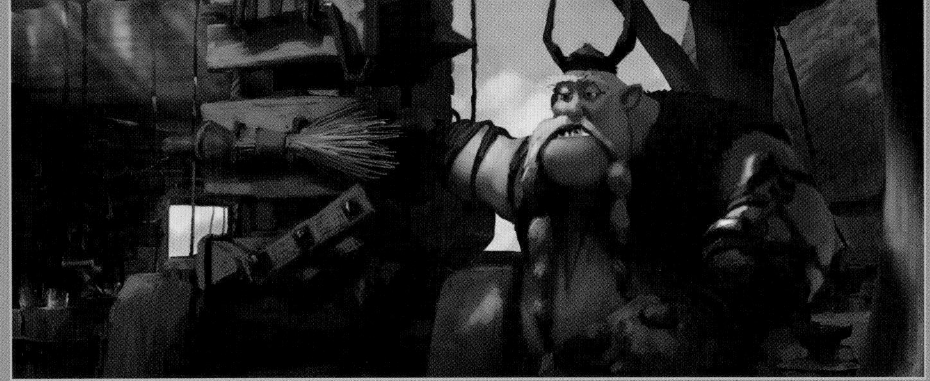
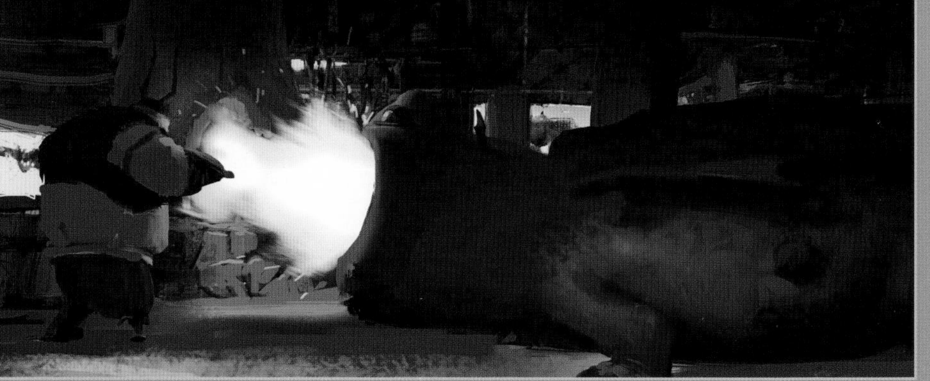

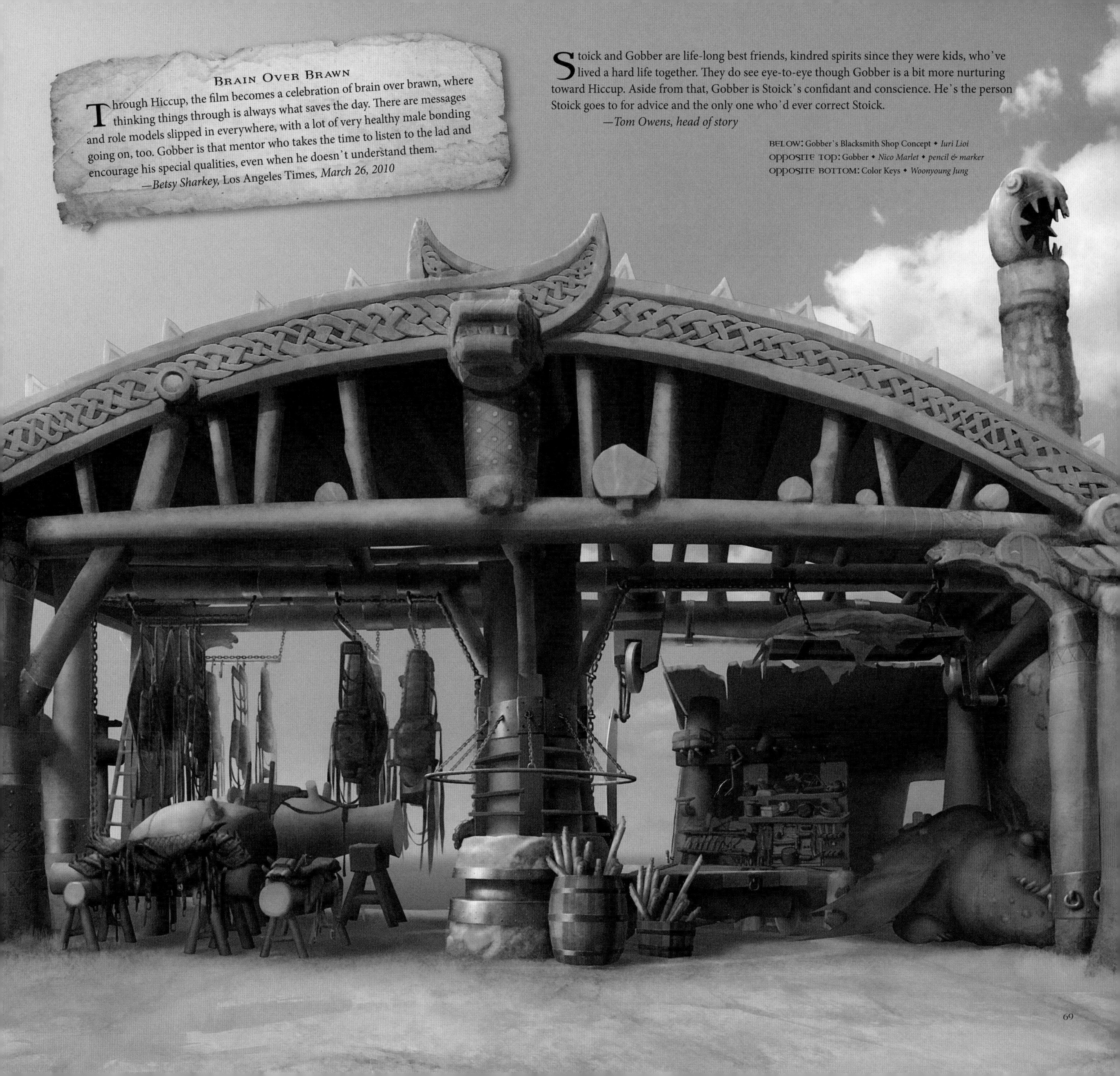

### Brain Over Brawn

Through Hiccup, the film becomes a celebration of brain over brawn, where thinking things through is always what saves the day. There are messages and role models slipped in everywhere, with a lot of very healthy male bonding going on, too. Gobber is that mentor who takes the time to listen to the lad and encourage his special qualities, even when he doesn't understand them.

—*Betsy Sharkey*, Los Angeles Times, *March 26, 2010*

Stoick and Gobber are life-long best friends, kindred spirits since they were kids, who've lived a hard life together. They do see eye-to-eye though Gobber is a bit more nurturing toward Hiccup. Aside from that, Gobber is Stoick's confidant and conscience. He's the person Stoick goes to for advice and the only one who'd ever correct Stoick.

—*Tom Owens, head of story*

BELOW: Gobber's Blacksmith Shop Concept • *Iuri Lioi*
OPPOSITE TOP: Gobber • *Nico Marlet* • *pencil & marker*
OPPOSITE BOTTOM: Color Keys • *Woonyoung Jung*

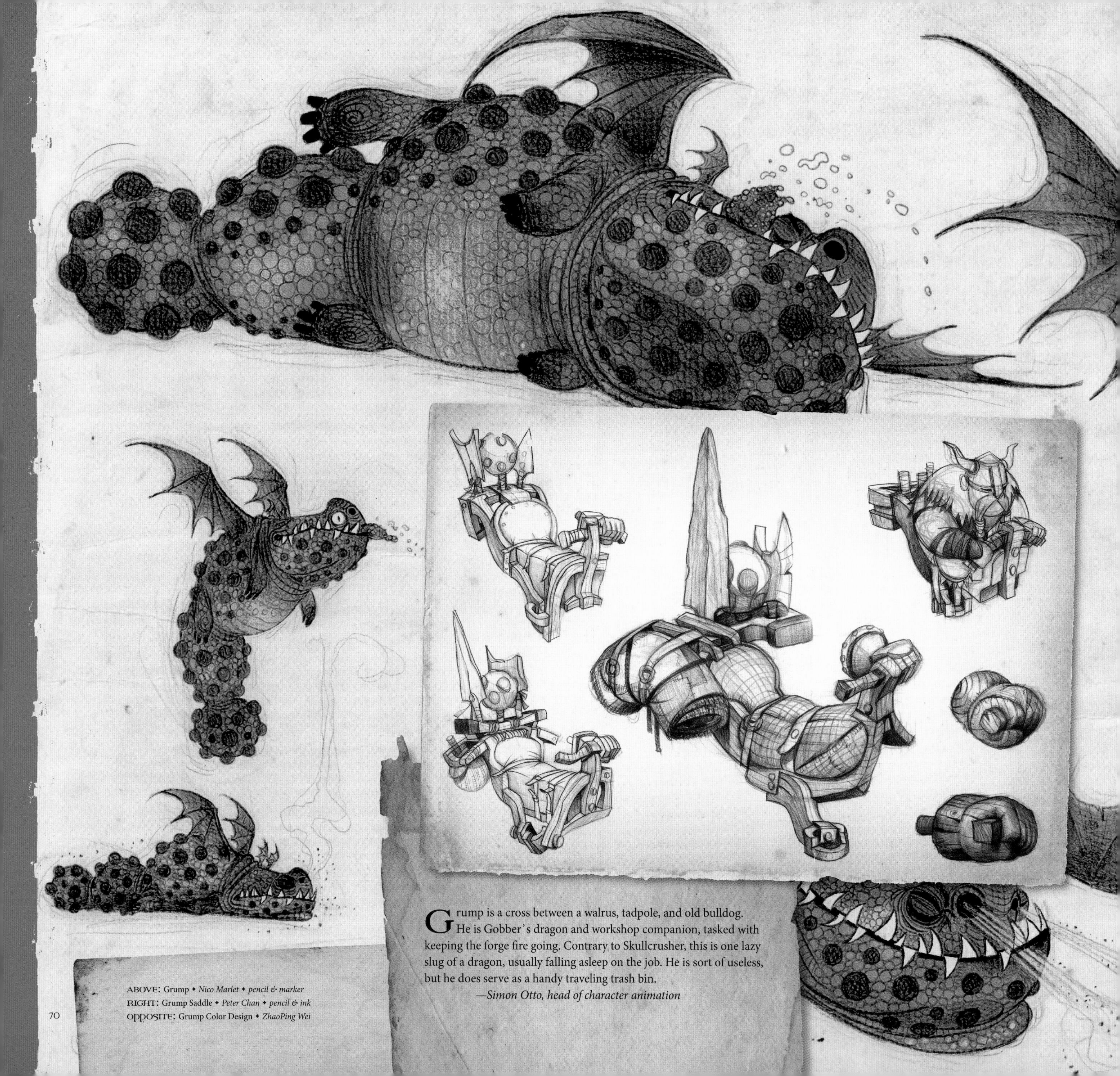

Grump is a cross between a walrus, tadpole, and old bulldog. He is Gobber's dragon and workshop companion, tasked with keeping the forge fire going. Contrary to Skullcrusher, this is one lazy slug of a dragon, usually falling asleep on the job. He is sort of useless, but he does serve as a handy traveling trash bin.

*—Simon Otto, head of character animation*

ABOVE: Grump • *Nico Marlet* • *pencil & marker*
RIGHT: Grump Saddle • *Peter Chan* • *pencil & ink*
OPPOSITE: Grump Color Design • *ZhaoPing Wei*

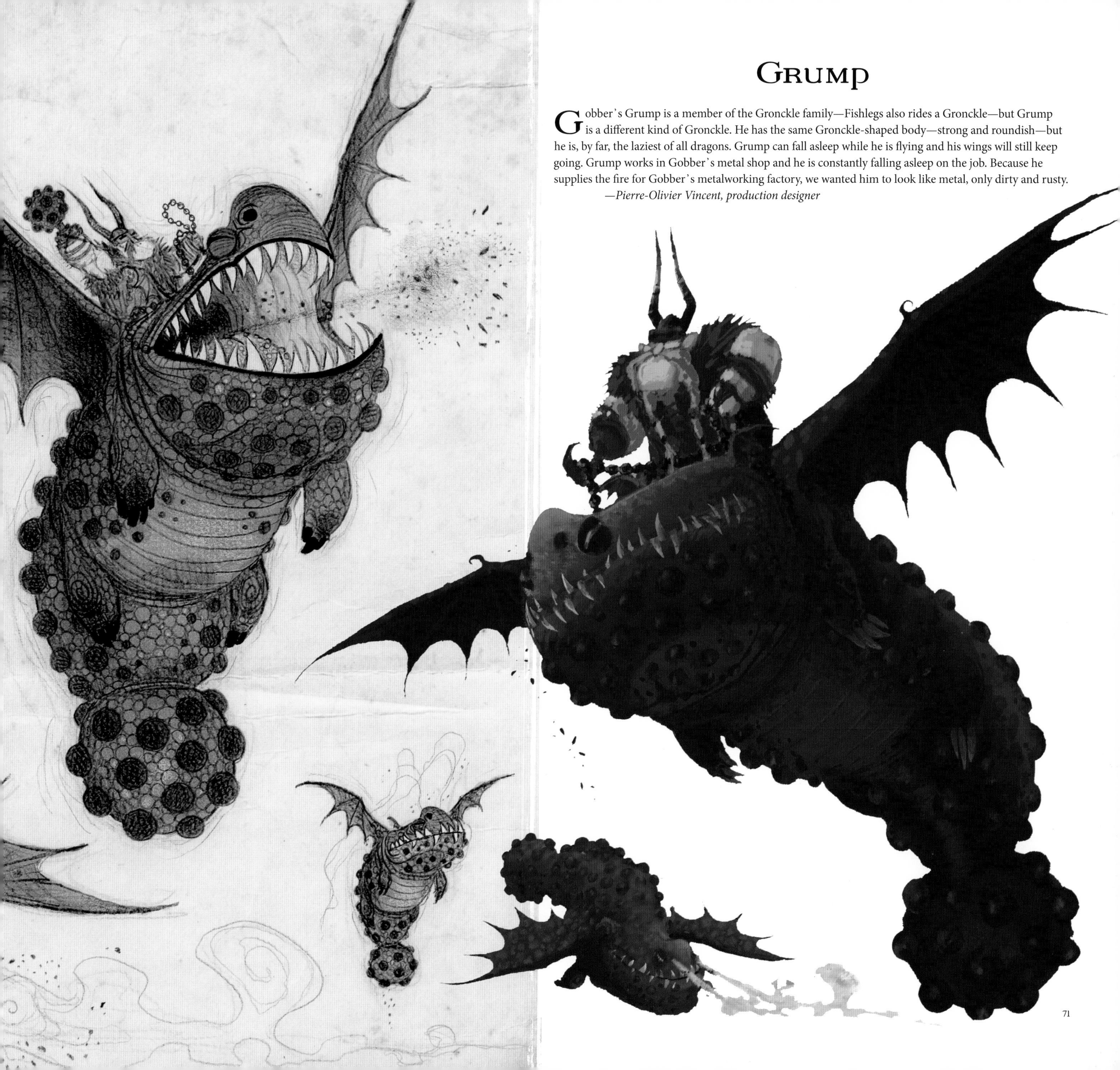

# GRUMP

Gobber's Grump is a member of the Gronckle family—Fishlegs also rides a Gronckle—but Grump is a different kind of Gronckle. He has the same Gronckle-shaped body—strong and roundish—but he is, by far, the laziest of all dragons. Grump can fall asleep while he is flying and his wings will still keep going. Grump works in Gobber's metal shop and he is constantly falling asleep on the job. Because he supplies the fire for Gobber's metalworking factory, we wanted him to look like metal, only dirty and rusty.

*—Pierre-Olivier Vincent, production designer*

# Berk Residents

We looked to Viking history when creating the characters that would make up the residents of Berk and the crowd scenes. We wanted to provide the audience with authentic pieces of everyday Viking life, so we looked at how they used natural materials to create their weapons, armor, clothes, and shelter. We also looked at the tools and technology they had in those days to help us construct a realistic setting.

—*ZhaoPing Wei, art director*

RIGHT: Berk Costume Colors ✦ *ZhaoPing Wei*
BELOW: Men's Facial Hair Studies ✦ *Nico Marlet* ✦ *pencil & marker*
OPPOSITE: Women's Head Studies ✦ *Nico Marlet* ✦ *pencil & marker*
OPPOSITE TOP LEFT: Berk Female Costume Colors ✦ *ZhaoPing Wei*
OPPOSITE TOP RIGHT: Female Designs ✦ *Tony Siruno*
FOLLOWING PAGES: New World Coastline ✦ *Pierre-Olivier Vincent*

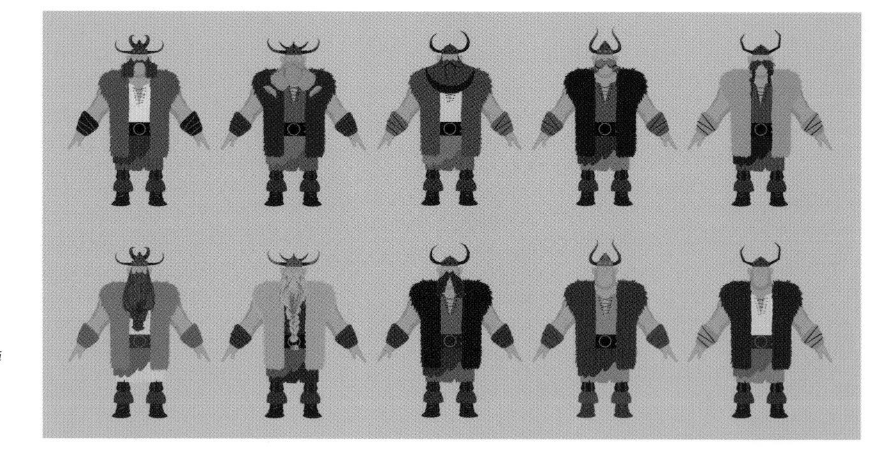

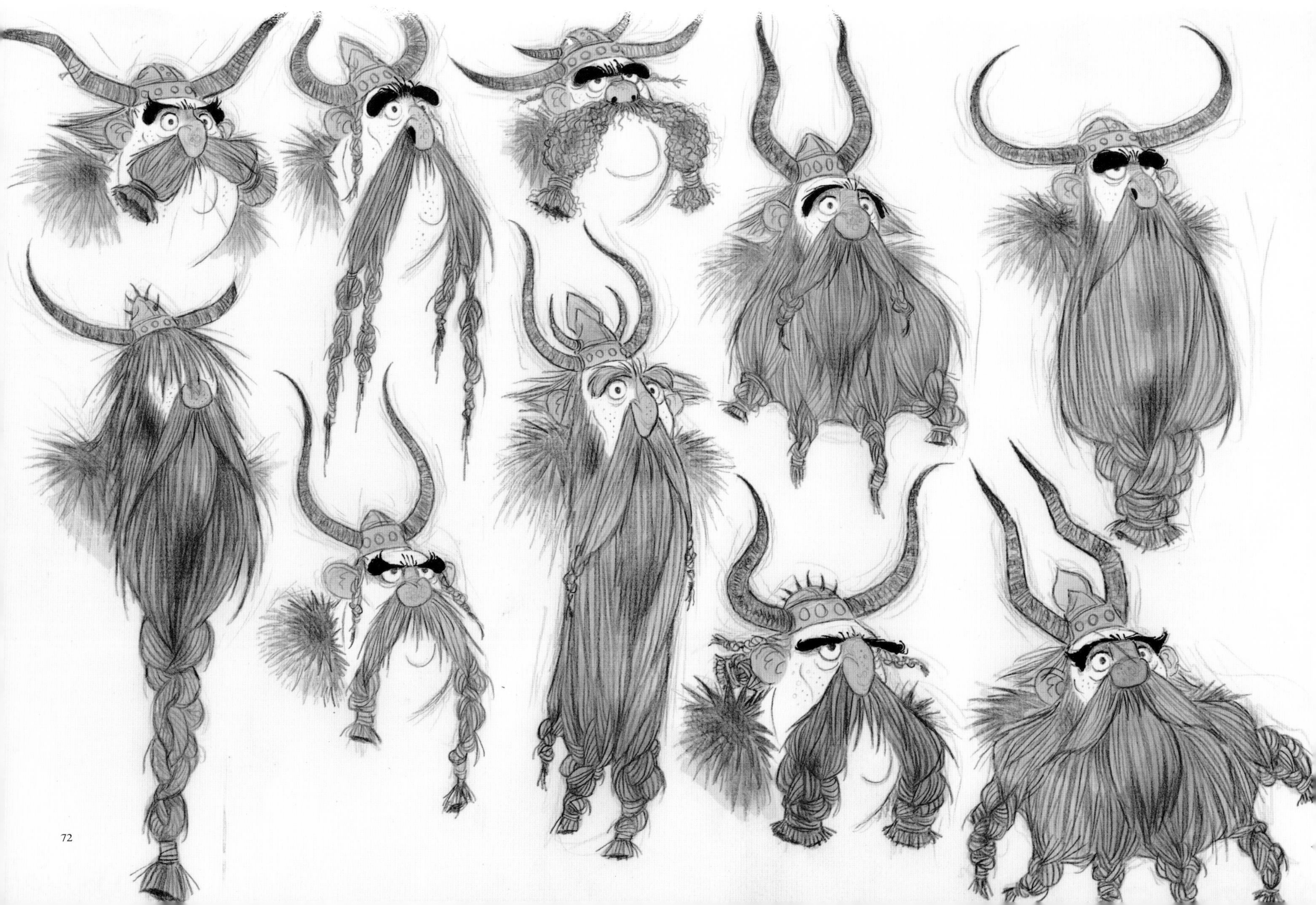

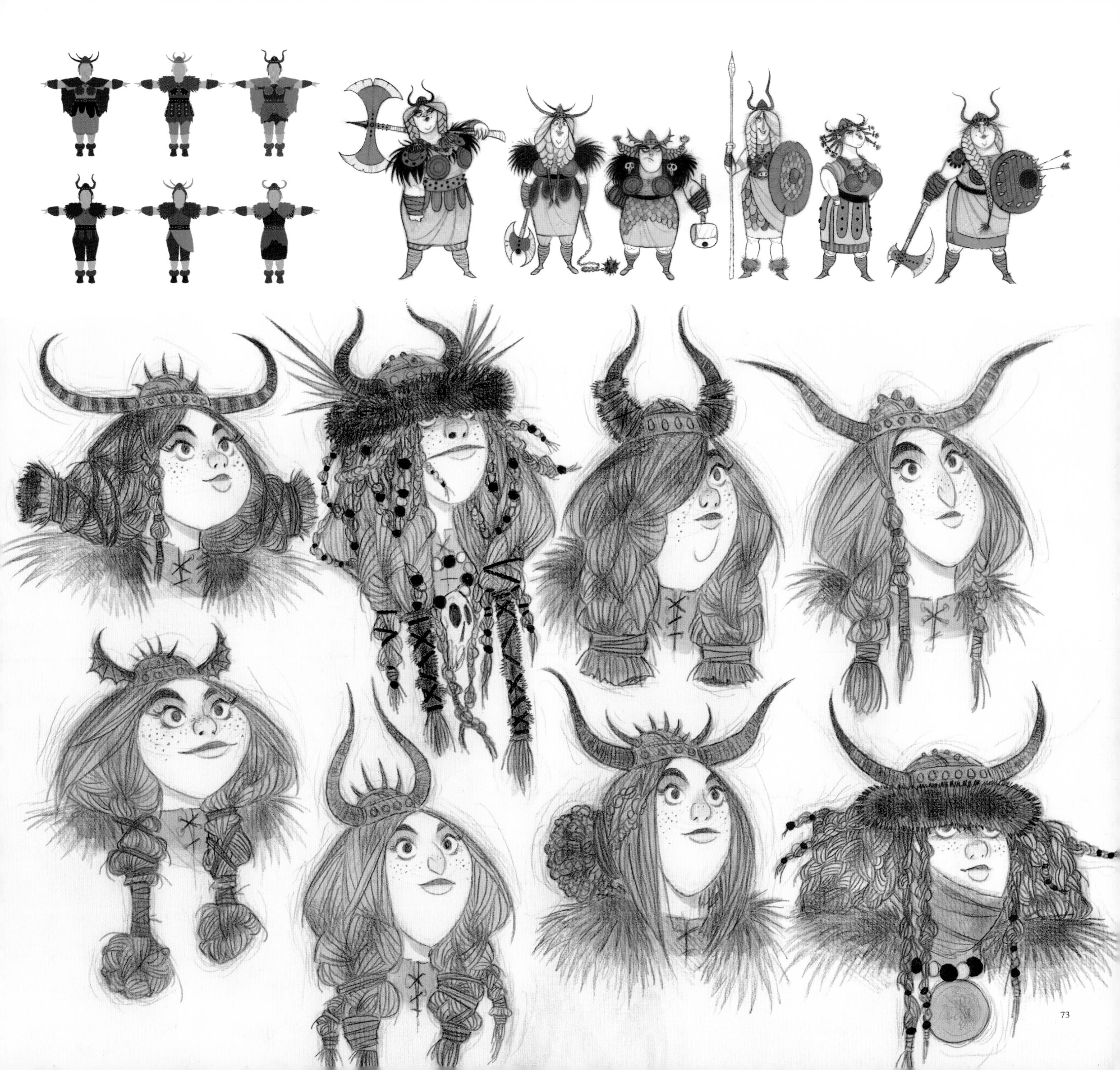

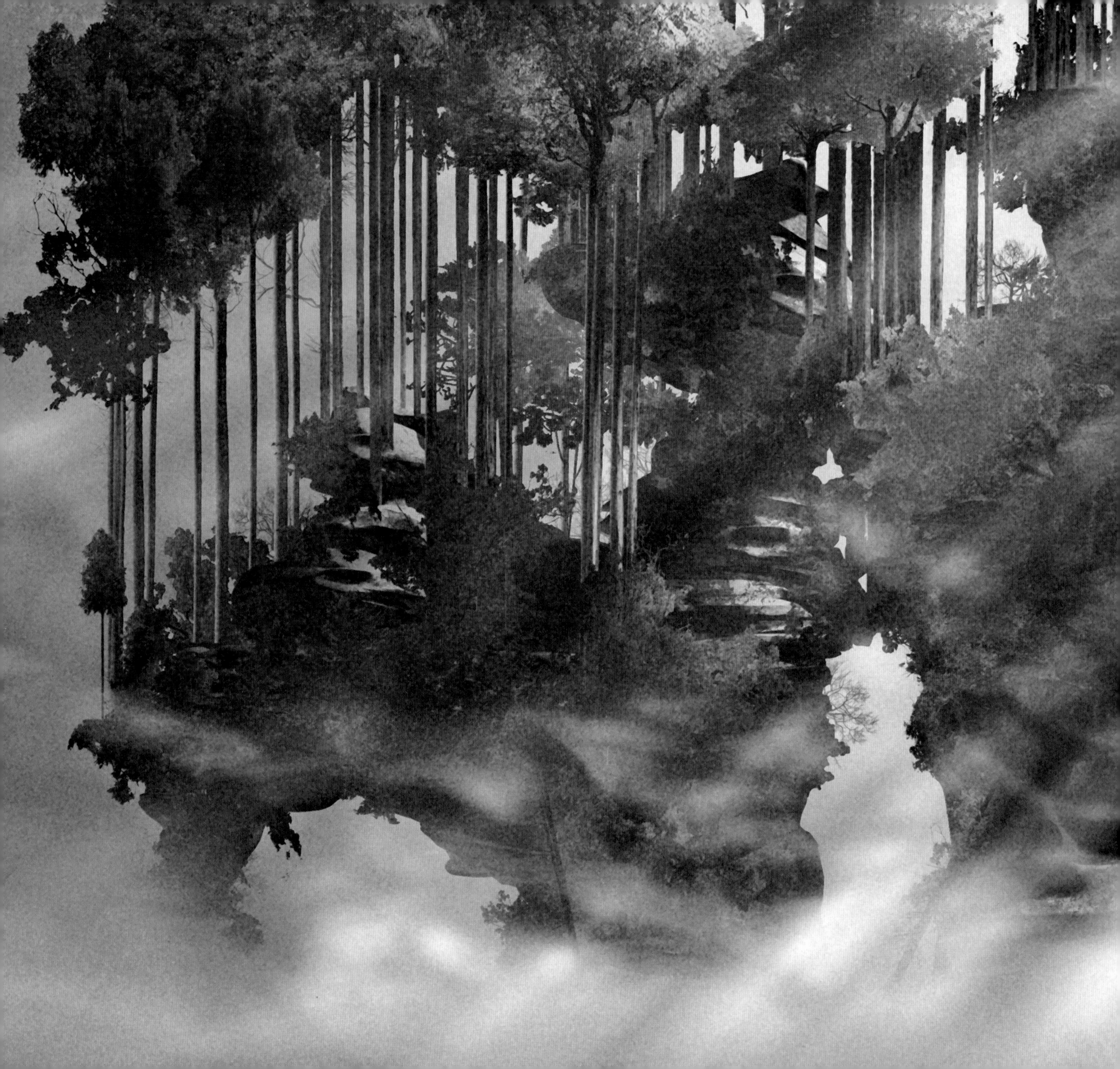

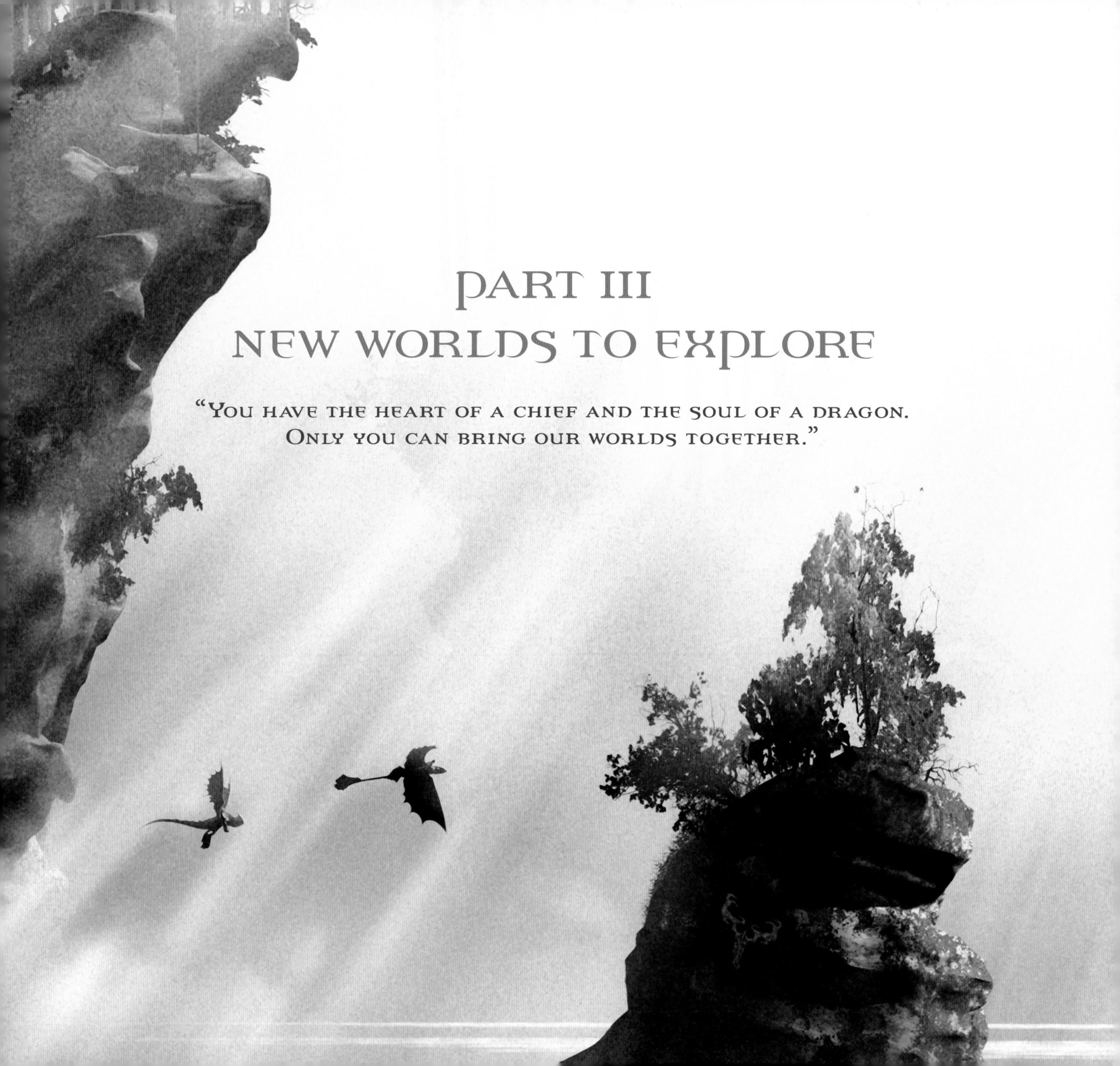

# PART III
# NEW WORLDS TO EXPLORE

"You have the heart of a chief and the soul of a dragon. Only you can bring our worlds together."

# New World Coastline

When we started this sequel, Dean was really into the idea that Hiccup is now exploring the world beyond Berk; therefore, we should make the map of the world much larger and introduce different cultures and aspects of the Nordic world. For inspiration, we looked at different landscapes from northern Norway and Finland.

In the first movie, Berk was all rocks, with some pine trees, or evergreens. We felt there would be a nice contrast if we added a different element so we introduced the Aspen trees that are turning yellow and red which added a new kind of drama. Drama can be created with shapes and scale but also with color. Here was a different kind of landscape and it was showing how far Hiccup had traveled from Berk to create his new map.

*—Pierre-Olivier Vincent, production designer*

BELOW LEFT: New World Concept Model ✦ *Facundo Rabaudi*
BELOW RIGHT: Color Key ✦ *Woonyoung Jung*
BOTTOM & OPPOSITE: New World Coastline Concept Artwork ✦ *Pierre-Olivier Vincent*

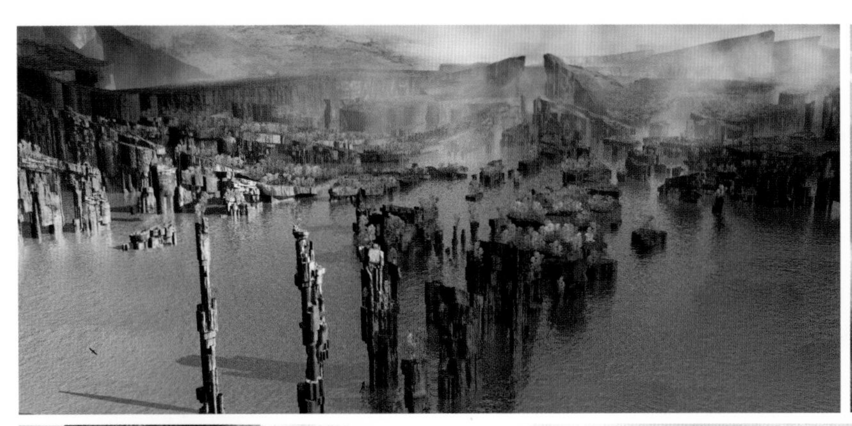

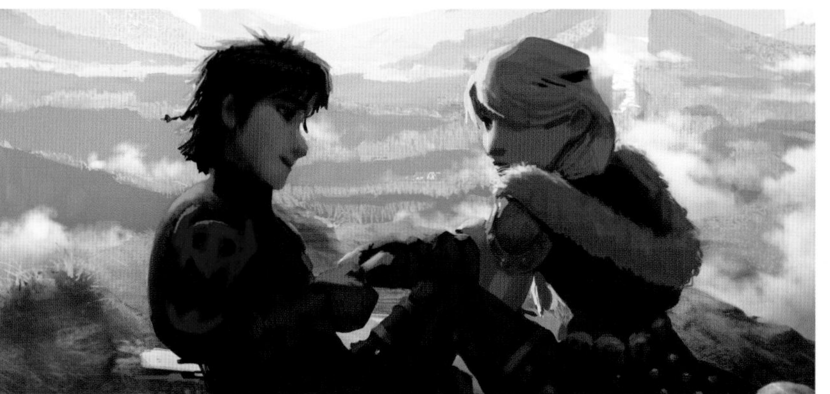

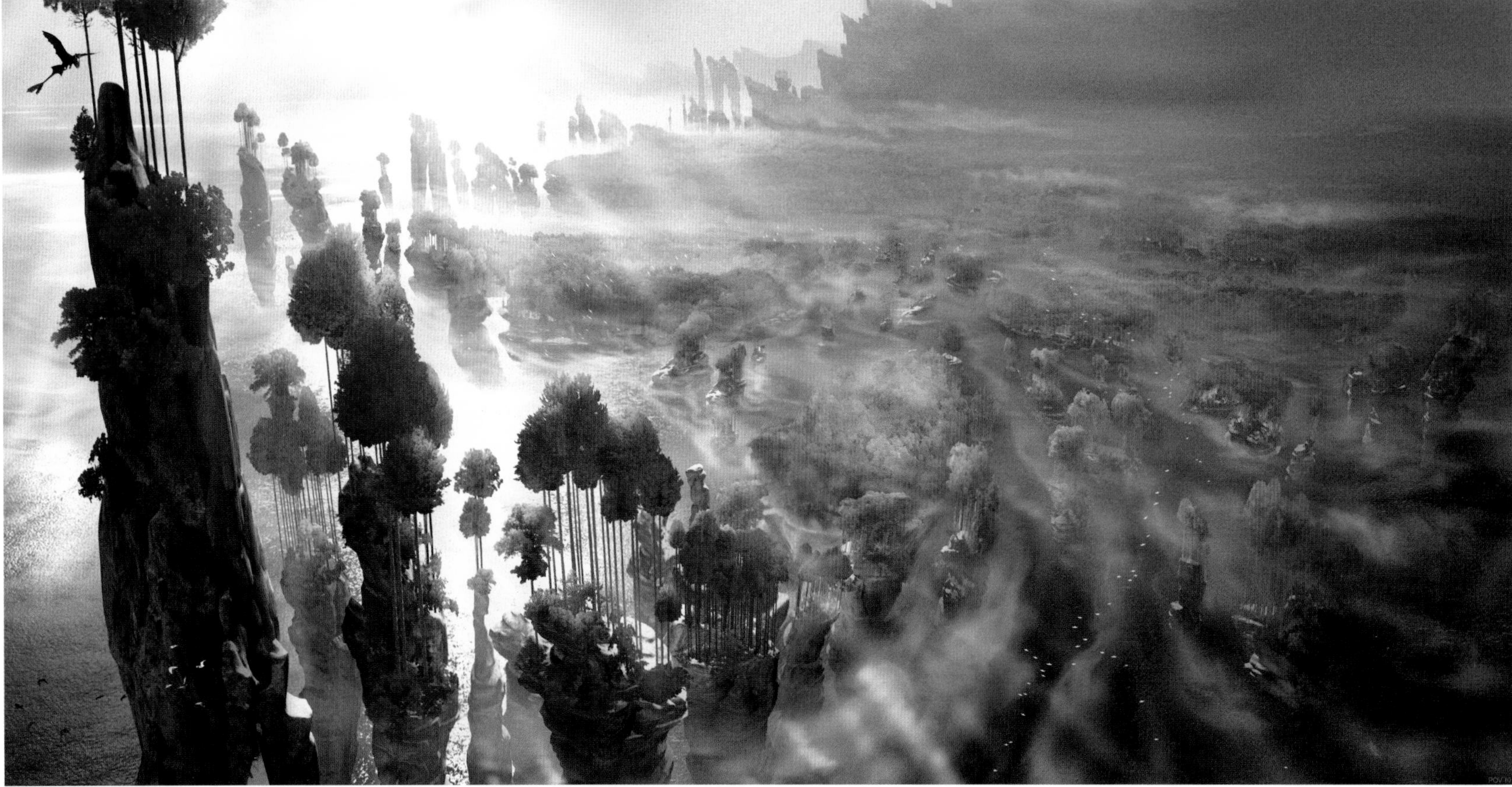

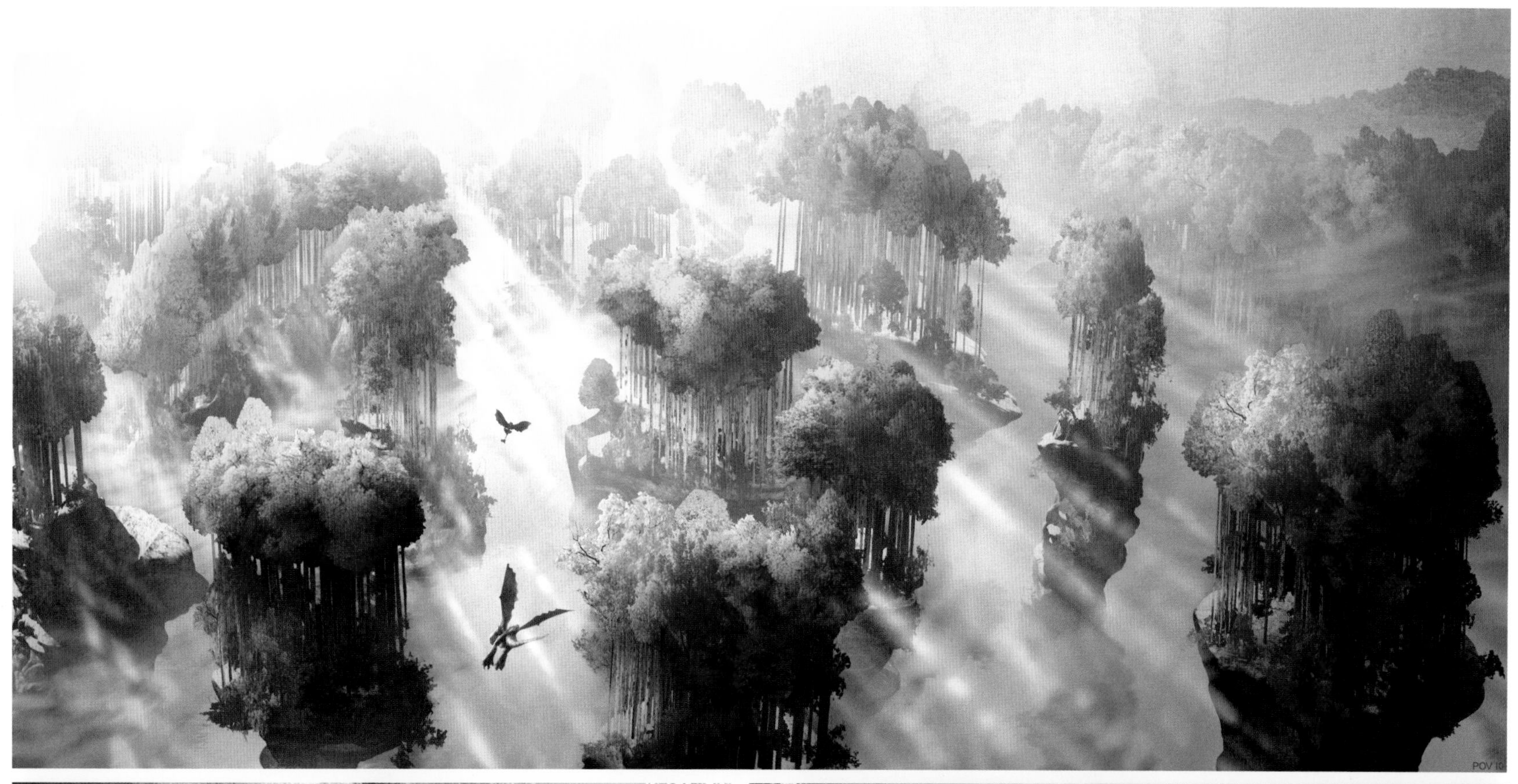

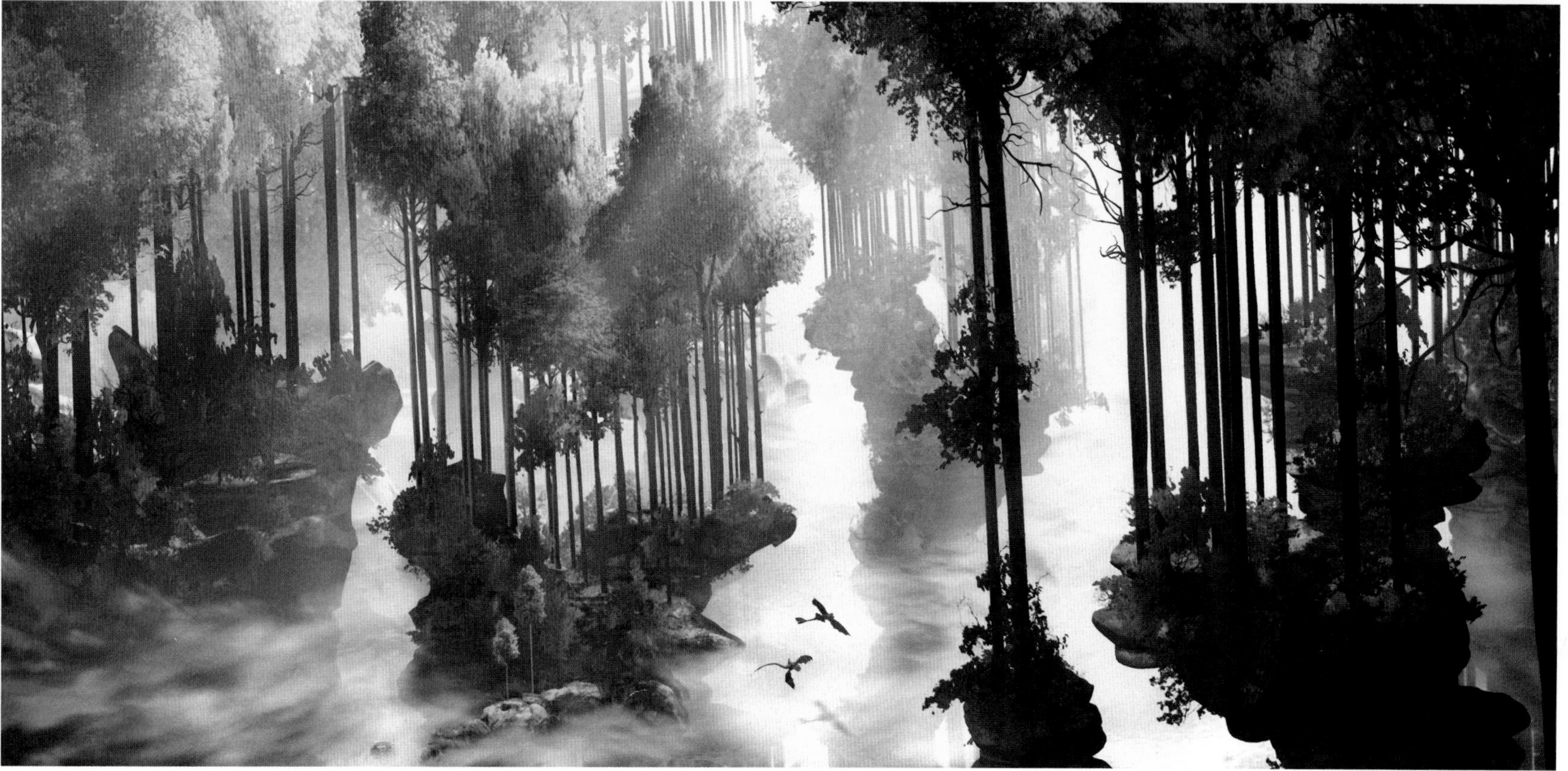

Being surrounded by those enormous cliffs was fantastic. Because of the intense beauty of the landscape in Norway, it's not a stretch to imagine those landscapes being created by volcanoes and other primitive forces. In the Nordic countries you have some vegetation but the more north you travel, the less vegetation you see. Basically, you lose those elements that make for a softer landscape. When there are only rocks and snow, everything is extremely contrasting and this has instant drama. When you want to support an epic movie, these are places you go.

*—Pierre-Olivier Vincent, production designer*

RIGHT: New World Concept Artwork • *Pierre-Olivier Vincent*
BELOW: Seastack Variations • *Peter Chan*

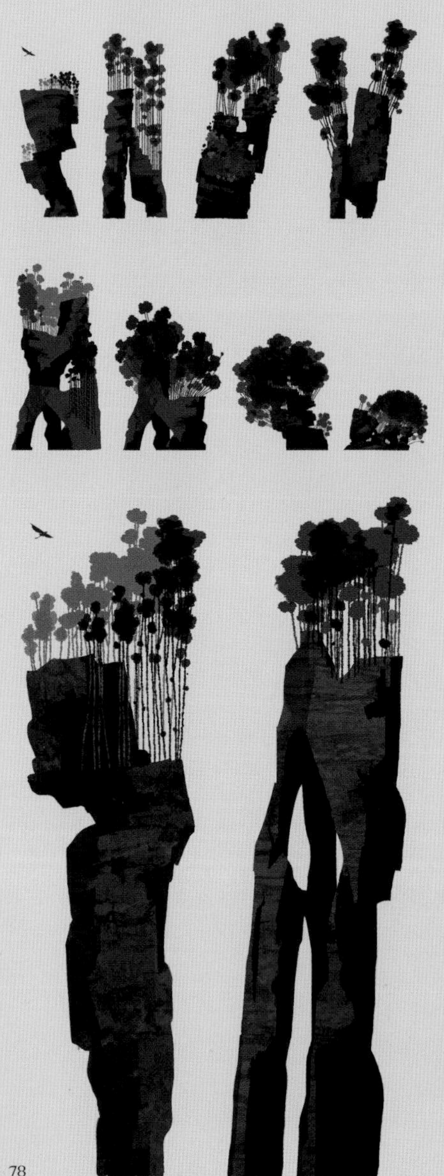

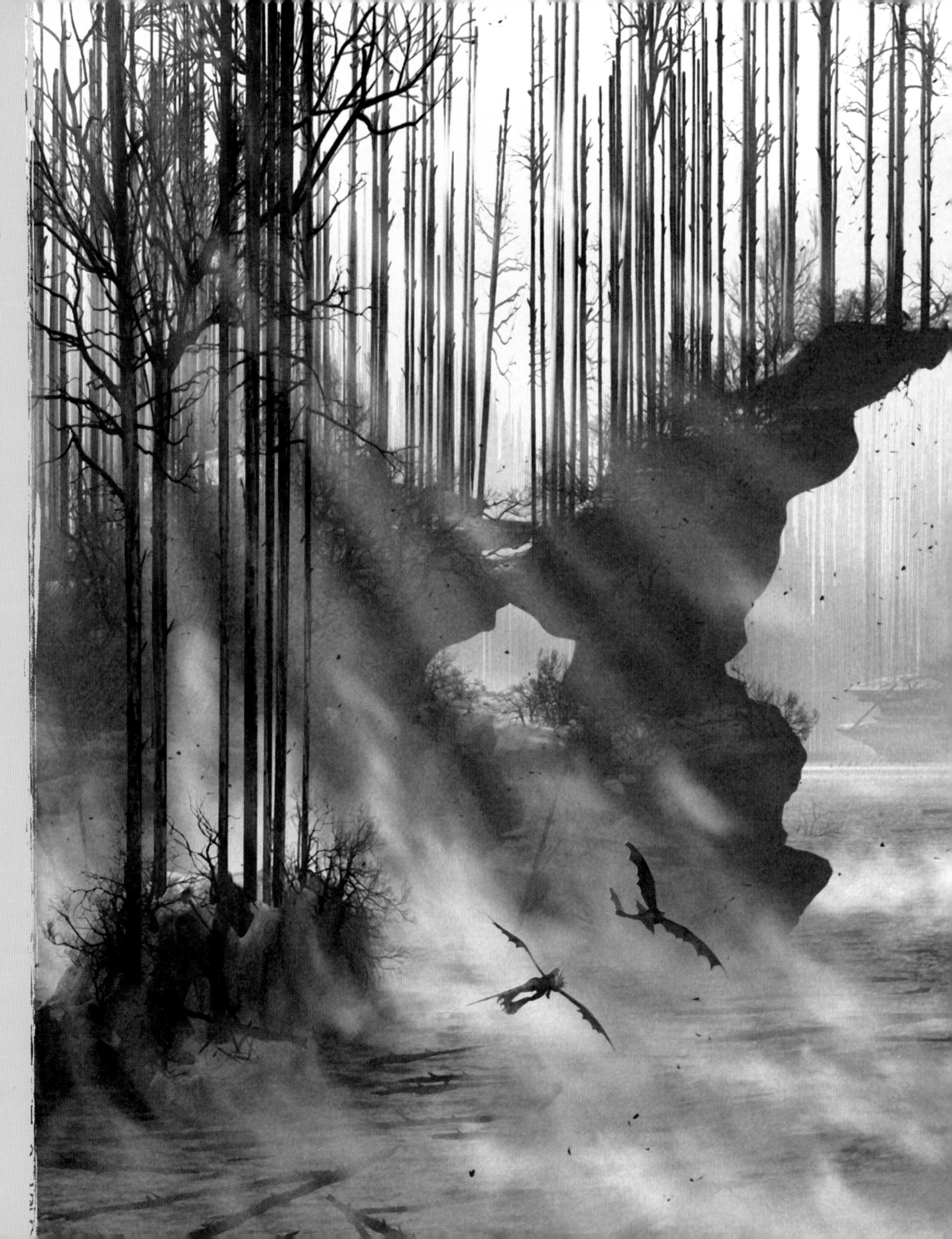

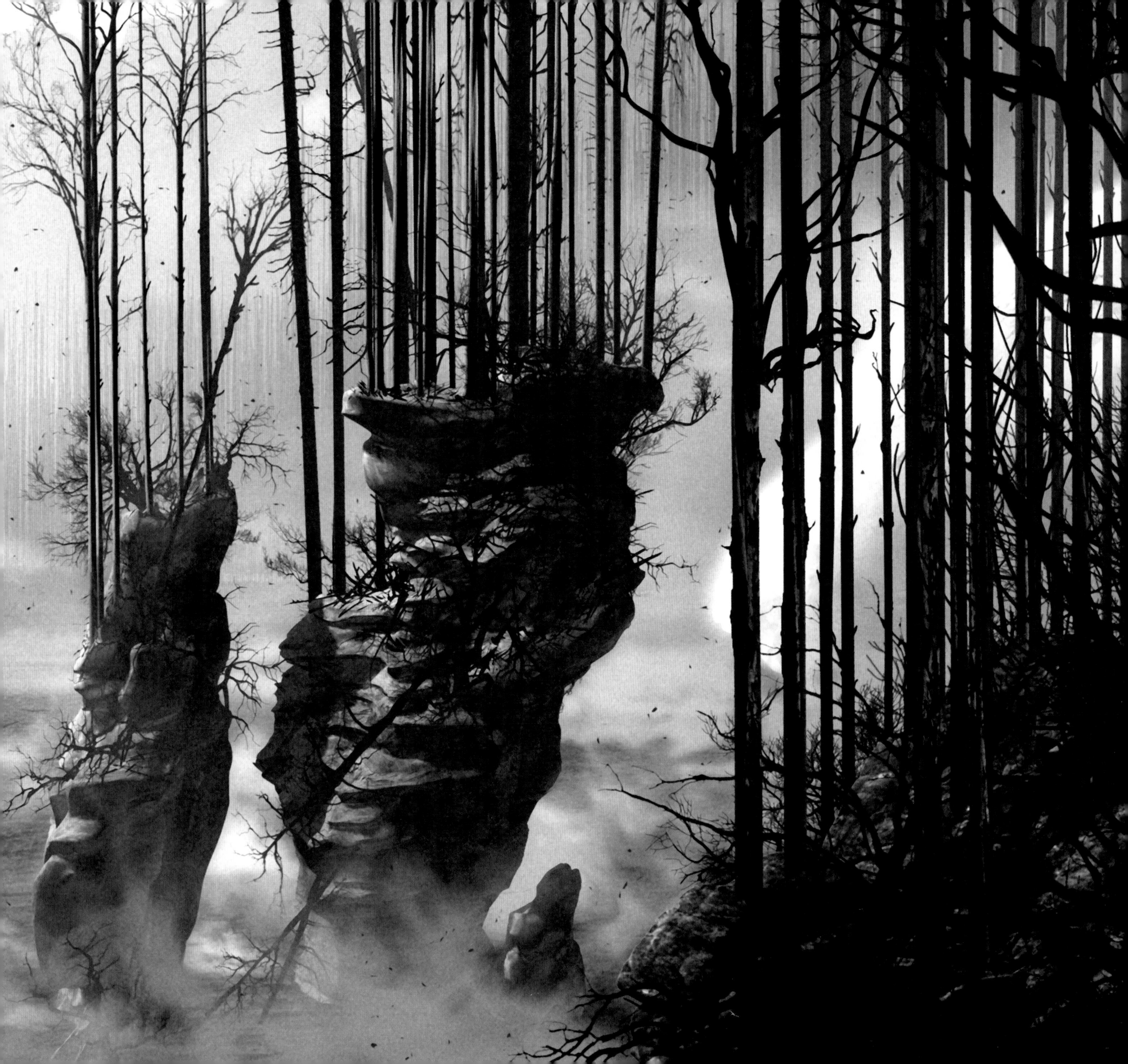

# The Destroyed Fort

Inevitably there are scenes in a movie that seem indispensable at first but then as the story evolves, they unexpectedly lose their significance. That's what happened to the original cold opening Dean conceived. It was always a terrific and surprising way to start the second installment. But eventually we decided it was more powerful for the audience to discover the villain plot through Hiccup rather than be ahead of him.

*—Gregg Taylor, head of feature development, DreamWorks Animation*

Early on in the production, we showed how Eret's fort was destroyed by Valka's Bewilderbeast, but the whole sequence got cut. Now, when we first see the fort, it has already been destroyed.

*—Pierre-Olivier Vincent, production designer*

BELOW: Destroyed Fort Reveal Concept Artwork ◆ *Pierre-Olivier Vincent*
OPPOSITE TOP LEFT: Destroyed Fort ◆ *Iuri Lioi*
OPPOSITE TOP RIGHT & OPPOSITE BOTTOM: Destroyed Fort Concept Artwork ◆ *Pierre-Olivier Vincent*

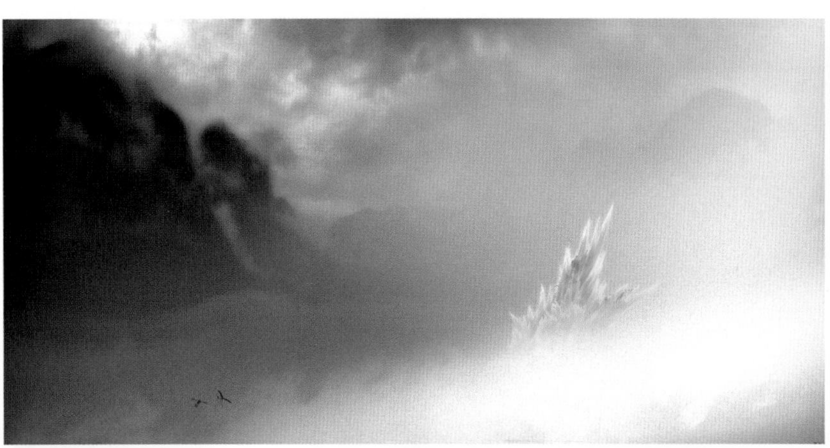

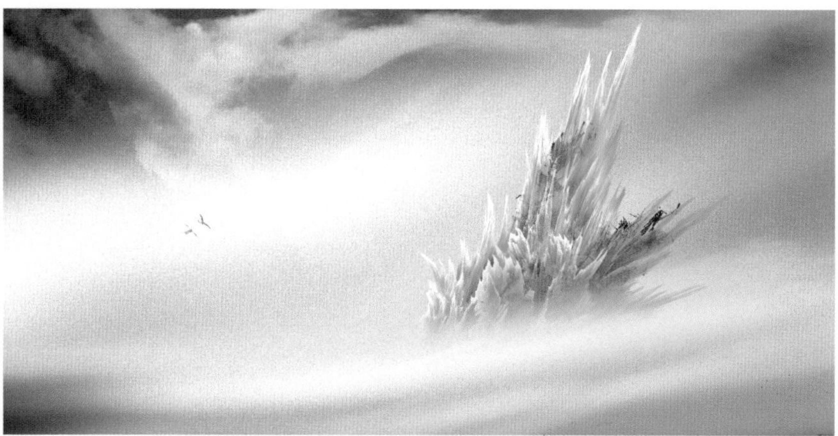

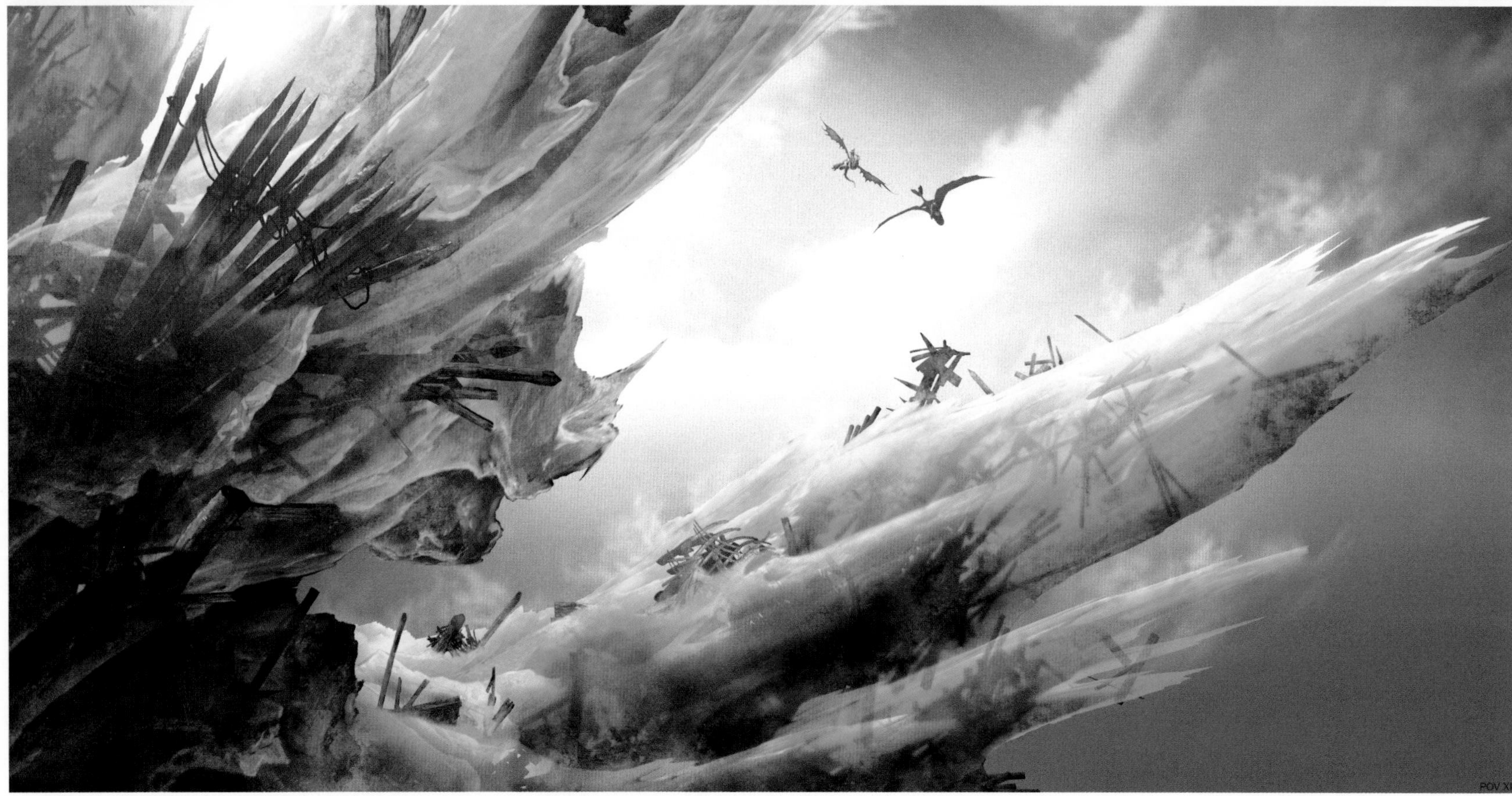

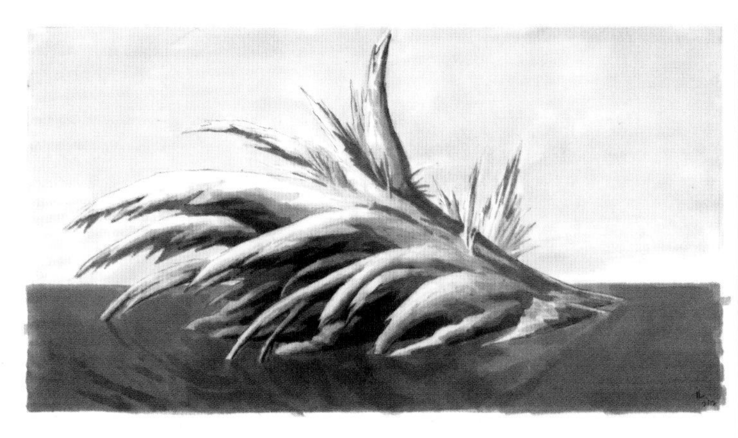

"Dragon trapping is hard enough work as it is without do-gooder dragon riders sneaking in to rescue them."

—Eret

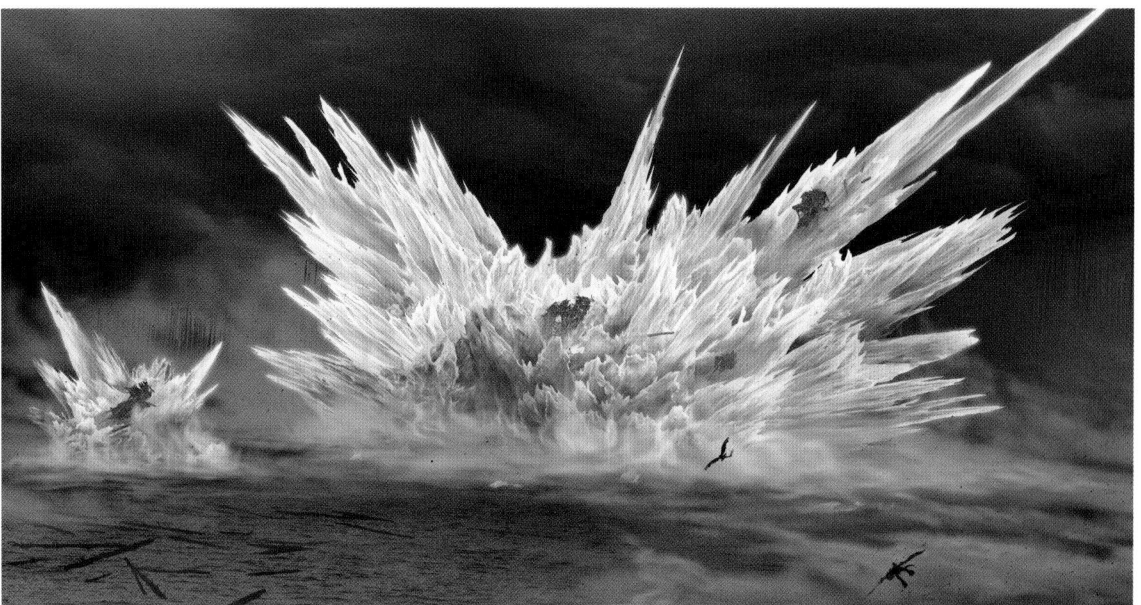

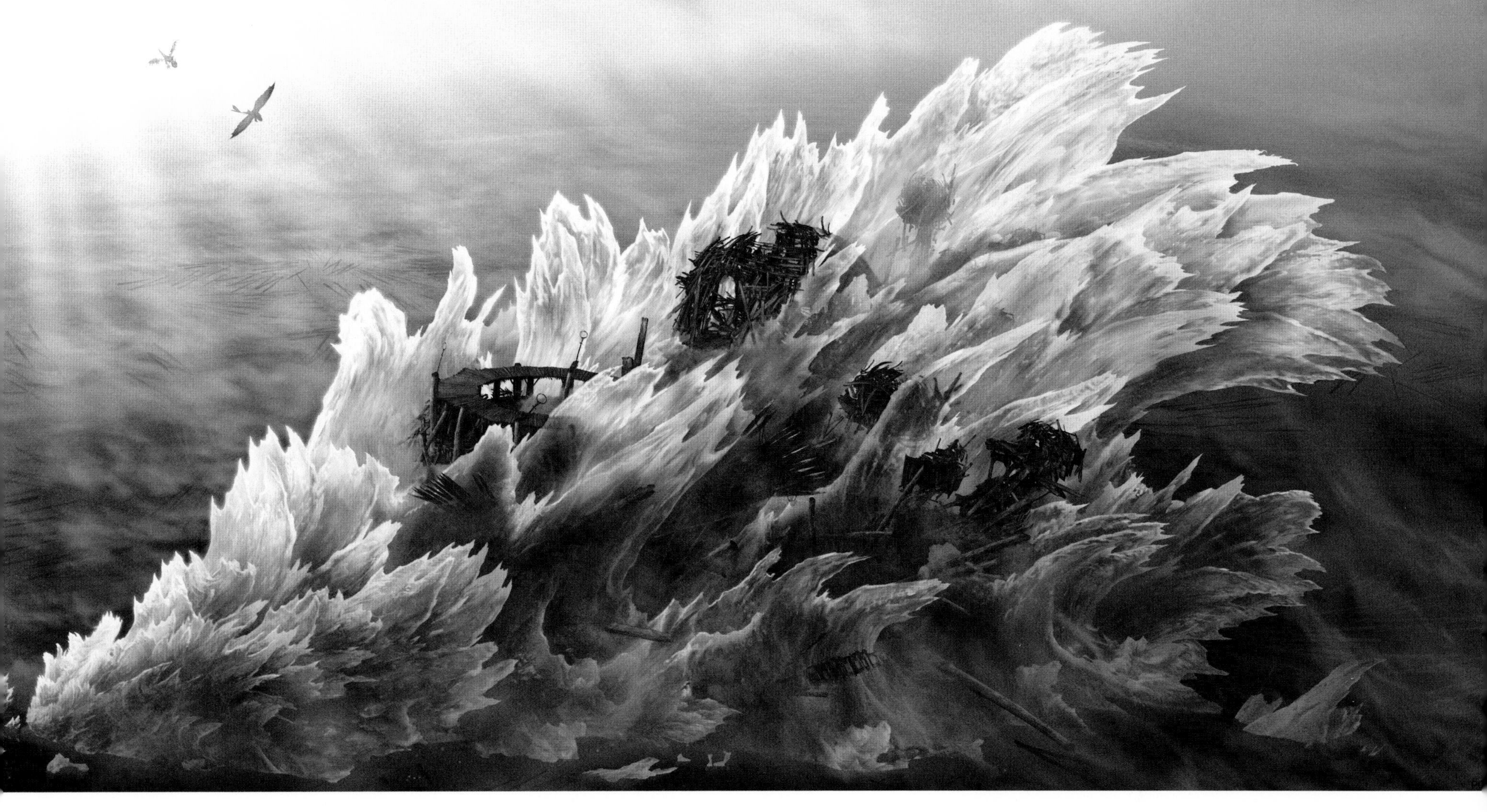

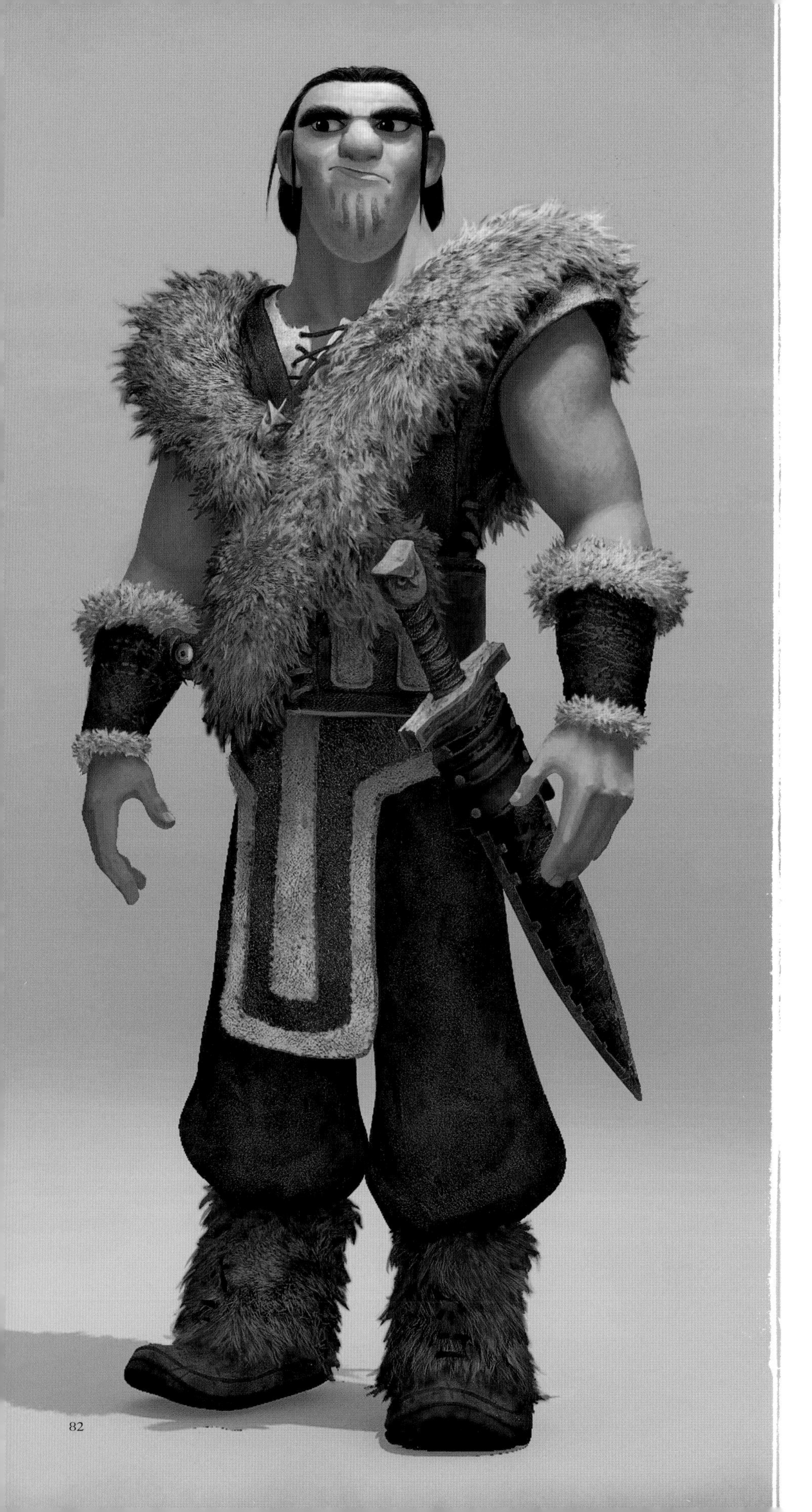



# Eret

Eret is a swashbuckling, northern pirate; he's a world-class trapper and he knows it. He surrounds himself with goons so that he can shine as their boss. We referenced Mafia movies and pegged Eret as the guy who enforces things. He's not the top guy and, in fact, he doesn't want to run the operation; he just wants to make his profit and get out. In the course of the story, he is little more than a tool for Drago, becoming a dragon slave driver for him.

Nico Marlet did some amazing drawings for Eret and most of the challenges of his design were solved on paper. There is also an aspect of humor about Eret. He is constantly flexing his muscles and is the beefcake for Ruffnut. A running gag in the movie is her attraction to him.

*—Simon Otto, head of character animation*

Nico Marlet had an incredible vision for Eret but he had drawn him quite short, which we discovered once we got him into 3-D. The director wanted Eret to have a strong, lean, muscular build, to be a heroic regal character with strength. For us, he was the Han Solo character of our movie, so he had to be attractive and not look too dopey or silly. He had to show some sort of leadership, so that when Stoick comes along there's a bit of tension between them.

*—Matt Paulson, modeling supervisor*

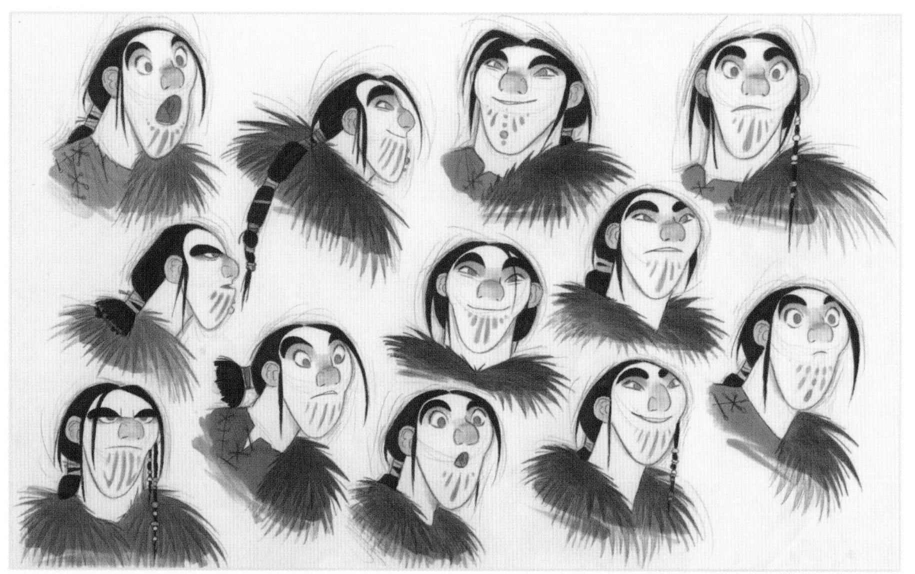

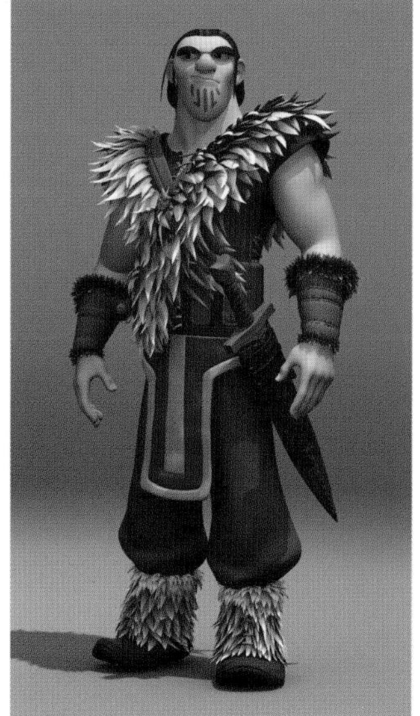

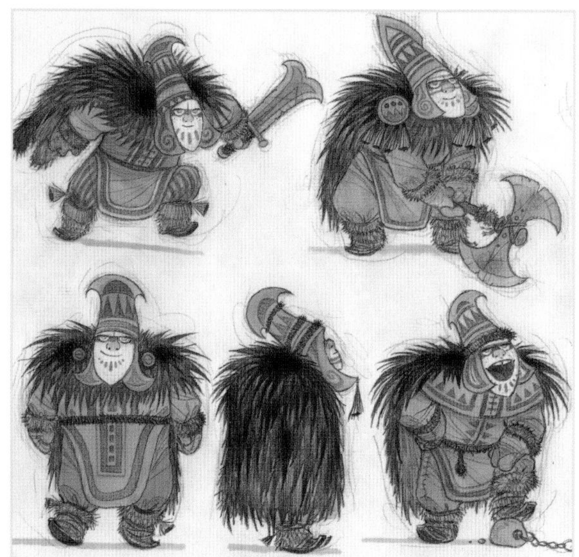

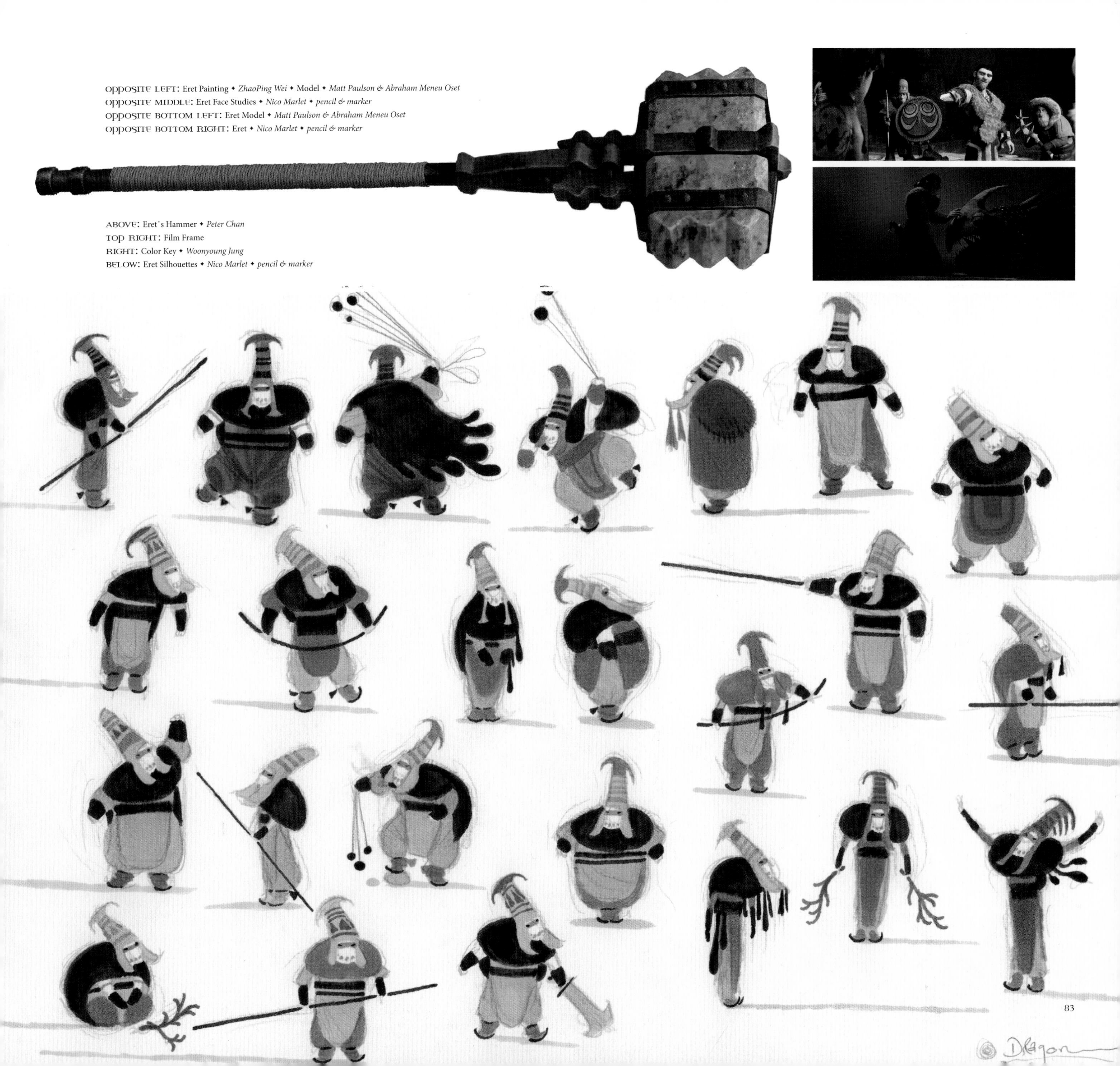

OPPOSITE LEFT: Eret Painting ✦ *ZhaoPing Wei* ✦ Model ✦ *Matt Paulson & Abraham Meneu Oset*
OPPOSITE MIDDLE: Eret Face Studies ✦ *Nico Marlet* ✦ *pencil & marker*
OPPOSITE BOTTOM LEFT: Eret Model ✦ *Matt Paulson & Abraham Meneu Oset*
OPPOSITE BOTTOM RIGHT: Eret ✦ *Nico Marlet* ✦ *pencil & marker*

ABOVE: Eret's Hammer ✦ *Peter Chan*
TOP RIGHT: Film Frame
RIGHT: Color Key ✦ *Woonyoung Jung*
BELOW: Eret Silhouettes ✦ *Nico Marlet* ✦ *pencil & marker*

BELOW: Eret's Fort Cutout ✦ *Iuri Lioi* ✦ Model ✦ *Manny Fragelus & James Stapp*
RIGHT: Fort Variations ✦ *Kirsten Kawamura*
BOTTOM RIGHT: Eret's Fort Color Concept ✦ *Kirsten Kawamura* ✦ Concept Model ✦ *Pierre-Olivier Vincent*
OPPOSITE TOP: Fort Sketches ✦ *Peter Chan* ✦ *pencil & ink*
OPPOSITE BOTTOM: Eret's Fort ✦ *Pierre-Olivier Vincent*

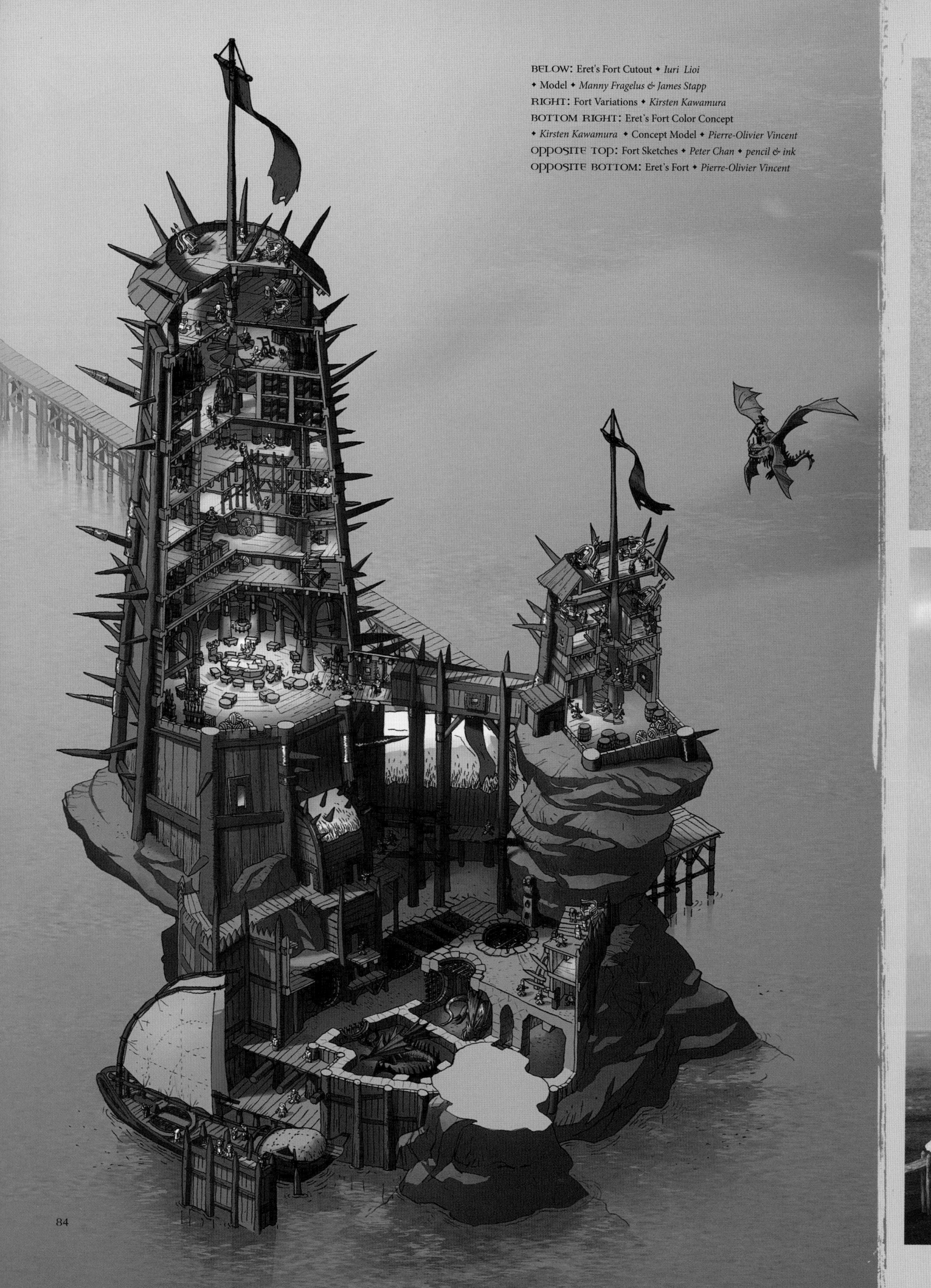

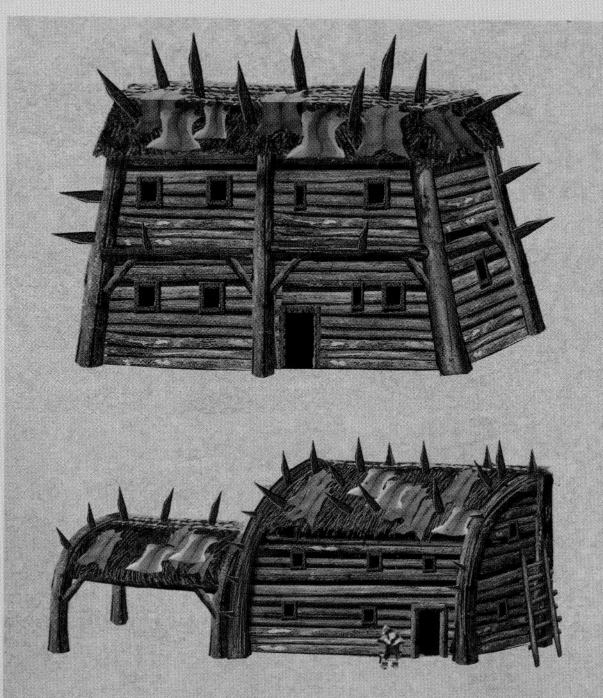

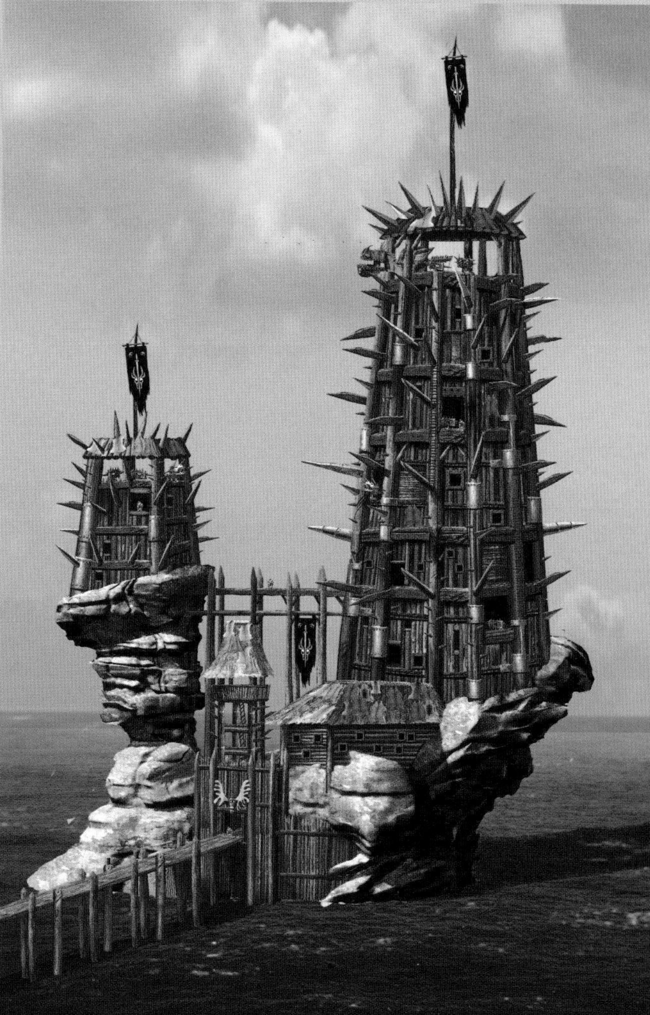

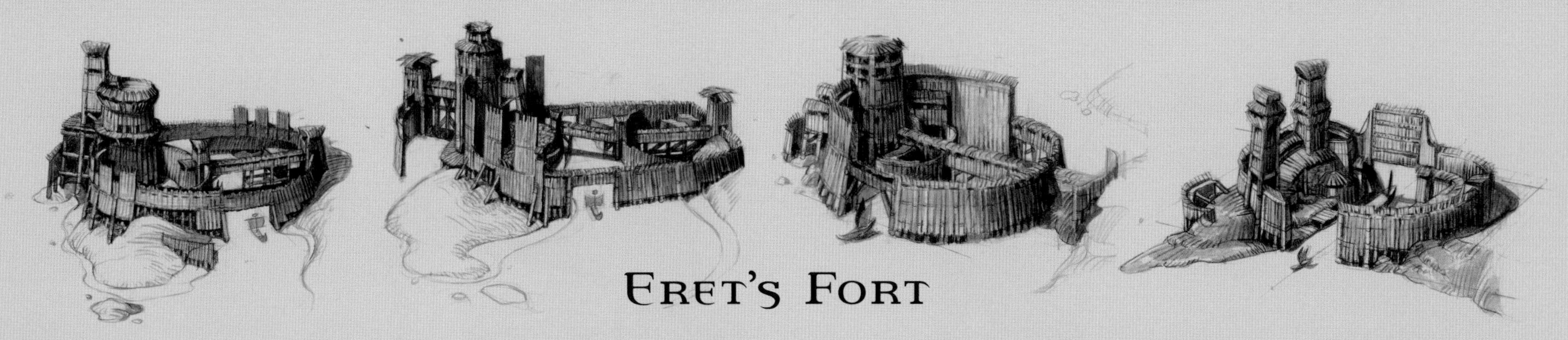

# Eret's Fort

For the longest time the movie was going to open in a completely different location with an unfamiliar group of new characters, to add an air of mystery. The idea was that we would introduce a remote trapper's fort, in the far reaches of Lapland, with its autumn leaves and beautiful Nordic fjords. In the midst of the grisly trapper's fort was a group of tough, seasoned cowboy-like dragon trappers. Their job was to trap dragons and ship them north to Drago Bludvist, who was building a dragon army to dominate the world.

The scene was going to be shot from the point of view of one of the trapped dragons in a holding cell, during a prison break incited by Valka and her dragon entourage. Valka stealthily arrives and deftly manages to take out a few of the trappers standing guard. Then she begins to pry the grate off of the cell where the captured dragons are being held. But the rescue operation gets botched, so she calls upon the Bewilderbeast to come to her aid. It rises up from the fjord and blasts the fort to bits with its regurgitated ice. Valka and the dragons get away, but the fort is left in ruins and the surrounding woods are aflame. Later, Hiccup and Astrid discover the eerie, ice-covered ruins of the fort and are shot down by the trappers, who believe they are cohorts of Valka.

The sequence was storyboarded many times and eventually went through pre-visualization, making it ready to animate. But the overall movie was suffering from a dark tone issue, so the scene was cut in the effort to lighten the mood. Though mysterious, interesting, and cool, it was deemed a little too dark. I still miss it.

Now the movie opens with a splashy, high-energy game sequence that reintroduces most of the main characters of Berk. It was originally slated to follow the destruction of Eret's fort, but as the opener, it makes for a celebratory, fun way to start the movie, and helps to establish what exactly is at stake in the story.

*—Dean DeBlois, director*

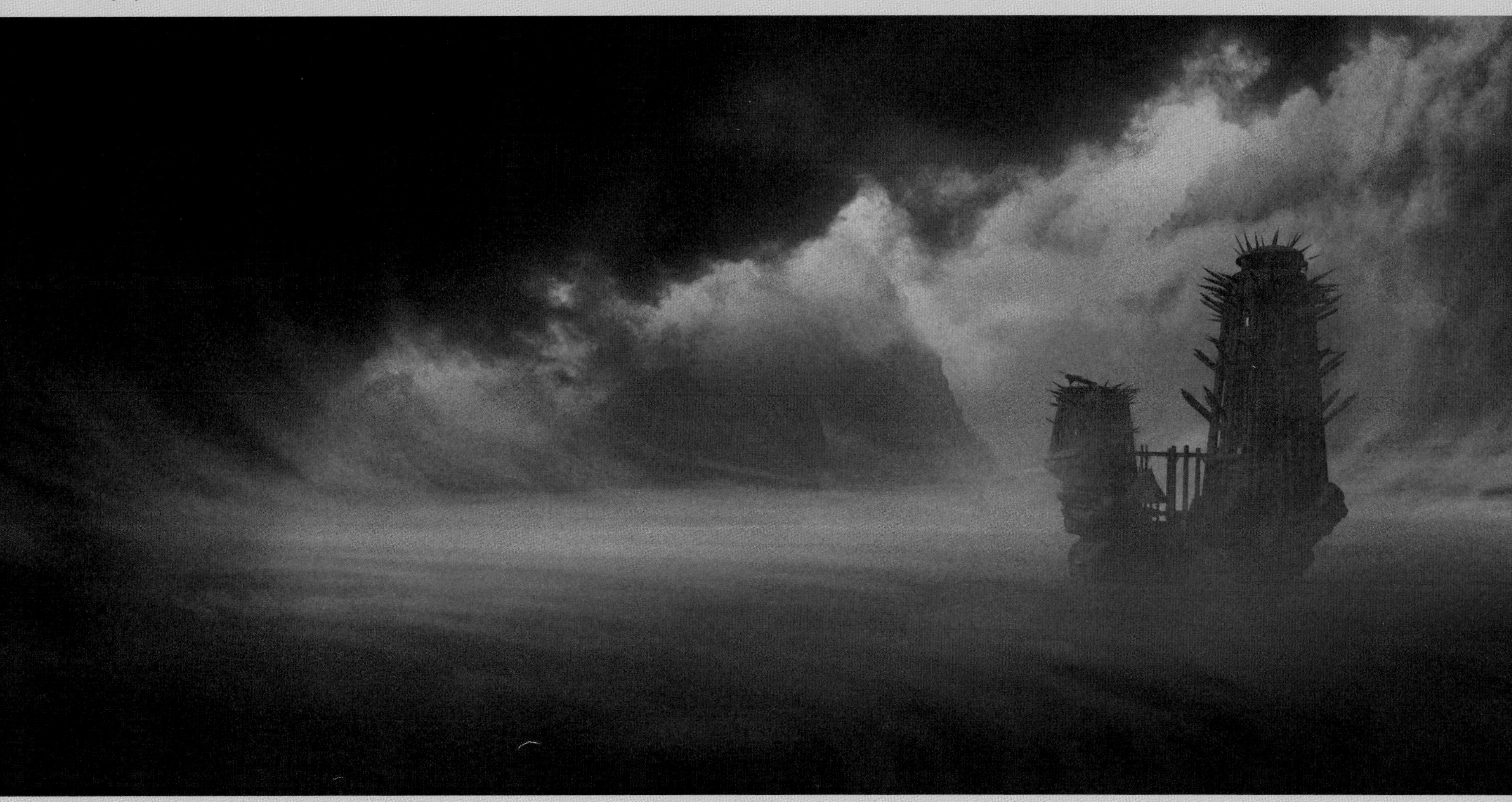

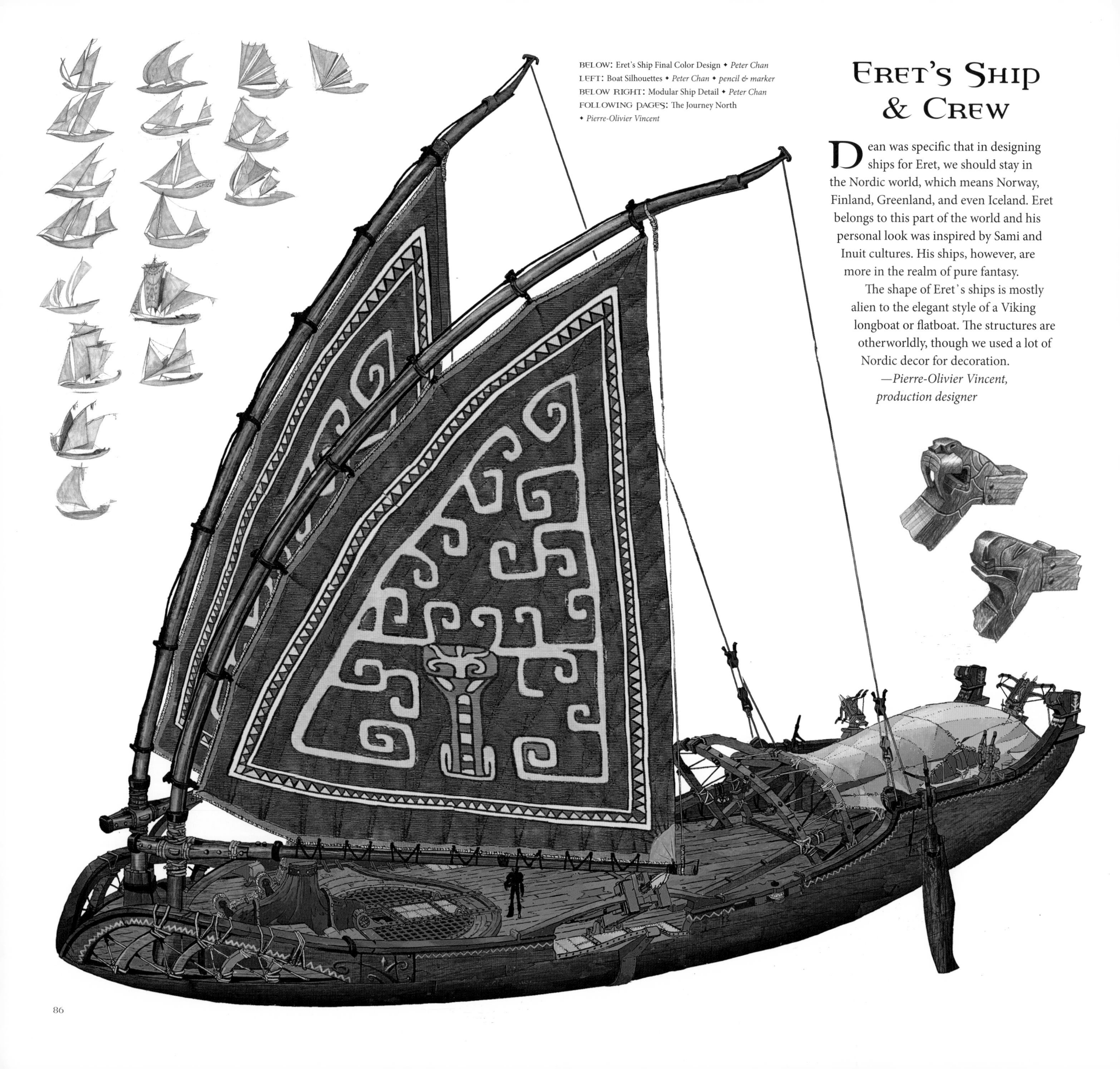

BELOW: Eret's Ship Final Color Design ✦ *Peter Chan*
LEFT: Boat Silhouettes ✦ *Peter Chan* ✦ *pencil & marker*
BELOW RIGHT: Modular Ship Detail ✦ *Peter Chan*
FOLLOWING PAGES: The Journey North
✦ *Pierre-Olivier Vincent*

# Eret's Ship & Crew

Dean was specific that in designing ships for Eret, we should stay in the Nordic world, which means Norway, Finland, Greenland, and even Iceland. Eret belongs to this part of the world and his personal look was inspired by Sami and Inuit cultures. His ships, however, are more in the realm of pure fantasy.

The shape of Eret's ships is mostly alien to the elegant style of a Viking longboat or flatboat. The structures are otherworldly, though we used a lot of Nordic decor for decoration.

*—Pierre-Olivier Vincent, production designer*

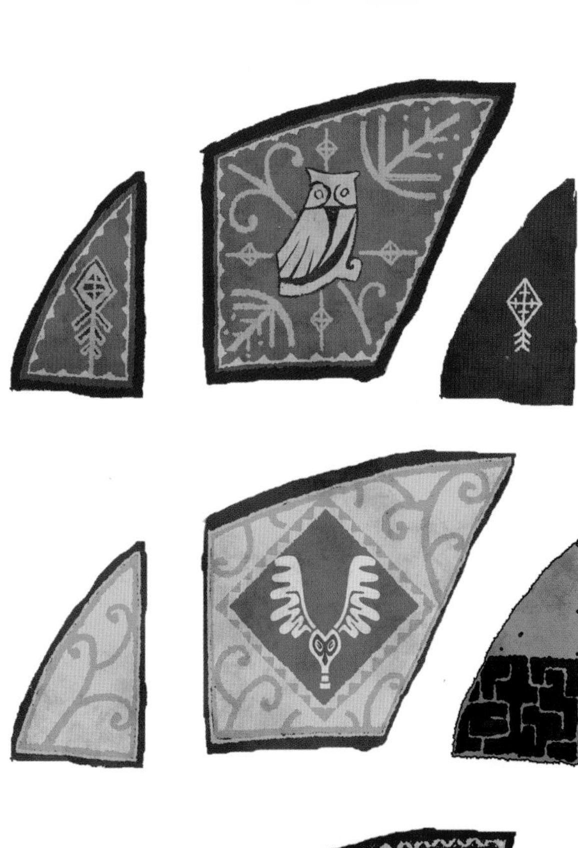
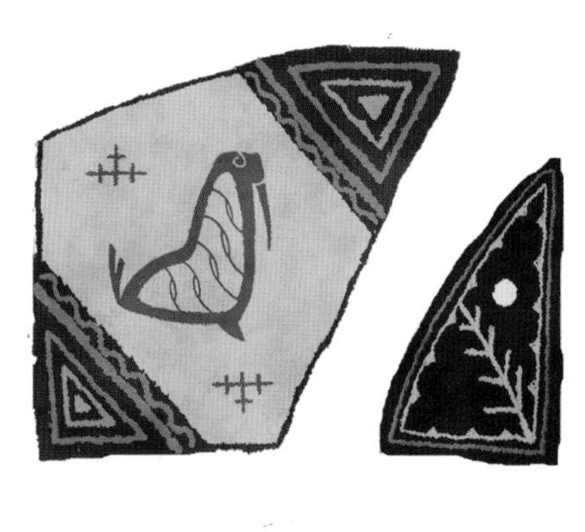
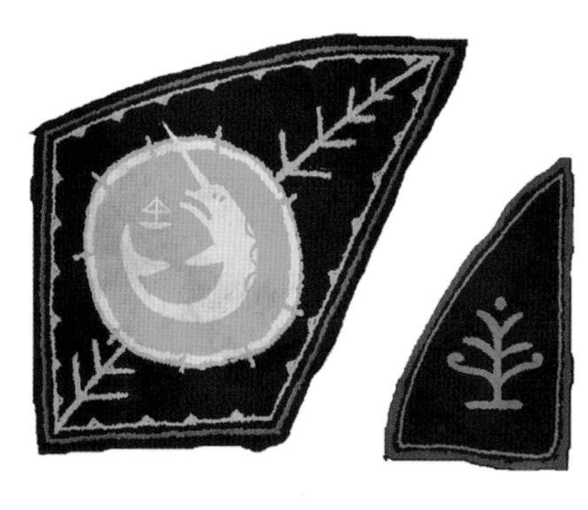
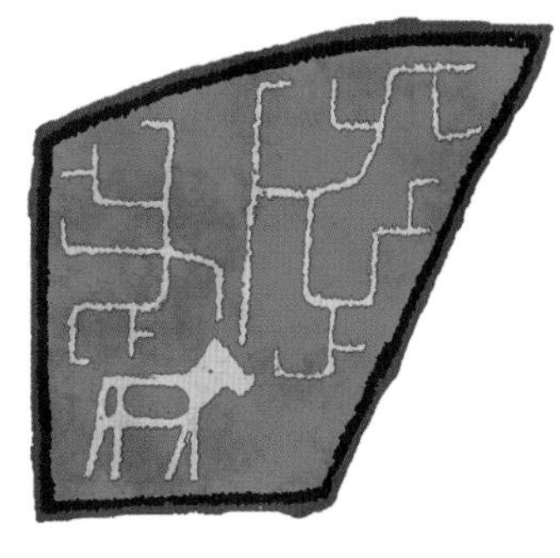
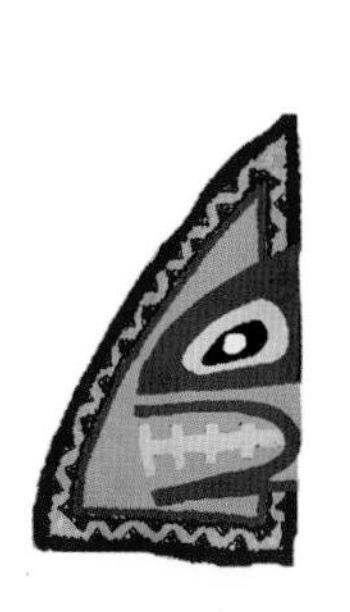
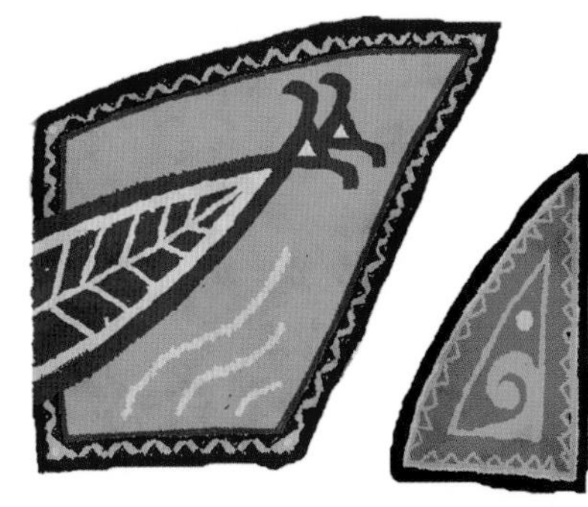
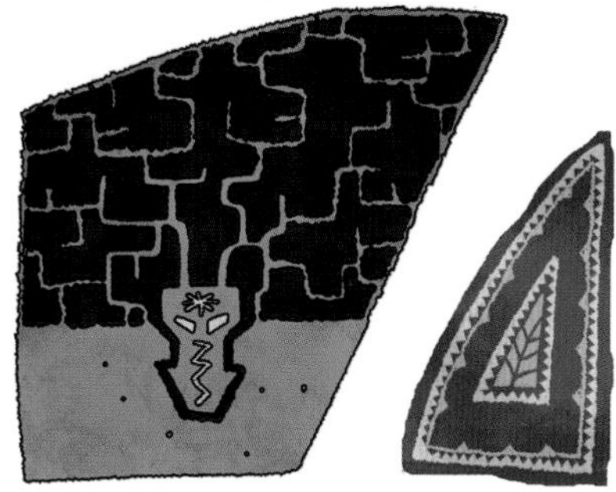

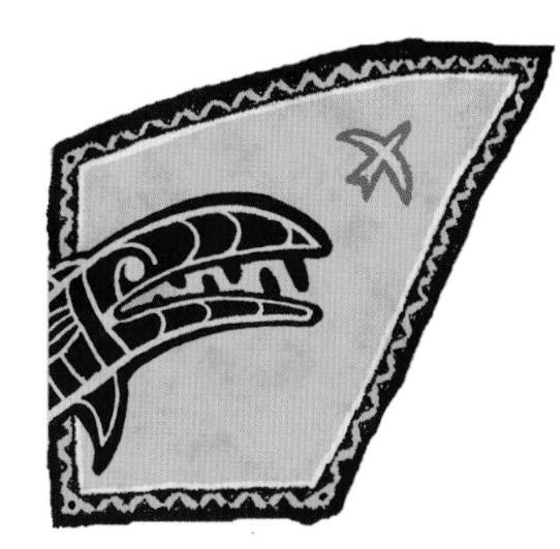
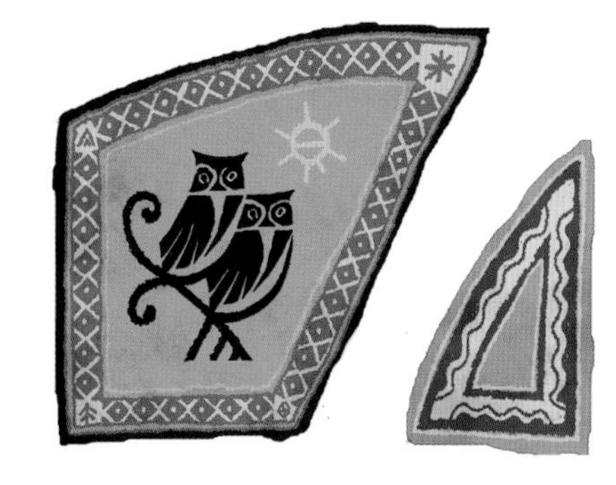
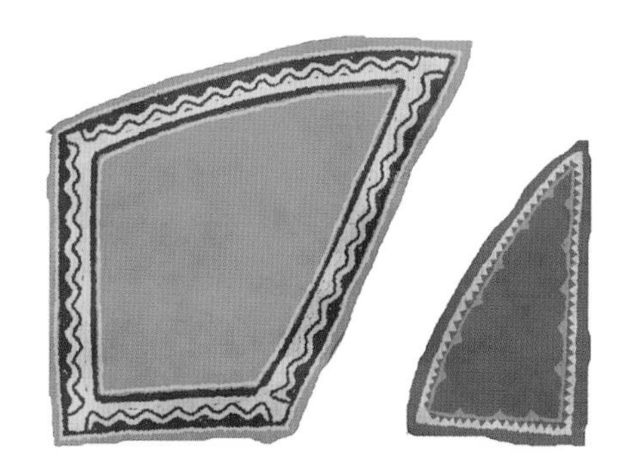
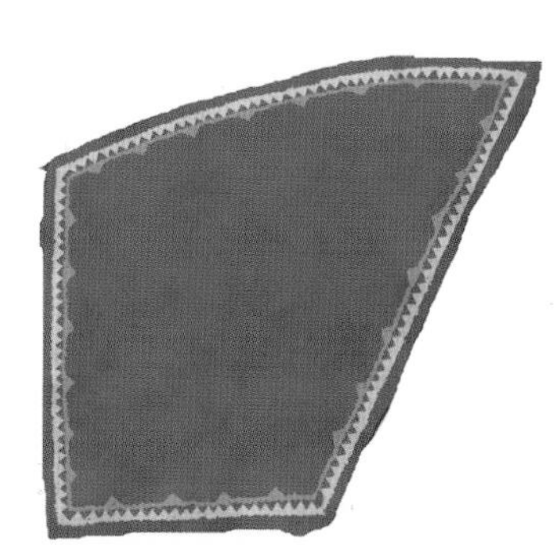
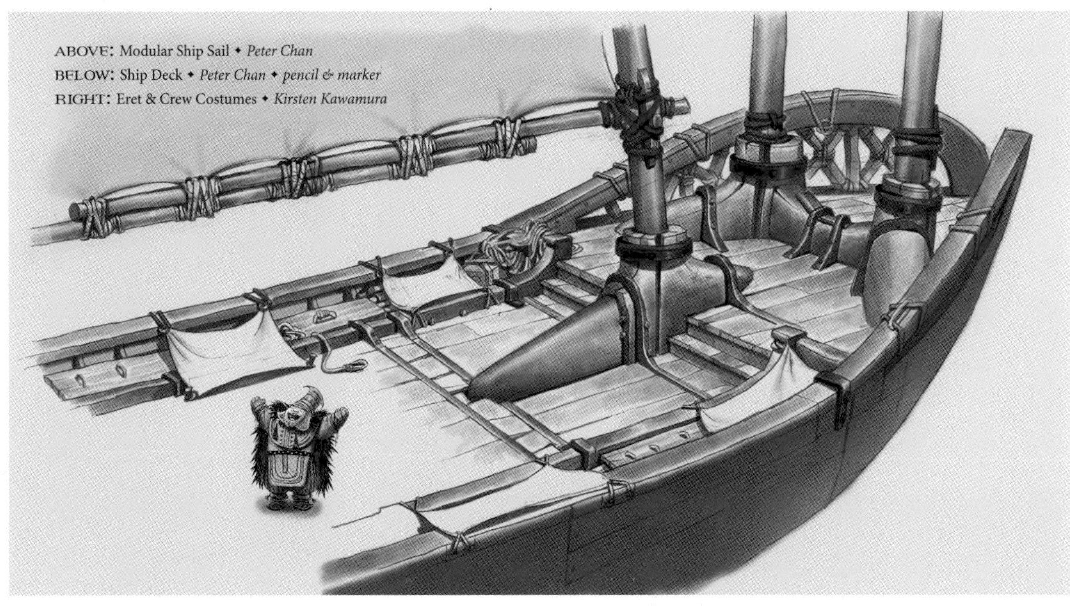

ABOVE: Modular Ship Sail ✦ *Peter Chan*
BELOW: Ship Deck ✦ *Peter Chan* ✦ *pencil & marker*
RIGHT: Eret & Crew Costumes ✦ *Kirsten Kawamura*

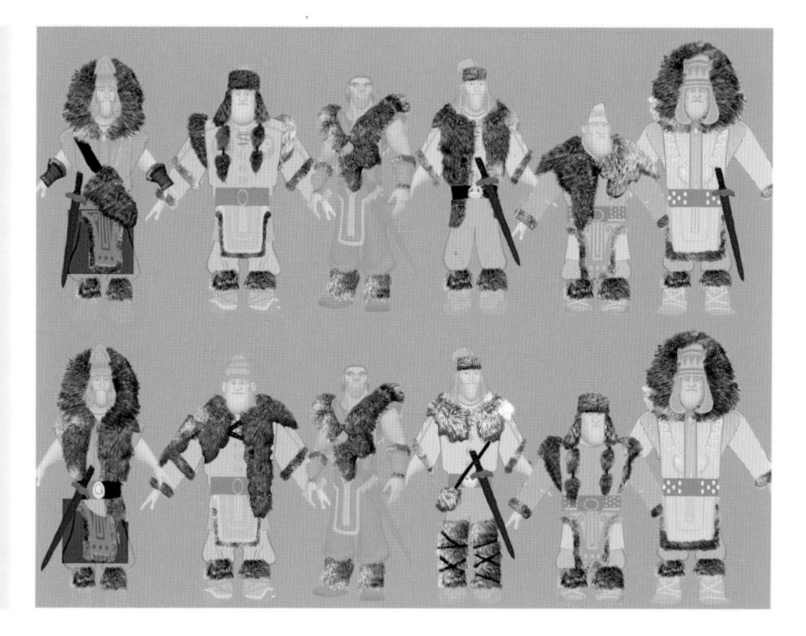

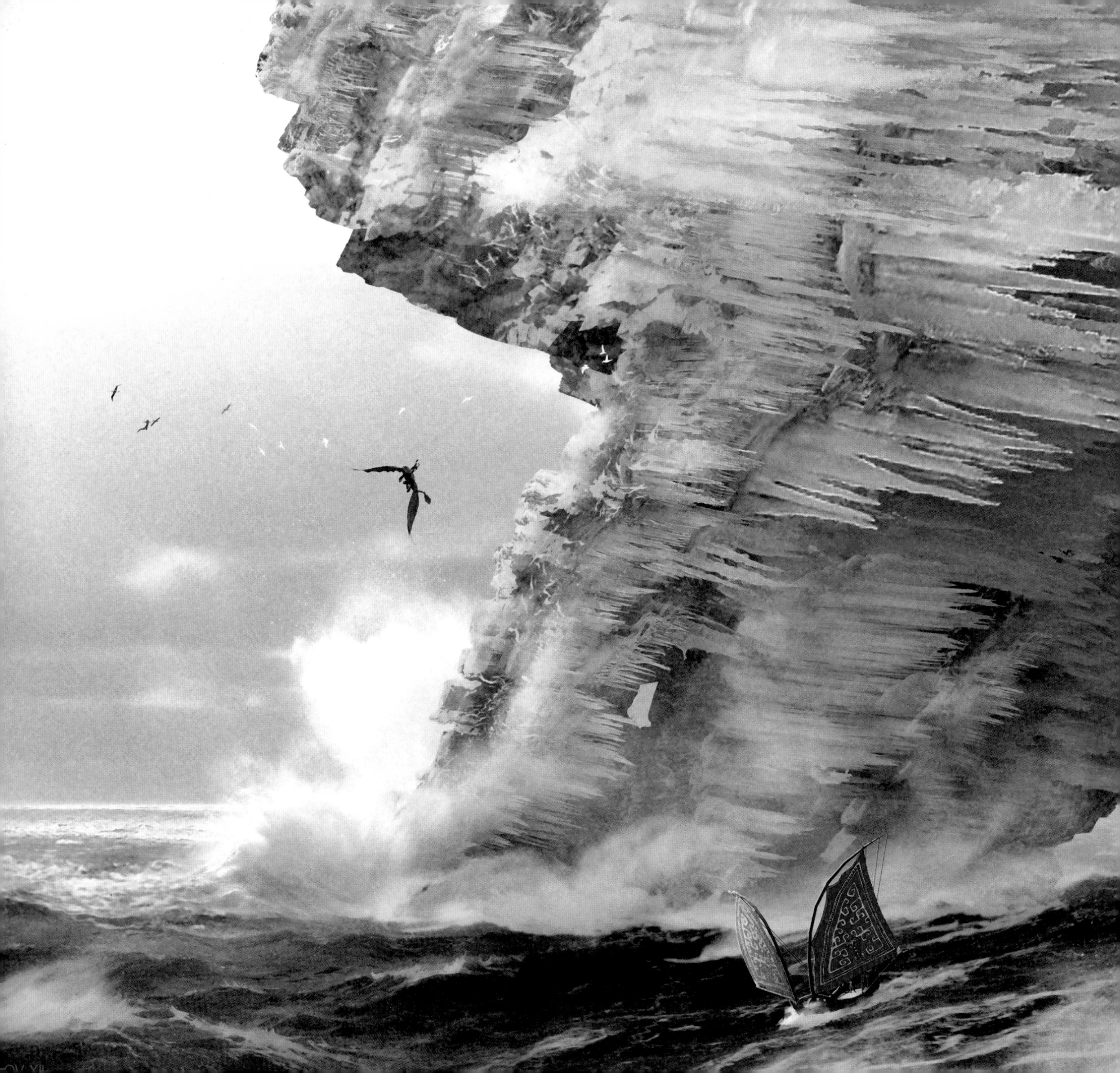

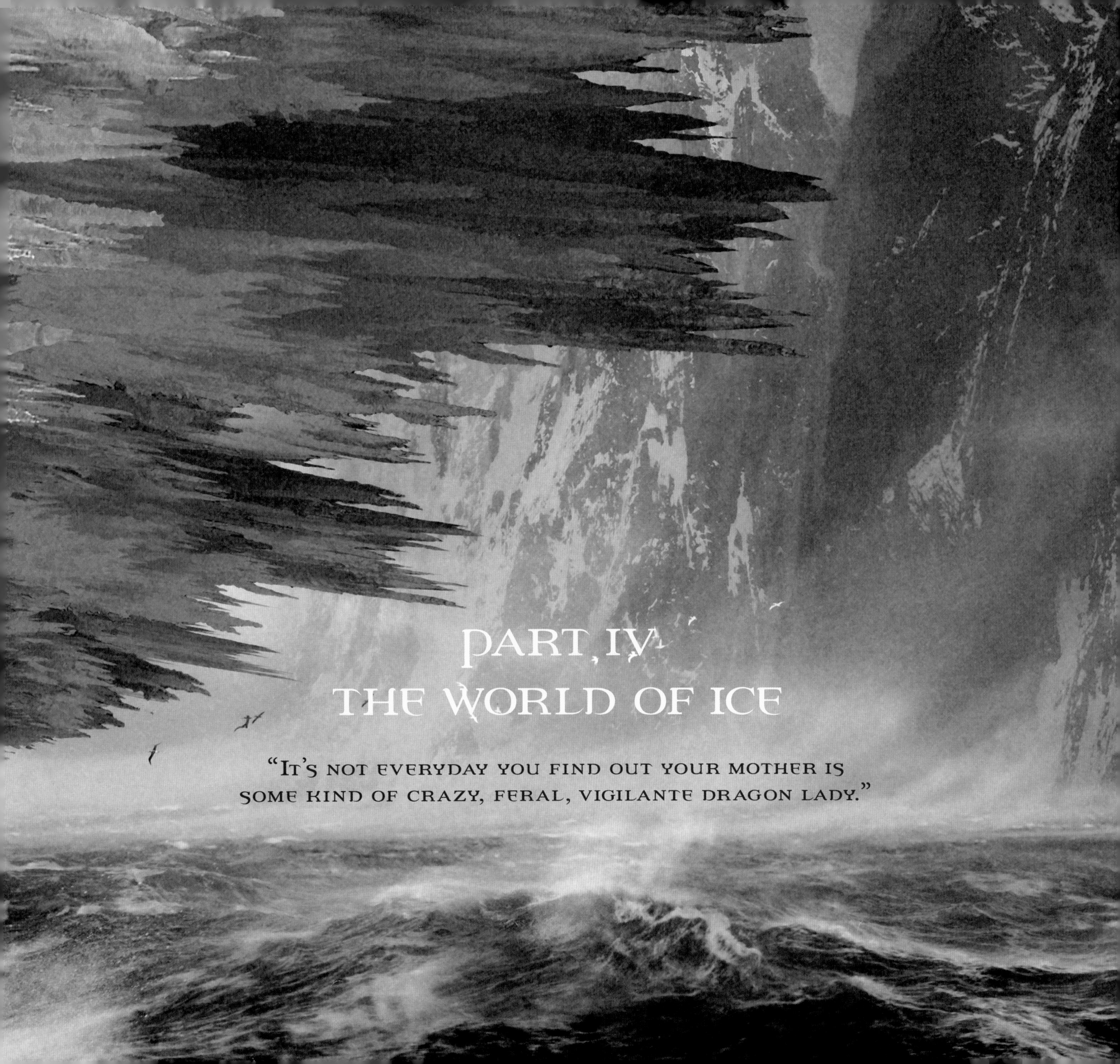

# PART IV
# THE WORLD OF ICE

"It's not everyday you find out your mother is some kind of crazy, feral, vigilante dragon lady."

# The Arctic World

This is kind of a traveling movie. The characters are always moving and we don't come back to locations very often. So whenever we have a traveling sequence, we try to inject those moments of Nordic light, that place you in that location. Hopefully it's not just the ice, it's also the lighting and everything around it that feels like that part of the world.

We used a massive collection of ice images and videos for reference, both from the team that went to Norway and from what we gathered through our own research. Some of the images are so out there that they don't seem quite real. That is the odd part of our business because sometimes we feel that if we re-created what nature really does, no one would believe it. But the truth is that ice does glow under water, trust me, I can show you a picture.

*—Pablo Valle, head of lighting*

BELOW LEFT: Frozen Waterfall Study ✦ *Iuri Lioi*
BELOW RIGHT: Iceberg Study ✦ *Peter Chan*
BOTTOM: Frozen Waterfall Concept ✦ *Peter Chan*
OPPOSITE TOP LEFT: Iceberg Concept ✦ *Pierre-Olivier Vincent*
OPPOSITE TOP RIGHT: Frozen Waterfall Concept ✦ *Iuri Lioi*
OPPOSITE BOTTOM: Islands Concept ✦ *Pierre-Olivier Vincent*

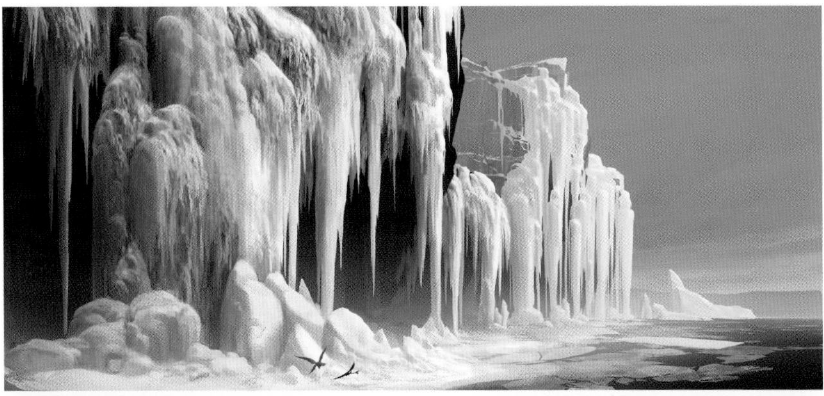

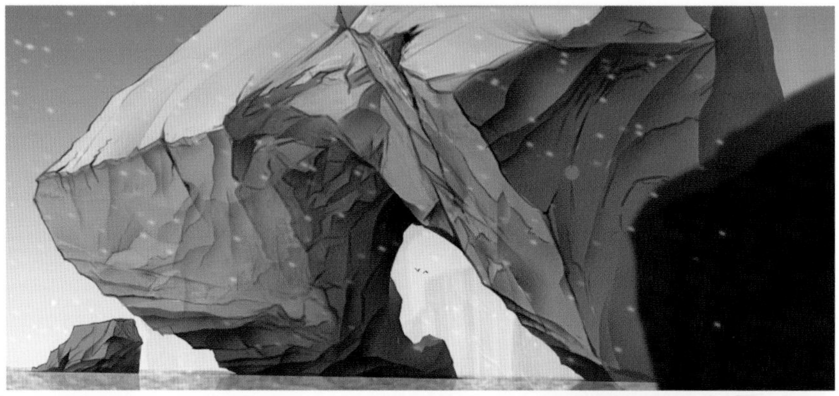

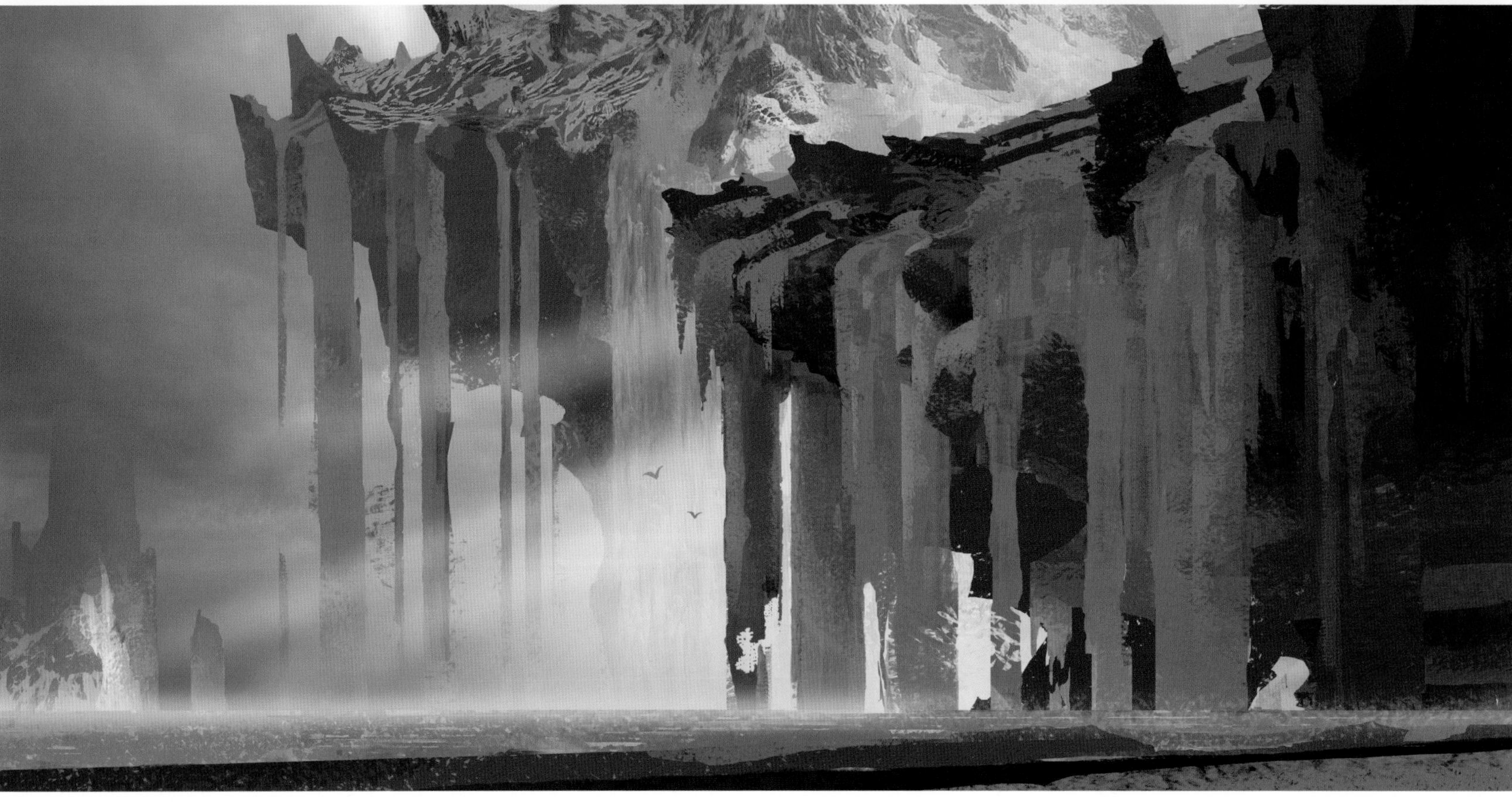

During our trip to Norway we got a firsthand look at ice landscapes. We were also able to see the costumes, tools, weapons, and ships of the native tribes. This helped us keep the film more authentic.

*—ZhaoPing Wei, art director*

The biggest challenge on this movie was the scale and vastness of the environments coupled with doing a lot of ice, which is traditionally a very hard look to simulate in computer graphics. There's a complex scattering of light in a piece of ice and replicating that into something believable, achievable, and affordable for our movie was really difficult.

*—Mike Necci, digital supervisor, environments*

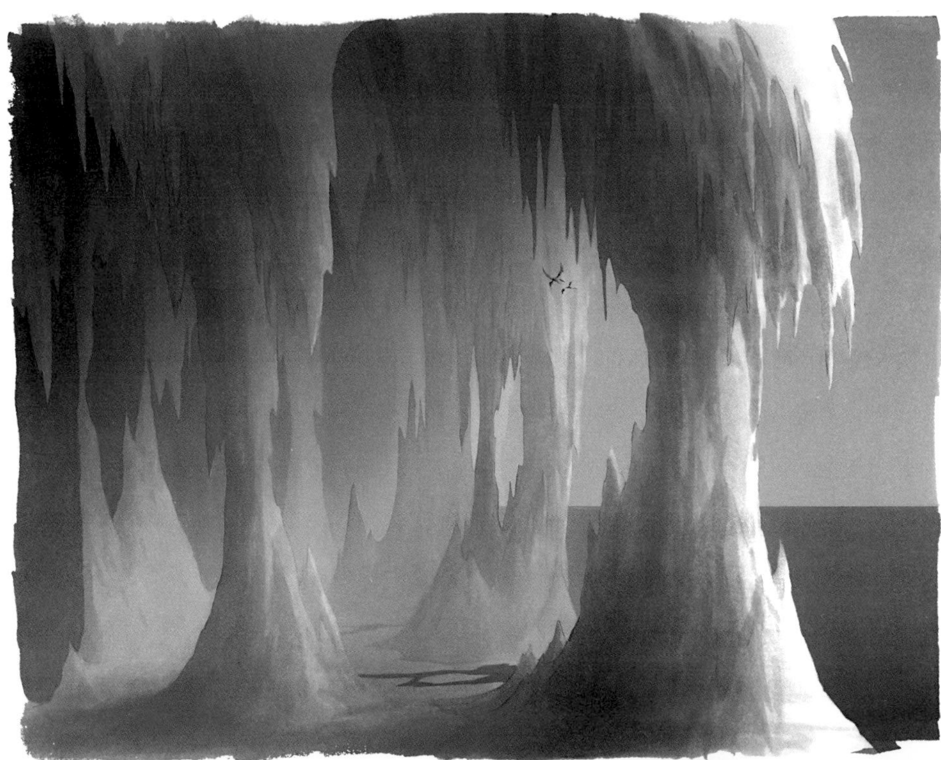

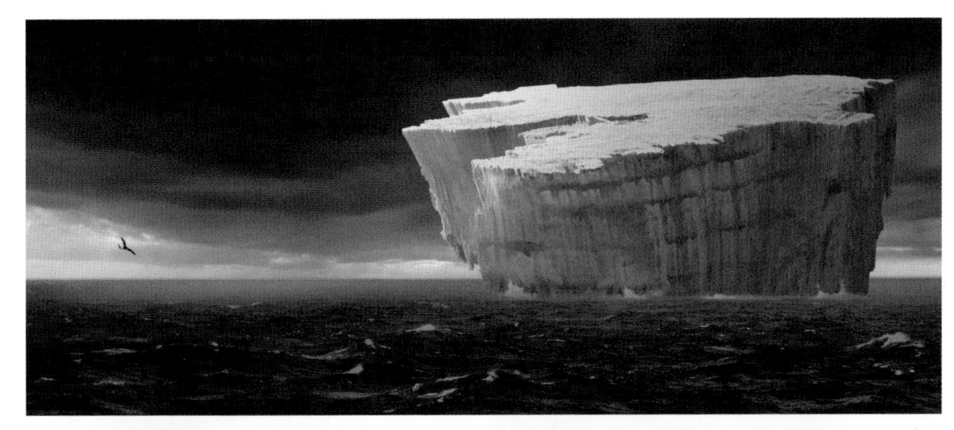

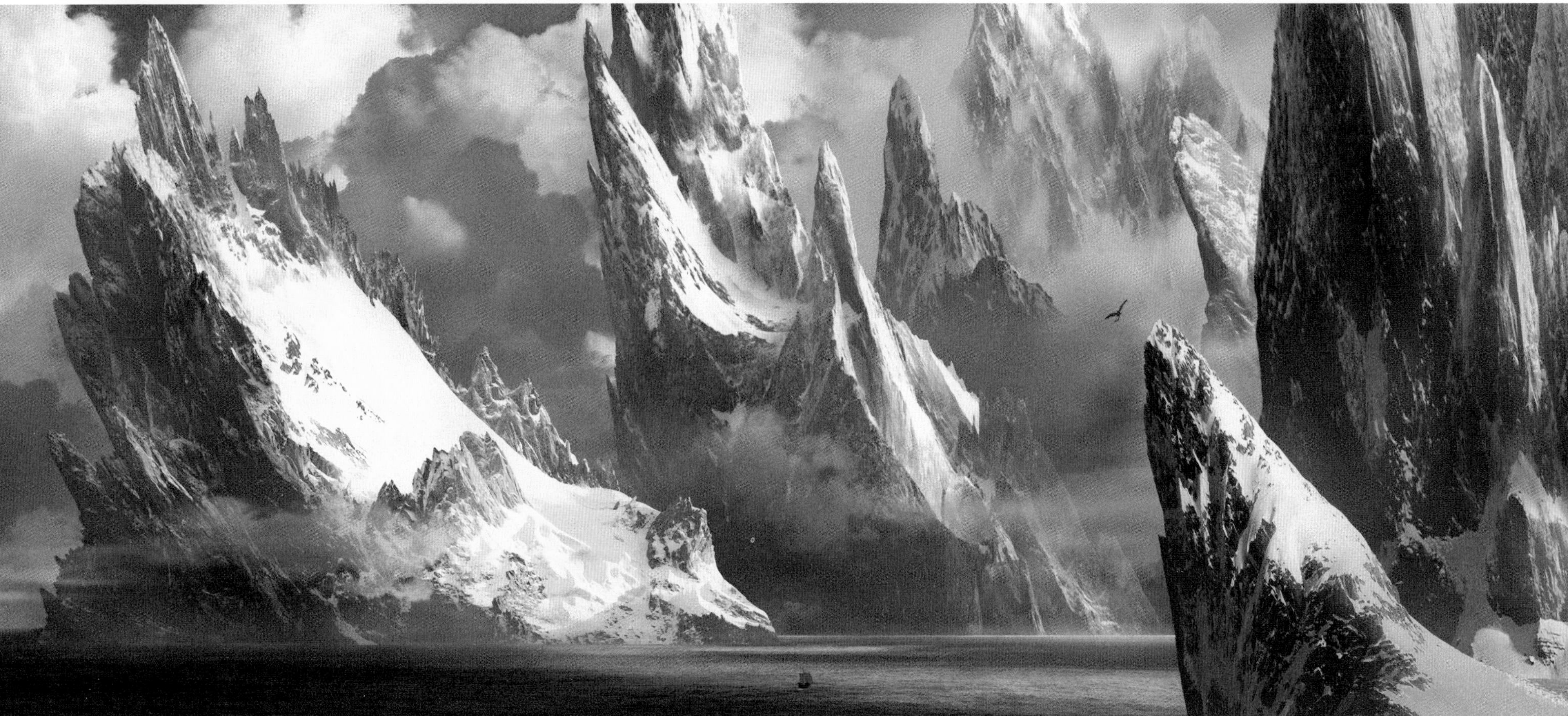

# Up in the Clouds

This sequence was all about Hiccup flying through the clouds with Toothless. When we started, we thought, Yeah, we can do these cool clouds, no problem, it's going to be great. The scene starts out really calm with this flat cloud deck. Hiccup is trying to get away from it all. It's very peaceful and reflective; Toothless is barely flapping his wings as they glide through the clouds.

When you think about flying through clouds (like on an airplane), not much happens. You see the cloud and you go through it. Since we wanted to do really dramatic things to stir up the clouds, we came up with this concept that the clouds would act more like water.

So, all of a sudden, from the first shot, Cloudjumper tears a hole through the cloudbank and it looks as if Valka is dragging the clouds behind and off of her. Then when the dragons start flapping their wings, they are pushing the clouds around as if the force of their wings were ten or twenty times what it would be.

Cloudjumper pulls up the clouds in such a way that they almost become a wall and Toothless has to stop, as if the clouds were solid. Then Cloudjumper circles around him in a dramatic way, his wings ripping through the clouds, almost creating an arena shape around Hiccup.

The difficulty in creating this sequence is that you have parts that were created by lighting, elements lit by special effects, and other parts that were painted by matte painting, all in one frame. If we did our job well, it is seamless and you can't tell how much work was involved.

What we thought would be easy turned out to be really challenging. Now we're all saying, let's not do clouds again.

*—Dave Walvoord, visual effects supervisor*

In this scene, we imagined being up above the cloud level with the sun setting. Dean, Dave, POV [Pierre-Olivier Vincent] and I each had a reference for this idea of a mass of clouds that almost feels like being above water with a kind of waving cloud and a low, pale, pink sun just edging the clouds. Above that is a blue sky but once Hiccup drops beneath the cloud line, he is in a different environment. We had the idea of the whirling of the clouds as Valka appears.

We wanted to get this feeling of going north into an empty landscape. It's important that every scene isn't the same; it is like the scenes in the snow, which can get monotonous. We wanted variations in textures and colors. The Arctic is a fascinating, otherworldly kind of place, where all the colors are really subtle.

*—Roger Deakins, visual consultant*

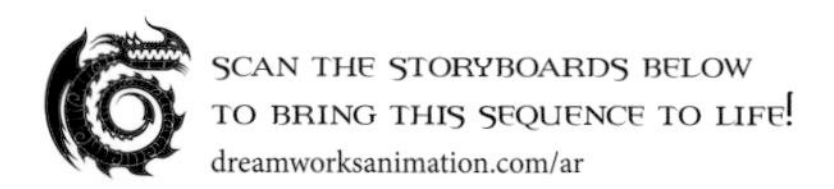


BELOW: Storyboards ✦ *Bolhem Bouchiba & Megan Nicole Dong*
OPPOSITE TOP: Lighting Study ✦ *Marcos Mateu-Mestre*
OPPOSITE BOTTOM: Film Frames

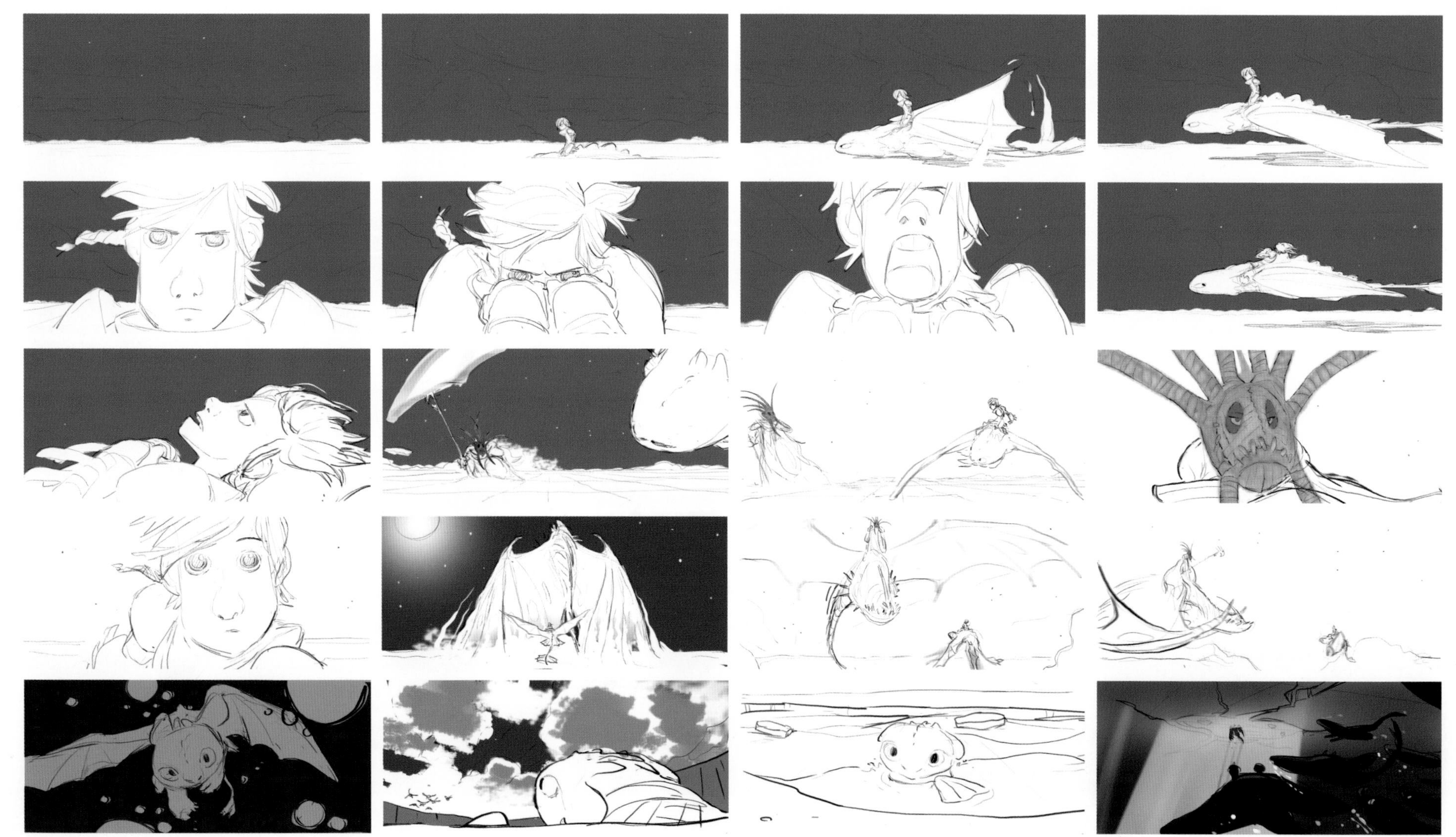

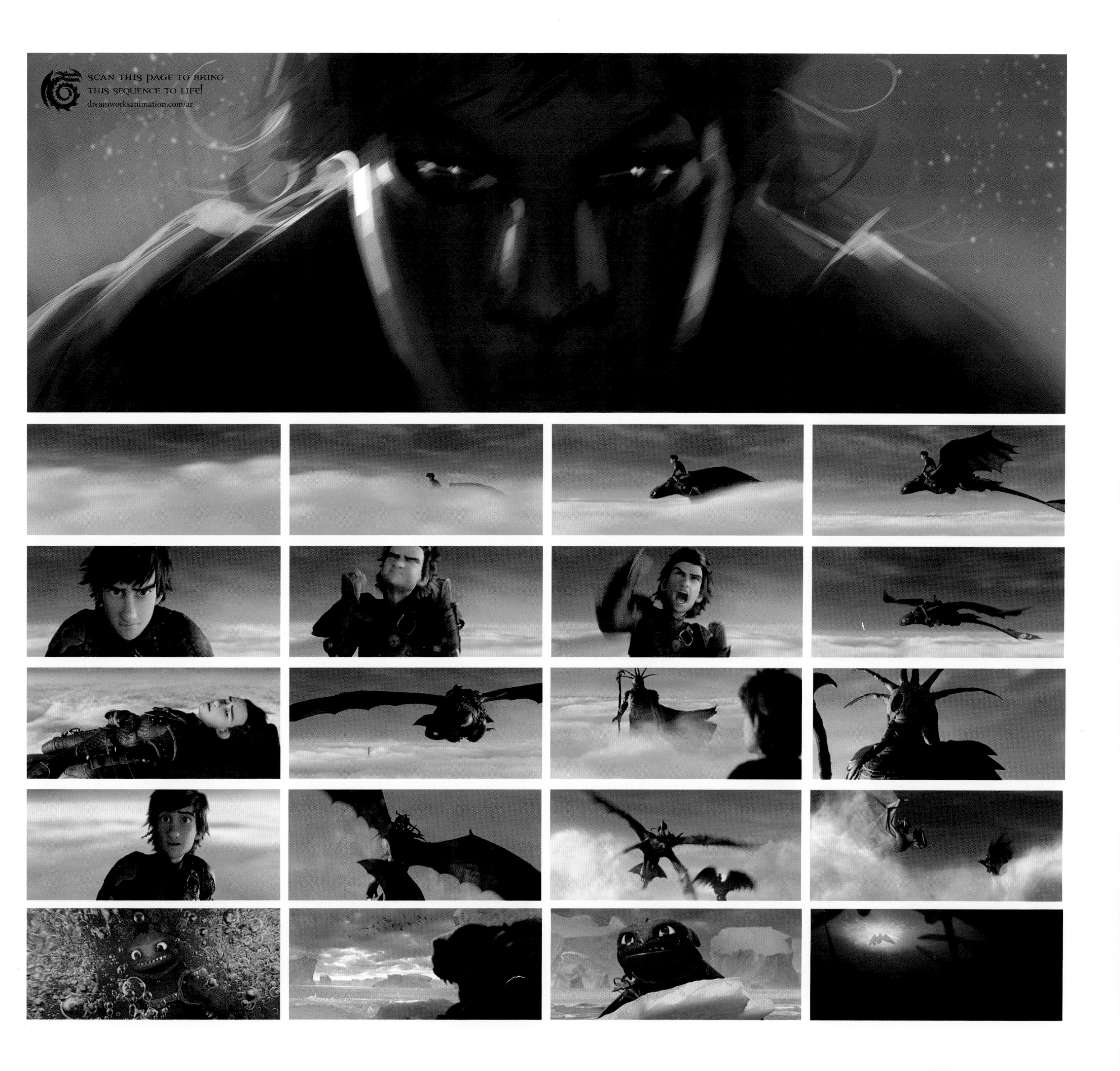
SCAN THIS PAGE TO BRING
THIS SEQUENCE TO LIFE!
dreamworksanimation.com/ar

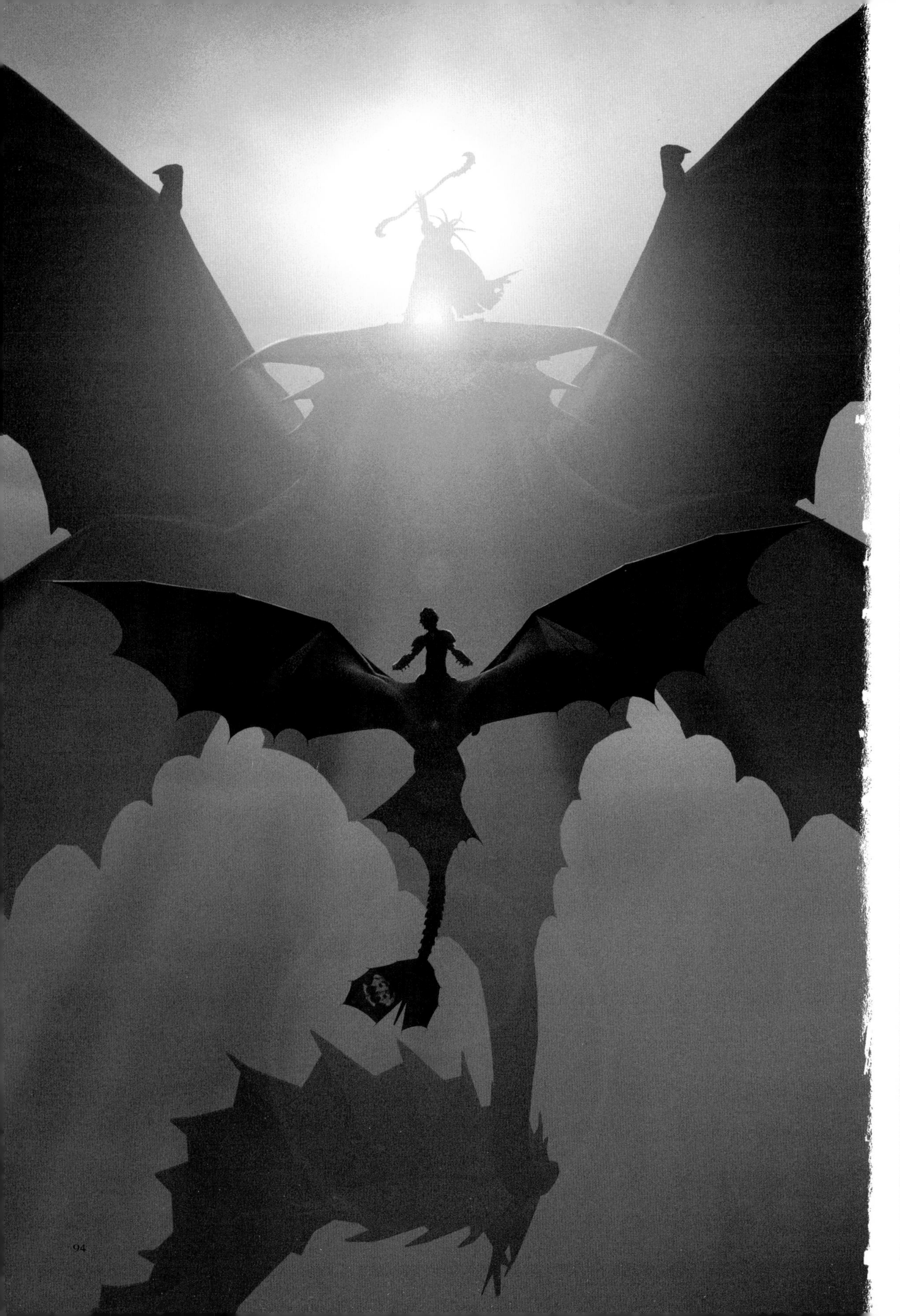



# Valka Rises, Toothless Falls

Keeping to the idea of shooting like a live-action film is really evident in the flying scenes especially in that moment where Cloudjumper flies around to show his four wings. The animators spent a lot of time adding a lot of detail to that move so the normal thing would have been to light him nice and bright. But we said no, if you are shooting against the sun, you have to let him go into silhouette. We went graphic with the shape and form and let that carry the shot instead of lighting every detail. It's much more cinematic, more like what you would get in a live-action film. It's a relatively small example but it's the language of our film, and we freed ourselves to be bolder and this is what is exciting. We are pushing the envelope with a lot of the departments because they spent a lot of time on these images but this kind of lighting is what serves the story.

*—Pablo Valle, head of lighting*

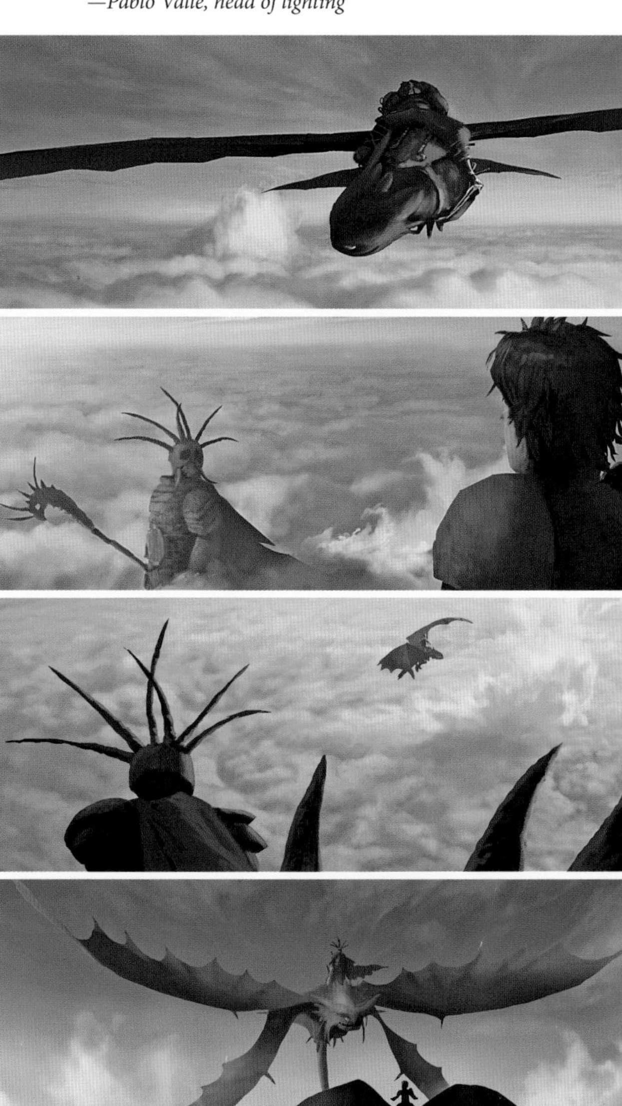

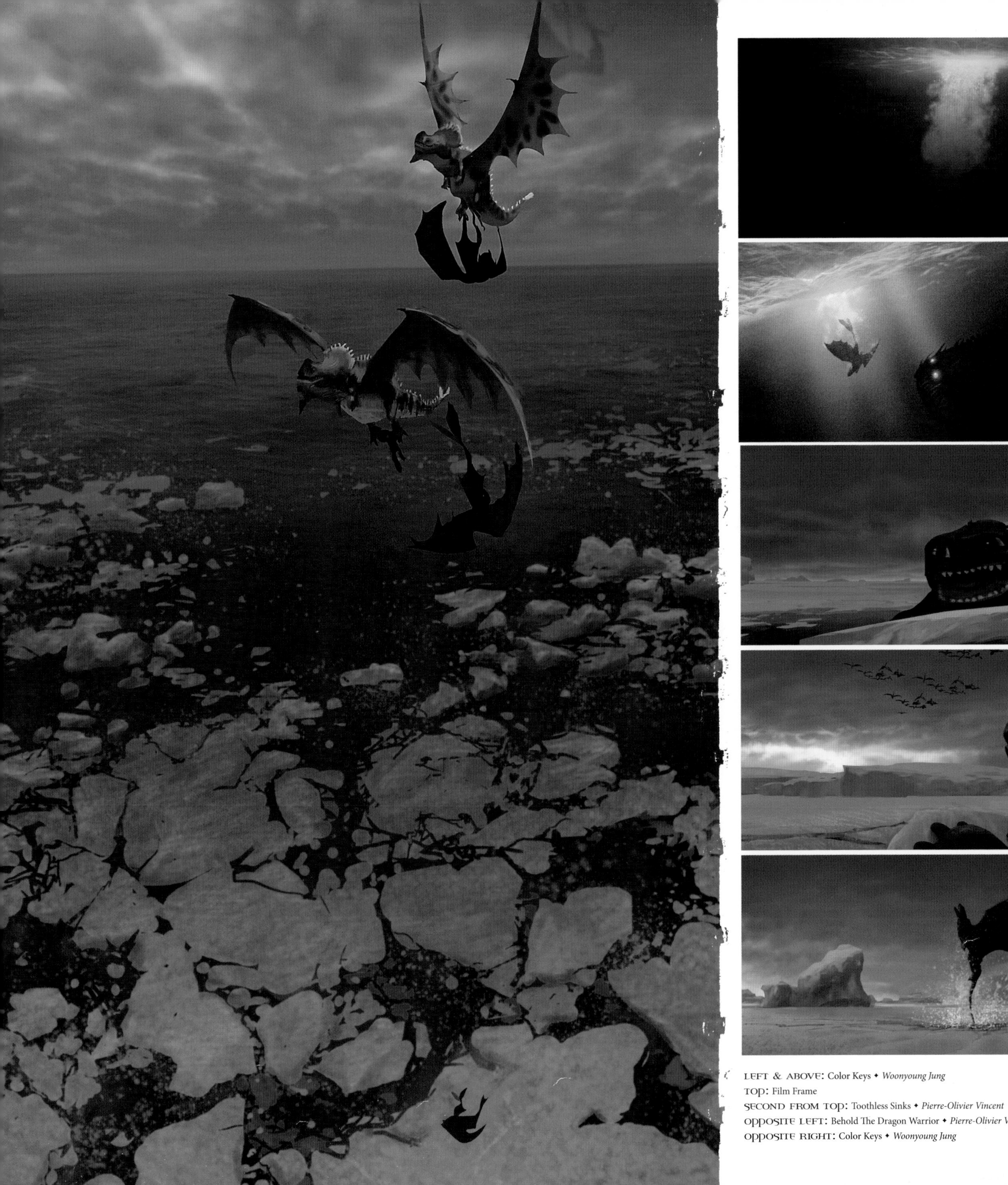

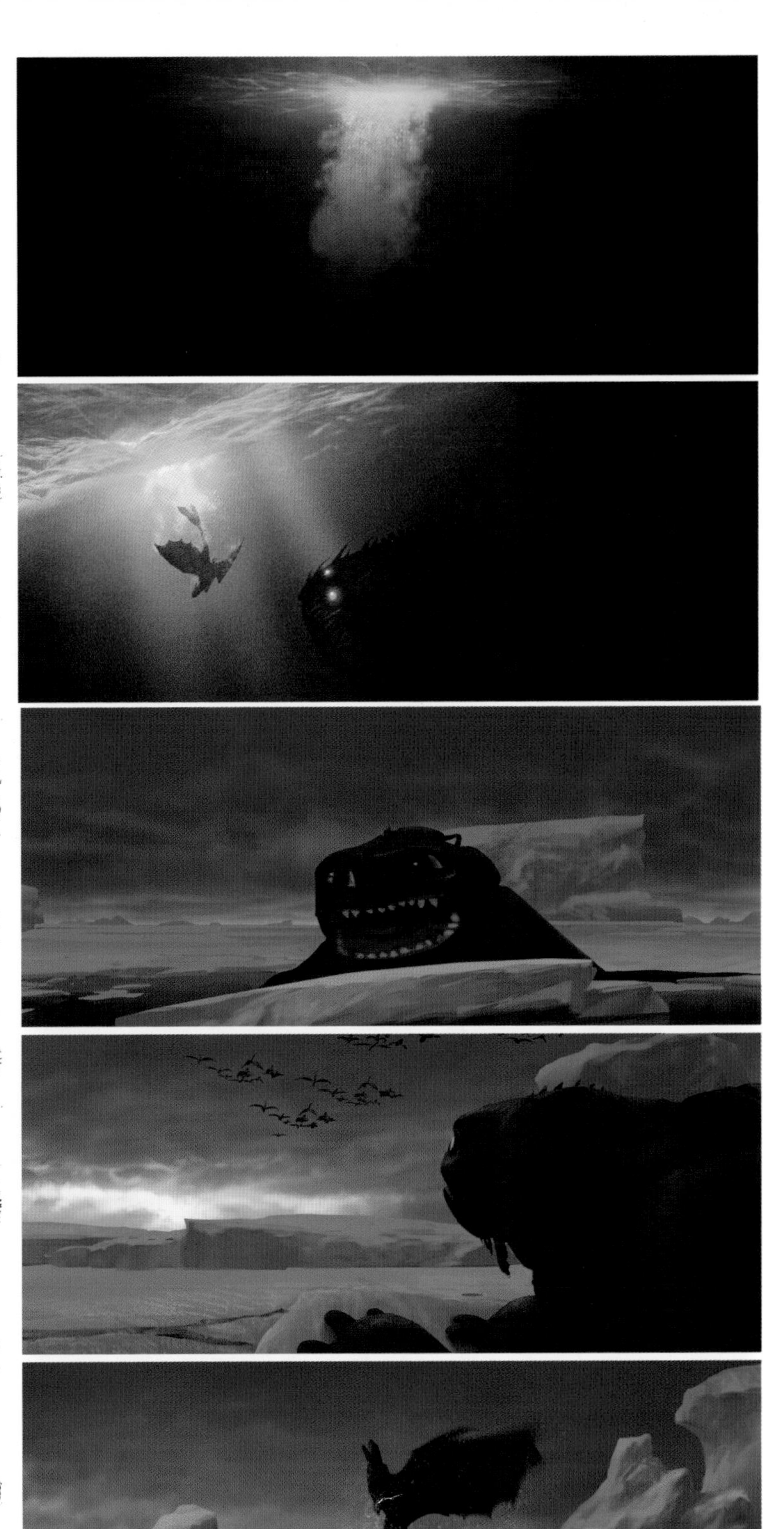

LEFT & ABOVE: Color Keys • *Woonyoung Jung*
TOP: Film Frame
SECOND FROM TOP: Toothless Sinks • *Pierre-Olivier Vincent*
OPPOSITE LEFT: Behold The Dragon Warrior • *Pierre-Olivier Vincent*
OPPOSITE RIGHT: Color Keys • *Woonyoung Jung*

# The Ice Maze

The first film was kind of localized to Berk and the villagers who lived there. In this sequel, we wanted to show a wide Nordic world filled with wonders but also danger. From the very beginning, we talked about how nature plays into this world.

A big portion of our movie happens around snow and ice. We spend less time in man-made environments as most of the film takes place in the vastness of nature. The scale is huge, the characters are big, and we introduce two enormous Bewilderbeasts. For us it was a discussion about nature, scale, and what role our characters play now that the dragons have given them the ability to fly to places they'd never have otherwise visited. How do we show that sense of scale and magnitude?

The language of the show is Viking, Nordic themes inhabited by hyper-real creatures that are kind of whimsical and funny but have a darker side. We wanted to keep everything as real as possible. Our lighting is meant to support a world that people have never seen but can believe exists.

*—Pablo Valle, head of lighting*

BELOW: Valka's Lagoon ✦ *Nicolas Weis*
OPPOSITE: Ice Maze Concepts ✦ *Pierre-Olivier Vincent*

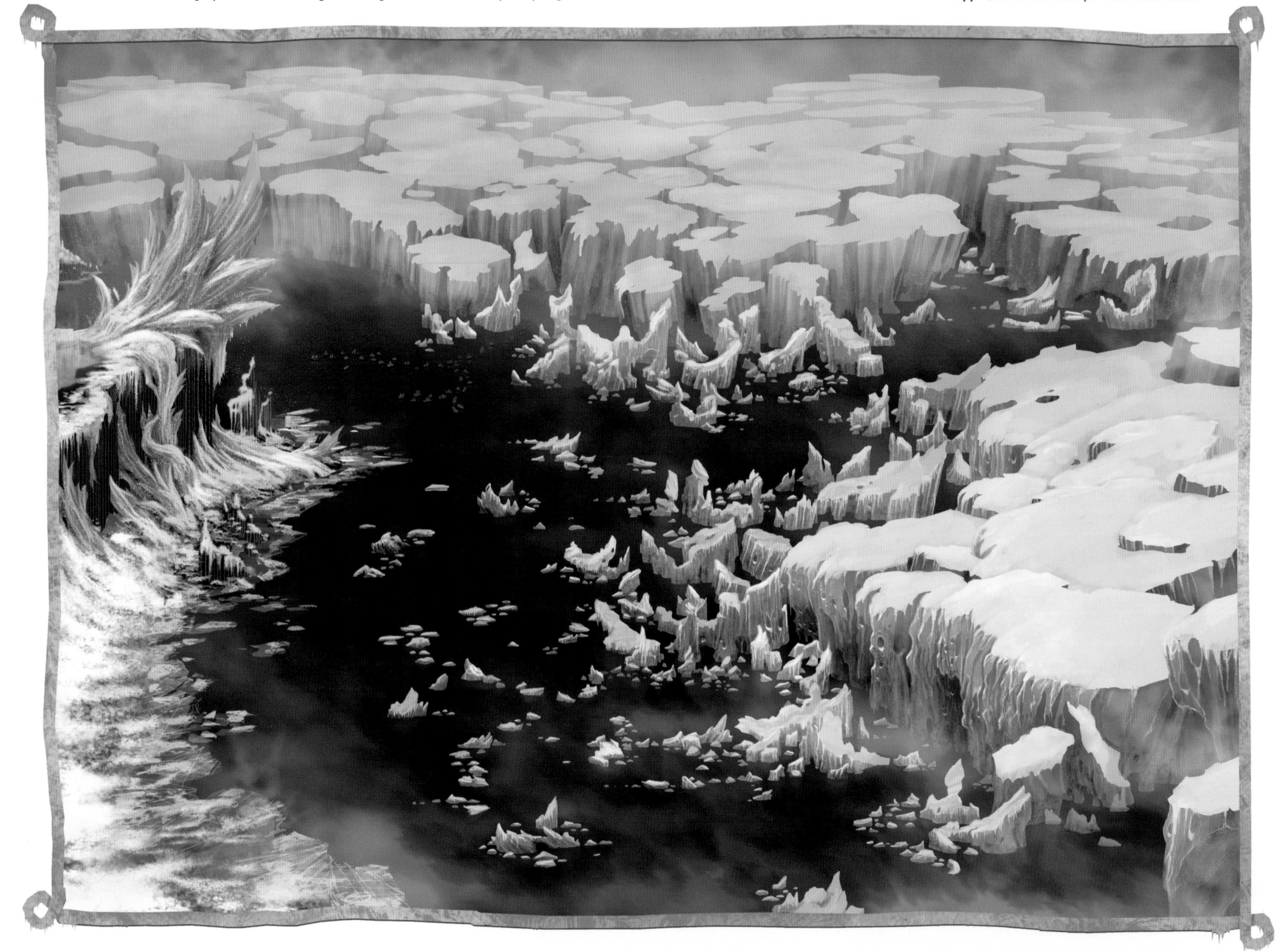

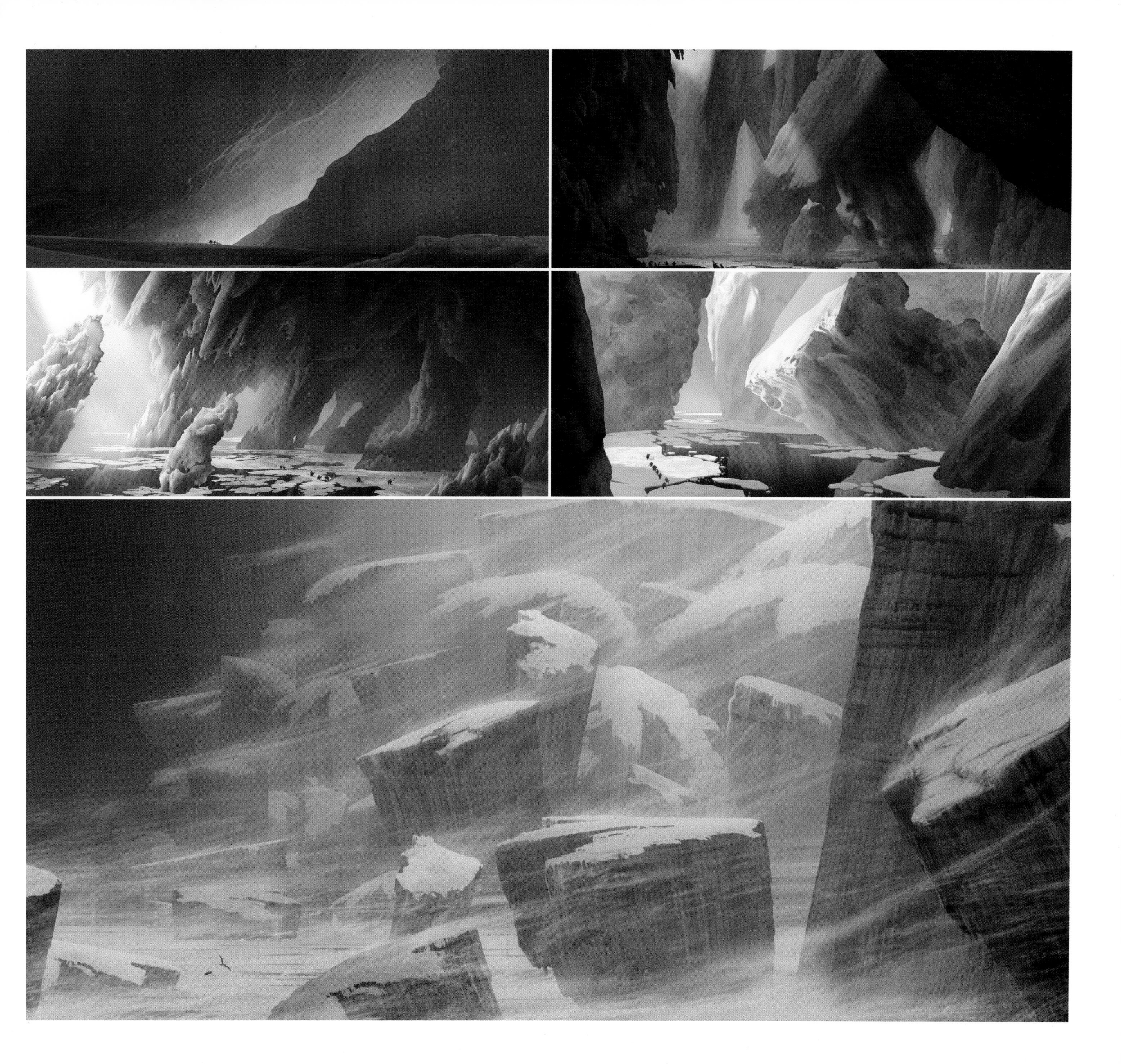

# Valka's Mountain Exterior

There are two kinds of ice in our movie. One is the realistic ice—the white, bluish ice of the glaciers and the icebergs. The other is the ice expelled by the Bewilderbeast, which has a very different texture, quality, and color. For example, the greenish tint of this ice tends to dominate the backdrop of Valka's cave. Both types of ice pose the challenge of re-creating the translucent quality of light shining through ice.

The other complexity of the cave was the oasis where the dragons are roosting. There is an immense amount of detail in the rock formations as well as in the mosses and ferns they are covered with.

*—Mike Necci, digital supervisor, environments*

BELOW & OPPOSITE BOTTOM: Valka's Mountain Exteriors ✦ *Pierre-Olivier Vincent*
OPPOSITE TOP LEFT: Color Key ✦ *Woonyoung Jung*
OPPOSITE TOP RIGHT: Film Frame

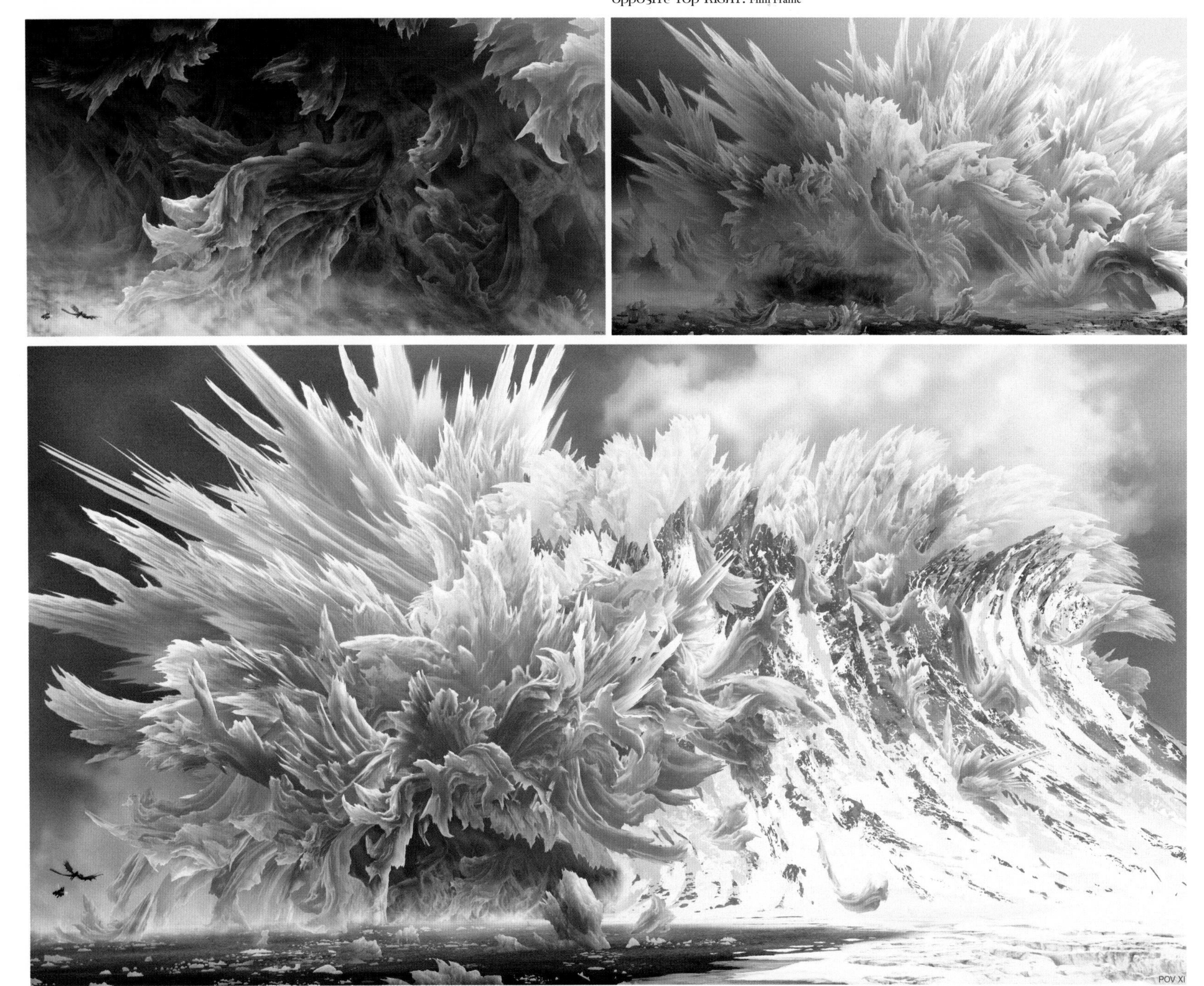

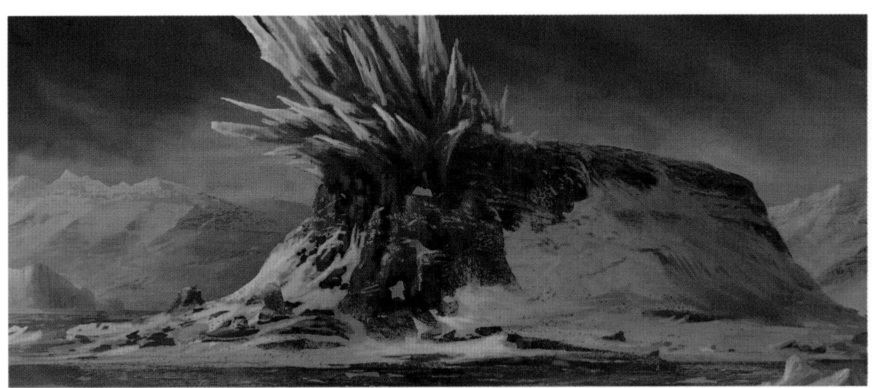
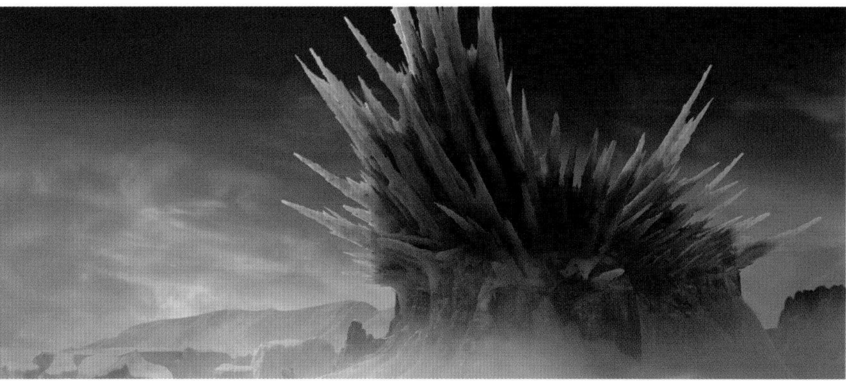
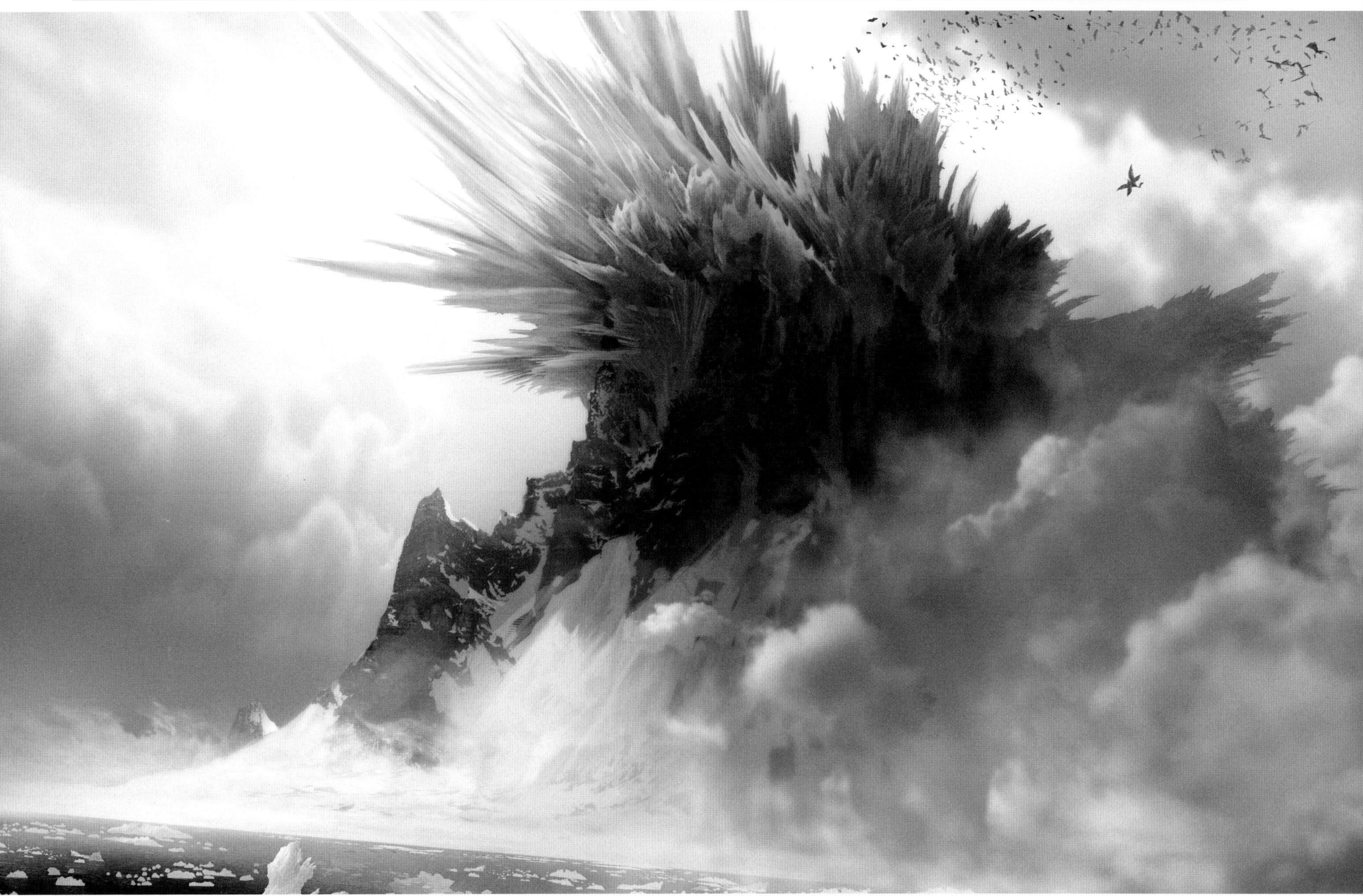

# The Ice Cave

We wanted this scene to be as creepy as possible. It's an emotional low point for Hiccup; he has lost Toothless and has been taken by this unknown dragon rider to a mysterious cave. Intentionally, this is the darkest part of the film, both emotionally and visually, as we are setting up the giant reveal that Valka is a woman and his mother.

Hiccup is now in a cave that almost looks like it's from another planet, like science fiction, because it has been formed by the Bewilderbeast. We've lit it by putting some light in the background and keeping everything up front dark and atmospheric. It's almost reminiscent of alien movies, in which you keep the monsters in darkness and see only shapes. The less the audience sees, the more they are freaked out by not knowing what is there. In any horror movie, once you see the villain, it's not so scary anymore. The only light source is the fire from the Dragon Blade and a tiny light behind Valka, so you can see her silhouette. This was one of the most fun scenes we did. I hope it makes people really uncomfortable.

*—Dave Walvoord, visual effects supervisor*

BELOW: Film Frames
MIDDLE: Color Key ✦ *Woonyoung Jung*
BOTTOM: Lighting Studies ✦ *Marcos Mateu-Mestre*

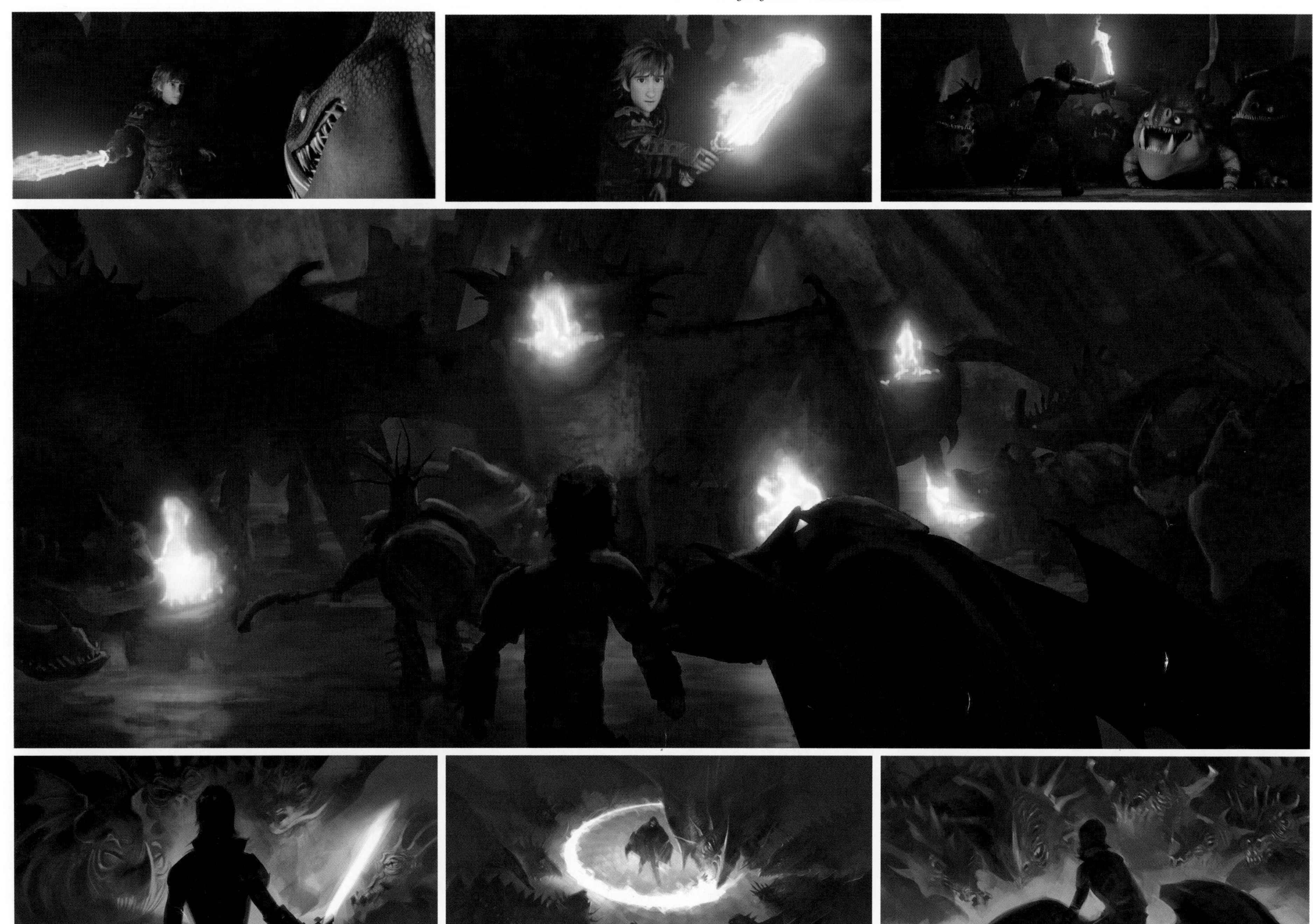

# The Dragon Warrior

I thought it would be interesting if Hiccup discovered that his mother was a dragon-loving enthusiast. Valka has been living in the wild and connecting with these animals, forming a familial relationship with them while she's been missing from her own home. The original idea was that over those twenty years of protecting dragons and bonding with them, she has lost her belief in humanity. She has come to believe that humans are not capable of change and they can't be trusted. She is emblematic of the part of Hiccup that connects with Toothless; only she has taken this concept to radical extremes.

*—Dean DeBlois, director*

On our first close-up of Valka, she is in silhouette, abstract and somewhat out of focus. This makes the scene more mysterious and poignant when you reveal someone who has only been a shape that is integrated into the clouds. This scene is all about the lighting. Here is a mysterious character wearing a strange mask; we don't know if she is good or evil. We want to keep it ambiguous, so we use the idea of bottom lighting her a bit.

Roger Deakins had a very significant influence on our show. Roger has always maintained that no matter how much of a fantasy world we create, people have to believe it exists. Our language is naturalism applied in such a way that it is still fantastical. We've been pushing lighting by making things more extreme and playing with graphic elements, which is unusual in an animated film. Generally, in CG animation, the principle is that you should see the character all the time.

We adopted another approach in this film. We are following the logic that we will tell the story and convey a picture as realistically as possible even if that means losing your character for a few frames or part of the shot. So, if the characters are going through a very dark tunnel, they go dark for a moment, just like you would in a cave when you are trying to get your bearings. We are treating it much more like a sophisticated live-action shoot, which is what Roger brought to the show. It's freeing to be able to do what works best for the scene and not just go by the rule that, well, we built the models and animated the characters so let's always show them.

*—Pablo Valle, head of lighting*

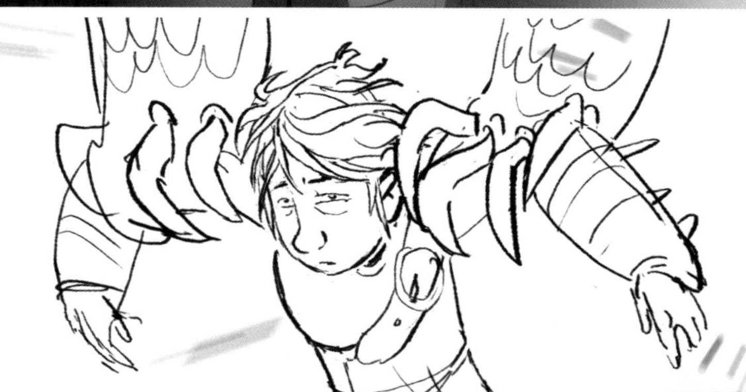

ABOVE RIGHT: Storyboards ◆ *Alessandro Carloni*
RIGHT & BELOW: Film Frames
BOTTOM LEFT: Color Key ◆ *Woonyoung Jung*
BOTTOM RIGHT: Rune ◆ *Kirsten Kawamura*

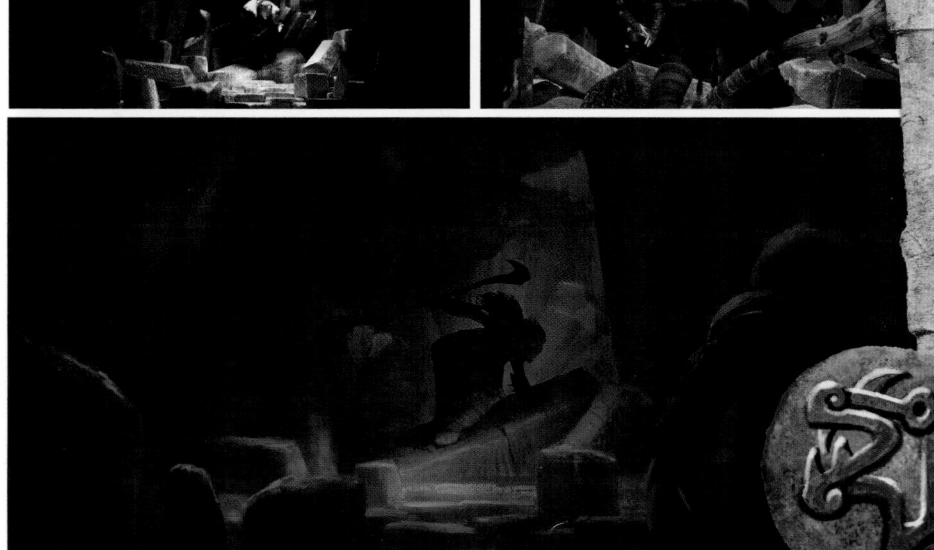

## A Lot of Story

We wanted a giant impact at the very end of the sequence that starts with Hiccup being taken off his dragon and left wondering if Toothless has drowned. Our goal was to keep the suspense alive while hiding the fact that this other person is a female. We want the audience to think this is some mysterious person, possibly related to dragons, but clearly ominous and otherworldly. By not knowing what you are dealing with, you get a big contrast when Valka sees the scar on Hiccup's face and realizes he might be the child she left behind at birth.

For a long time, that was all the scene was meant to reveal and it ended with Valka saying she was Hiccup's mother and his shocked reaction. We played around with that for a long time, working on how we might improve that scene. Now, although the entire scene is shot from Hiccup's perspective, Valka has more of a beat where she effectively reveals herself and then gets the idea that if Hiccup can control his dragon and has a relationship with him, he might be interested in what she's been doing for the past twenty years. Is it possible that she has something in common with her son? In this way, we end the scene on a much more positive note and the next time we see them, she is leading Hiccup through a dark tunnel to see her dragons.

There is a lot of story to be told in this movie and not a lot of time to tell it. We are constantly trying to take a very sophisticated story and break it down in the simplest way possible. For Hiccup and his mother, there are precious few moments for them to go from being estranged family members to being mother and child again, and this scene helped bridge that story line.

*—Gil Zimmerman, head of layout*

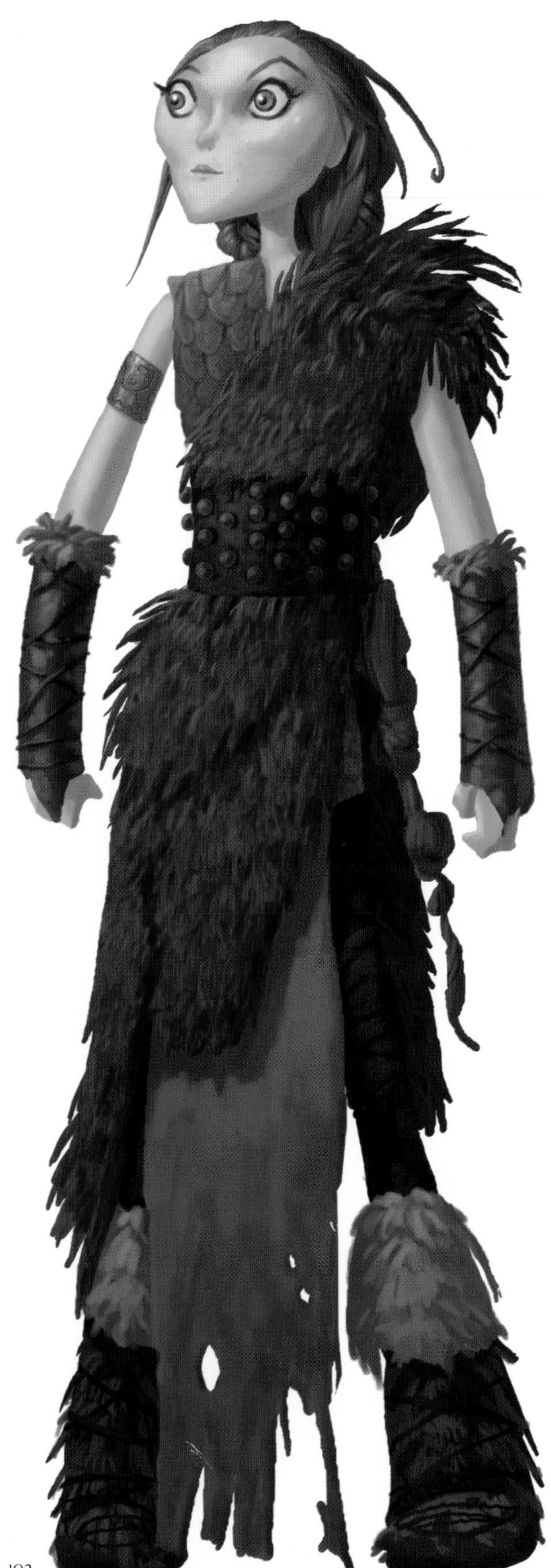

# Valka

The first character we designed for the sequel was Valka. She lives with dragons and respects them so much that Dean had this idea she'd want to make herself look and behave like one of them. I tried to find a shape for her costume that resembled a dragon. Valka was supposed to be very athletic so we had to incorporate that into the design. She had to wear a mask as well.

*—Nico Marlet, character designer*

For all of Hiccup's accomplishments as a dragon rider, Valka blows him away. She rides without a saddle, standing on her dragon's back and walking around him as he barrel rolls, just like a logger. She has a kind of silent communication with dragons, honed through many years of living with them, studying them, and discovering their secrets. She is meant to embody what Hiccup could become years down the road if left alone to immerse himself in the world of dragons.

We wanted her to look arresting but a bit peculiar and intimidating in her own right. She lives a minimal existence, only taking what she needs. She is definitely very physical, lean, and athletic due to her years of rescuing dragons from Drago's forces. Because we ended up cutting the opening scene that was meant in part to show off her vigilante prowess as a force to be reckoned with, we now only suggest what she is capable of according to people's accounts and brief moments of battle.

*—Dean DeBlois, director*

First we had to find a striking face for her. We didn't know at first that Cate Blanchett would do the voice but we had her in mind because she has portrayed strong-minded, intelligent women like Queen Elizabeth I. We wanted Valka to be physical in a Nordic way.

We talked for a long time about her acting and how she could almost have a gesture inspired by one of the dragons. Ultimately, we didn't do it because it made her too alien and we felt she was already quite removed from the world.

*—Pierre-Olivier Vincent, production designer*

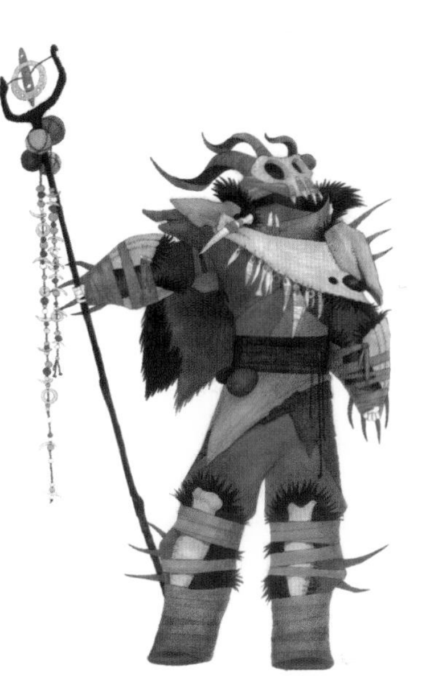

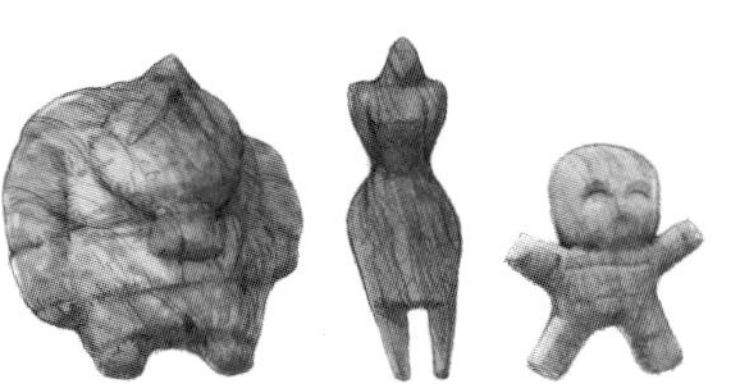

LEFT: Young Valka ✦ *Bill Kaufmann*
TOP: Valka ✦ *Iuri Lioi* ✦ *pen & marker*
ABOVE: Props ✦ *Iuri Lioi* ✦ *pen & marker*
BELOW: Valka Face Studies ✦ *Nico Marlet* ✦ *pencil & marker*

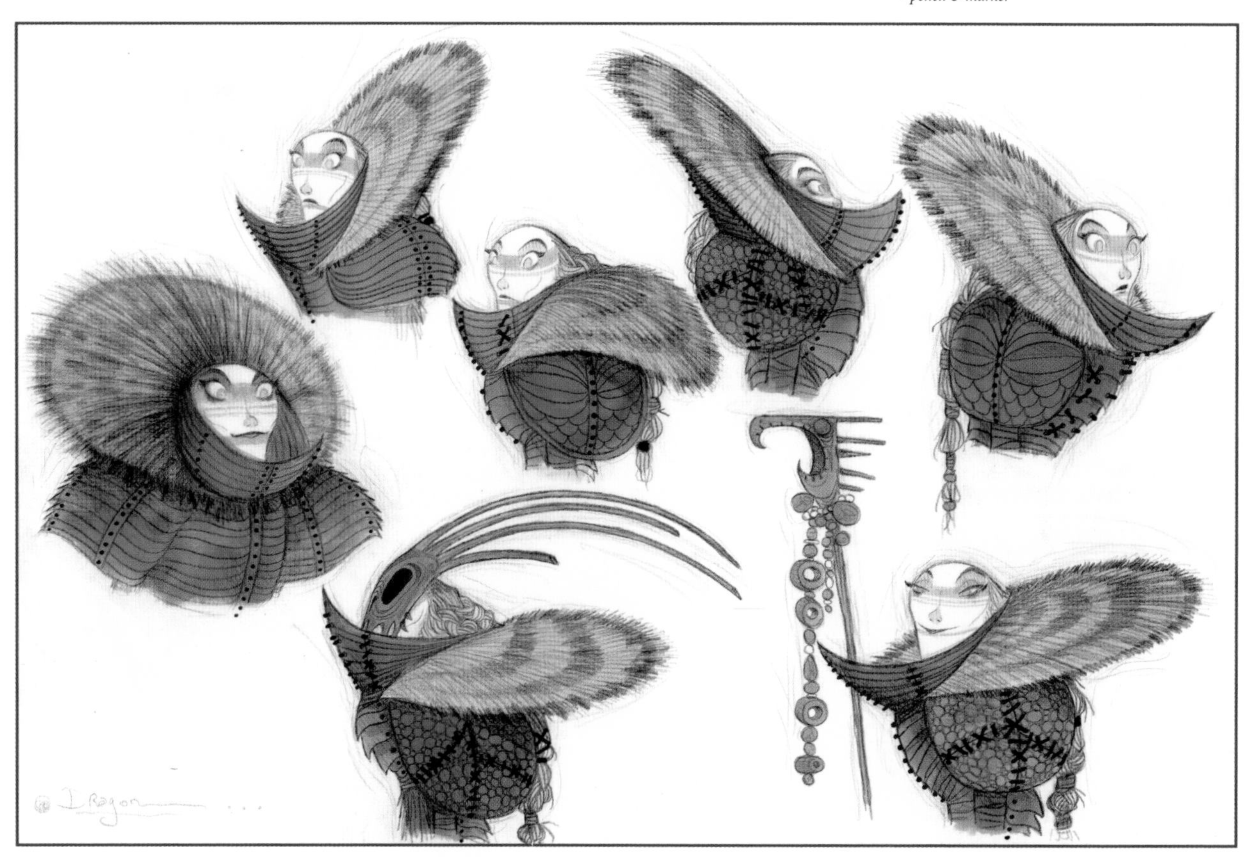

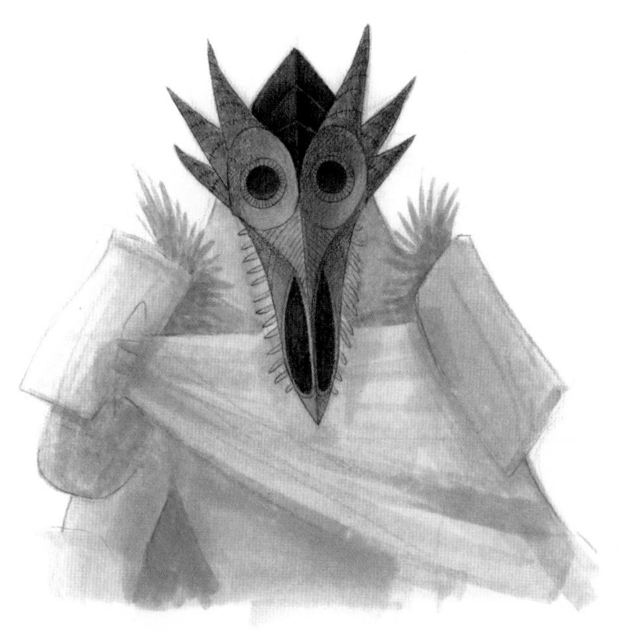

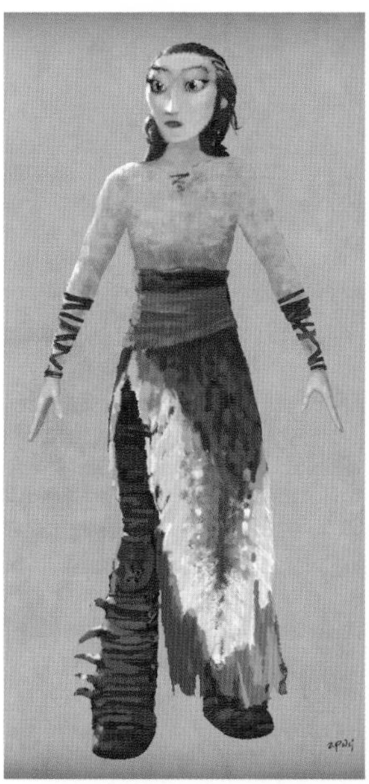

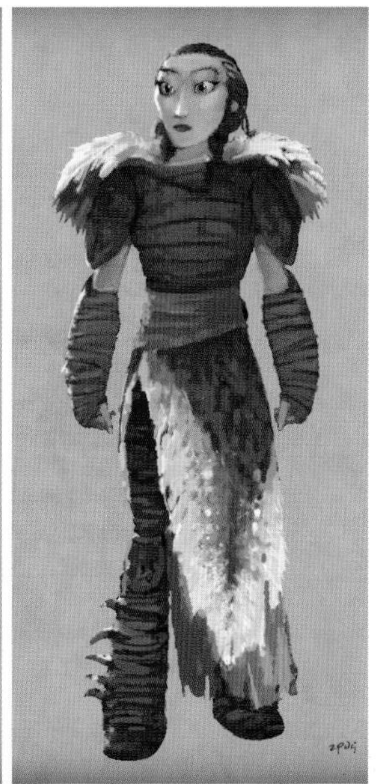

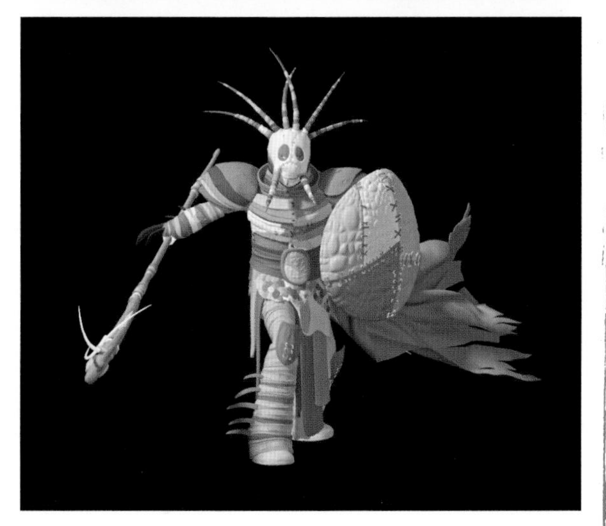

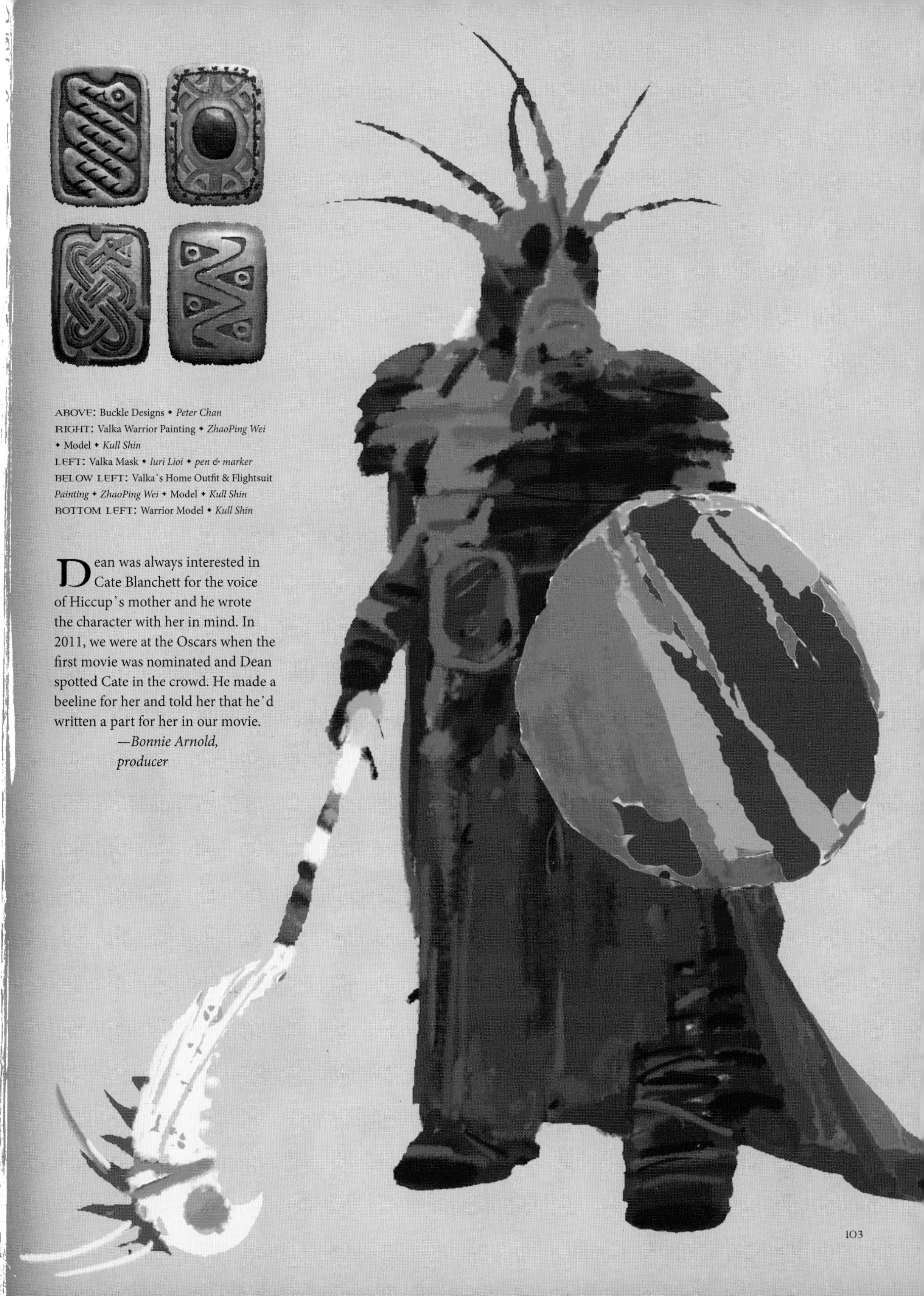

ABOVE: Buckle Designs ◆ *Peter Chan*
RIGHT: Valka Warrior Painting ◆ *ZhaoPing Wei* ◆ Model ◆ *Kull Shin*
LEFT: Valka Mask ◆ *Iuri Lioi* ◆ *pen & marker*
BELOW LEFT: Valka's Home Outfit & Flightsuit *Painting* ◆ *ZhaoPing Wei* ◆ Model ◆ *Kull Shin*
BOTTOM LEFT: Warrior Model ◆ *Kull Shin*

Dean was always interested in Cate Blanchett for the voice of Hiccup's mother and he wrote the character with her in mind. In 2011, we were at the Oscars when the first movie was nominated and Dean spotted Cate in the crowd. He made a beeline for her and told her that he'd written a part for her in our movie.

*—Bonnie Arnold,*
*producer*

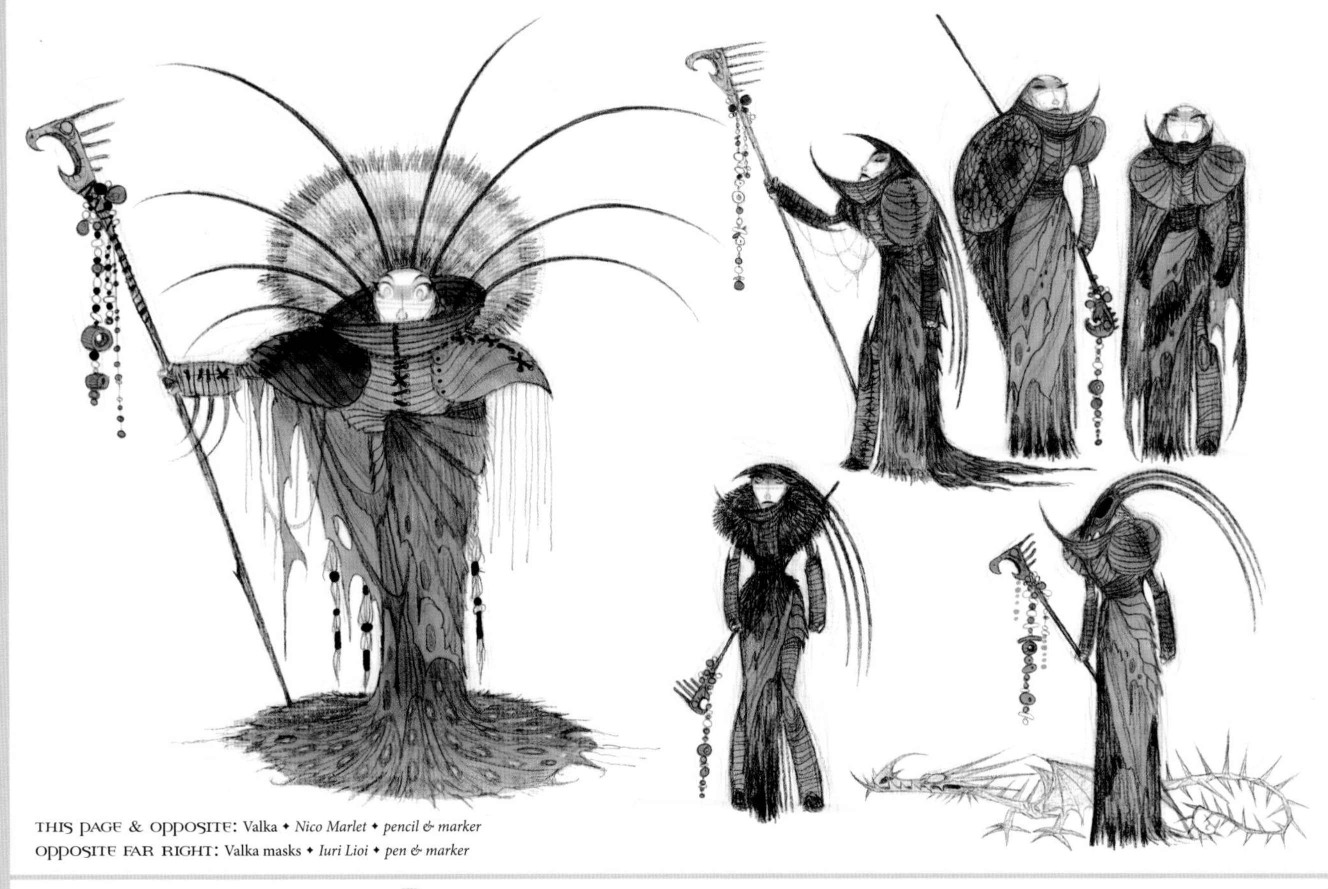

THIS PAGE & OPPOSITE: Valka ✦ *Nico Marlet* ✦ *pencil & marker*
OPPOSITE FAR RIGHT: Valka masks ✦ *Iuri Lioi* ✦ *pen & marker*

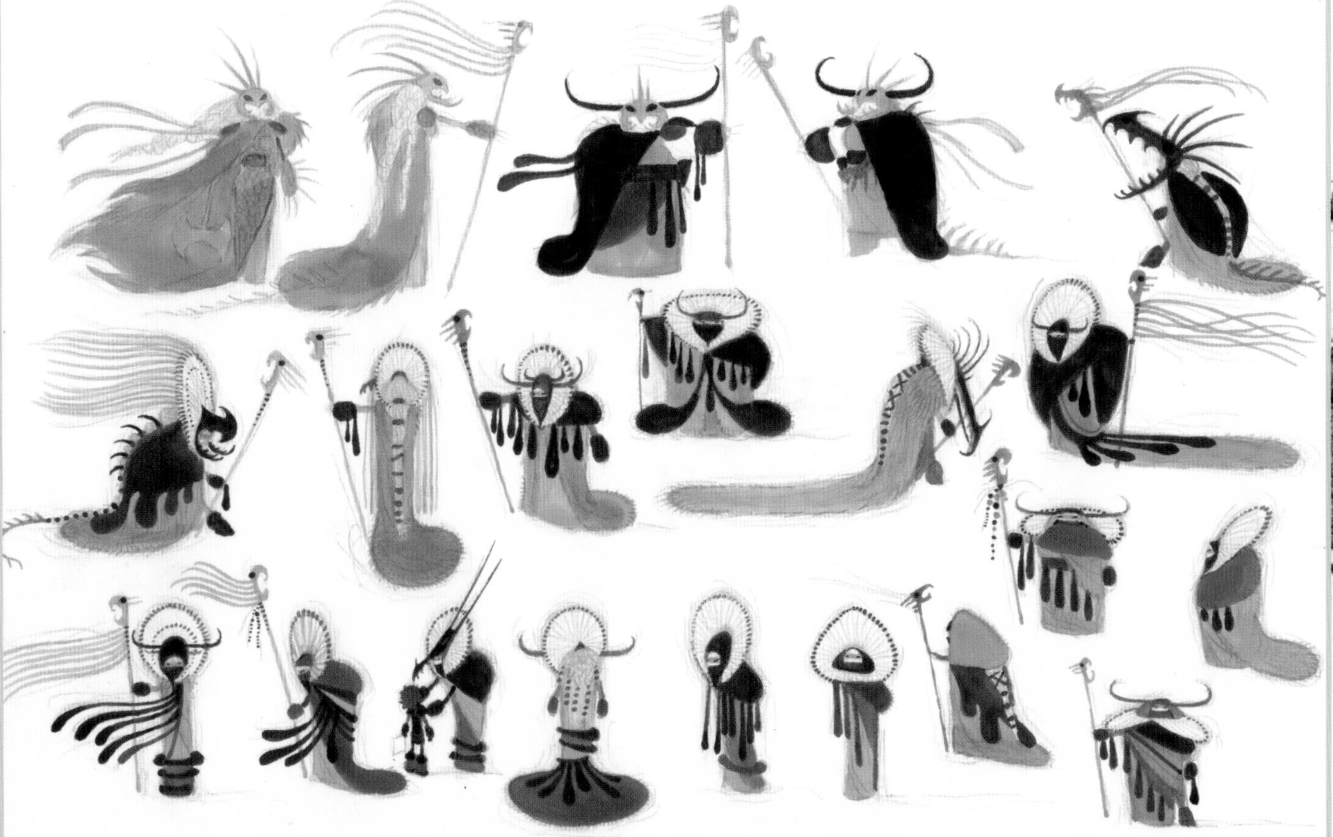

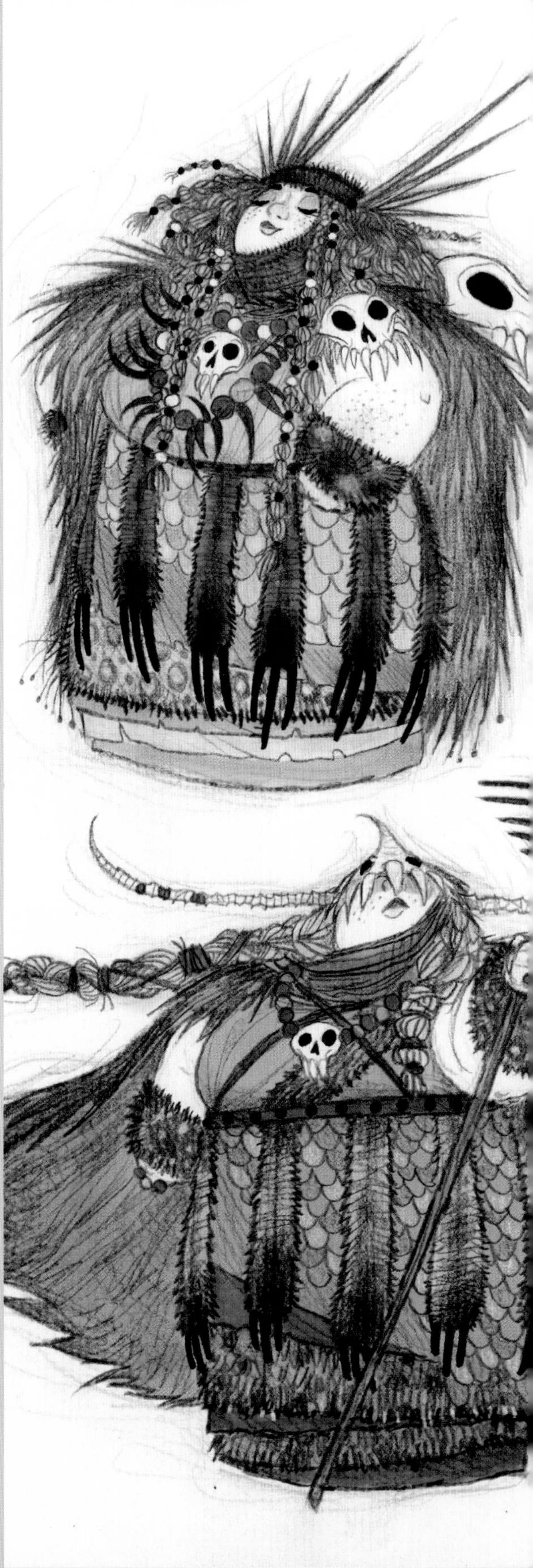

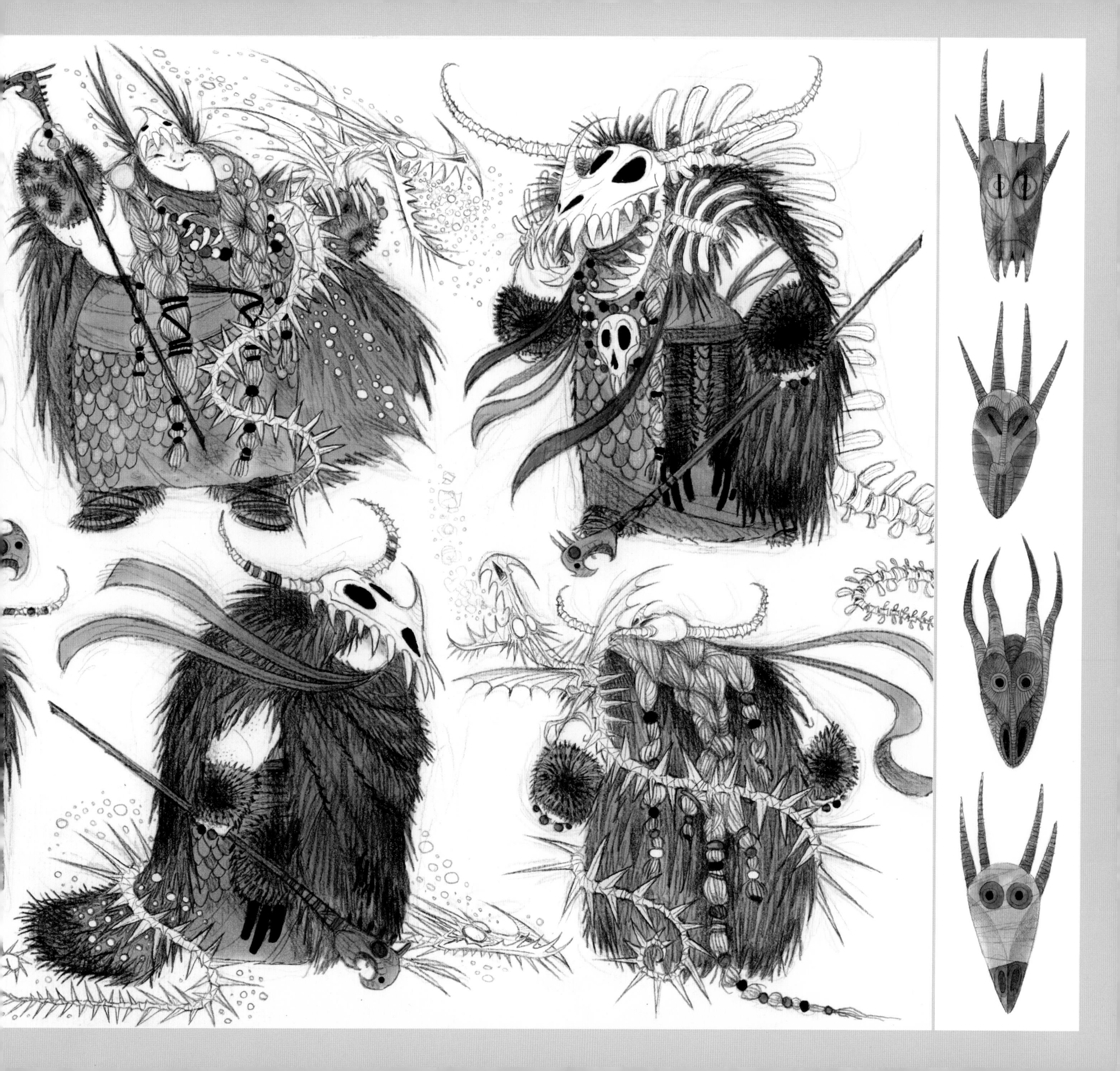

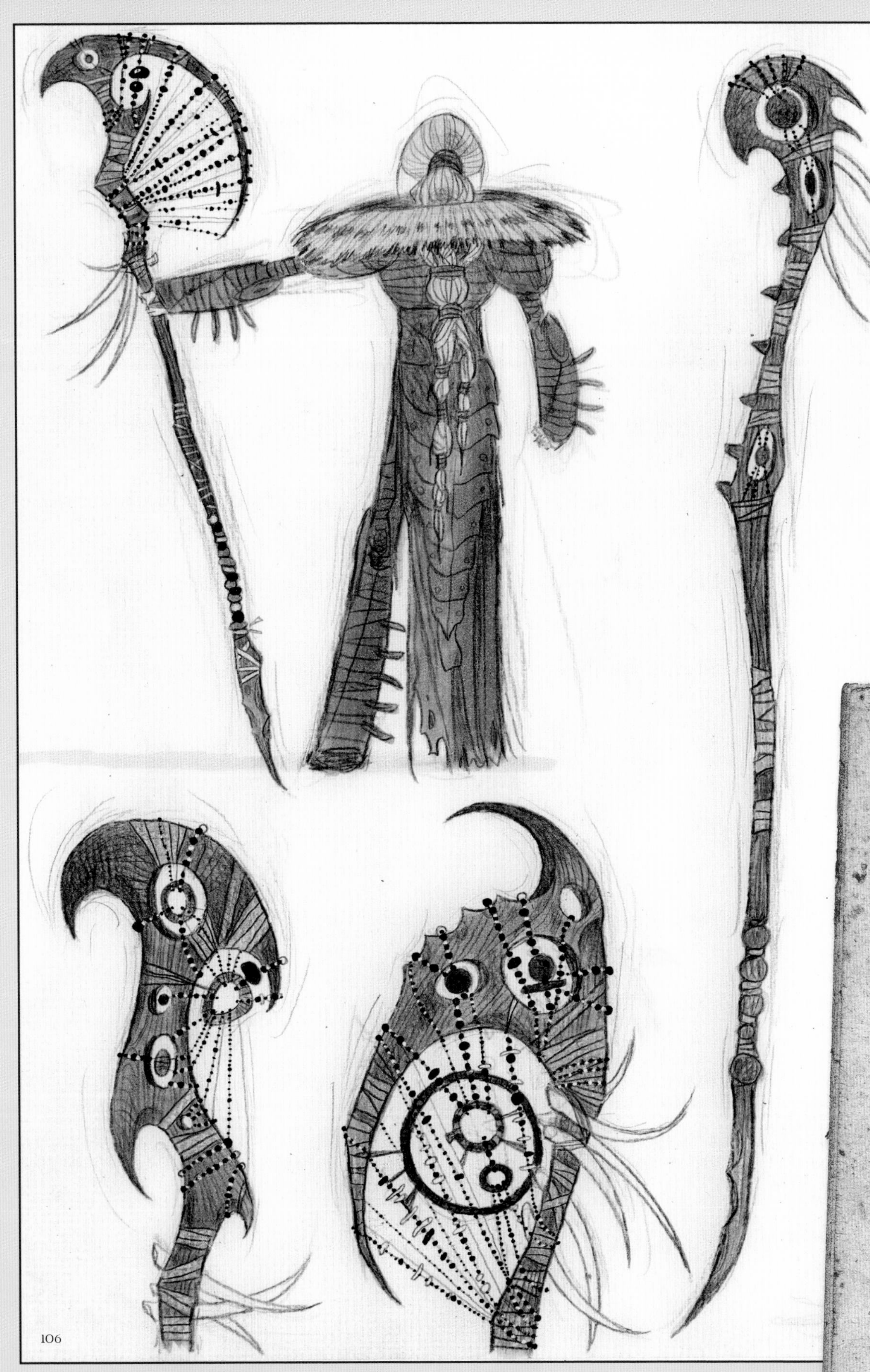

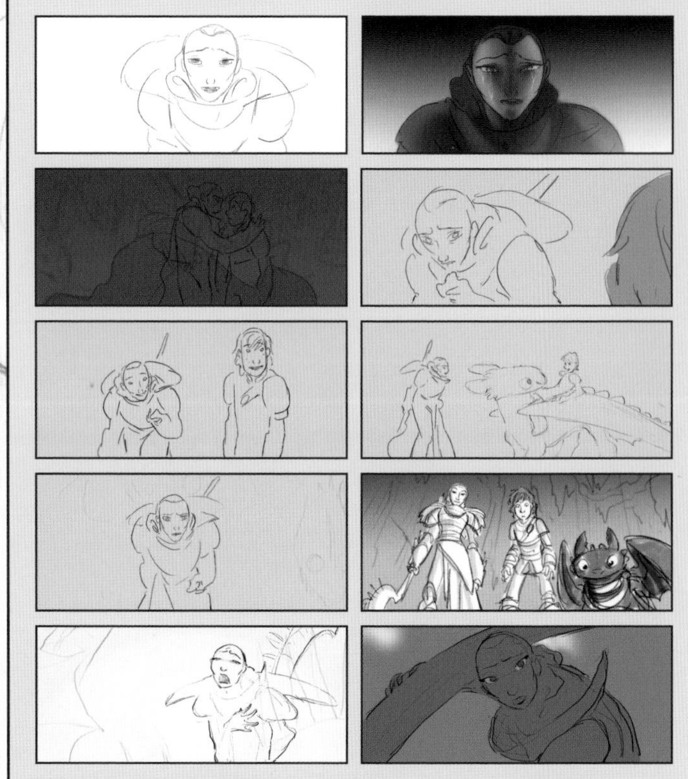

ABOVE: Storyboards ✦ *Tron Mai, Bolhem Bouchiba, Alessandro Carloni, Johane Matte*
LEFT: Valka's Staff ✦ *Nico Marlet* ✦ *pencil & marker*
BELOW: Film Frame

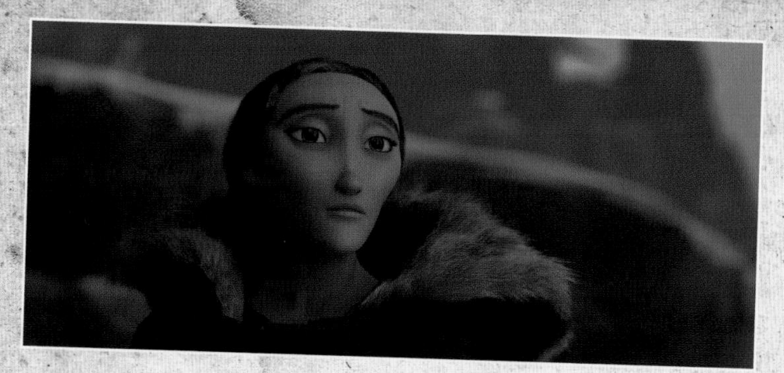

# Mother Issue

Over the course of development and early production, Valka certainly evolved as a character, but in every version she was inspired by the Jane Goodall's and Diane Fossey's of the world who studied and protected primates. Valka is no different. In a time when Vikings were at war with dragons, Valka saw them as something more than the enemy. She saw them as equals and she dedicated her life to protecting them when no one else would.

It takes a person of great character to be so selfless, especially when that person is a woman in a male-dominated society. And what makes Valka even more layered is that she's also the mother of a son she hasn't seen in twenty years. Even so, she quickly realizes she and Hiccup are not so different. They share a deep bond in their love of dragons. In Valka, the director has created one of the most complicated and interesting female heroines I've ever seen in film.

*—Gregg Taylor, head of feature development, DreamWorks Animation*

We started developing Valka in animation before we knew exactly how she would look. At first she looked a little more like a witch in disguise; and for a while, she had a kind of scarecrow look. Nico Marlet did many versions of her costume, which needed to look like a medieval warrior who didn't have access to any metal or advanced tools and needed to be made out of leather or animal skin. We pushed her design to such an extreme point that we needed to back off a little bit to find the warmth in the character.

We needed to sell the idea that she was a character who has lived among dragons for twenty years. We started thinking about Tarzan and Mowgli as prototypes. But they were taken away as children and Valka was twenty when she went to live with the dragons. We had to consider: Had Valka forgotten how to function socially in the human world? Had she started to copy dragon behavior? Or was she somebody who was completely human but just a good dragon rider?

In the end, through this process of trial and error, James Baxter, the supervising animator, and his team managed to make her look as off-kilter and socially awkward as possible, while retaining a crucial sense of appeal. The audience experiences the movie through Hiccup and the idea that all of a sudden he is standing in front of his mother, which is so powerful that you want this character to have some warmth and tenderness. We wanted the audience to fall in love with Valka, but we also needed to maintain the pivotal story conflict.

*—Simon Otto, head of character animation*

Valka was a marvellous character to light. She is introduced to the audience in her warrior attire and is almost inhuman with gaping black holes for eyes. We keep the light behind her to increase the tension. Then as Valka and Hiccup face-off above the clouds we light her very dramatically with hard light and dark shadows. When Hiccup finds himself face to face with Valka in the cave we use very little light on Valka and mostly rim her, making her feel threatening up until the moment she removes her mask and suddenly, as we see her face, we wrap soft romantic light around her and reveal her to be Hiccup's beautiful mother. Her face has sharp angles and strong planes, making her one of the most stylized characters in the film. While she was being designed there was concern that it would be difficult to light her attractively, but when the character came together she turned out to be one of the easiest characters to flatter with light. She was a real surprise.

*—Dave Walvoord, visual effects supervisor*

RIGHT: Valka Masks ✦ *Nico Marlet* ✦ *pencil & marker*
BELOW: Valka ✦ *Nico Marlet* ✦ *pencil & marker*
FAR LEFT: Rune ✦ *Kirsten Kawamura*

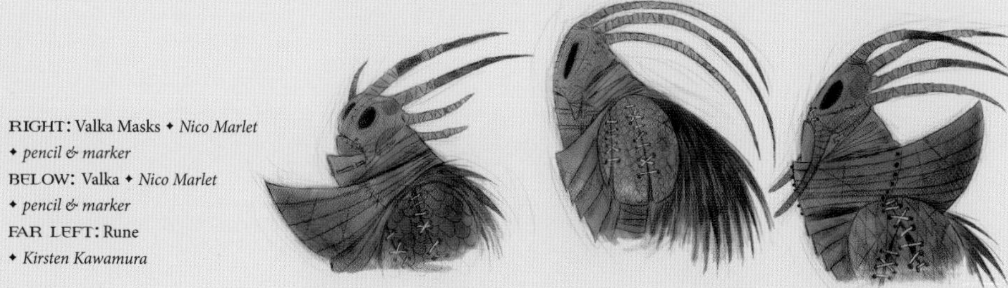

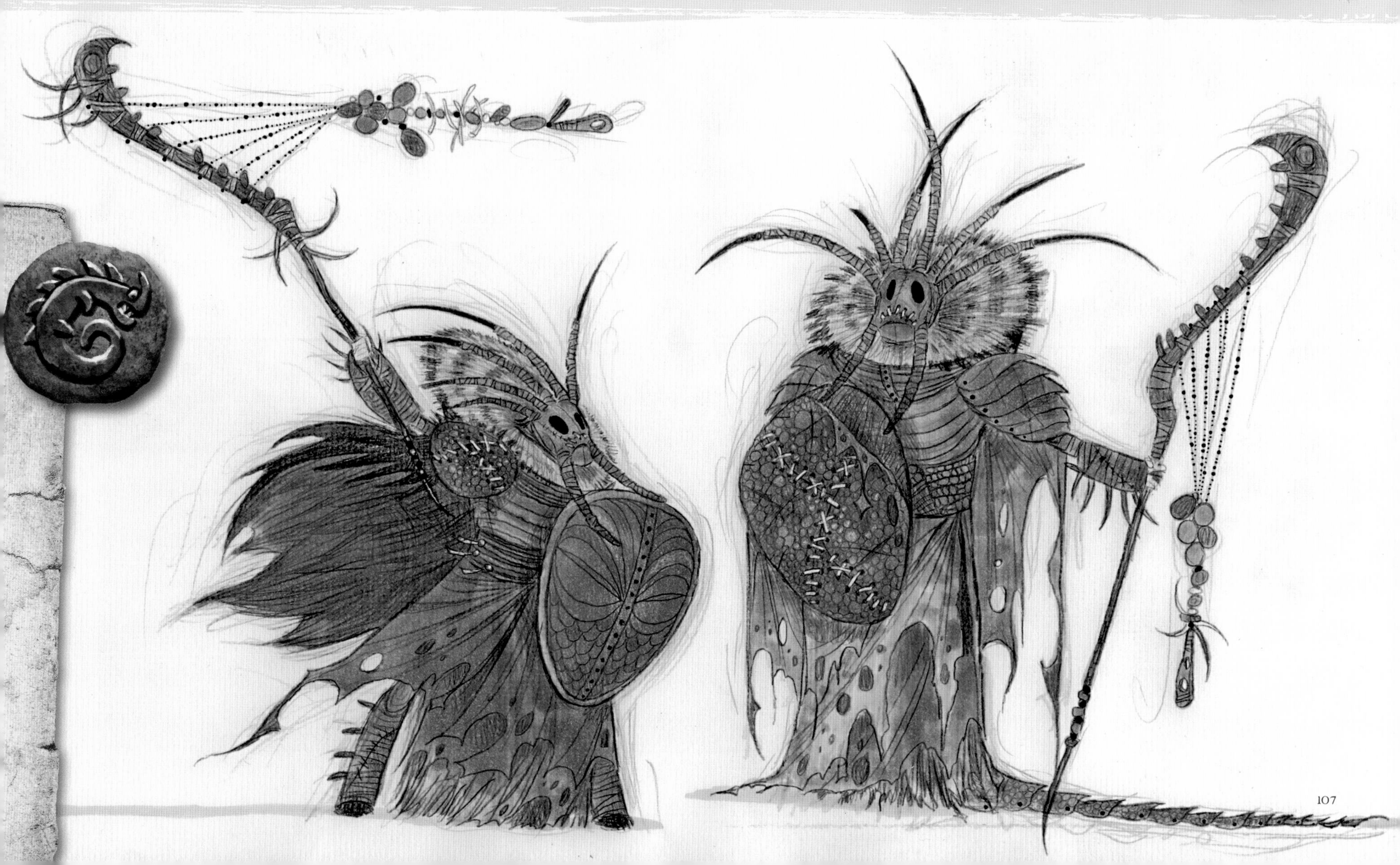

# Nest of Dragons

Here we are inside Valka's mountain, which is created from natural hot springs that were protected and fortified by the Bewilderbeast with massive ice floes. It creates a lush greenhouse, a perfect nest for dragons in the Arctic. It was important to bring Hiccup to the understanding that other people have been in contact with dragons and have a powerful knowledge of them. This scene is the turning point in the story where Hiccup discovers his mother and how much he has in common with her. We wanted to plant this idea that both Hiccup and his mother are fighting for a similar cause.

*—Pierre-Olivier Vincent, production designer*

The oasis presented the challenge of trying to convey an enormous, lush, and humid environment enshrined in the frigid ice columns created by the Bewilderbeast. We had to convincingly combine massive ice structures with hundreds of waterfalls and tropical ferns and moss.

*—Paolo deGuzman, head of surfacing*

BELOW: Film Frames
BOTTOM: Oasis • *Pierre-Olivier Vincent*

OPPOSITE TOP: Storyboards • *Johane Matte*
OPPOSITE BOTTOM LEFT: Color Key • *Woonyoung Jung* • Model • *Shannon Thomas* • OPPOSITE BOTTOM: Color Key • *Woonyoung Jung*

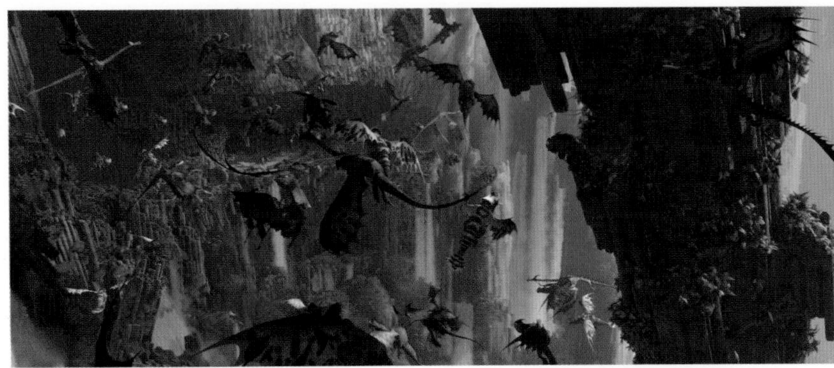

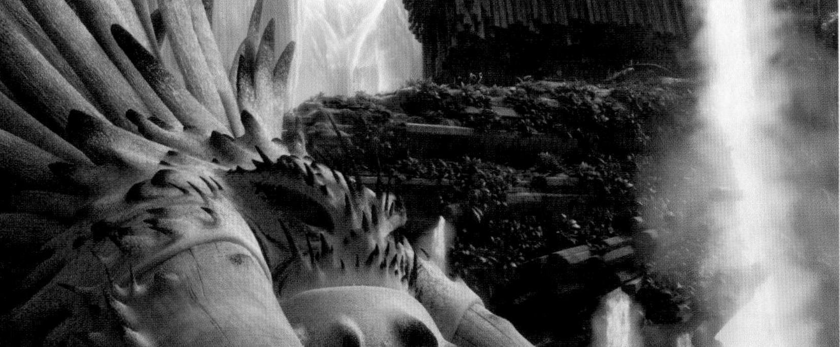

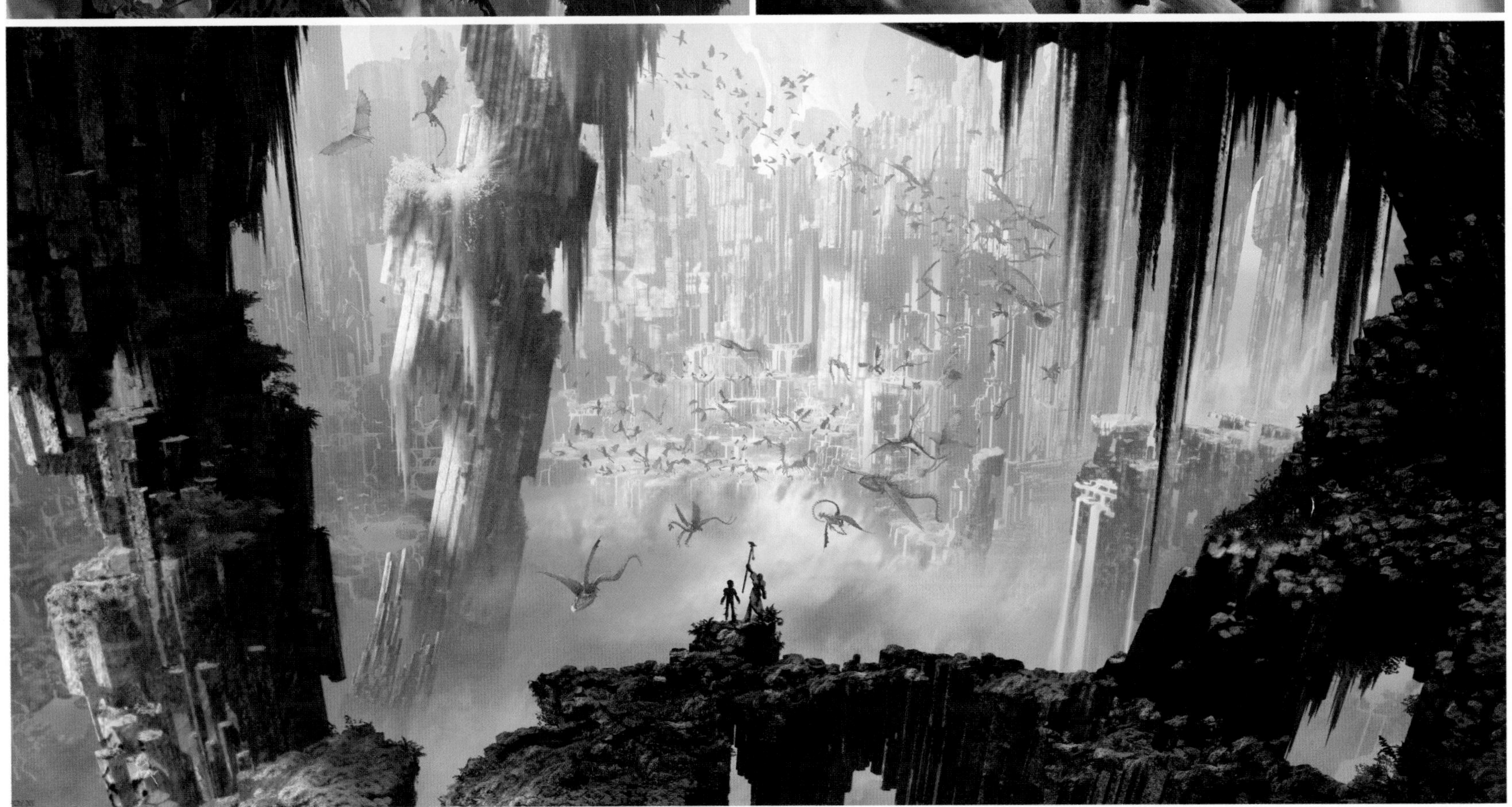

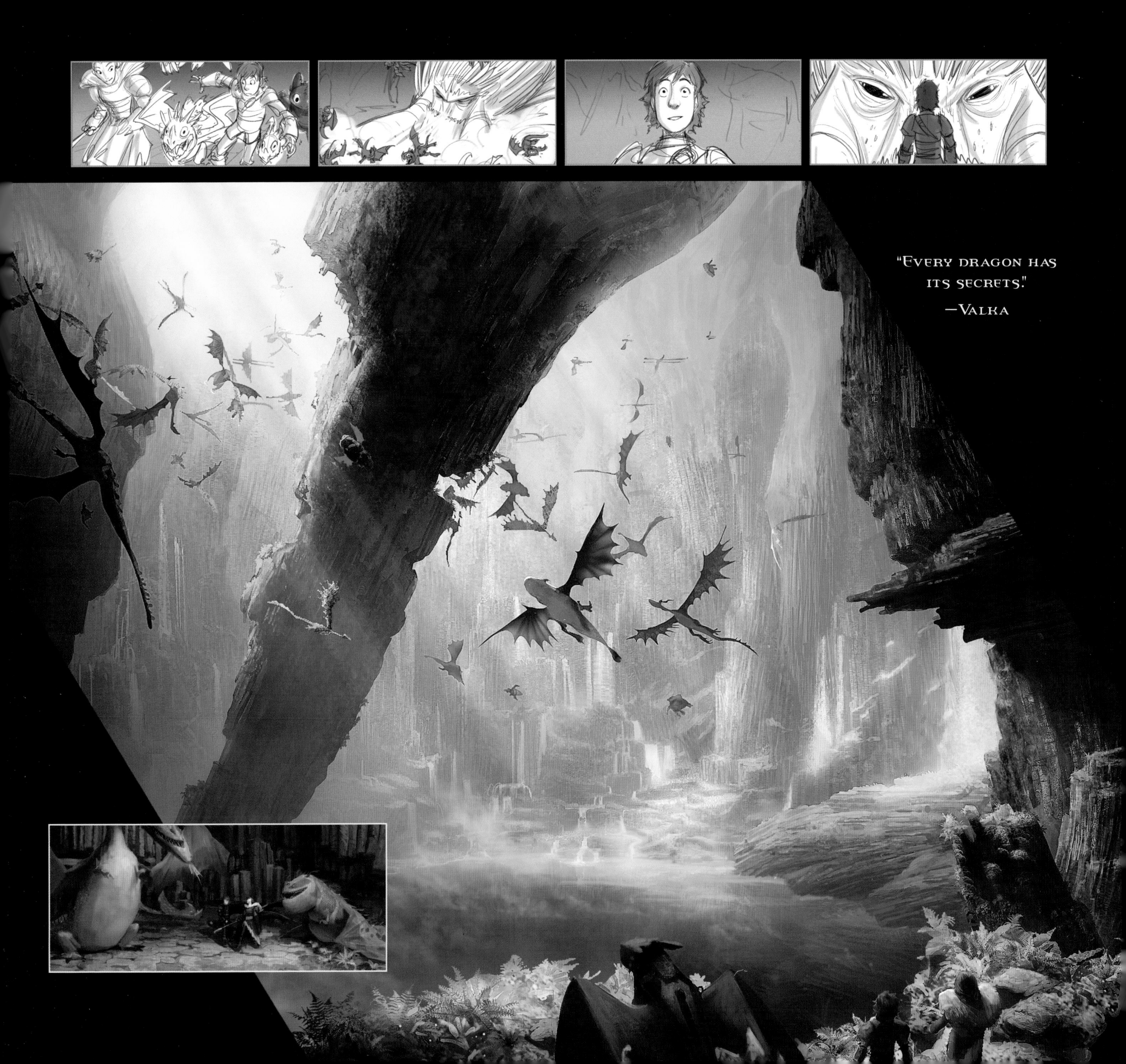

"Every dragon has its secrets."
—Valka

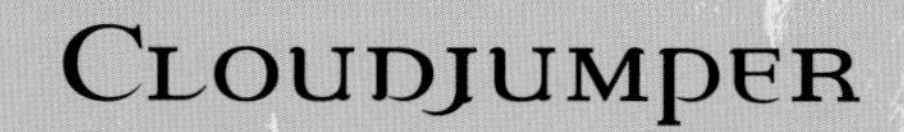

# Cloudjumper

Cloudjumper was designed to be surprising. We knew that we would have scenes in which Toothless and he would fly together, so we were looking for a bold statement to help differentiate them, even at a distance. I liked the idea of two sets of wings that form an X in the sky. They could be stowed into one another so as to create a surprise reveal. Personality-wise we thought of Cloudjumper as a bit of an elitist within the Arctic dragon colony—Valka's chosen one—and somewhat stuffy and mature to contrast with Toothless's youthful energy and ignorance of rank. His animal references are a Great Dane mixed with an owl. It makes for a unique and interesting dragon.

*—Dean DeBlois, director*

TOP RIGHT: Cloudjumper Painting ✦ *ZhaoPing Wei* ✦ Model ✦ *Ming Hao Yu*
ABOVE: Cloudjumper Fire Pattern ✦ *Nicolas Weis*
BELOW: Cloudjumper Studies ✦ *Nico Marlet* ✦ *pencil & marker*
BELOW (INSETS): Head Studies ✦ *Jean-Francois Rey*
OPPOSITE: Cloudjumper ✦ *Jean-Francois Rey*

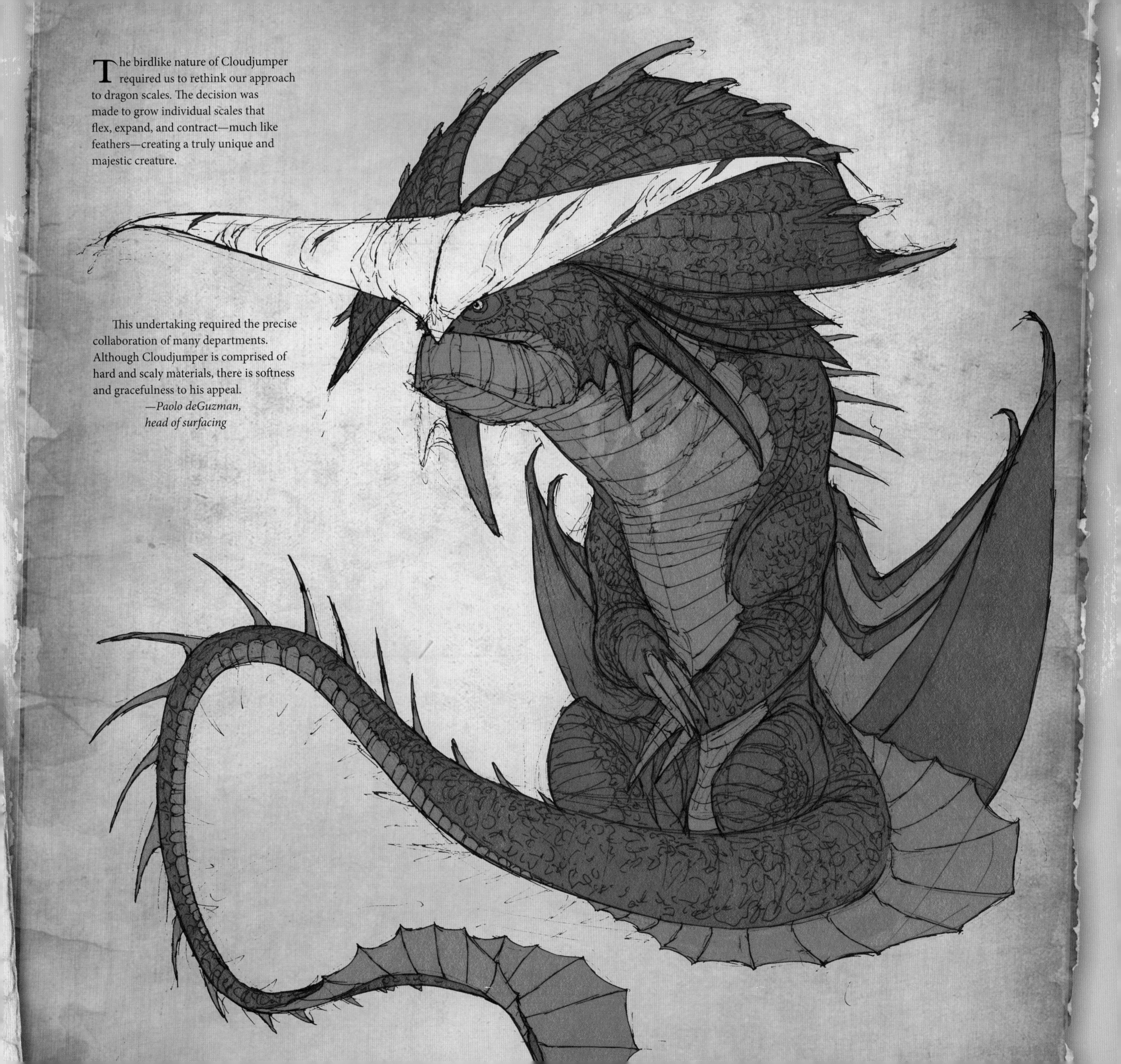

The birdlike nature of Cloudjumper required us to rethink our approach to dragon scales. The decision was made to grow individual scales that flex, expand, and contract—much like feathers—creating a truly unique and majestic creature.

This undertaking required the precise collaboration of many departments. Although Cloudjumper is comprised of hard and scaly materials, there is softness and gracefulness to his appeal.

—*Paolo deGuzman, head of surfacing*

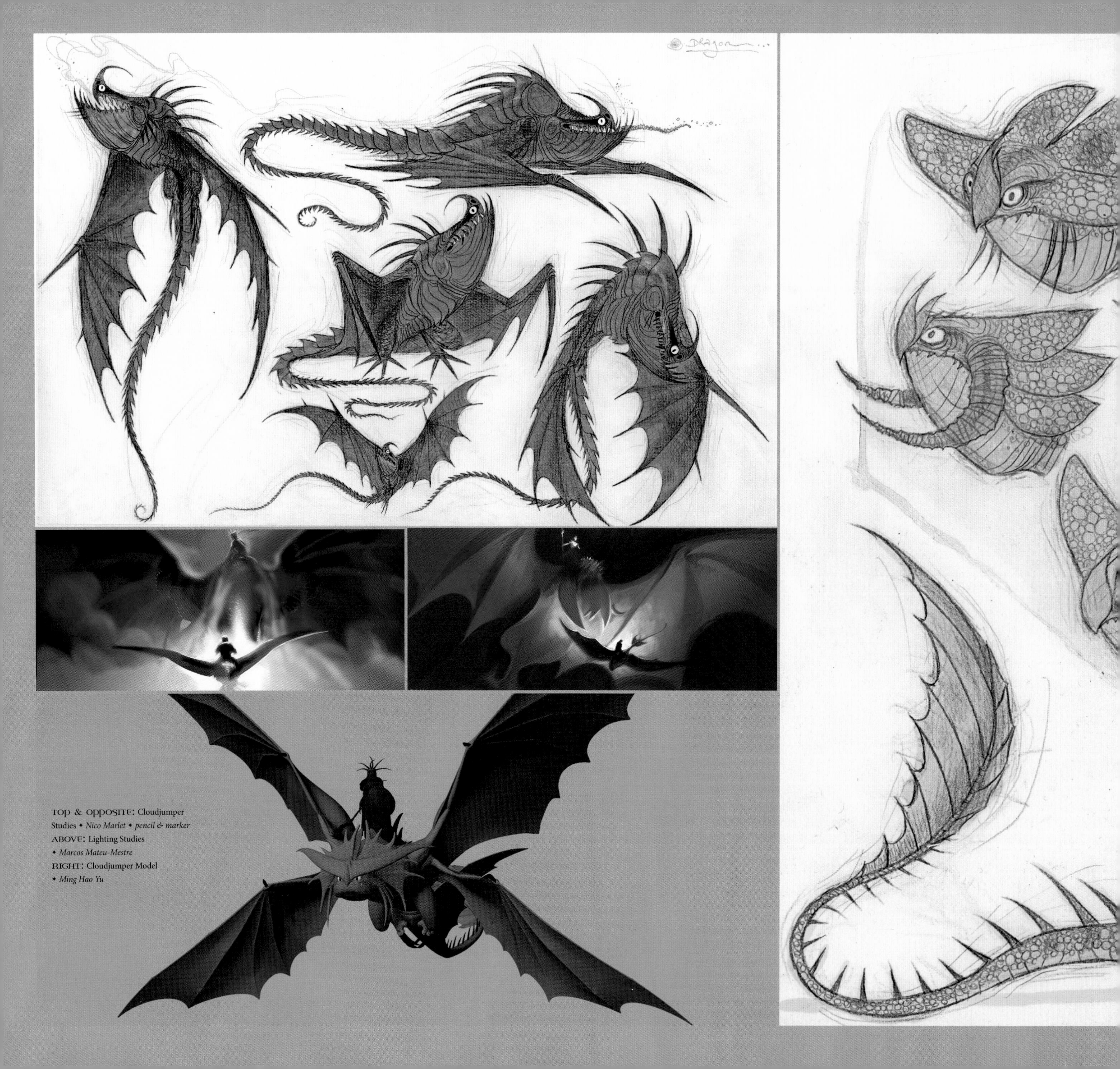


TOP & OPPOSITE: Cloudjumper Studies ✦ *Nico Marlet* ✦ *pencil & marker*
ABOVE: Lighting Studies ✦ *Marcos Mateu-Mestre*
RIGHT: Cloudjumper Model ✦ *Ming Hao Yu*

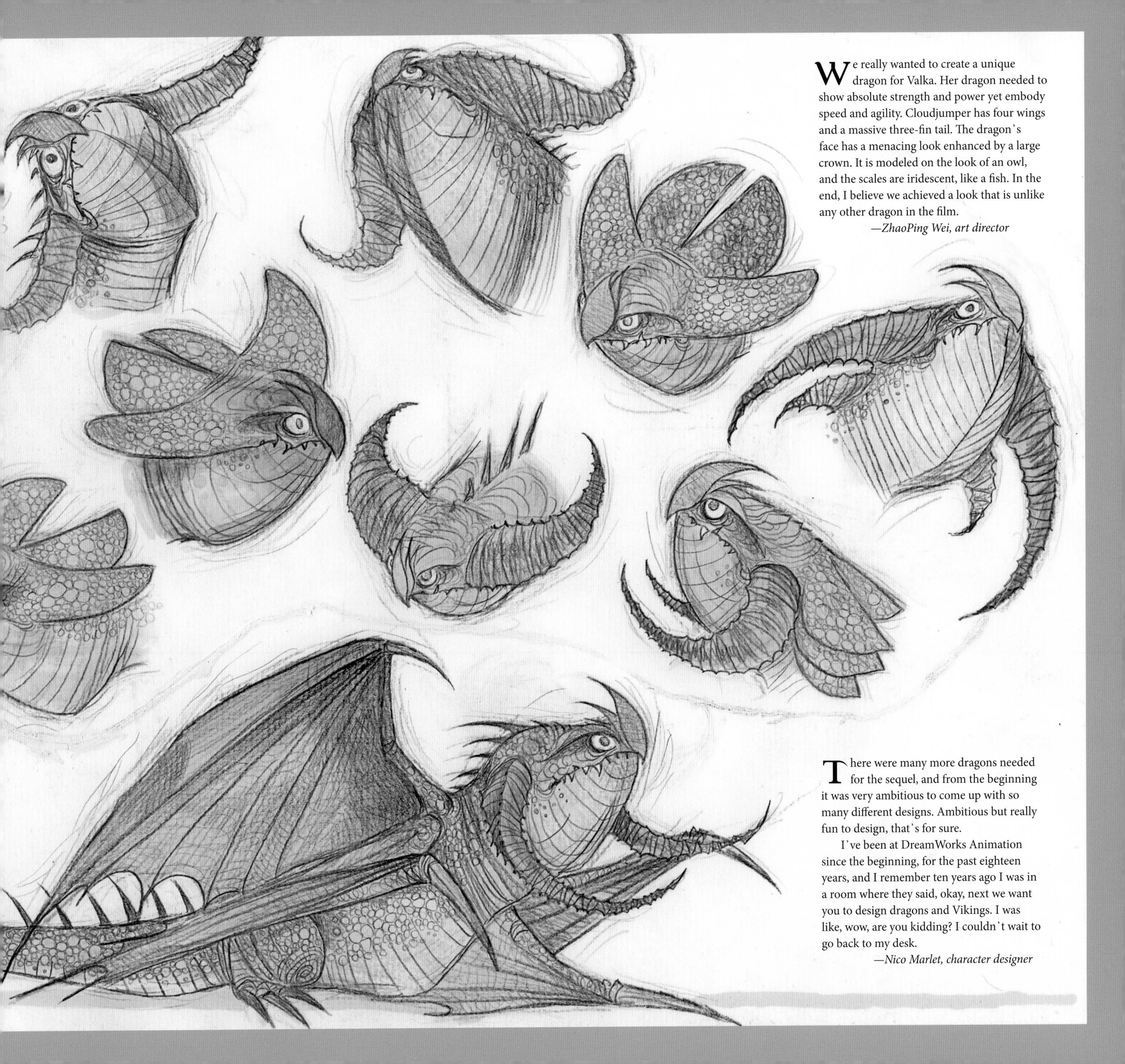

We really wanted to create a unique dragon for Valka. Her dragon needed to show absolute strength and power yet embody speed and agility. Cloudjumper has four wings and a massive three-fin tail. The dragon's face has a menacing look enhanced by a large crown. It is modeled on the look of an owl, and the scales are iridescent, like a fish. In the end, I believe we achieved a look that is unlike any other dragon in the film.

*—ZhaoPing Wei, art director*

There were many more dragons needed for the sequel, and from the beginning it was very ambitious to come up with so many different designs. Ambitious but really fun to design, that's for sure.

I've been at DreamWorks Animation since the beginning, for the past eighteen years, and I remember ten years ago I was in a room where they said, okay, next we want you to design dragons and Vikings. I was like, wow, are you kidding? I couldn't wait to go back to my desk.

*—Nico Marlet, character designer*

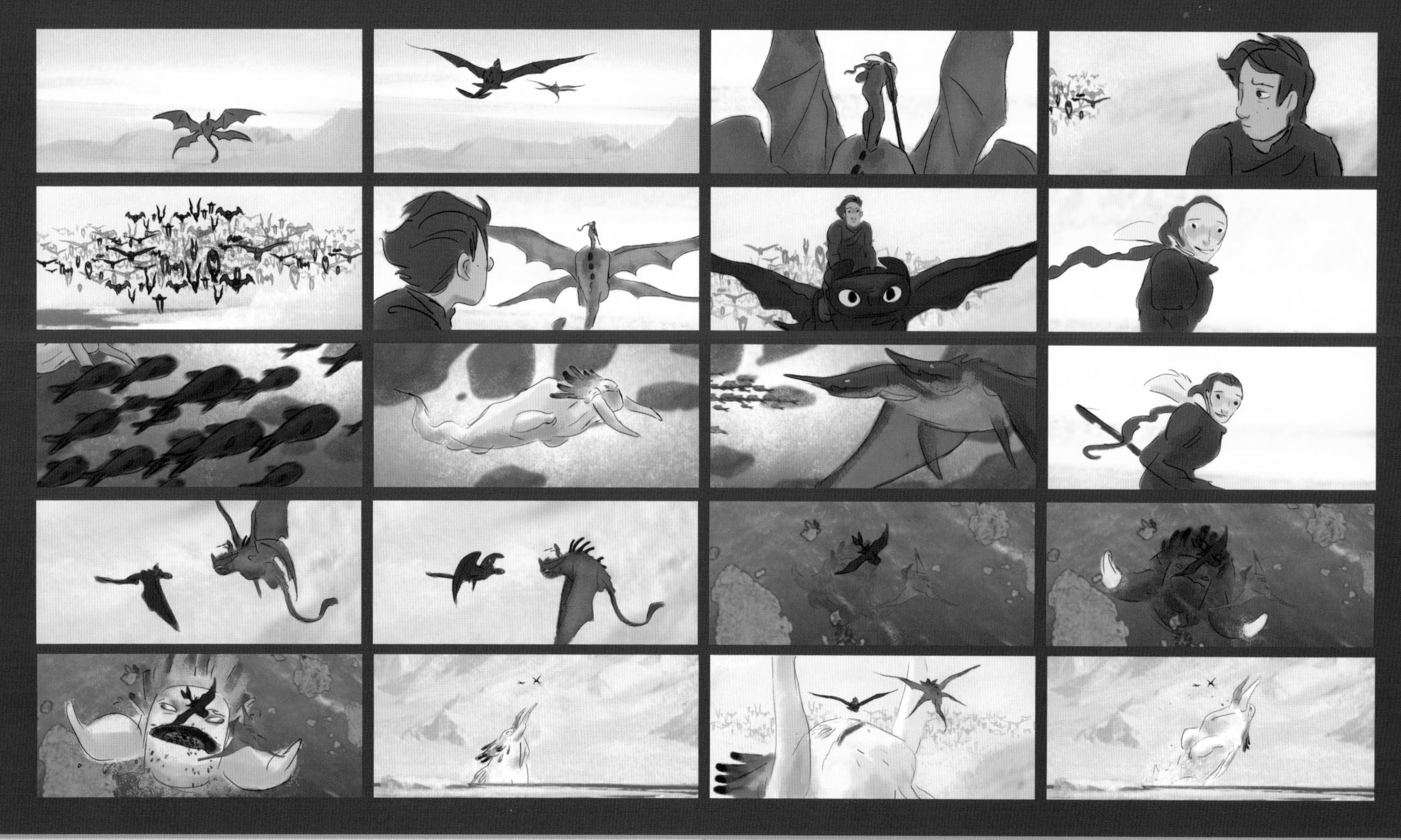

# World of Dragons

We wanted to create believable creatures that feel familiar to us, like our own pets but sized up considerably. Our main challenge was how we would make these creatures realistic and believable. We accomplished this by referencing real animals for each dragon and by adding a lot more structure and a sense of flesh and bone to each of the body shapes, which greatly improved the surfacing and texturing. The uniqueness of our movie is that we had the freedom to create a stylized dragon world that had a sense of humor and that could break free from the restraints of a live-action film.

—*Simon Otto, head of character animation*

In order to achieve the depth and numbers of the dragons in Valka's sanctuary, a modular system was devised, where a variety of horns, spikes, nose pieces, and tails were mixed-and-matched to fit into several different body types. To further give the illusion of even more dragons, several simple color variations were created for all the variants.

—*Paolo deGuzman, head of surfacing*

ABOVE & OPPOSITE: Storyboards ✦ *Tron Mai*
RIGHT: Hiccup Dragon Logo ✦ *Nico Marlet*
FAR RIGHT: Dragon Head Sketches ✦ *Nico Marlet* ✦ *pencil*
OPPOSITE BOTTOM: Dragon Heads ✦ *Nico Marlet* ✦ *pencil & marker*

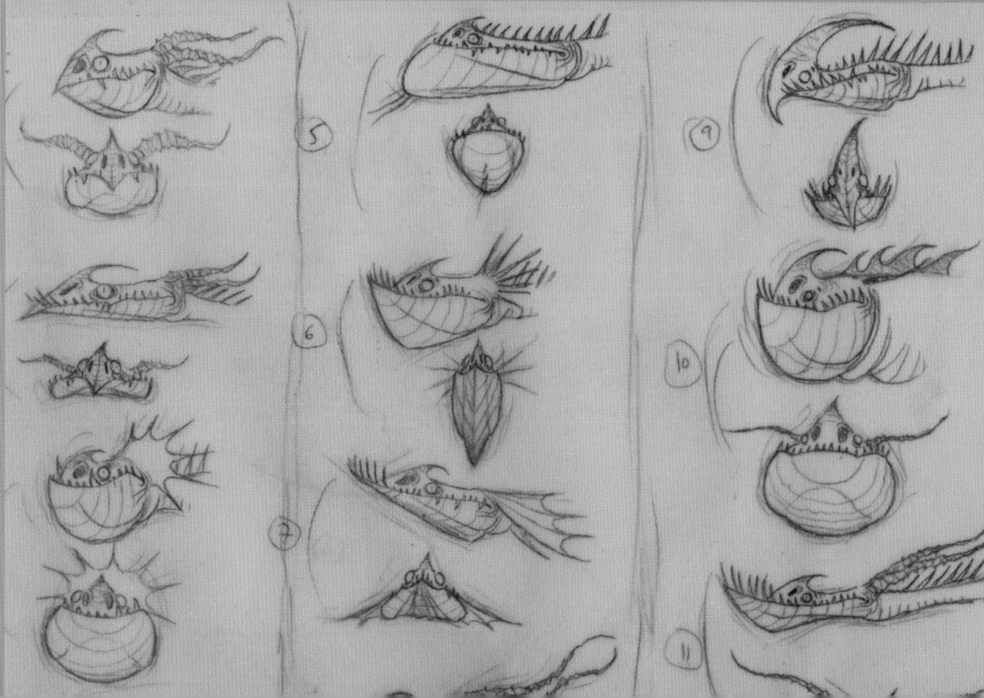

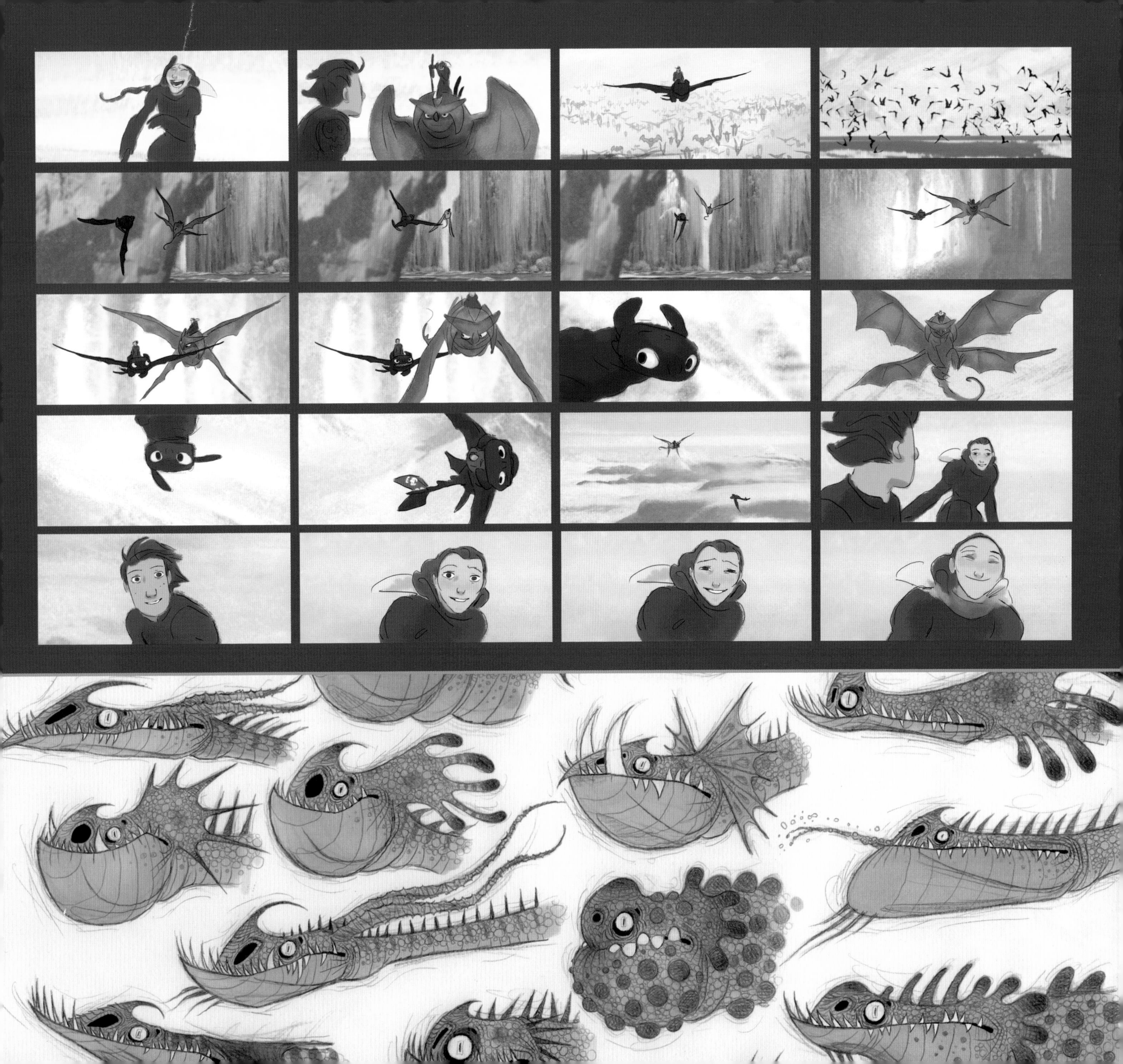

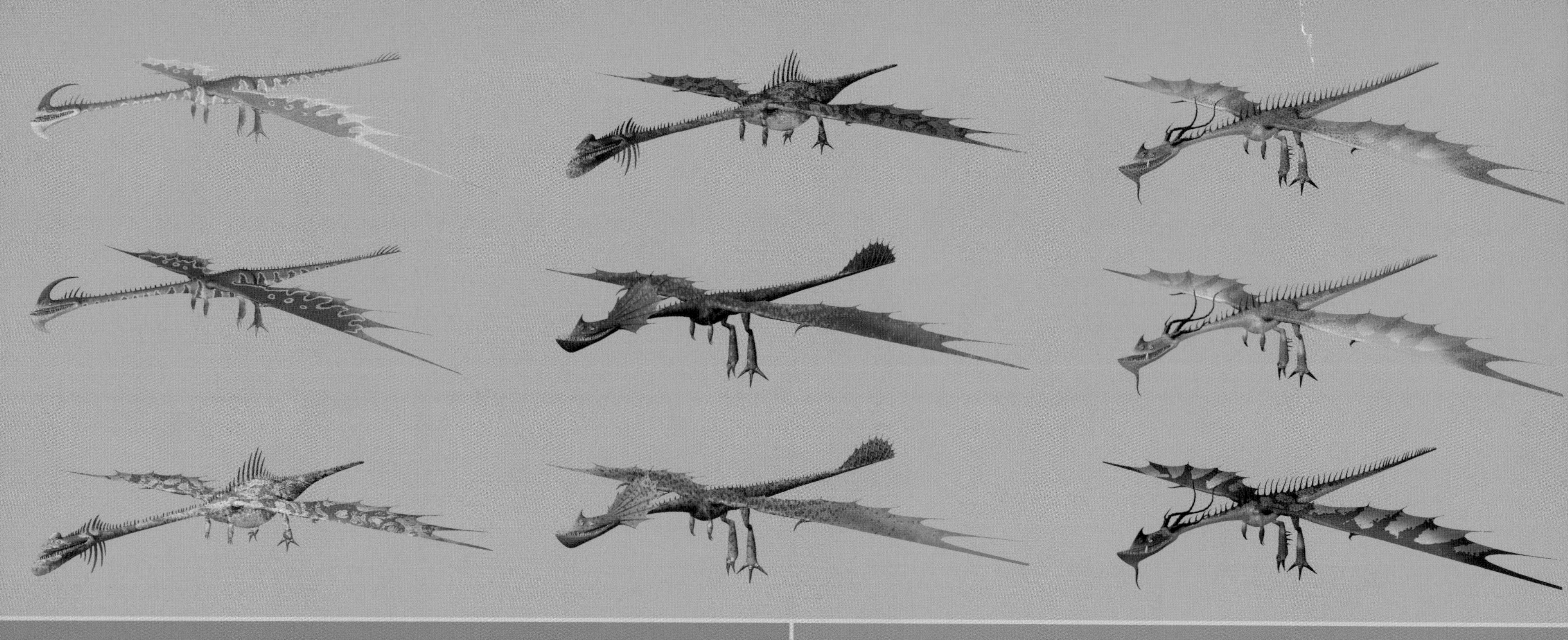

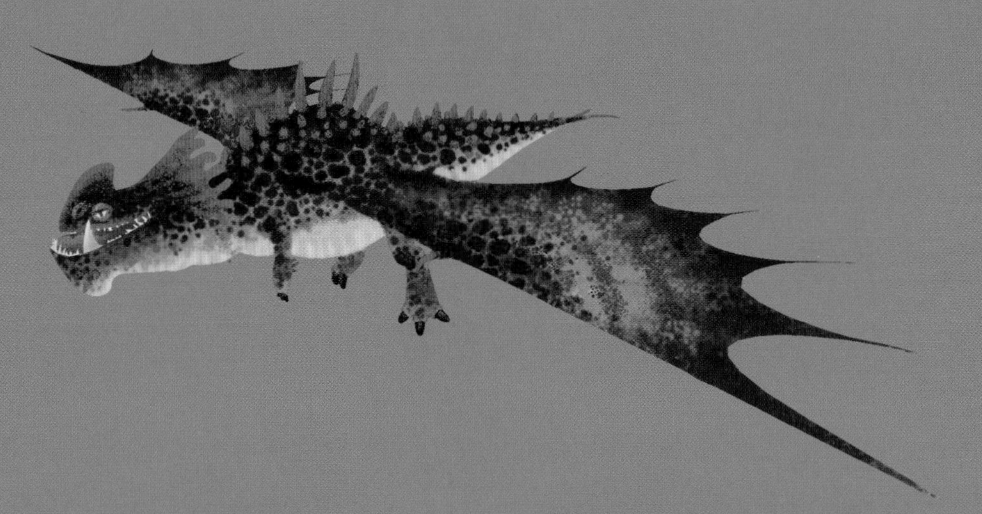

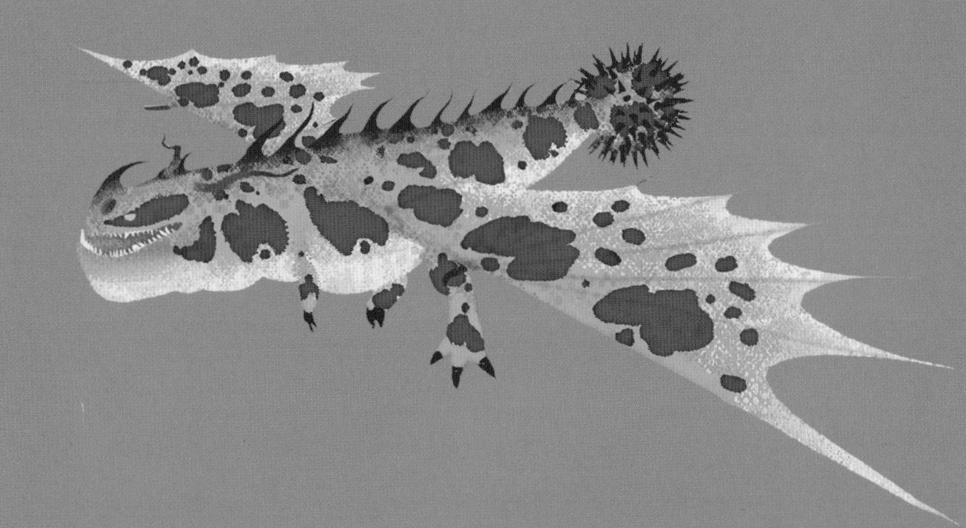

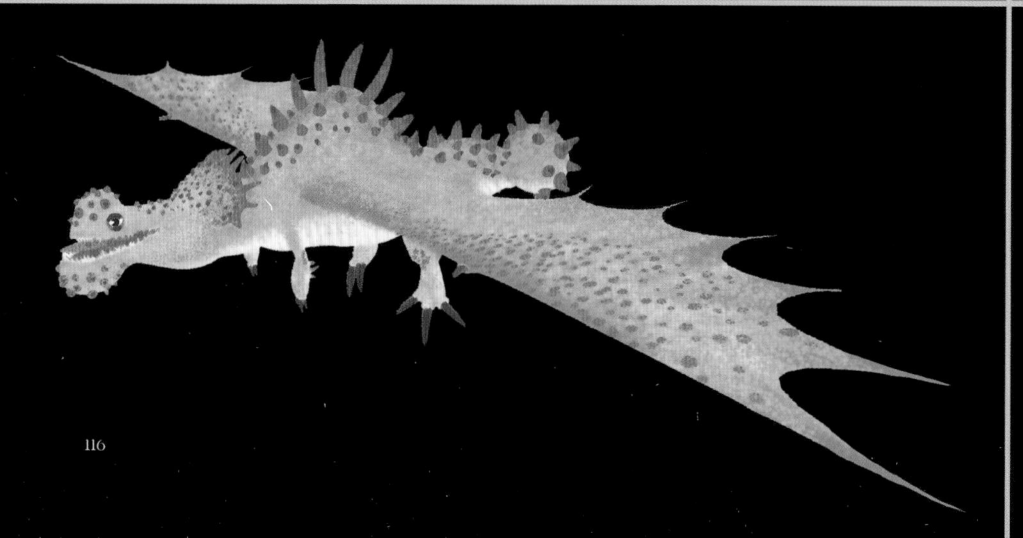

Due to Hiccup's travels and experiences in the sequel we wanted to broaden the variety of dragons. In order to achieve this we came up with a modular dragon design system. Think of it as an à la carte menu to build your own unique dragon with multiple choices for claws, spikes, wings, and even body types. The art department used this idea to design the physical elements of a dragon that then could be mixed and matched together to create a new breed of dragon when it was needed. Coupling this with surfacing treatments, we were able to provide large diverse crowds of dragons for important moments of the movie.

*—Kevin Ochs, character technical direction supervisor*

THIS PAGE: Dragon Coloring Variations • *ZhaoPing Wei* • Models • *Abraham Meneu Oset*
OPPOSITE: Seashocker Painting • *Pierre-Olivier Vincent* • Model • *Ming Hao Yu*
OPPOSITE BOTTOM LEFT: Rune • *Kirsten Kawamura*

# Seashocker Dragon

All of our designs for the dragons and their behavior patterns are essentially constructed through mixing and matching interesting characteristics from the animal world or from objects that surround us. We combined different animals and gave them various textures. So some dragons look like horned lizards, rhinos, pit bulls, parrots, or walruses, but may have the shell of a beetle or the skin of a snake. We also used the concept of trash cans, motorcycles, and helicopters for style, shape, and movement. We came up with personality characteristics and behavior patterns for all of our dragons. We researched all the elements that inspired us and studied them in great detail. Nothing was too far out of the box for us as long as we could relate to it in some way and recognize what it caricatured.

—*Simon Otto,*
*head of character animation*

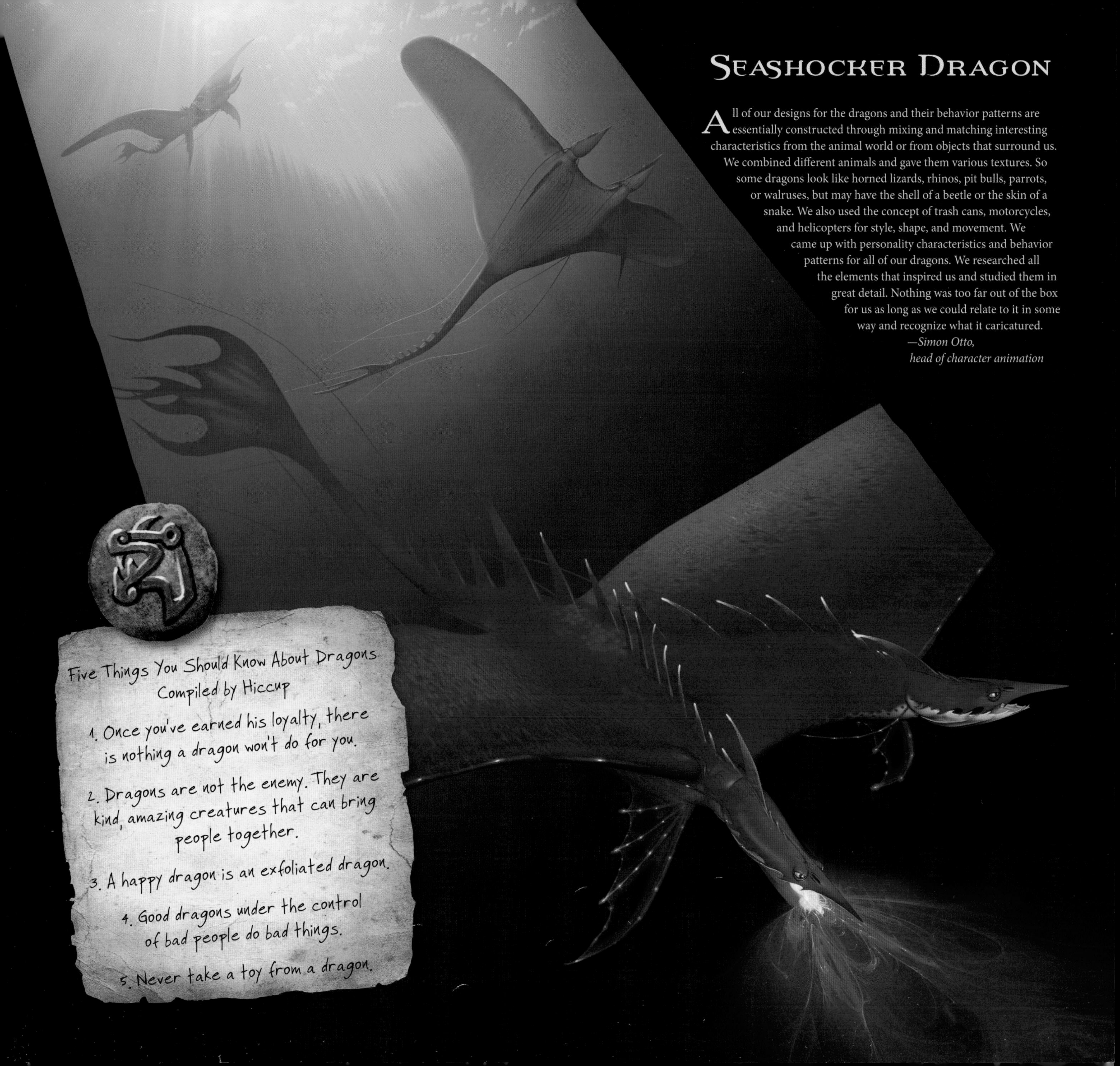

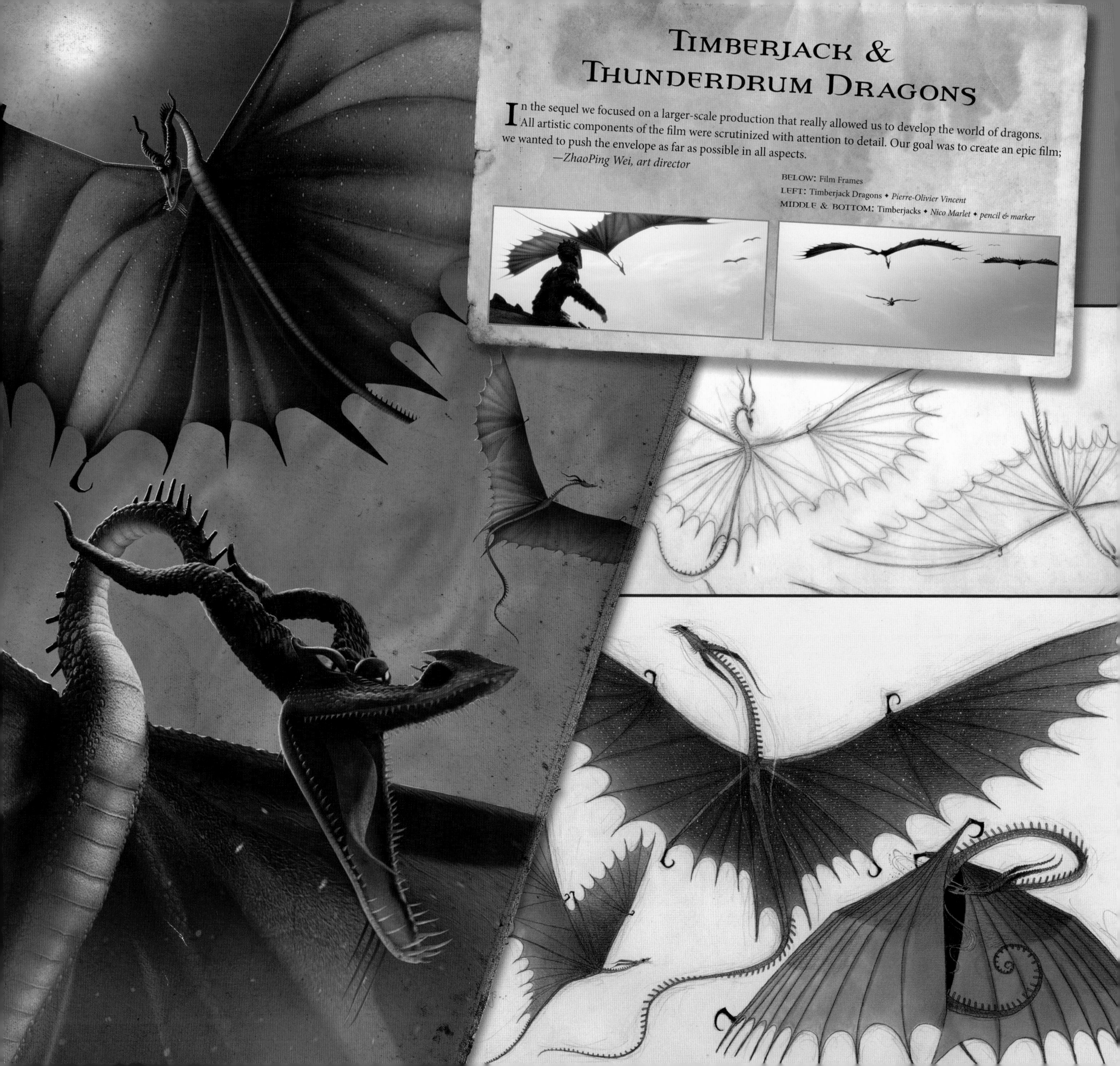

# Timberjack & Thunderdrum Dragons

In the sequel we focused on a larger-scale production that really allowed us to develop the world of dragons. All artistic components of the film were scrutinized with attention to detail. Our goal was to create an epic film; we wanted to push the envelope as far as possible in all aspects.

—*ZhaoPing Wei, art director*

BELOW: Film Frames
LEFT: Timberjack Dragons ✦ *Pierre-Olivier Vincent*
MIDDLE & BOTTOM: Timberjacks ✦ *Nico Marlet* ✦ *pencil & marker*

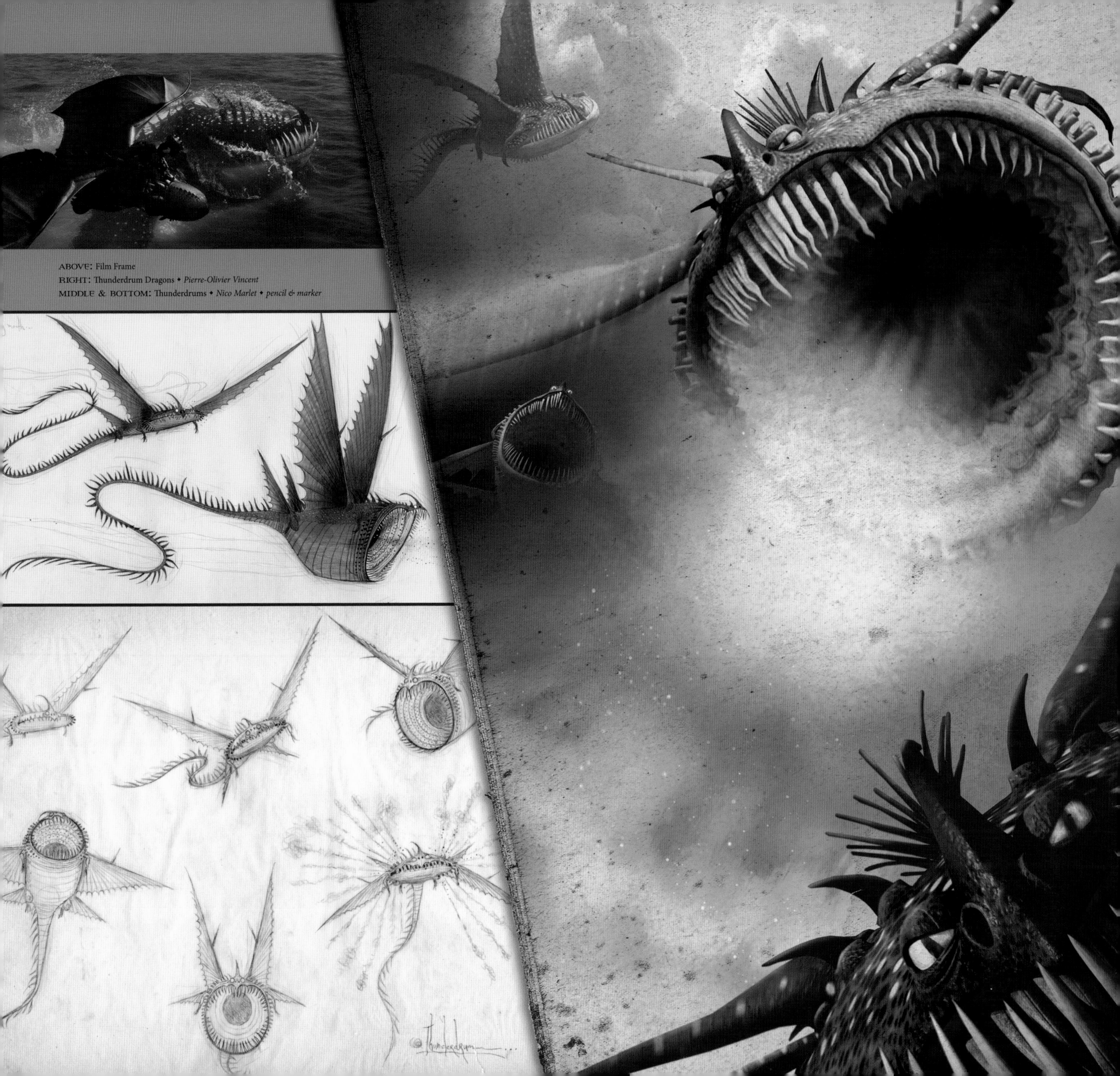


ABOVE: Film Frame
RIGHT: Thunderdrum Dragons • *Pierre-Olivier Vincent*
MIDDLE & BOTTOM: Thunderdrums • *Nico Marlet* • *pencil & marker*

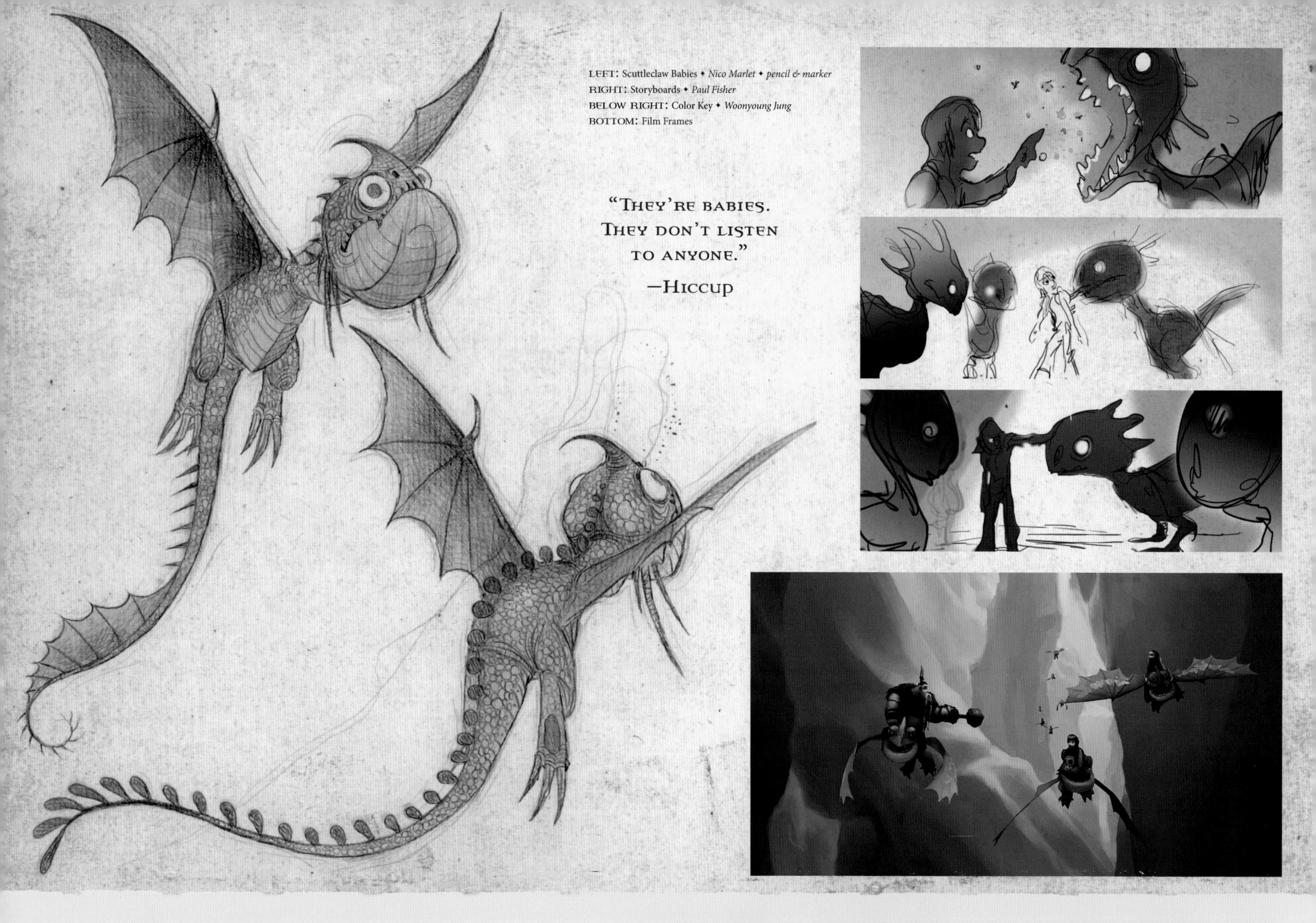

LEFT: Scuttleclaw Babies ✦ *Nico Marlet* ✦ *pencil & marker*
RIGHT: Storyboards ✦ *Paul Fisher*
BELOW RIGHT: Color Key ✦ *Woonyoung Jung*
BOTTOM: Film Frames

"They're babies. They don't listen to anyone."
—Hiccup

# Scuttleclaw Babies

Because the Scuttleclaw babies are so young, they are not submissive to the hypnotic power of the Bewilderbeast. They are in fact very disrespectful to their elders and don't really listen to anyone. We wanted them to look like cute, turbulent, adolescent dragons; therefore they have those big eyes and huge heads like toddlers. We were going for that look that toddlers sometimes have, where their heads are so big they look like they will just topple over. The babies are meant to be gawky, awkward, and not in control of themselves.

The Scuttleclaw babies are mostly comedic, so they needed to look a little bit off-balance and unfinished. We wanted them to look like they were still growing.

*—Pierre-Olivier Vincent, production designer*

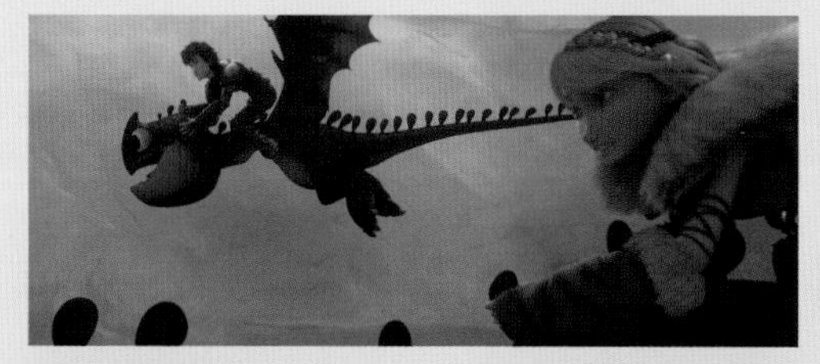

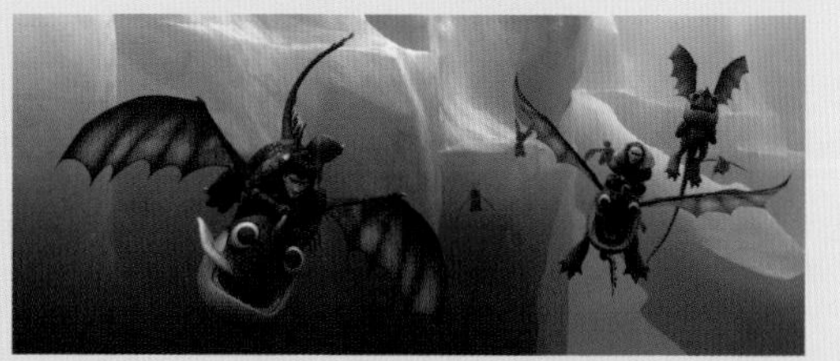

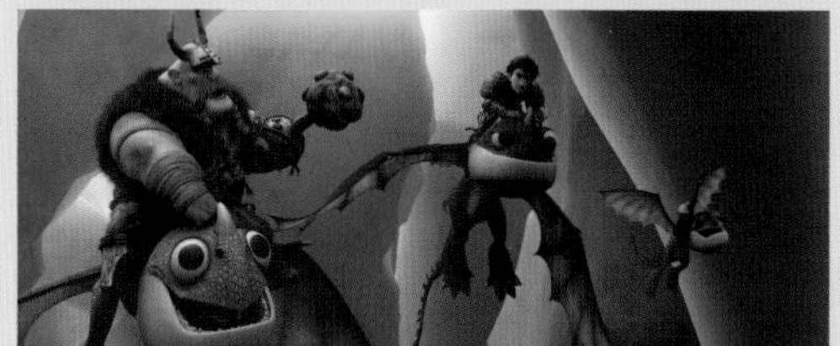

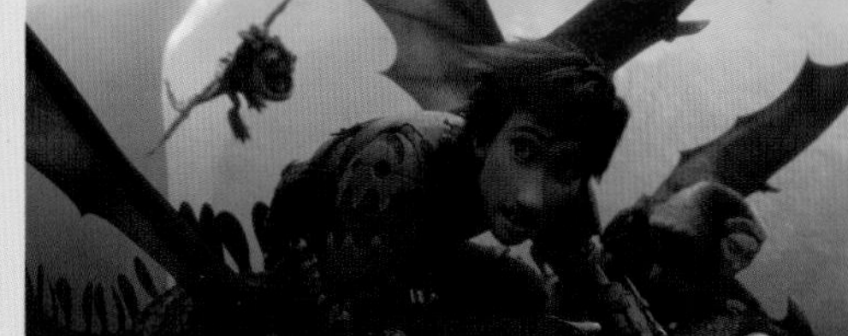

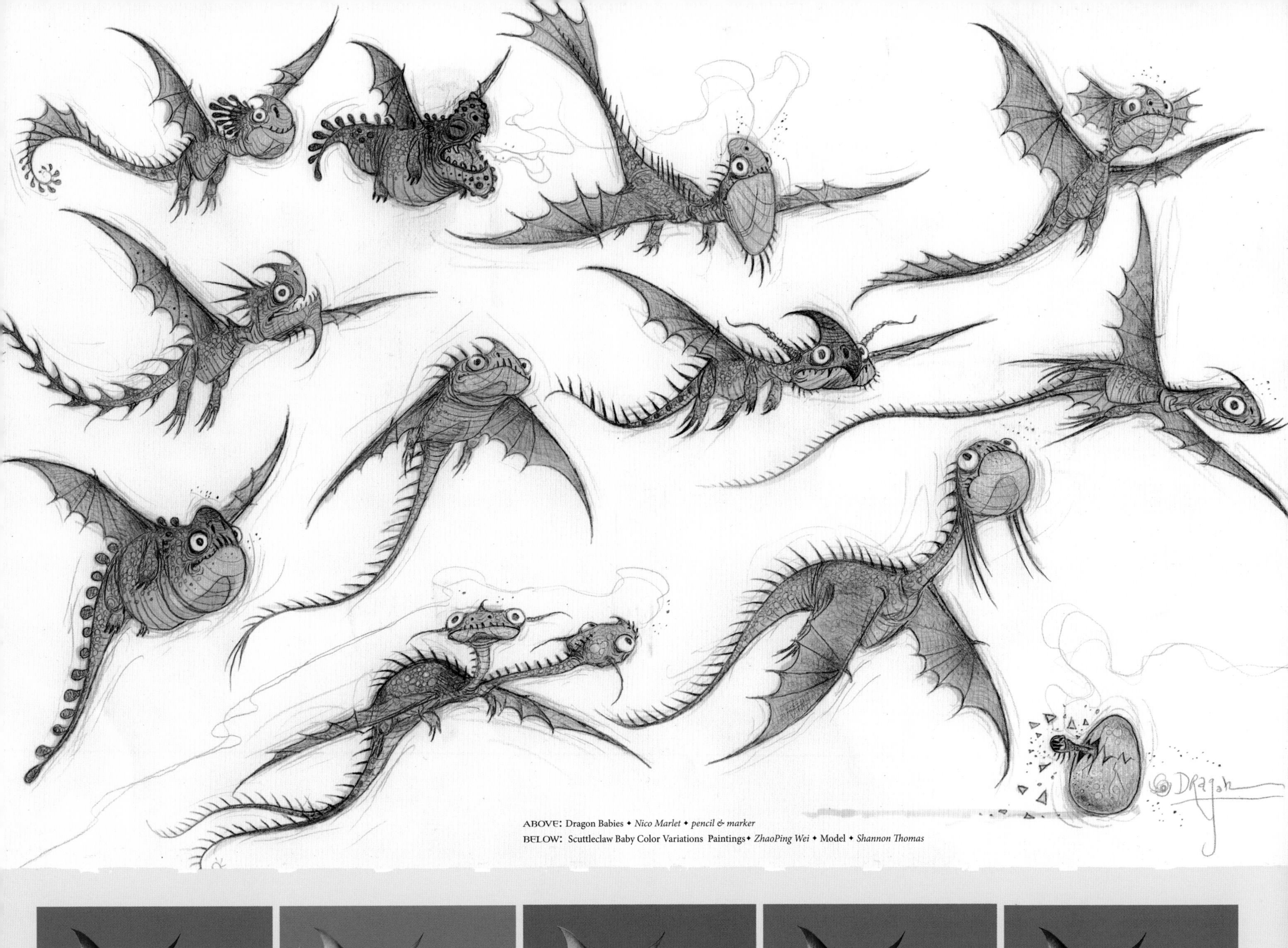


ABOVE: Dragon Babies ✦ *Nico Marlet* ✦ *pencil & marker*

BELOW: Scuttleclaw Baby Color Variations Paintings ✦ *ZhaoPing Wei* ✦ Model ✦ *Shannon Thomas*

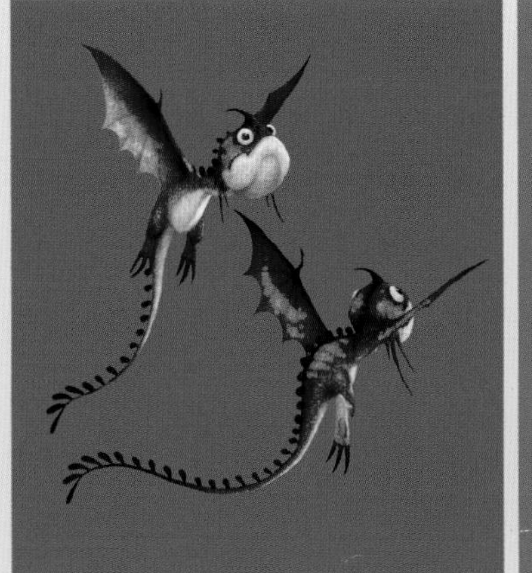
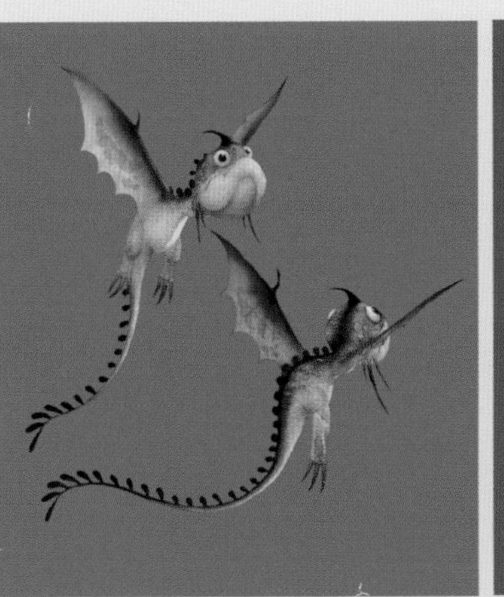
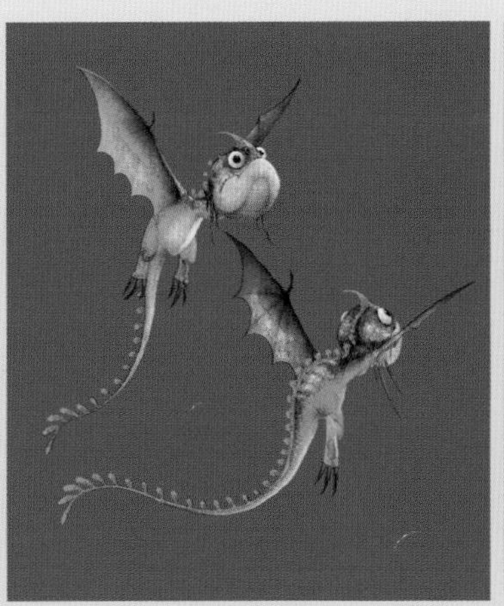
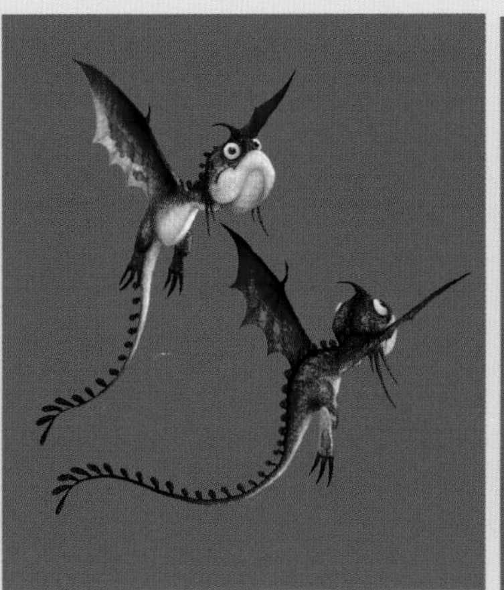
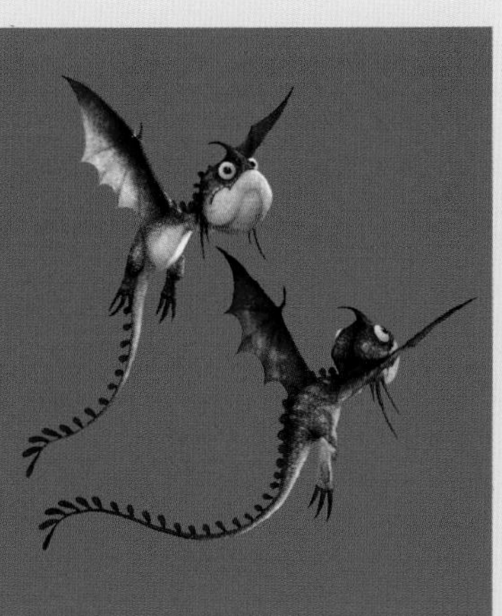

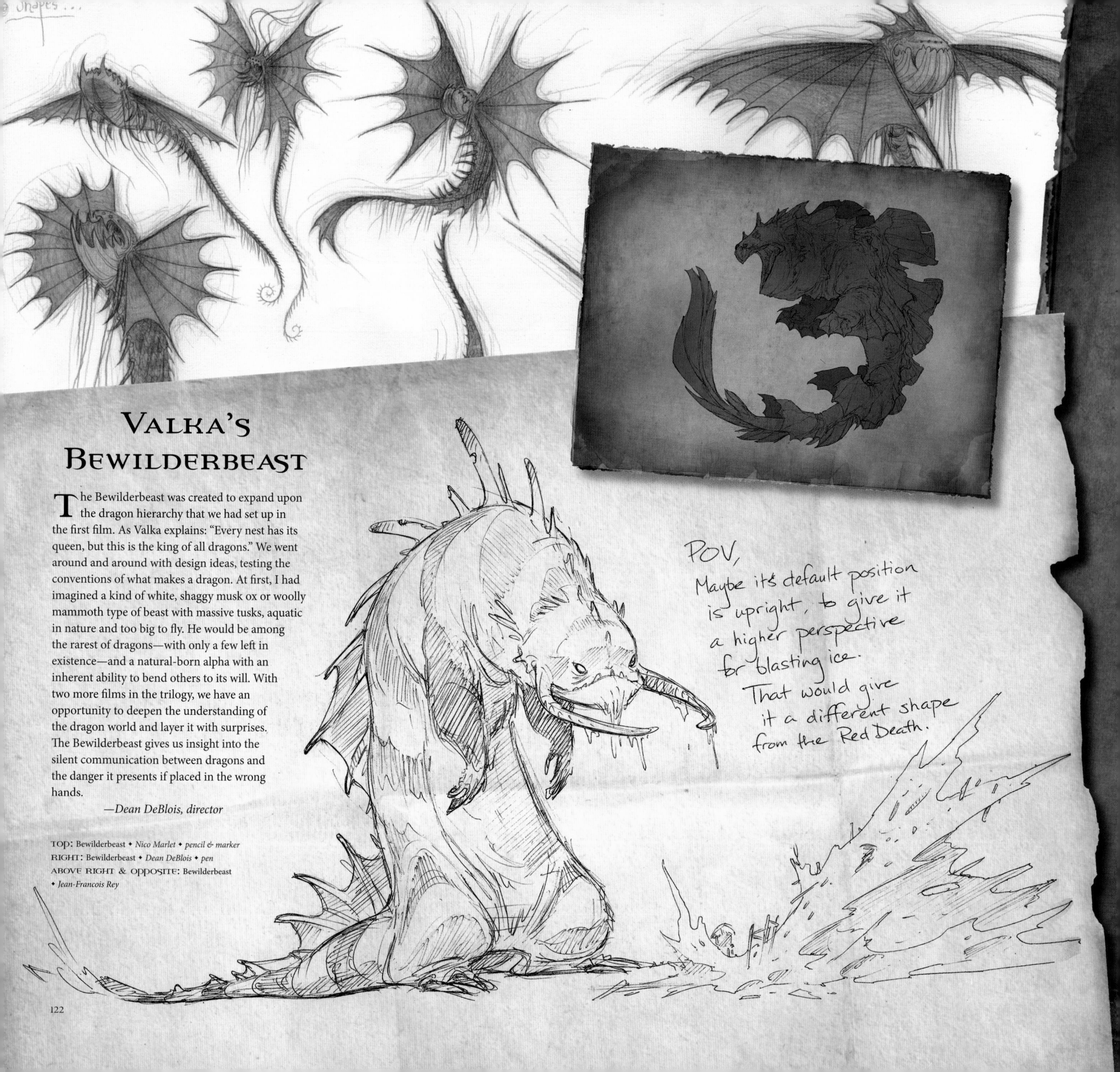


# Valka's Bewilderbeast

The Bewilderbeast was created to expand upon the dragon hierarchy that we had set up in the first film. As Valka explains: "Every nest has its queen, but this is the king of all dragons." We went around and around with design ideas, testing the conventions of what makes a dragon. At first, I had imagined a kind of white, shaggy musk ox or woolly mammoth type of beast with massive tusks, aquatic in nature and too big to fly. He would be among the rarest of dragons—with only a few left in existence—and a natural-born alpha with an inherent ability to bend others to its will. With two more films in the trilogy, we have an opportunity to deepen the understanding of the dragon world and layer it with surprises. The Bewilderbeast gives us insight into the silent communication between dragons and the danger it presents if placed in the wrong hands.

*—Dean DeBlois, director*

TOP: Bewilderbeast ✦ *Nico Marlet* ✦ *pencil & marker*
RIGHT: Bewilderbeast ✦ *Dean DeBlois* ✦ *pen*
ABOVE RIGHT & OPPOSITE: Bewilderbeast ✦ *Jean-Francois Rey*

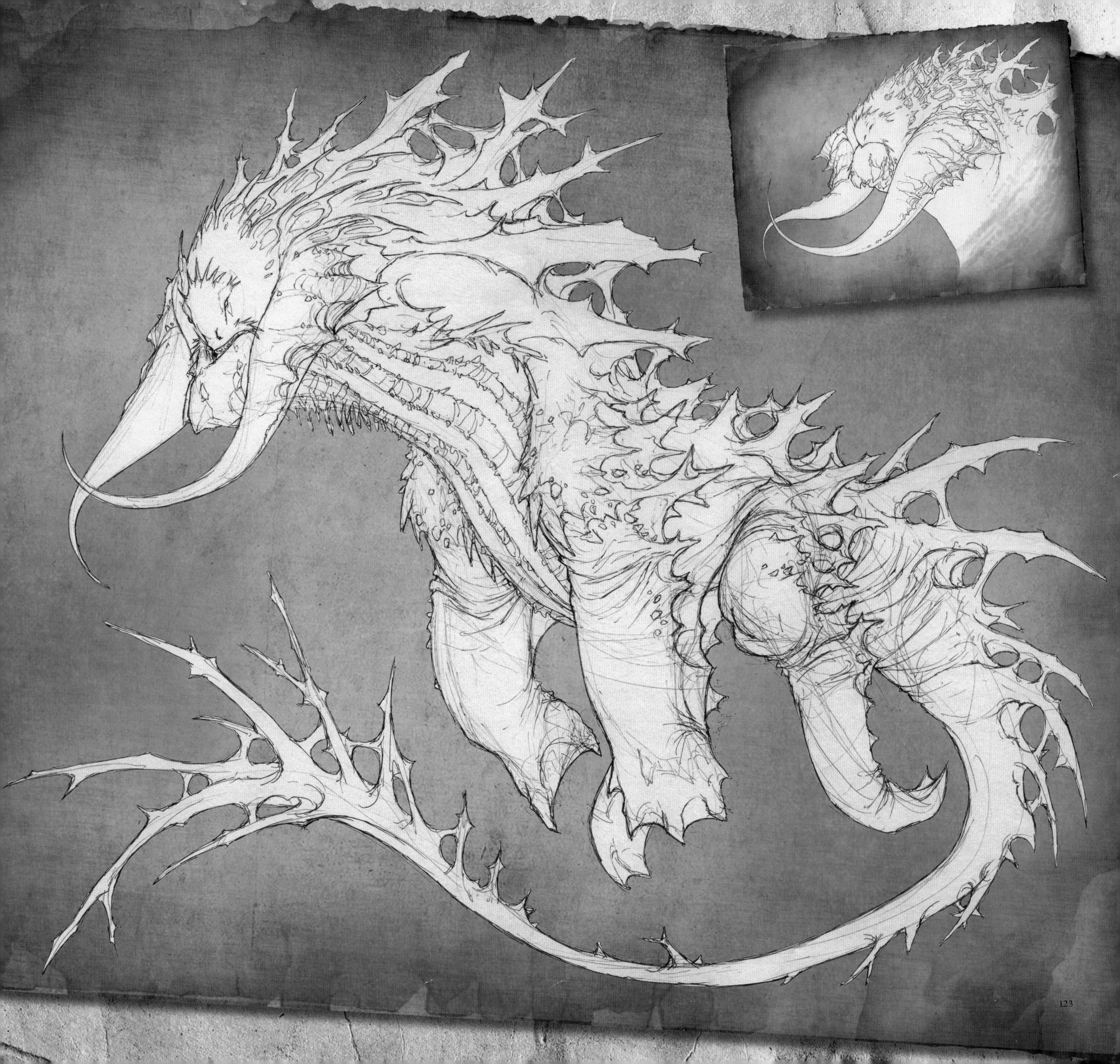

The Bewilderbeast is this absolutely massive reptile; the sheer size of this dragon made him different from any other beast in the movie. We wanted him to convey a sense of sheer superiority and supremacy.

*—ZhaoPing Wei, art director*

The Bewilderbeast was a huge undertaking due to its colossal size and how close the camera gets to him. Our main challenge was to create textures that worked in ultra-close-up to reveal his coral-like amphibian skin and in wide shots to underscore his imposing scale.

*—Paolo deGuzman, head of surfacing*

BELOW: Color Key ◆ *Woonyoung Jung*
BOTTOM: Bewilderbeast Concept Model ◆ *Leo Sanchez*

RIGHT: Bewilderbeast Studies ◆ *Nico Marlet* ◆ *pencil & marker*
OPPOSITE: Bewilderbeast Painting ◆ *ZhaoPing Wei* ◆ Model ◆ *Seungyoung "Sean" Choi*

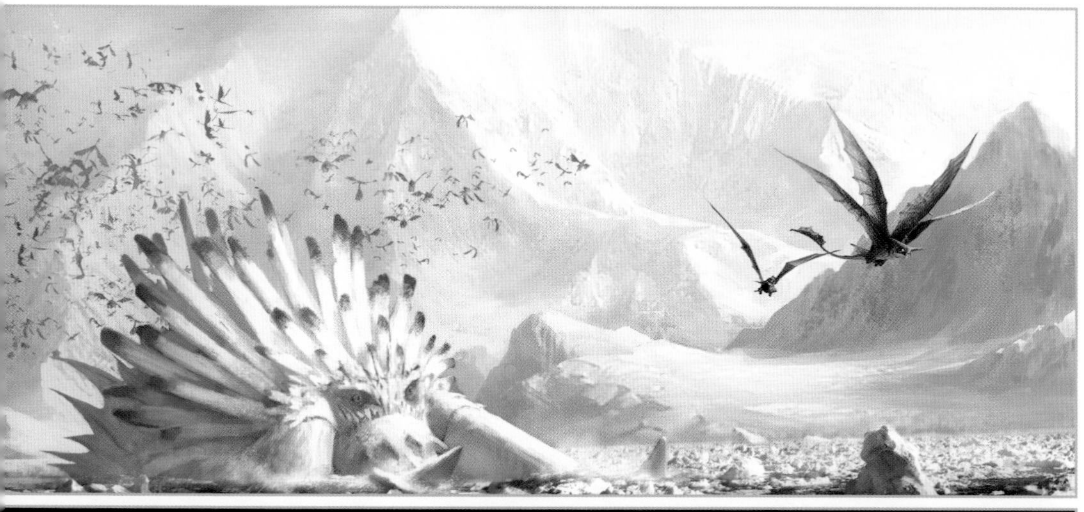

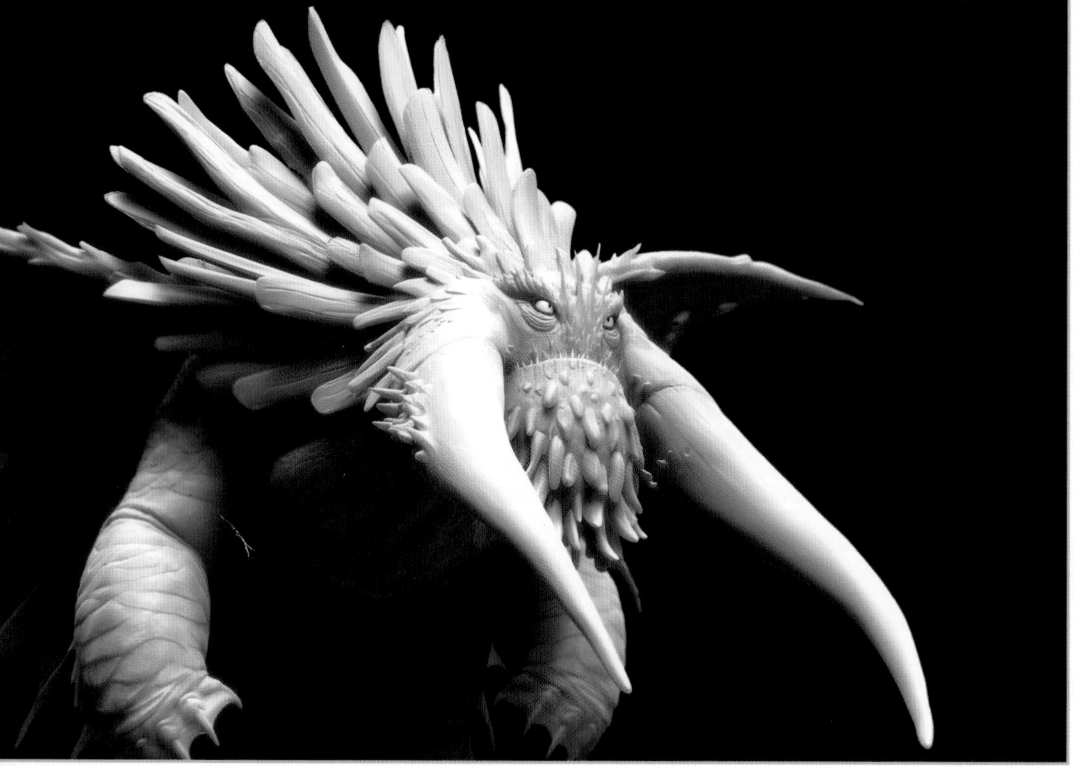



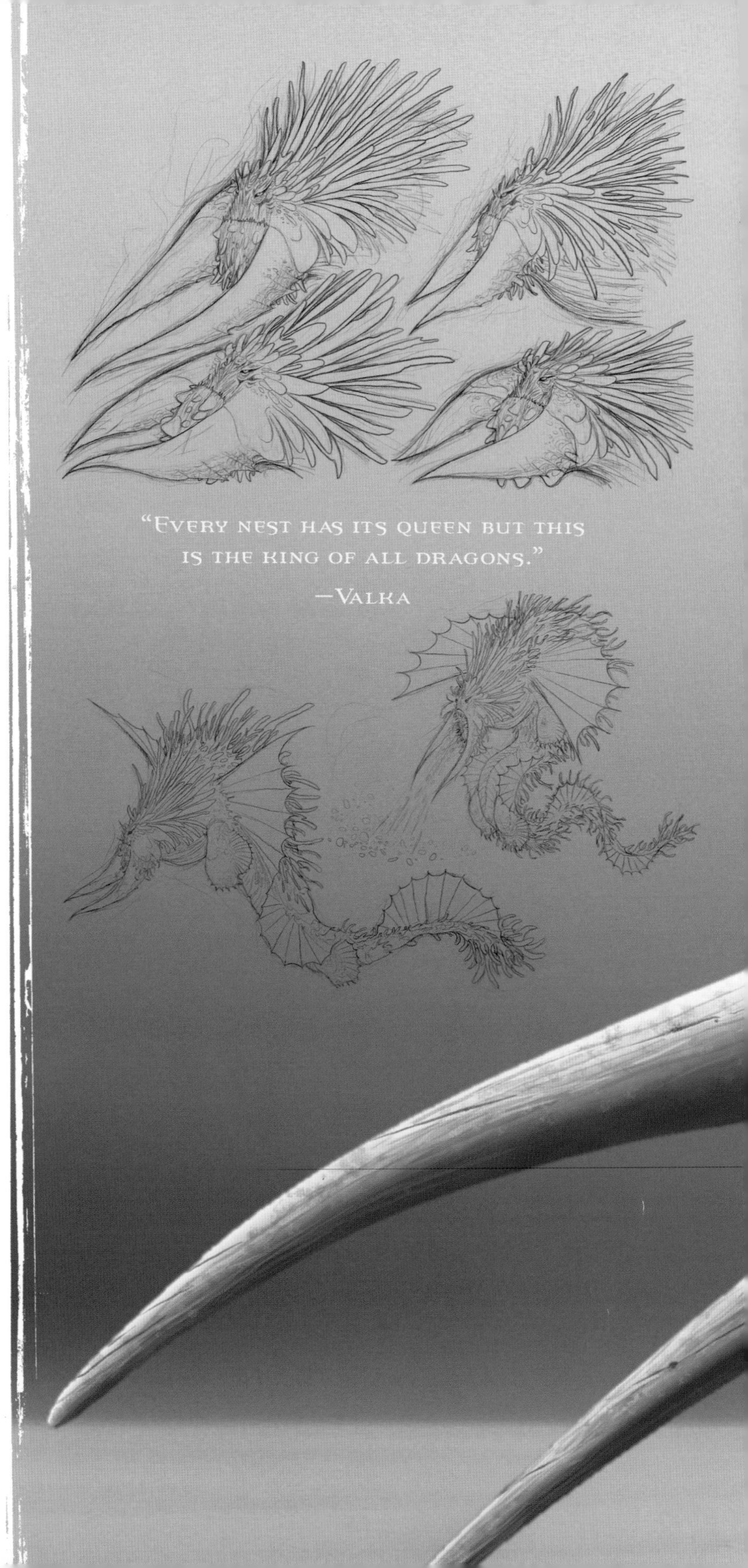

"Every nest has its queen but this is the king of all dragons."

—Valka

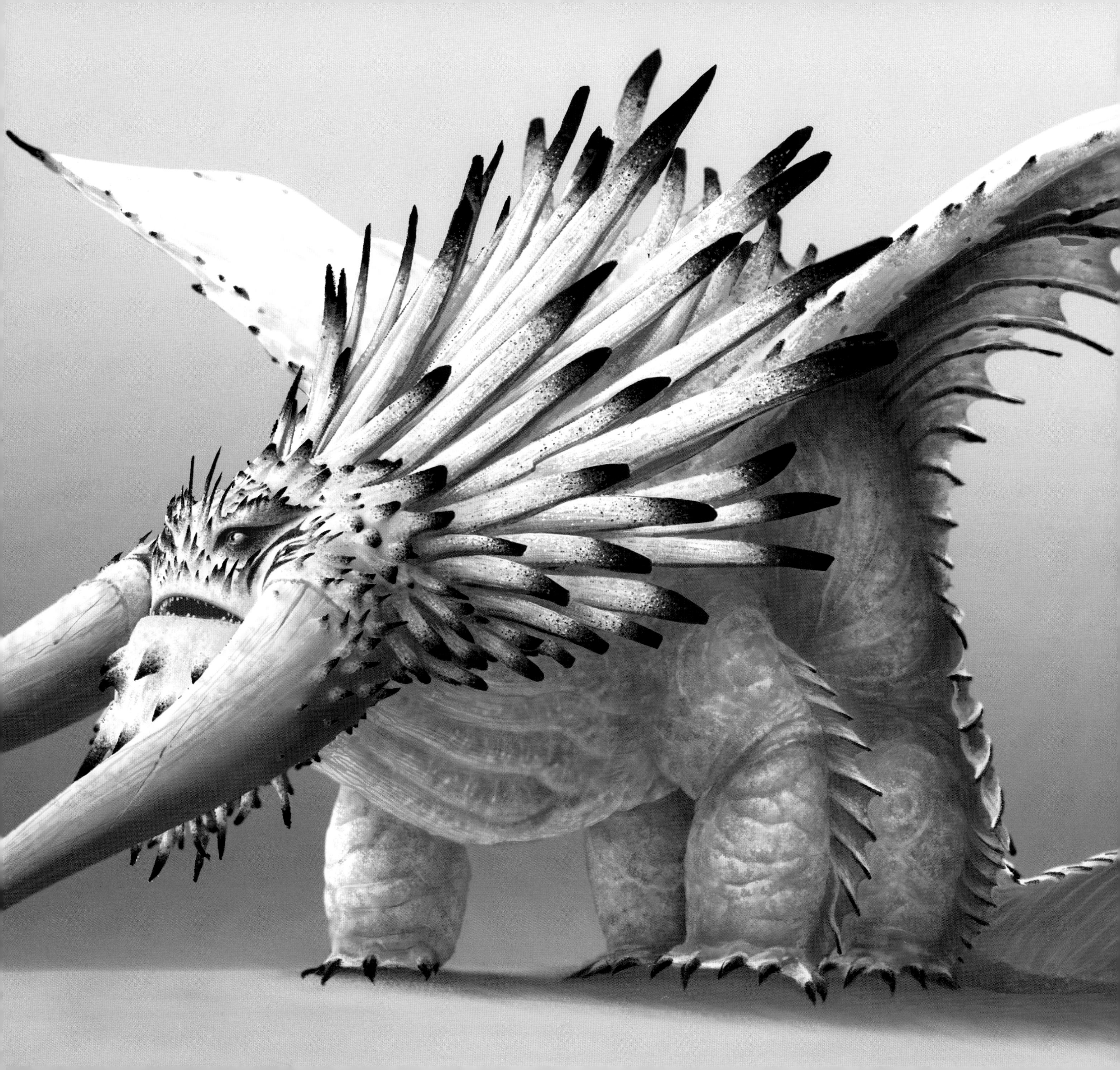

# The Reunion

One of the scenes that remained true to its original concept was called "Family Reunion," in which Stoick comes face-to-face with his long-lost wife. It was intended from the start that Stoick would be rendered speechless, as though seeing a ghost, while Valka would nervously fill the awkward silence, rattled by her own guilt. Stoick's slow, steady approach first amplifies then disarms Valka's guarded justifications for being gone so long, leaving her tearful and full of remorse. Then, with a few soft and sincere words, Stoick melts away the tension and seals it with a kiss—a potent demonstration of true love transcending time and regret.

It was followed by a scene entitled "The Last Dance," in which Stoick and Hiccup do their best to convince Valka to return home with them. She's spent twenty years living among dragons and learning to distrust humans. Now, suddenly surrounded by family and the realization that people *can* change, Valka's world has once again come apart, leaving her overwhelmed. To ease the sudden impact of their unexpected reunion and to remind her of who they had been in happier times, Stoick whistles and then clumsily sings his part of a duet intended to feel like "their" song. It was written to suggest an old Viking courting ballad, one that would have been passed down through generations and known to everyone. At first, Valka rejects Stoick's invitation to join in, but nostalgia soon gets the better of her and she sings her part with increasing gusto, bridging the gap between them. The moment is magical for Hiccup, seeing his parents laughing, arm in arm—something he'd never expected to witness. By the song's end, Stoick proposes anew, asking Valka to come home and leading her to accept him back wholeheartedly. The danger was that the scene would feel hokey and cringe-worthy, so we went about it very carefully. It needed to be honest and sweet, yet jaunty and joyous by the end. John Powell and Jónsi wrote a beautiful melody, to which Shane MacGowan added poignant lyrics. The result is one of the most memorable moments in the film.

*—Dean DeBlois, director*

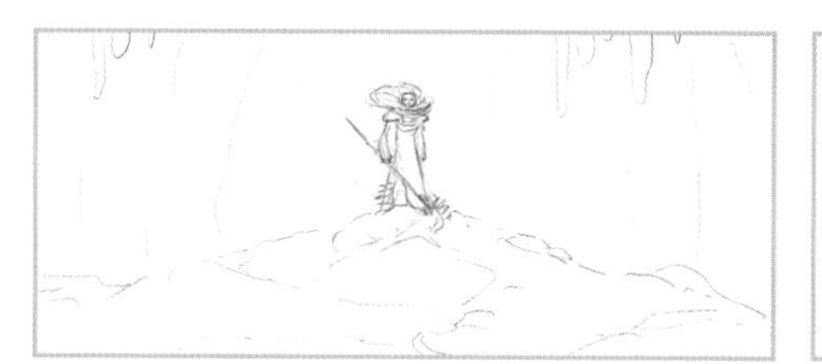
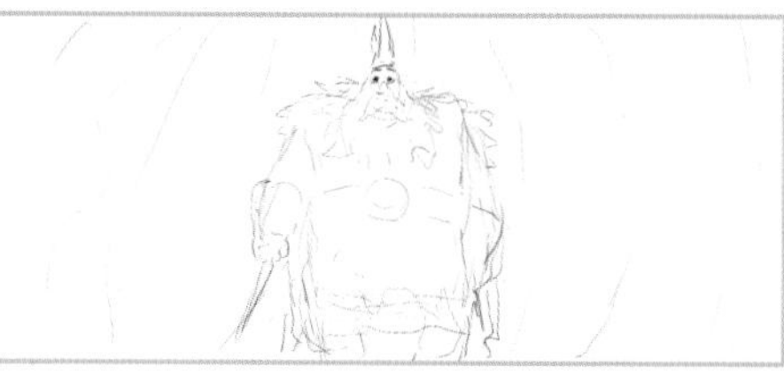
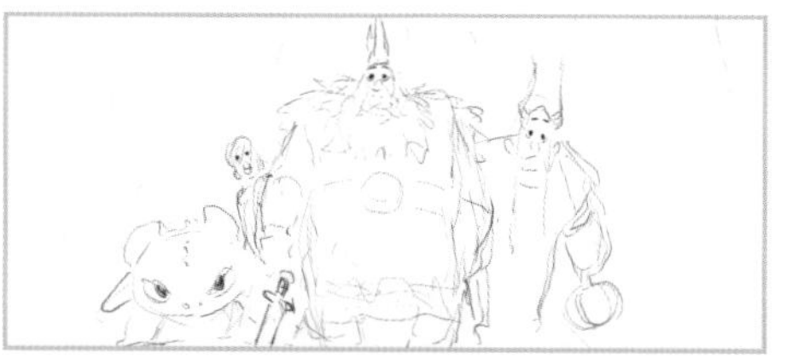
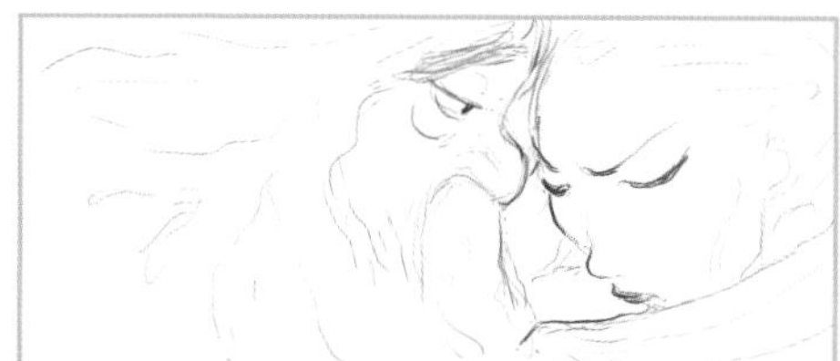
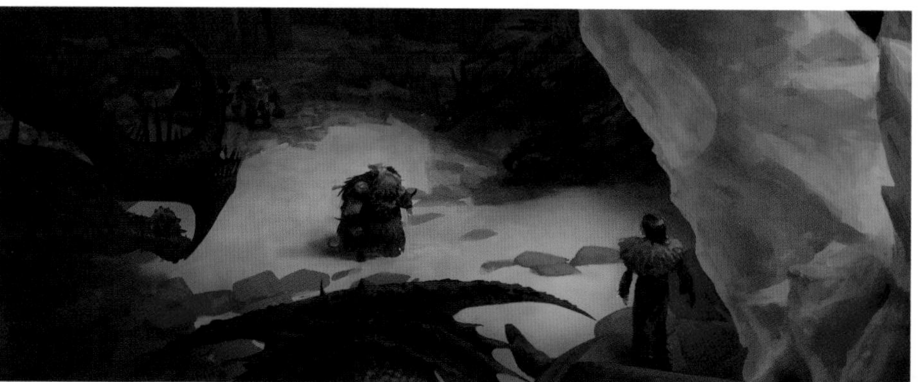

ABOVE RIGHT: Storyboards • *Bolhem Bouchiba*
RIGHT: Color Key • *Woonyoung Jung*
BELOW: Lighting Study • *Marcos Mateu-Mestre*

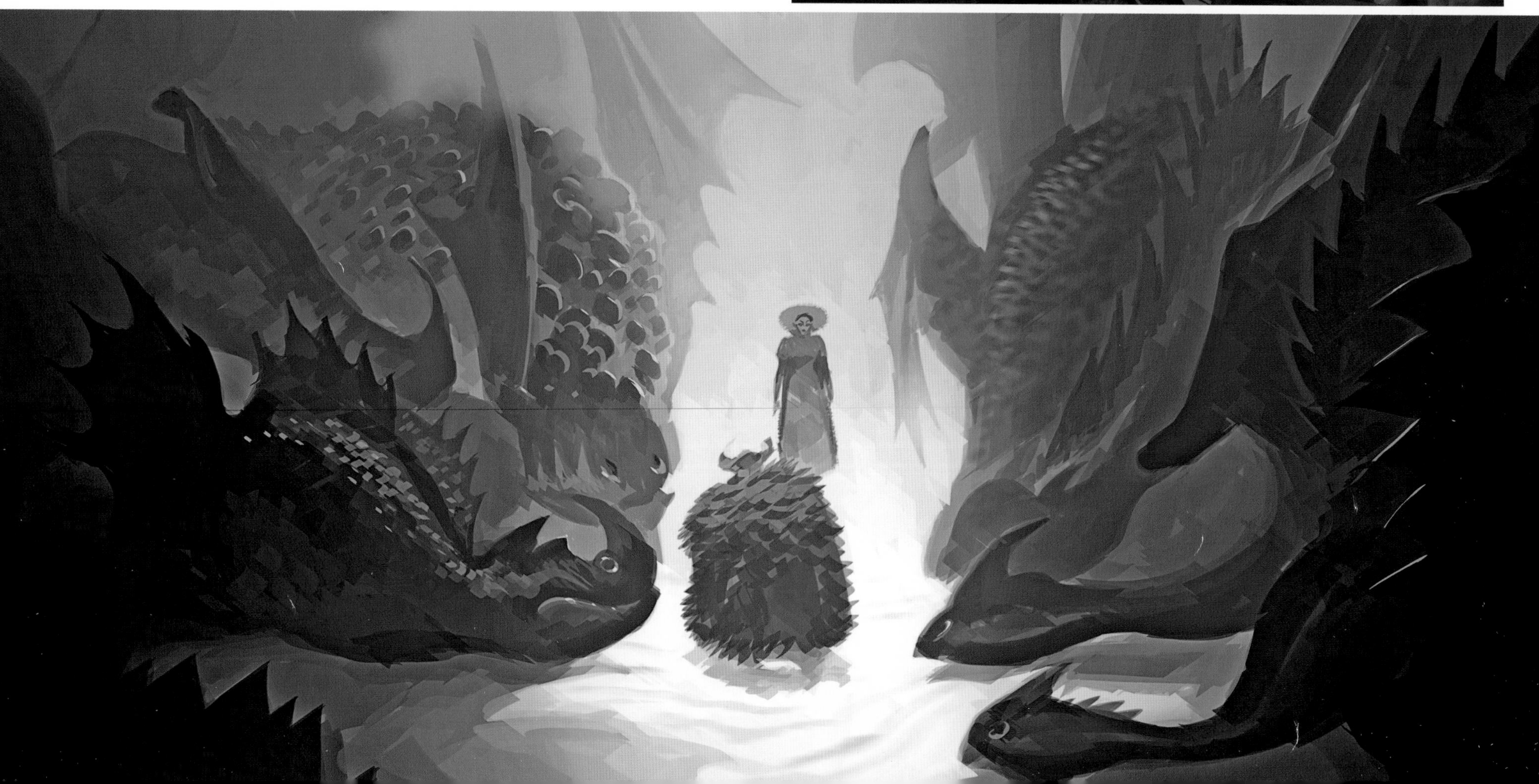

# Dance to the Music

I am most moved by music when I hear a melancholy Irish ballad, which reminds me of who I am, where I come from, and everything I love about being a Celt. So it was fascinating to be singing this kind of song about love, joy, romance, chivalry, and valor from a guy who seems the least likely to understand that. The song I sing with Valka reveals a whole new layer of the story; we learn that Stoick is really a hopeless romantic! The song also explains everything they had together. It's like when you sit with your parents and they start telling you stories about when they were young and in love.

*—Gerard Butler, actor and voice of Stoick*

The dance sequence between Valka and Stoick was not so much of a visual problem as it was contextual. We are kind of a serious movie and then we have this musical number in the middle of the story. This scene takes place right before the most serious part of the movie so there are some people who wanted us to punch this up with a lot of joy and happiness. But you don't want it to seem so completely different from the rest of the movie.

We have the elation of Hiccup now that his parents are finally united and all the promise of that. But we didn't want to have the equivalent of the three-way hug because it could get too syrupy. We wanted to keep it both innocent and natural in order to fit the general tone of the film.

We certainly didn't want to go *Beauty and the Beast* in a Broadway style of choreography. Instead, we wanted to keep it more like the way your parents might actually dance in your living room. We were also trying to shoot it so that midway through we see it through Hiccup's point of view, as a realization of a dream he's harbored for a long time.

*—Gil Zimmerman, head of layout*

Jónsi Birgisson is the lead singer for an Icelandic band called Sigur Rós. Dean had done a documentary about the band and asked Jónsi to do the end credit song for the first movie, which was lovely. On this film, we brought him in for the Viking love ballad that Stoick and Valka sing to each other. He and John Powell collaborated on that song and the plan is for them to write more songs together.

John Powell was the composer for the first film and he completely got the story and delivered the single most unbelievable element of the movie. John took things that were great and made them brilliant. His work here was far from traditional, but he was able to play to the tone that we wanted. The music he created for us is heartwarming, heroic, romantic, sad, funny, happy, wondrous, and believable. It came as no surprise to me when he was nominated for an Academy Award for the first film.

*—Bonnie Arnold, producer*

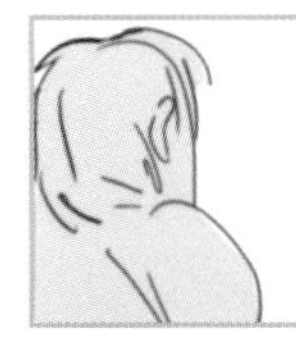

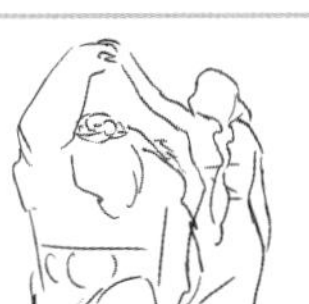

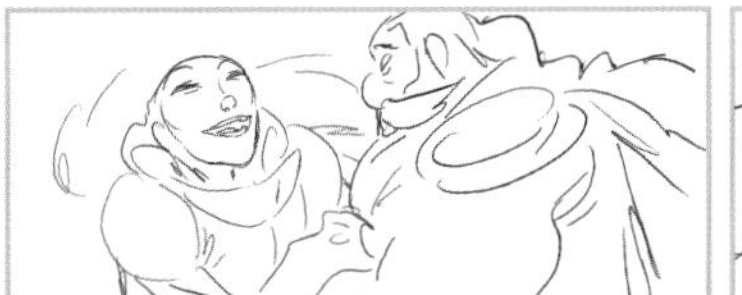

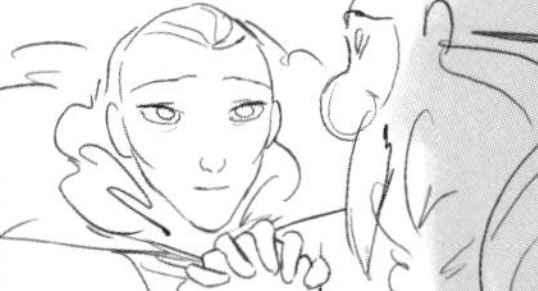

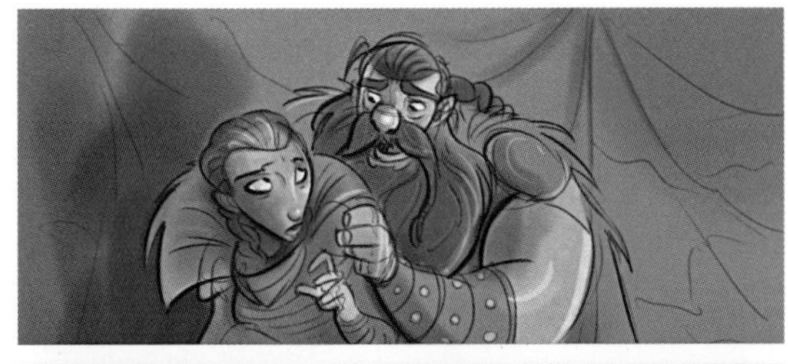

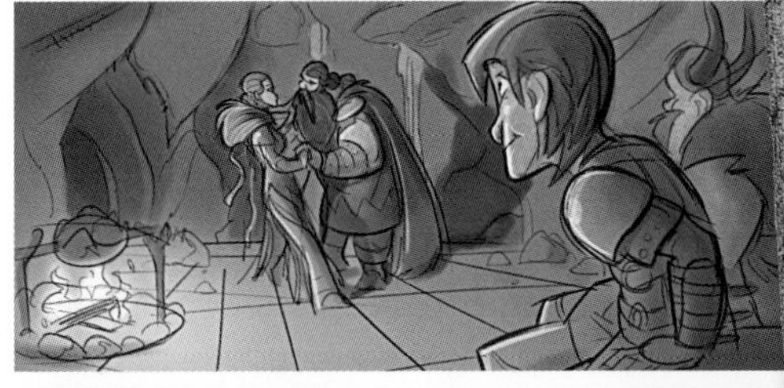

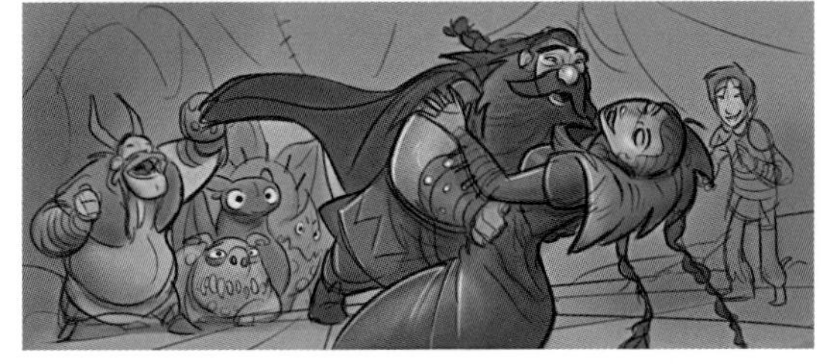

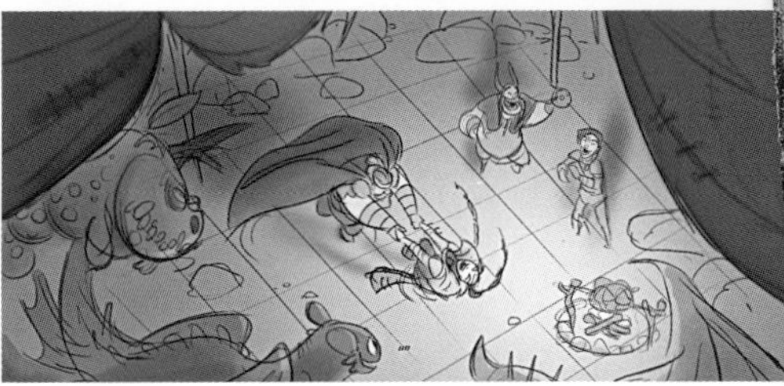

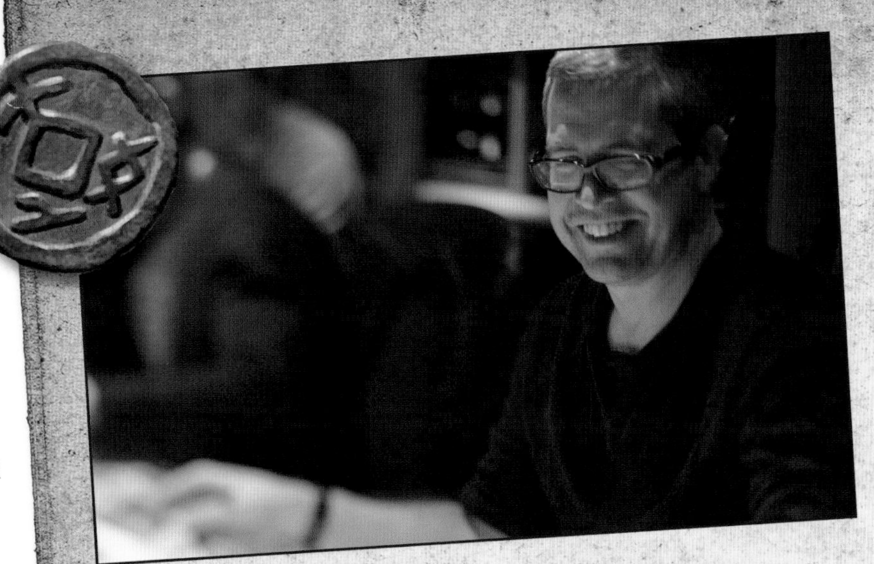

# About the Music

Working on a sequel is like any challenge when writing music, which is to always better yourself. For the first movie, I was able to work with the directors and write a score that was better than anything I'd done before, and receiving an Oscar nomination was a great honor. For the second movie, everyone wants the score to be as good (or better) than the first: to be the same but different. Right now it's early in the process for me, as the film is not yet completed. I won't get it for another two months and won't record for six months so lately I've been focusing on some thematic material.

For the second movie I want to make sure there is a very strong theme for Toothless, who is the catalyst for the whole story. So if he's in the scene—whether he's in the exact shot or not—we keep with his theme. It's the most important melody you can attach to the idea of what is happening.

Also, I've been working on the love ballad between Stoick and Valka. It was great to sit down with Dean and figure out how to make this song work dramatically without being a musical indulgence. We didn't want a moment when everyone breaks out in song. It had to be organic and allow the story to turn on that one moment of music. We decided that since this was a culture with a deep tradition of singing, music and storytelling, these two people could start singing as a kind of memory.

I worked on the music with Jónsi Birgisson from the Icelandic band Sigur Rós. Jónsi writes melodies without words; it was just sounds. We got the structure and the form, knew the melody and figured out what we wanted the song to be doing dramatically. Then we had to find the words. I had a conversation with Jónsi and Dean about songs we loved and strangely we all fell upon Shane MacGowan, the singer/songwriter of The Pogues, who wrote the genius words to "Fairytale of New York." We contacted Shane and he rewarded us with amazing lyrics. In all, the song was a wonderful collaboration of people from very different backgrounds and worlds. It really worked for us once we got Gerard Butler to sing and emote from within the backstory.

What I'm hoping to achieve in the second movie is a maturation in the structure of the music. I want the music to be reminiscent of the first film but grown up a little. That can mean taking the same joyful theme and making it darker or taking a darker theme and making it joyful. It will be the same fun music, but more developed in every aspect of composition.

*—John Powell, composer*

ABOVE LEFT: Storyboards ✦ *Tron Mai*
LEFT: Storyboards ✦ *Ryan Savas*
TOP LEFT: Rune ✦ *Kirsten Kawamura*

TOP: John Powell Working at the AirLyndhurst Studio in London ✦ *Photo by Melinda Lerner*
FOLLOWING PAGES: Destroyed Village ✦ *Pierre-Olivier Vincent*

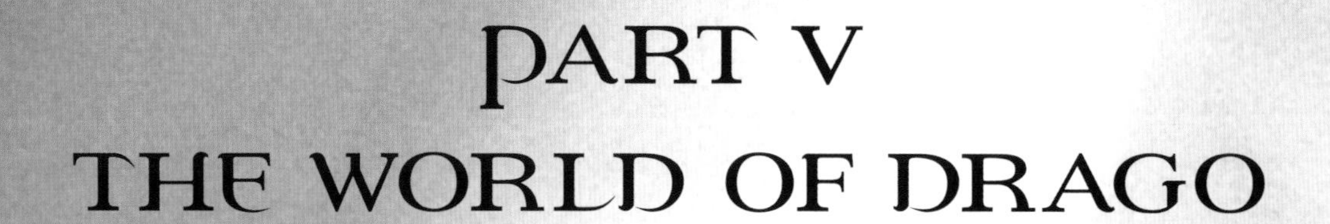

# PART V
# THE WORLD OF DRAGO

"DRAGO BLUDVIST IS A MADMAN WITHOUT CONSCIENCE OR MERCY AND IF HE'S BUILT A DRAGON ARMY . . . GODS HELP US ALL."

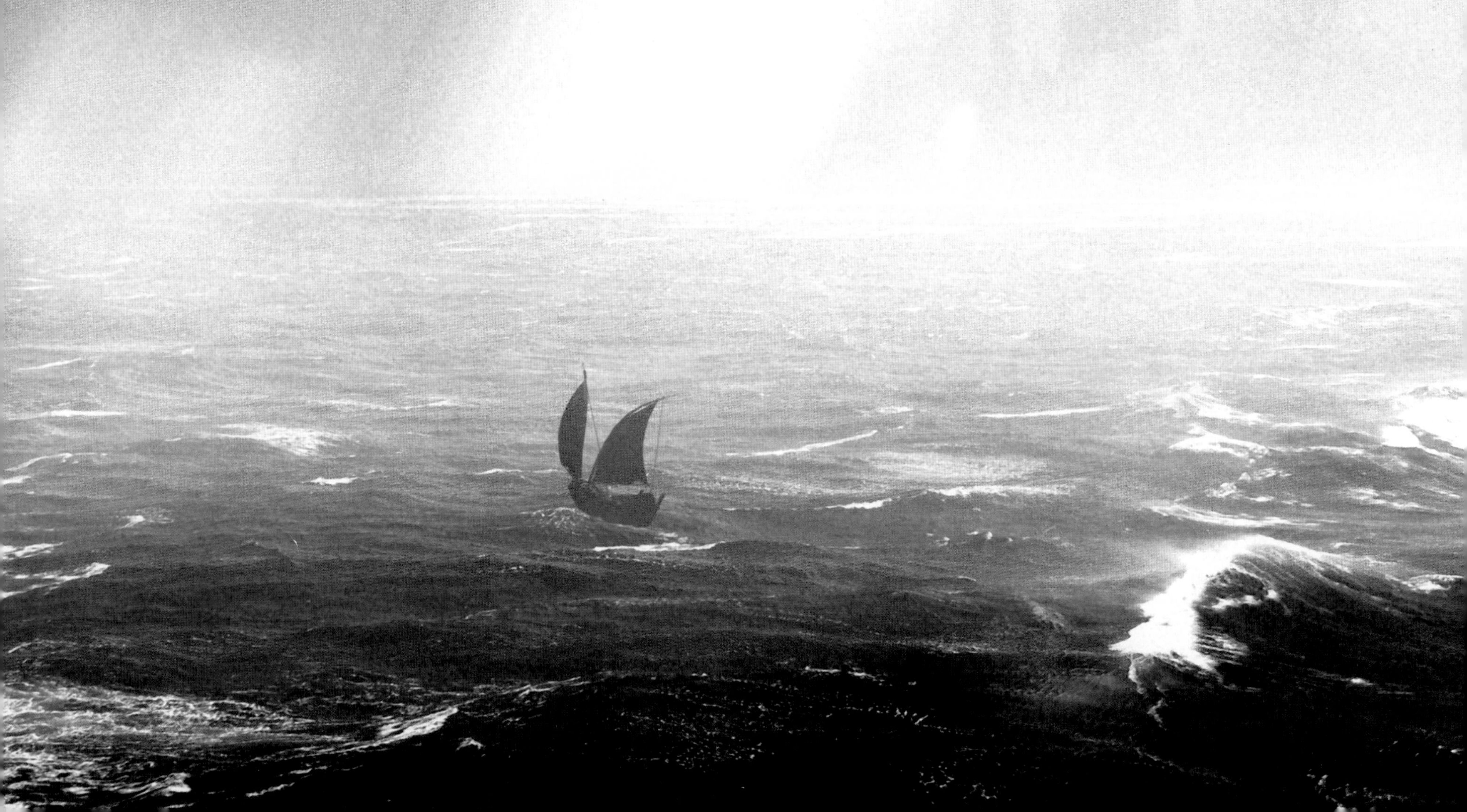

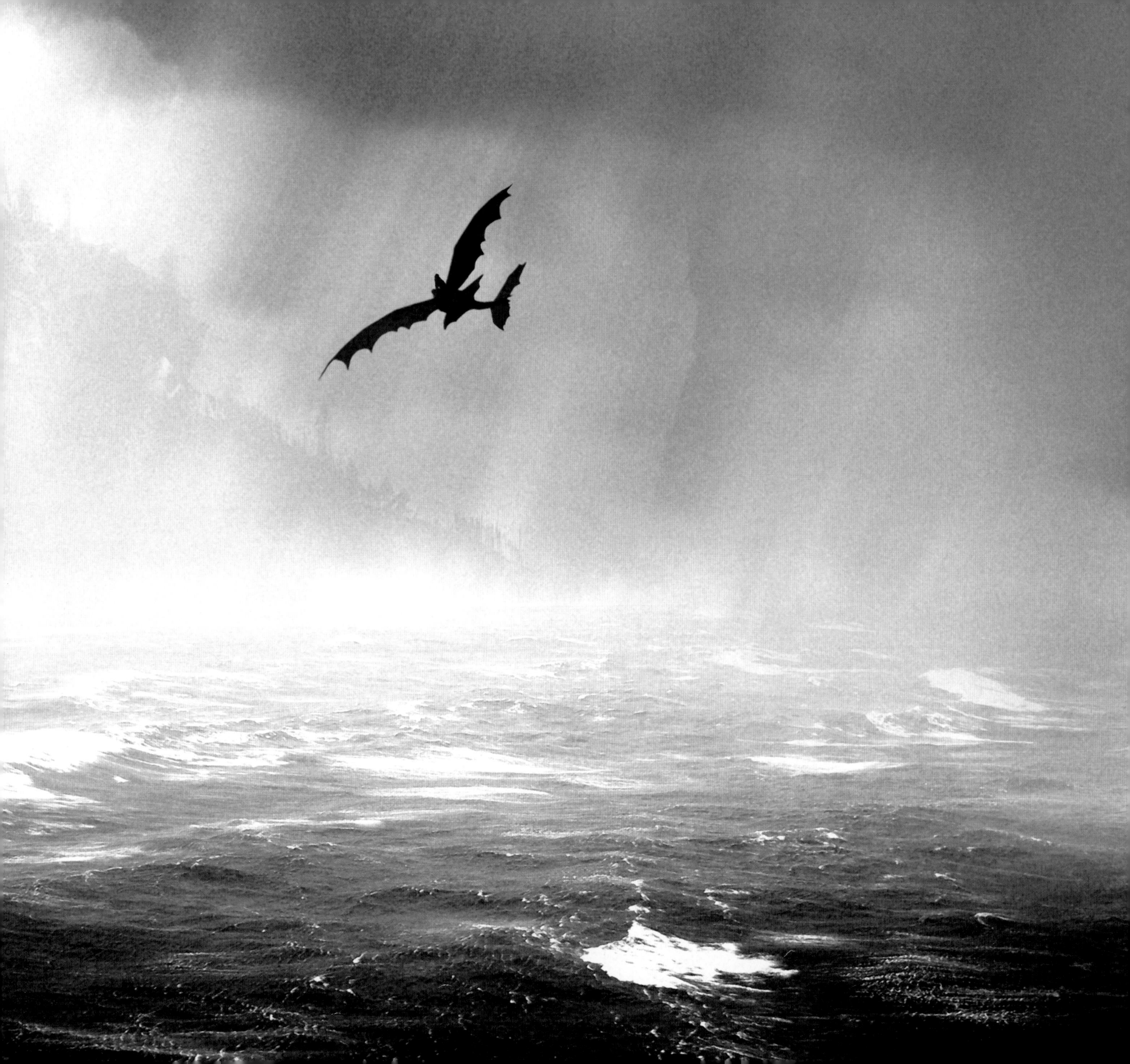

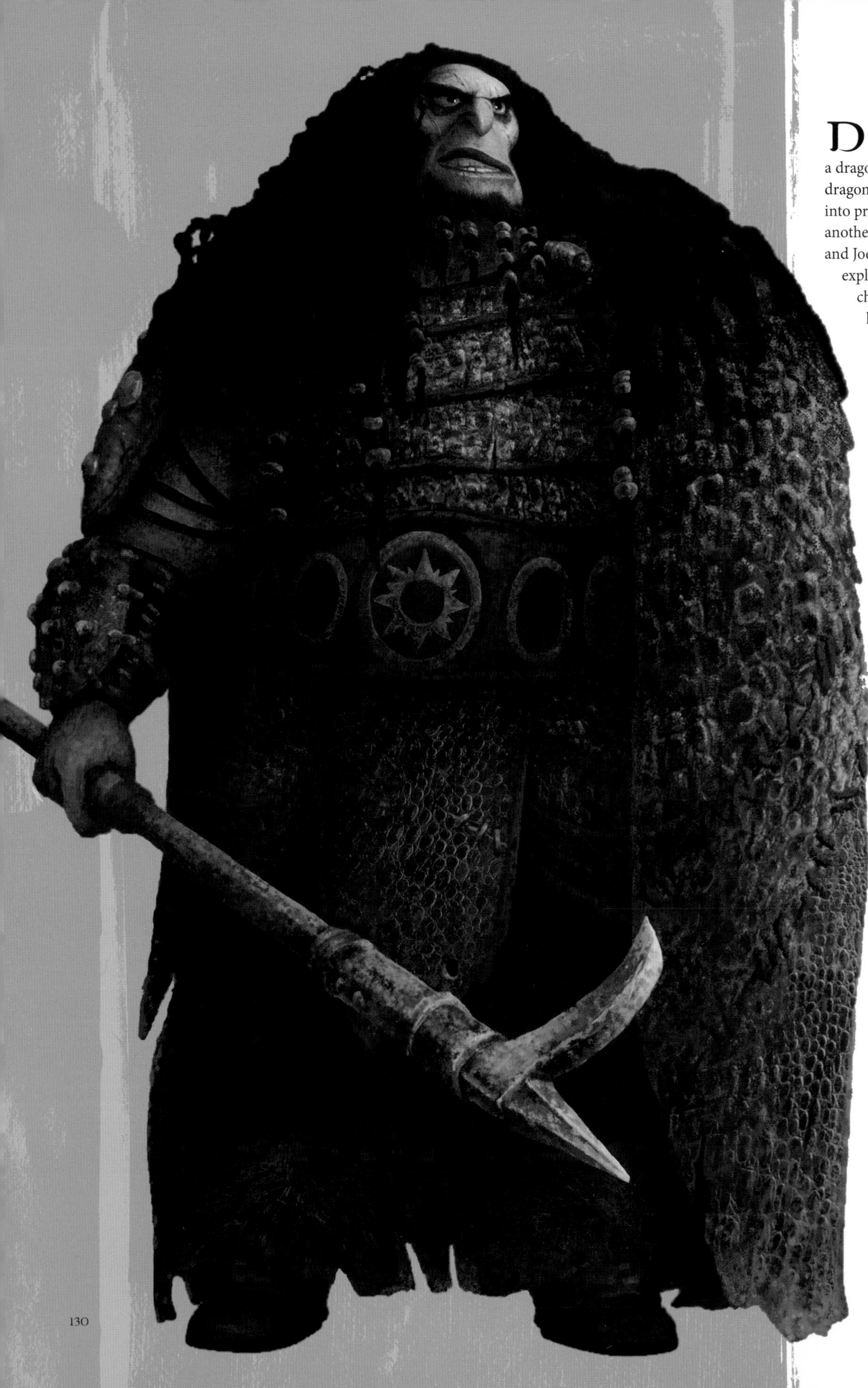

# Drago

Drago needed to be memorable and striking, but for the longest time, all we had was a generic-looking brute. We knew he had to look strong enough to overpower a dragon. We gave him some scars, presumably from his early days of learning to control dragons, but otherwise he didn't have much of an interesting look. As we were heading into production with him we had a moment of pause and thought we should take another stab at designing him, so we hired two character designers, Carter Goodrich and Joe Moshier. We only gave them three things: a description of the character, an explanation of his role in the movie, and a recording of Djimon Hounsou's voice in character. Both artists went off and came up with ideas of what that character might look like. Interestingly, even though the two artists had not spoken to each other, they both landed on the same look for Drago. Then we brought their sketches to Nico Marlet who added to the concept and pulled it into the style of the film.

We described Drago as a bit of a predator, so his profile has almost an eagle-like beak in the way his forehead sweeps into his nose. The long dreads give him an arresting quality because in every previous version, he was either bald or had minimal hair. We decided to give him an injury brought about by a dragon. He is missing an arm but he covers it up because he wants to appear invincible to the people who follow him.

Drago is steadily gaining control over the world by reinforcing the belief that he alone can control the dragons. Therefore, he alone can keep people safe. His aim is to gather the world's dragons in order to keep the threat alive and close. With them, he can control those who follow him, and get rid of those who won't.

Dragon riders, with their symbiotic relationships with dragons, make the animals seem sympathetic and not to be feared. Living in harmony with dragons would be Drago's undoing and mean the loss of any power he has garnered. He breaks the dragons and turns them into beasts of burden so the idea of dragon riders is poison in the well and he is actively trying to destroy the dragon riders. He thought Valka was the only one but through the course of the story he comes to learn that there is an entire island full of dragon riders on Berk.

*—Dean DeBlois, director*

We started with a version of Drago that was bald, with a thin mustache and a kind of Asian quality, but he looked like a villain we'd seen before. We wanted to give him a fresh, unique look. So we changed the profile into one with a strong, hawkish presence from the side or three-quarter view. We added hair but didn't want him to look too vain. If he had trimmed hair or even braids, it would look like he was taking care of himself. There was a delicate balance of trying to make him look really fierce without being vain. Drago's hair is a little crazy and the dreadlocks lend themselves to this I-don't-care attitude.

*—Matt Paulson, modeling supervisor*

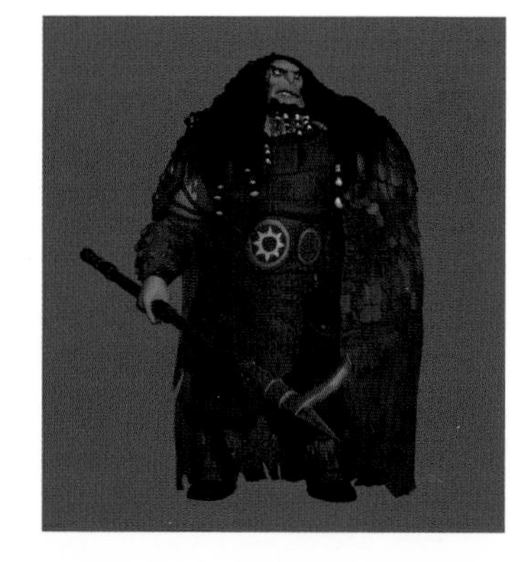

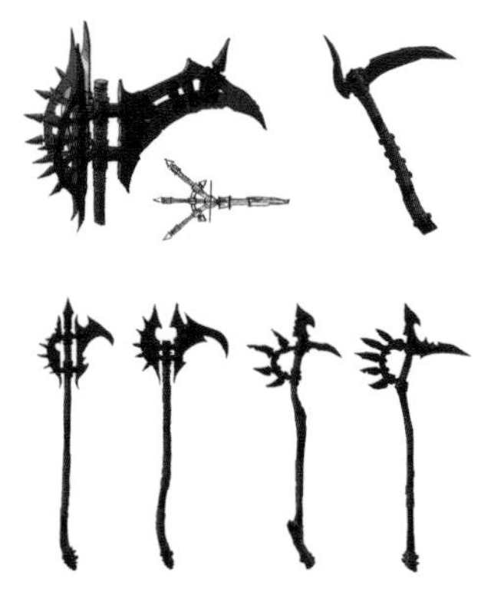

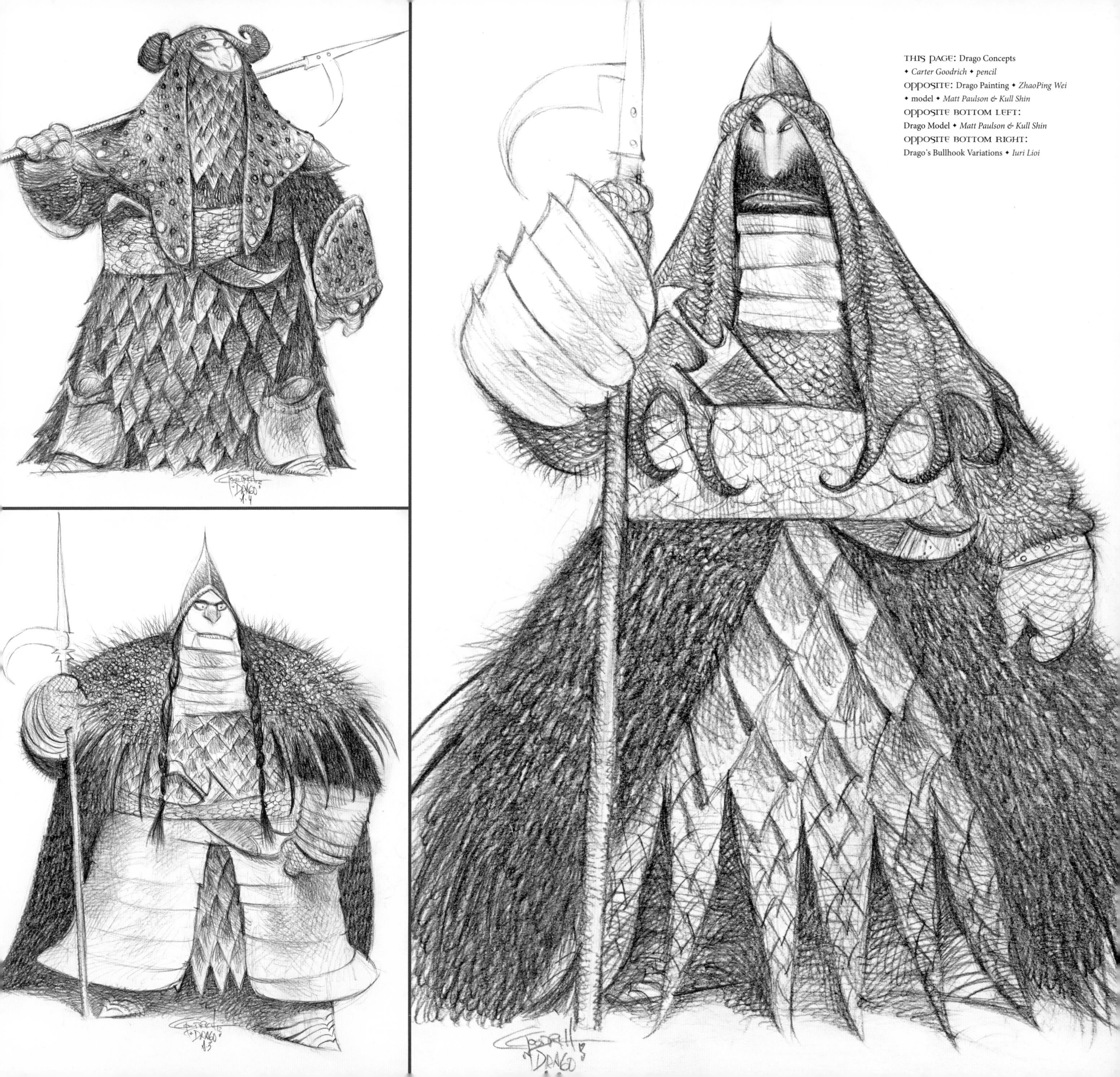

THIS PAGE: Drago Concepts ✦ *Carter Goodrich* ✦ *pencil*
OPPOSITE: Drago Painting ✦ *ZhaoPing Wei* ✦ model ✦ *Matt Paulson & Kull Shin*
OPPOSITE BOTTOM LEFT: Drago Model ✦ *Matt Paulson & Kull Shin*
OPPOSITE BOTTOM RIGHT: Drago's Bullhook Variations ✦ *Iuri Lioi*

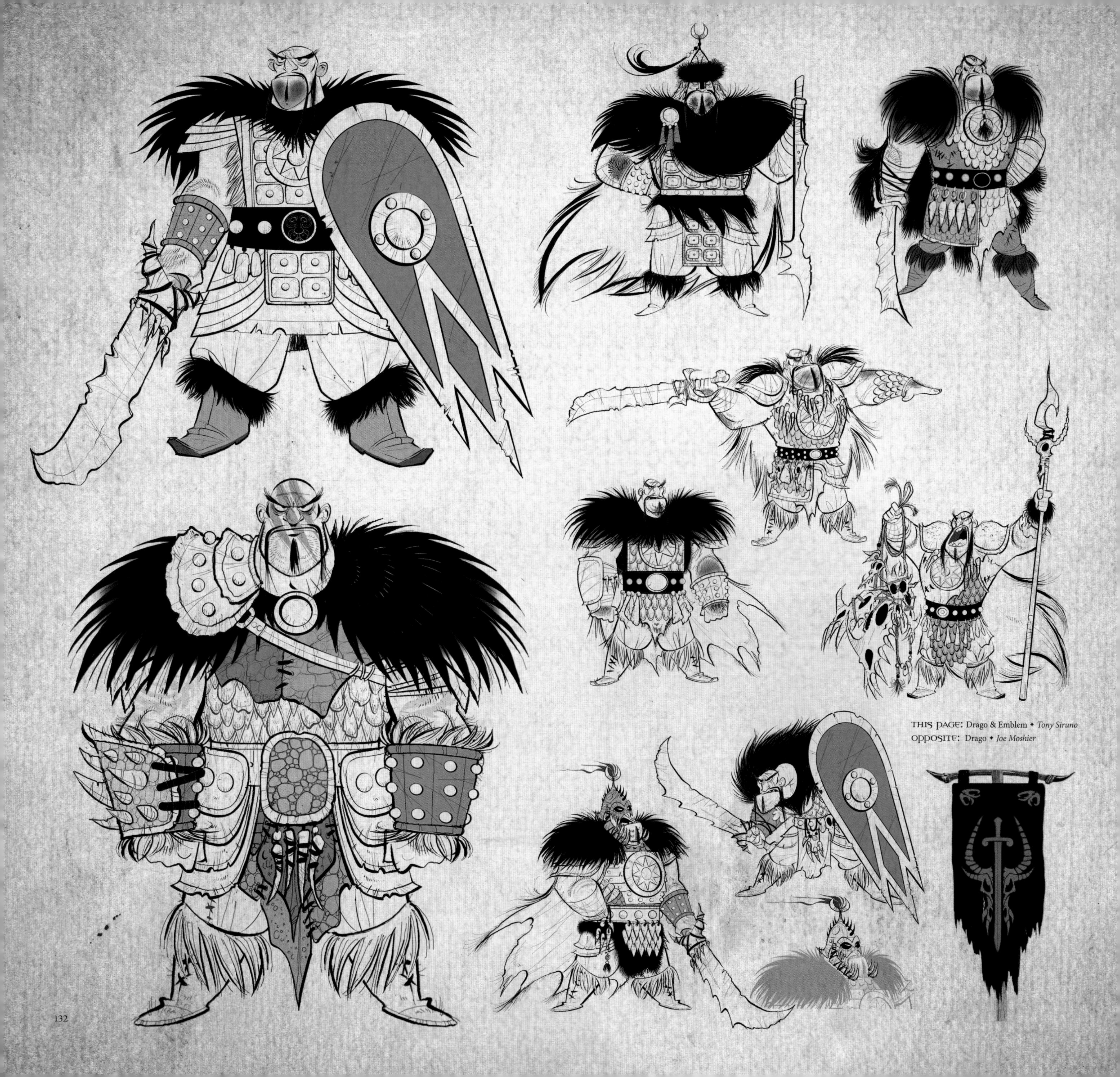

THIS PAGE: Drago & Emblem ✦ *Tony Siruno*
OPPOSITE: Drago ✦ *Joe Moshier*

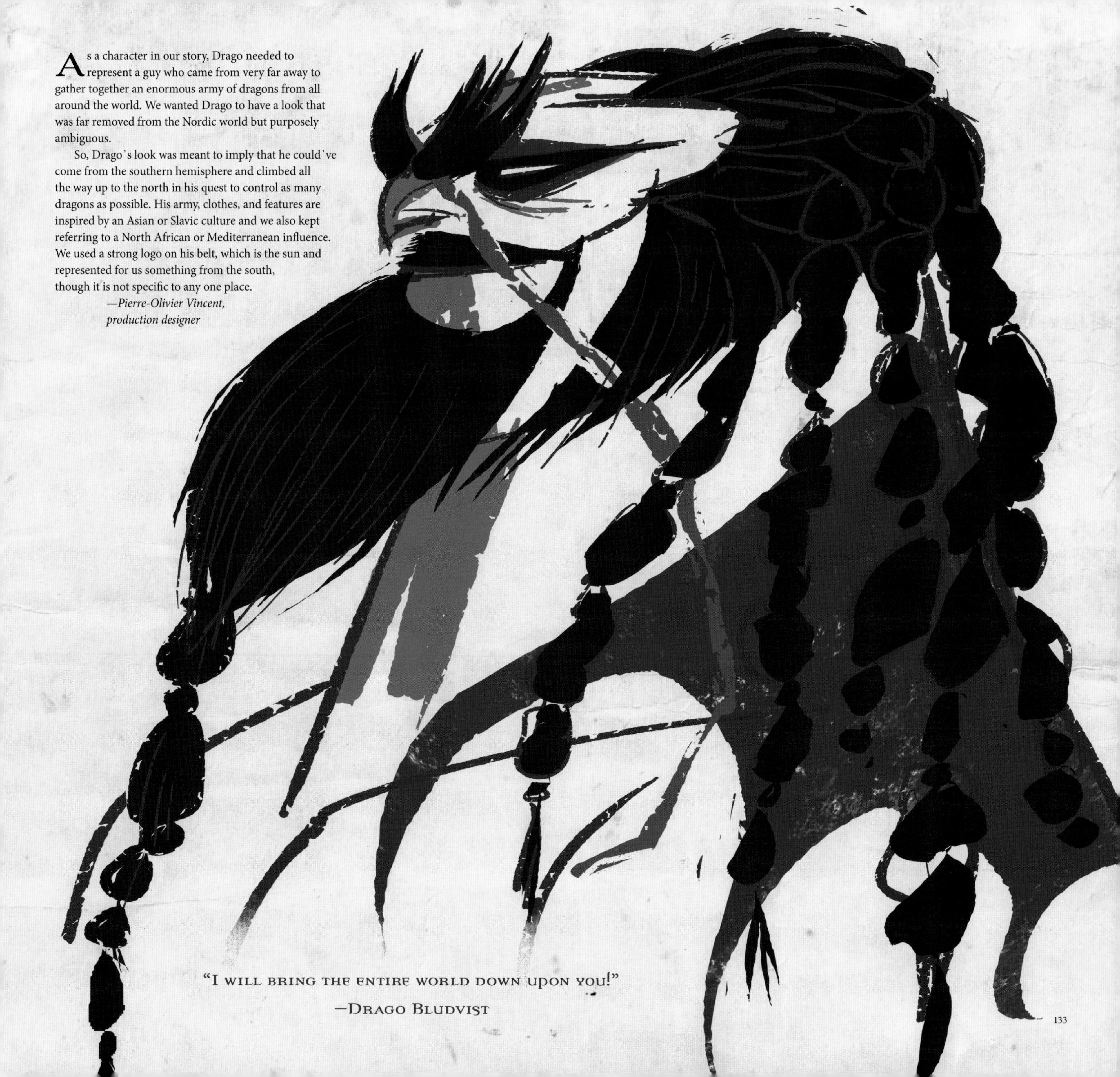

As a character in our story, Drago needed to represent a guy who came from very far away to gather together an enormous army of dragons from all around the world. We wanted Drago to have a look that was far removed from the Nordic world but purposely ambiguous.

So, Drago's look was meant to imply that he could've come from the southern hemisphere and climbed all the way up to the north in his quest to control as many dragons as possible. His army, clothes, and features are inspired by an Asian or Slavic culture and we also kept referring to a North African or Mediterranean influence. We used a strong logo on his belt, which is the sun and represented for us something from the south, though it is not specific to any one place.

*—Pierre-Olivier Vincent, production designer*

"I WILL BRING THE ENTIRE WORLD DOWN UPON YOU!"

—DRAGO BLUDVIST

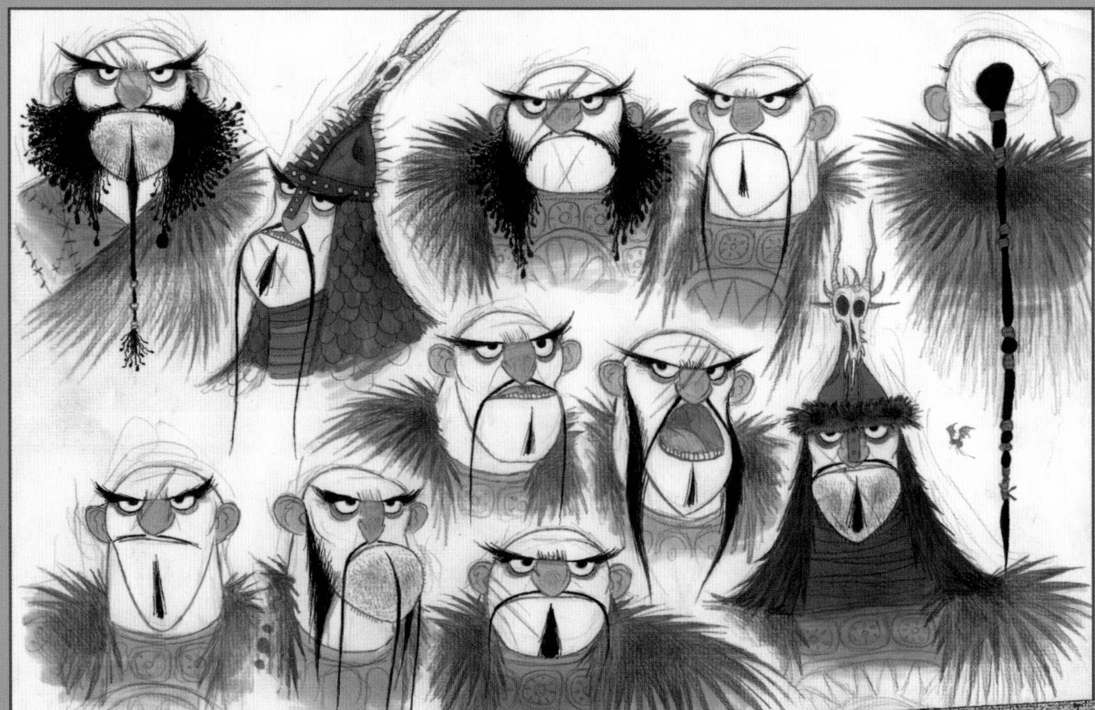

The story drove the idea that Drago lost a limb to the dragons. We wanted to show that he has been scarred in a similar way to Hiccup, who lost a foot to the dragons. But Hiccup has a completely different view on it. Drago is using the dragon power to dominate the world while Hiccup wants to coexist with them.

There is always more freedom when you are designing a villain, and for Drago we had some solid ideas. We knew he had to be someone from a strange land that no one had seen before. We wanted him to look capable of commanding great armies from different lands, so if you look closely at Drago's men, they are all from different places.

We wanted an original design for Drago and explored many different hair and beard styles. In the first version, he was essentially bald. We needed a design that felt like it was not from the Viking world, but we didn't want to be too specific about where he was from. He needed to be an amalgam of different cultures. The design was also influenced when Djimon Hounsou was cast. Now Drago is from somewhere in the larger Mediterranean world and sports a healthy set of dreadlocks. That was a home run everyone loved, so we went with it.

*—Simon Otto, head of character animation*

LEFT: Drago Head Studies • *Nico Marlet* • *pencil & marker*
BELOW (FROM LEFT): Drago Evolution • *Carter Goodrich, Joe Moshier, Nico Marlet*
BOTTOM: Rune • *Kirsten Kawamura*
OPPOSITE: Drago • *Nico Marlet* • *pencil & marker*
OPPOSITE BOTTOM LEFT: Drago Emblem Variations • *Iuri Lioi*

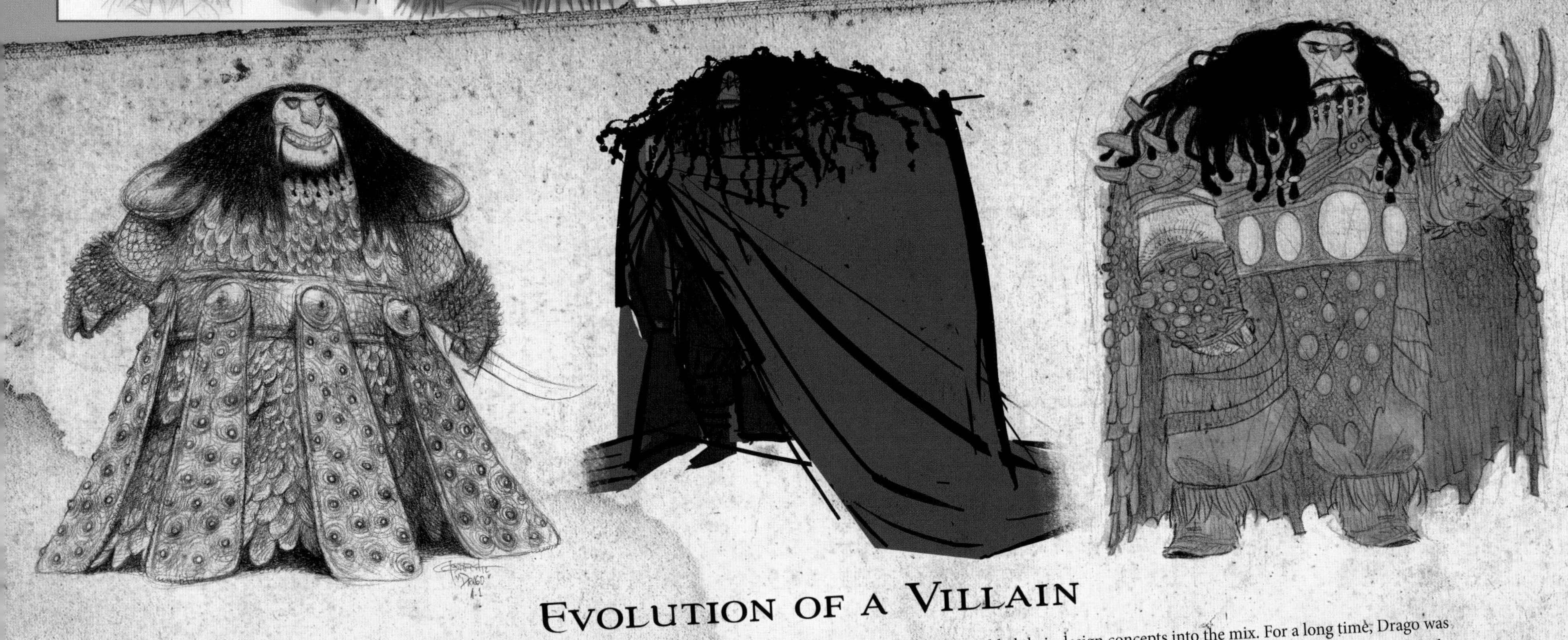

# Evolution of a Villain

These three drawings demonstrate the evolution of the design of the Drago character. The filmmakers particularly liked the top half of the Carter Goodrich drawing (left) and the feeling of the Joe Moshier drawing (center). These ideas were relayed to character designer Nico Marlet who incorporated them into his final design (right). Filmmaking is a collaborative effort, even in terms of developing the look of a particular character. The drawings by Nico Marlet at the top of this page show the character as he was imagined before Carter and Joe added their design concepts into the mix. For a long time, Drago was bald, though no one felt that was 100 percent right for the character. Now he has long dark locks of unruly hair. The amazing thing was that Carter and Joe came up with such similar concepts for the character even though they never saw each other's work. Interestingly, they were able to imagine a look that, along with refinements from Nico, appealed to all the filmmakers.

*—Pierre-Olivier Vincent, production designer*

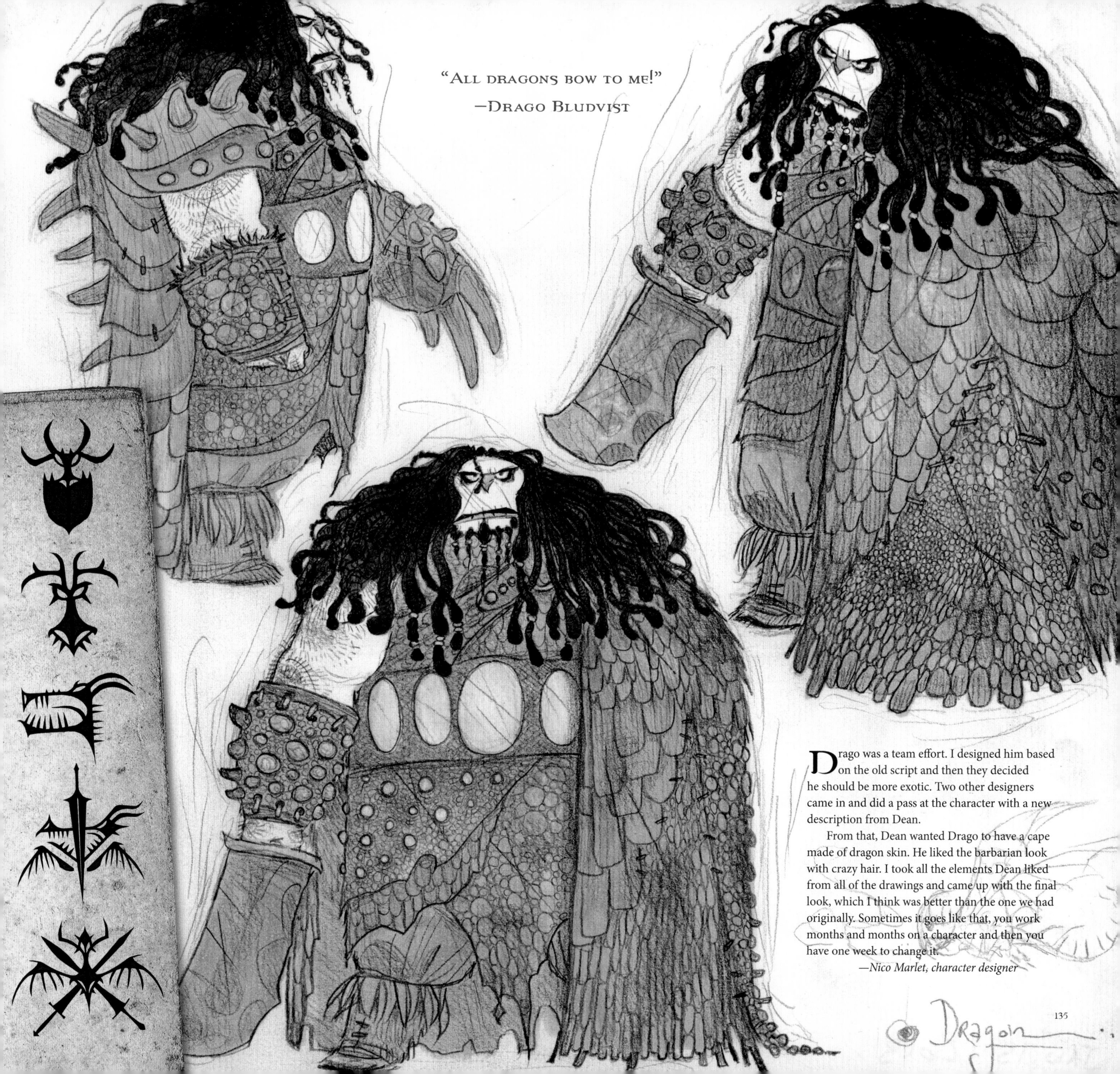

"All dragons bow to me!"
—Drago Bludvist

Drago was a team effort. I designed him based on the old script and then they decided he should be more exotic. Two other designers came in and did a pass at the character with a new description from Dean.

From that, Dean wanted Drago to have a cape made of dragon skin. He liked the barbarian look with crazy hair. I took all the elements Dean liked from all of the drawings and came up with the final look, which I think was better than the one we had originally. Sometimes it goes like that, you work months and months on a character and then you have one week to change it.

*—Nico Marlet, character designer*

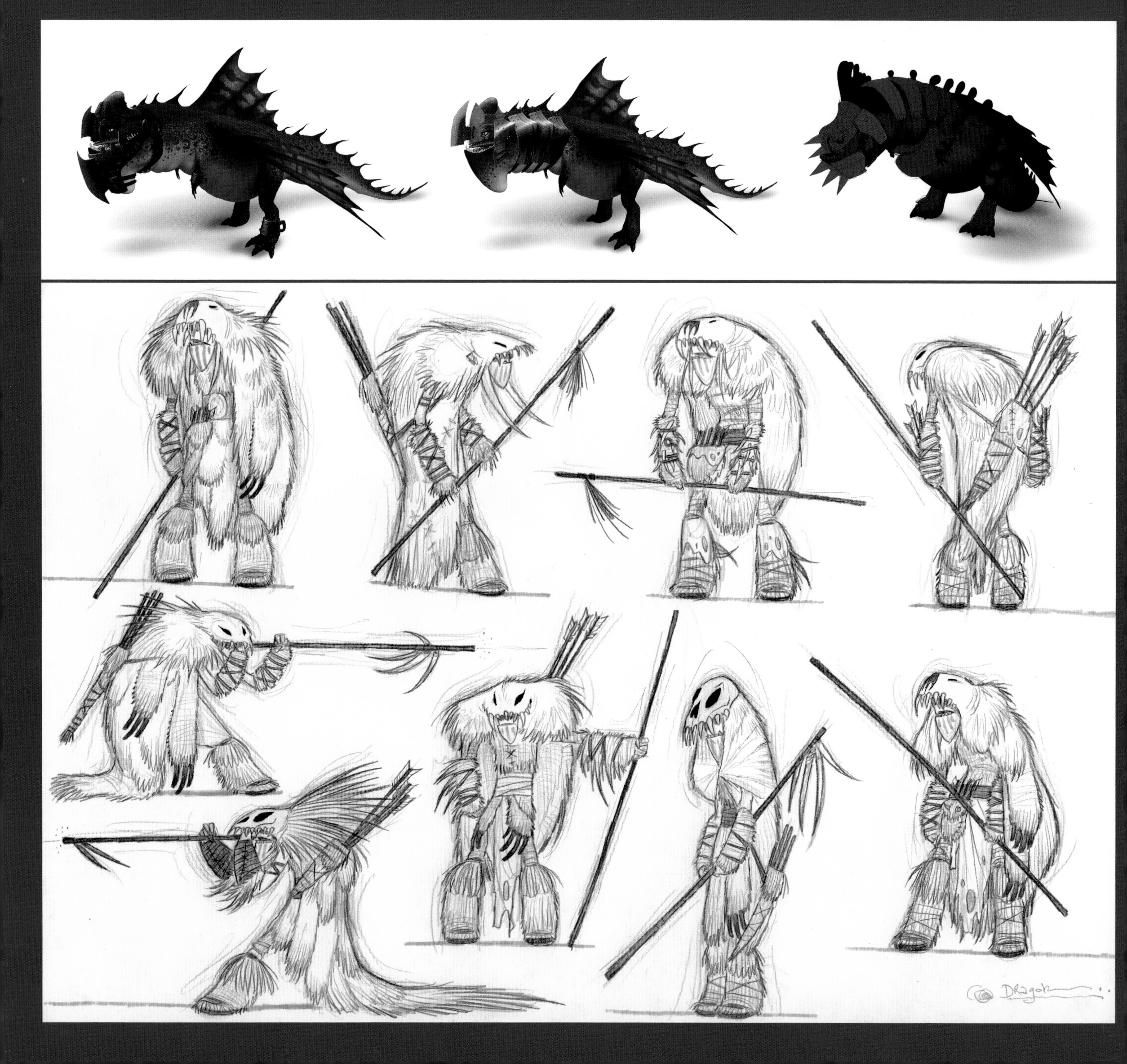
Dragon

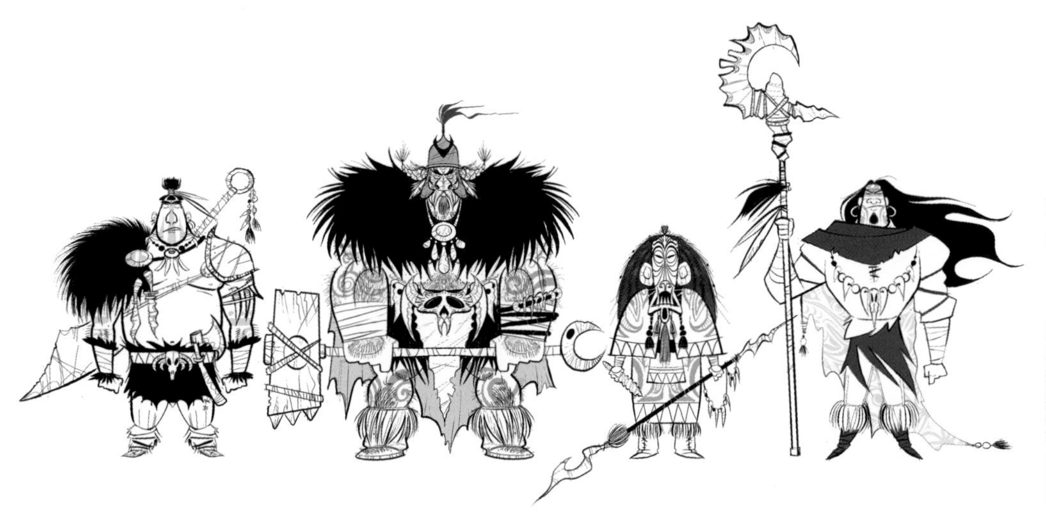

# Drago's Army

We looked to Slavic and Asiatic influences in the design of Drago's army and his ships. We sampled the traditional clothing and armor of those cultures. We also looked at the material and the colors of their costumes to keep everything authentic. The Slavic colors were mostly on the cold side: grays, blues, blacks, and magentas.

—*ZhaoPing Wei, art director*

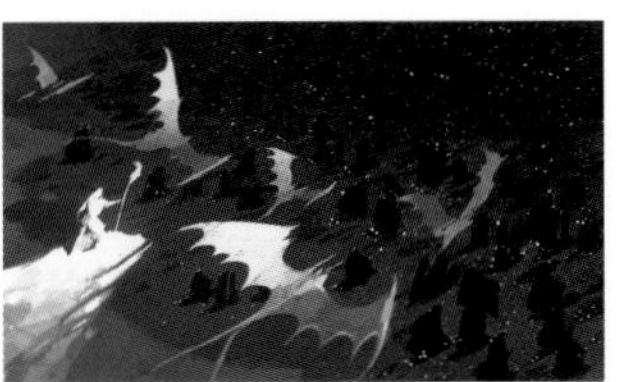

LEFT: Lighting Study • *Marcos Mateu-Mestre*
FAR LEFT: Drago's Army • *Tony Siruno*
BELOW: Sled Variations • *Peter Chan* • *pencil & marker*
BOTTOM: Army Banners • *Peter Chan, Iuri Lioi & Kirsten Kawamura* • Models • *Vinay Hegde, Jayanta Mazumder & Vaibhav Shah*
OPPOSITE TOP: Dragon Armor Variations • *Iuri Lioi* • Models • *Abraham Meneu Oset*
OPPOSITE BOTTOM: Disguised Army • *Nico Marlet* • *pencil & marker*

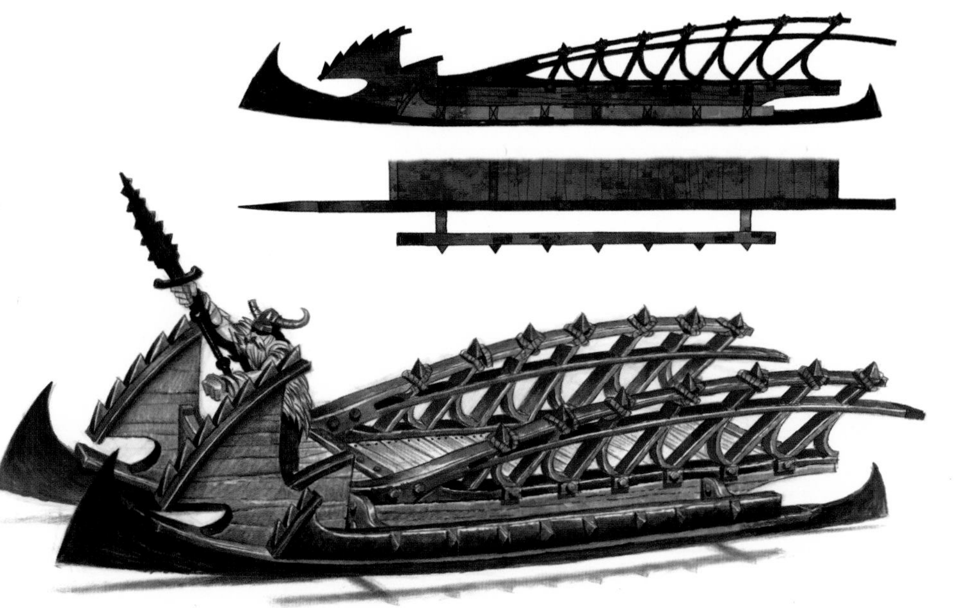

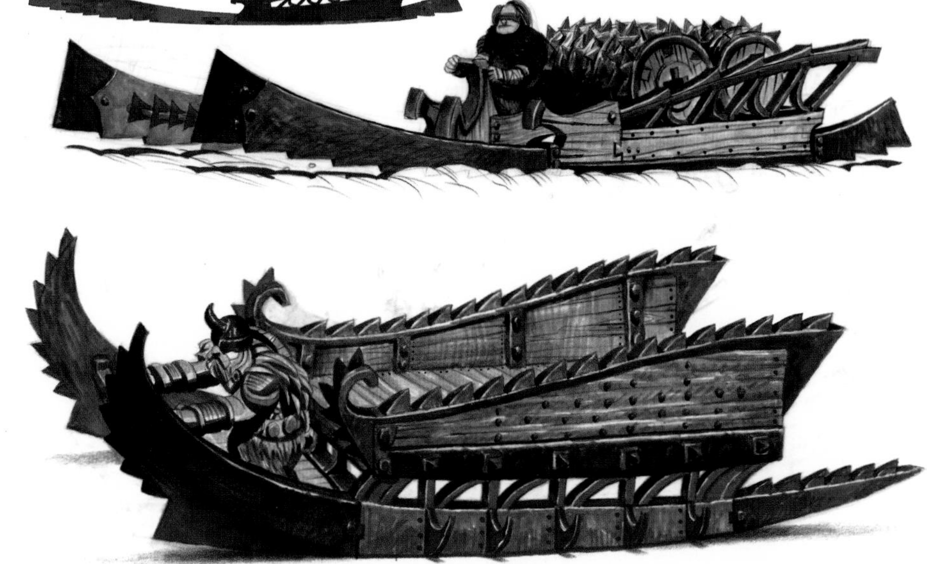

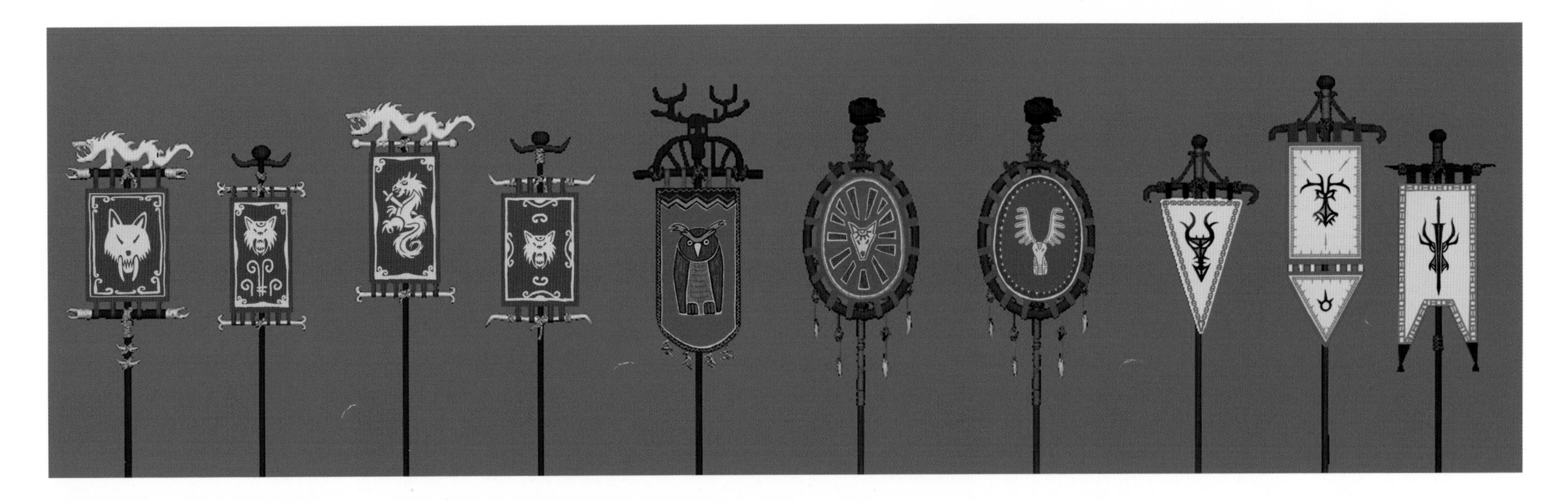

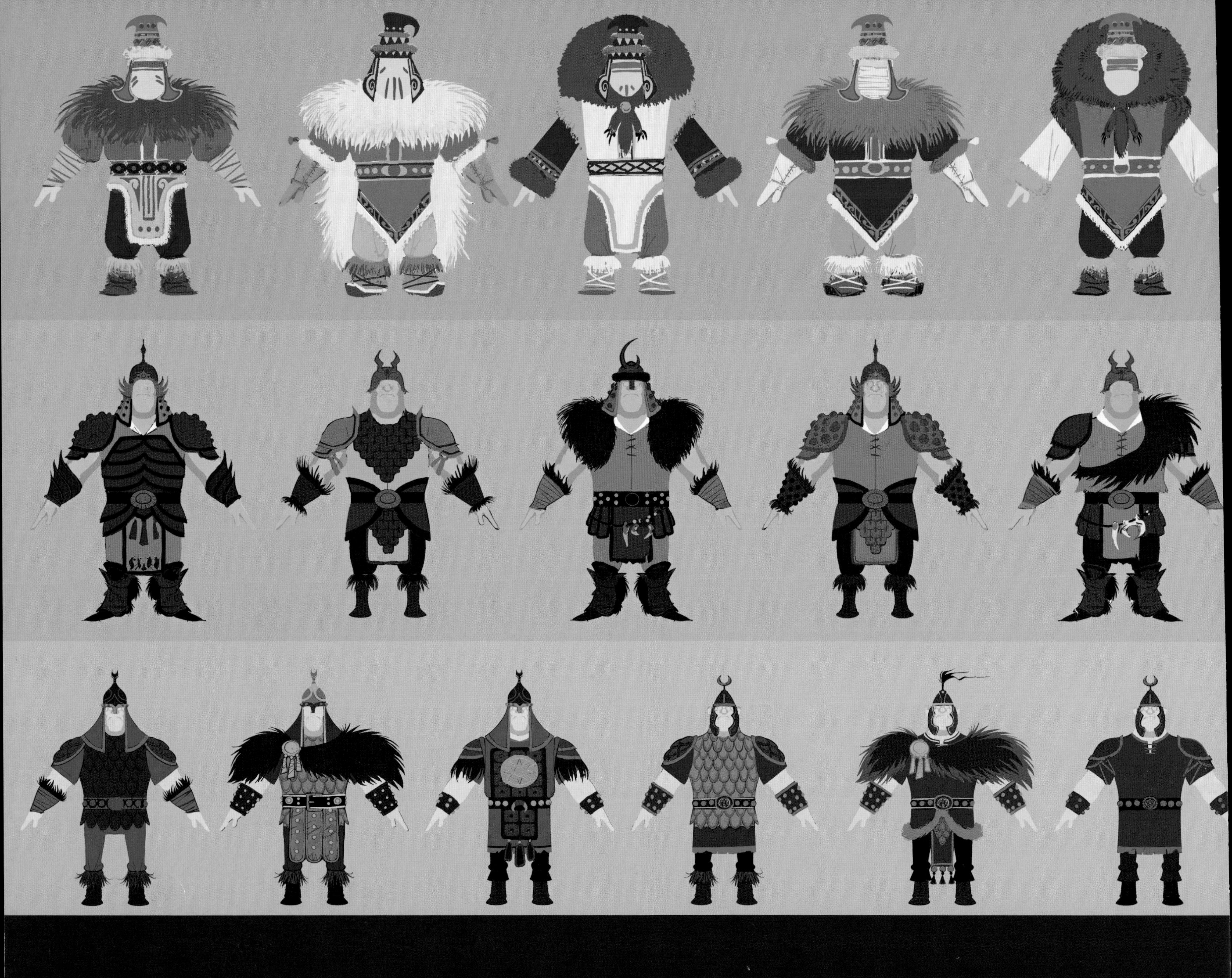

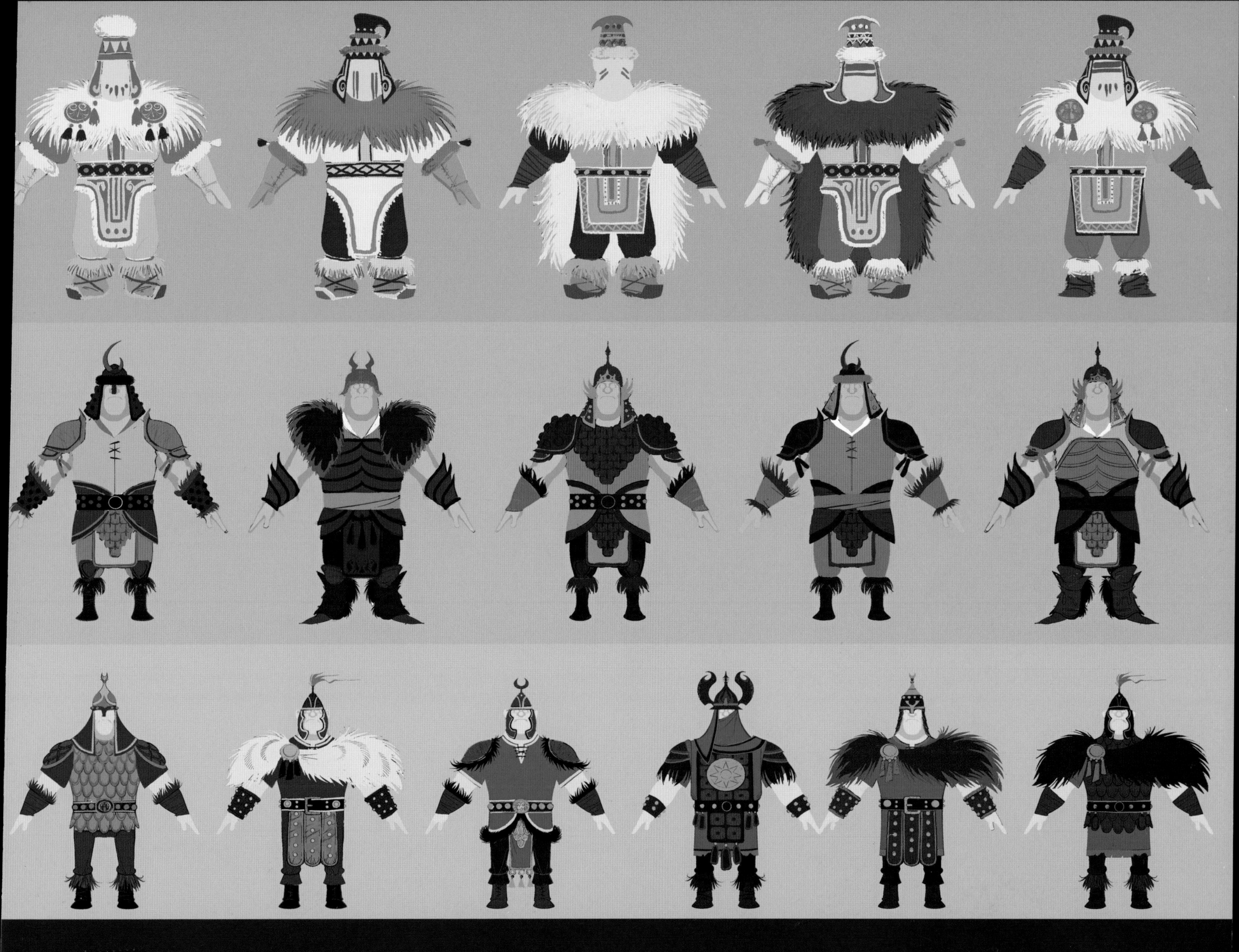

THIS PAGE & OPPOSITE: Army Costume Color Variations • *ZhaoPing Wei* • Costume Designs • *Tony Siruno*

# Drago's Ship

The ships we designed for Drago are very different than the elegant Viking ships that have many functions such as fishing, racing, and sailing, as well as war. Drago's ships are designed solely to capture dragons and carry weapons of war—we think of them as the giant aircraft carriers of the Dark Ages.

The designs for Drago's ships are very primitive and aggressive. We used a lot of heavy metal and decorated the ships with skeletons, bones, and pointy spears, which are meant to instill fear.

*—Pierre-Olivier Vincent, production designer*

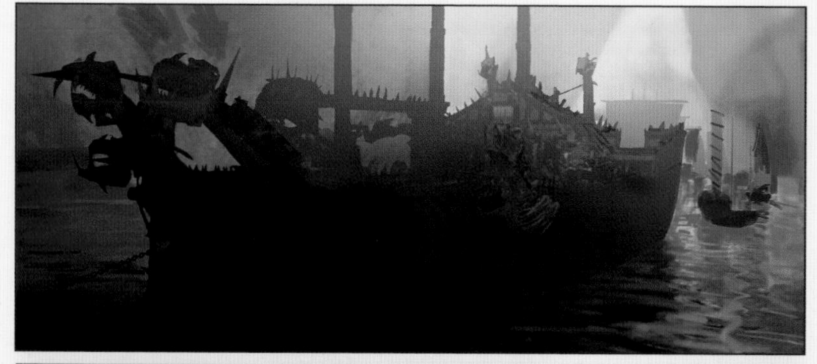

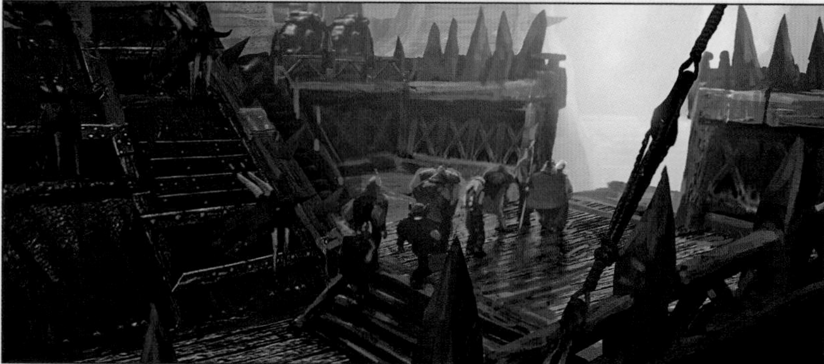

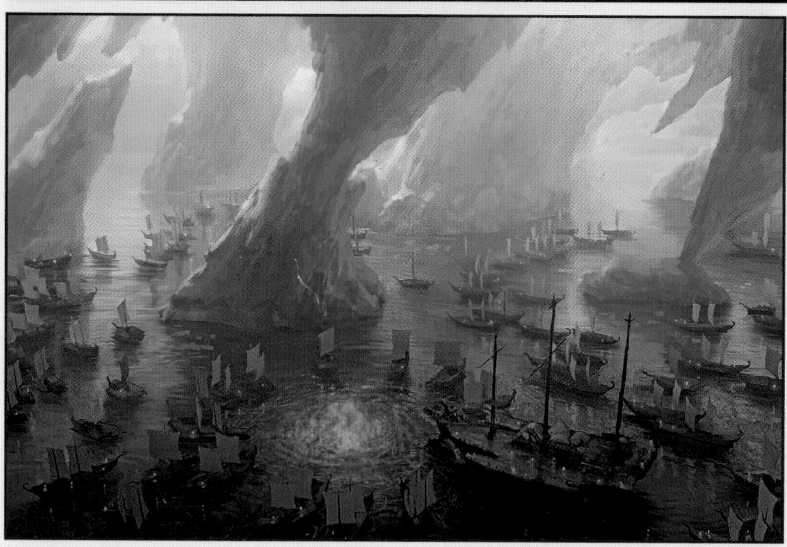

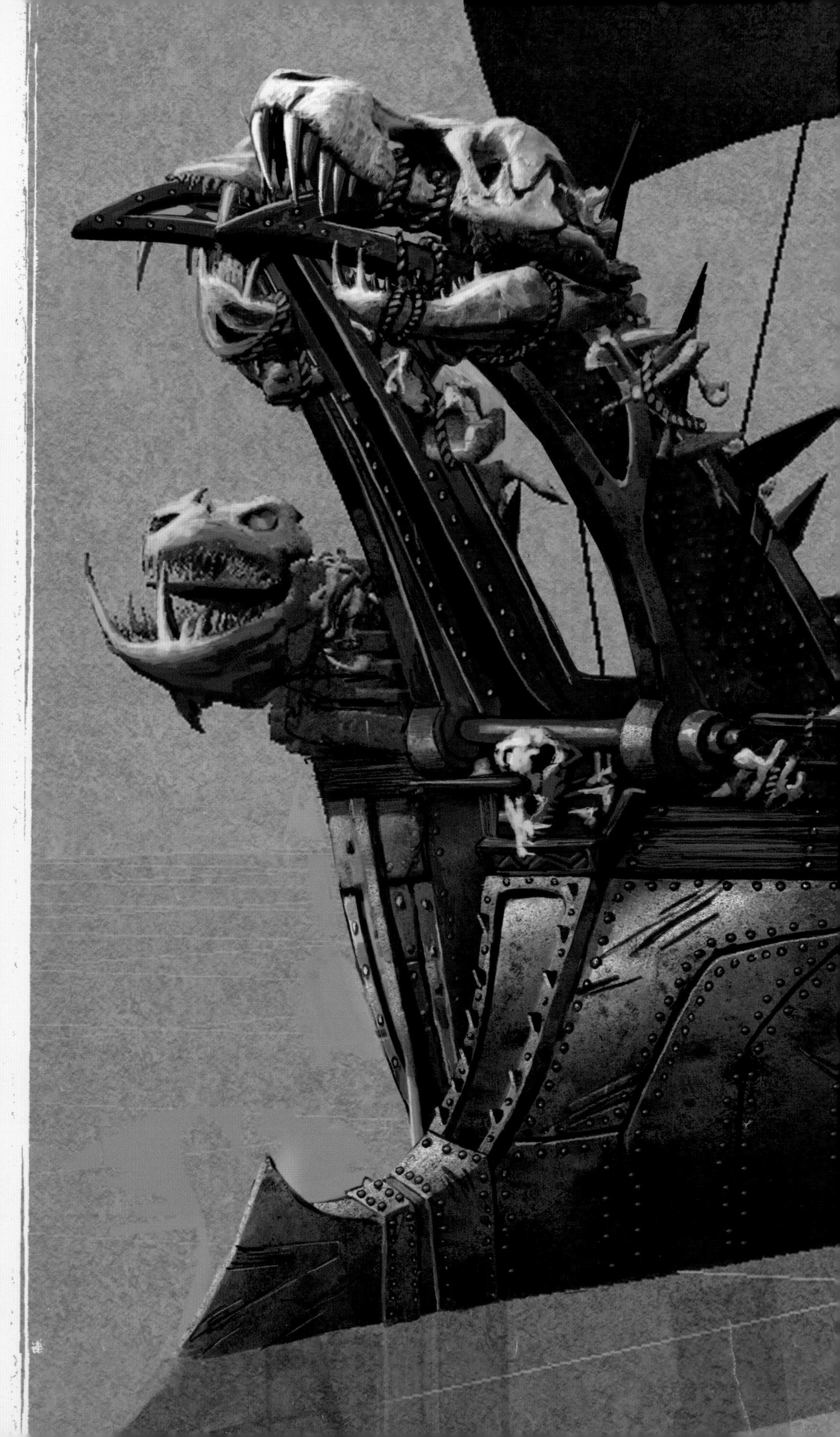

ABOVE: Color Keys ✦ *Woonyoung Jung*
RIGHT: Drago's Ship ✦ *Kirsten Kawamura*

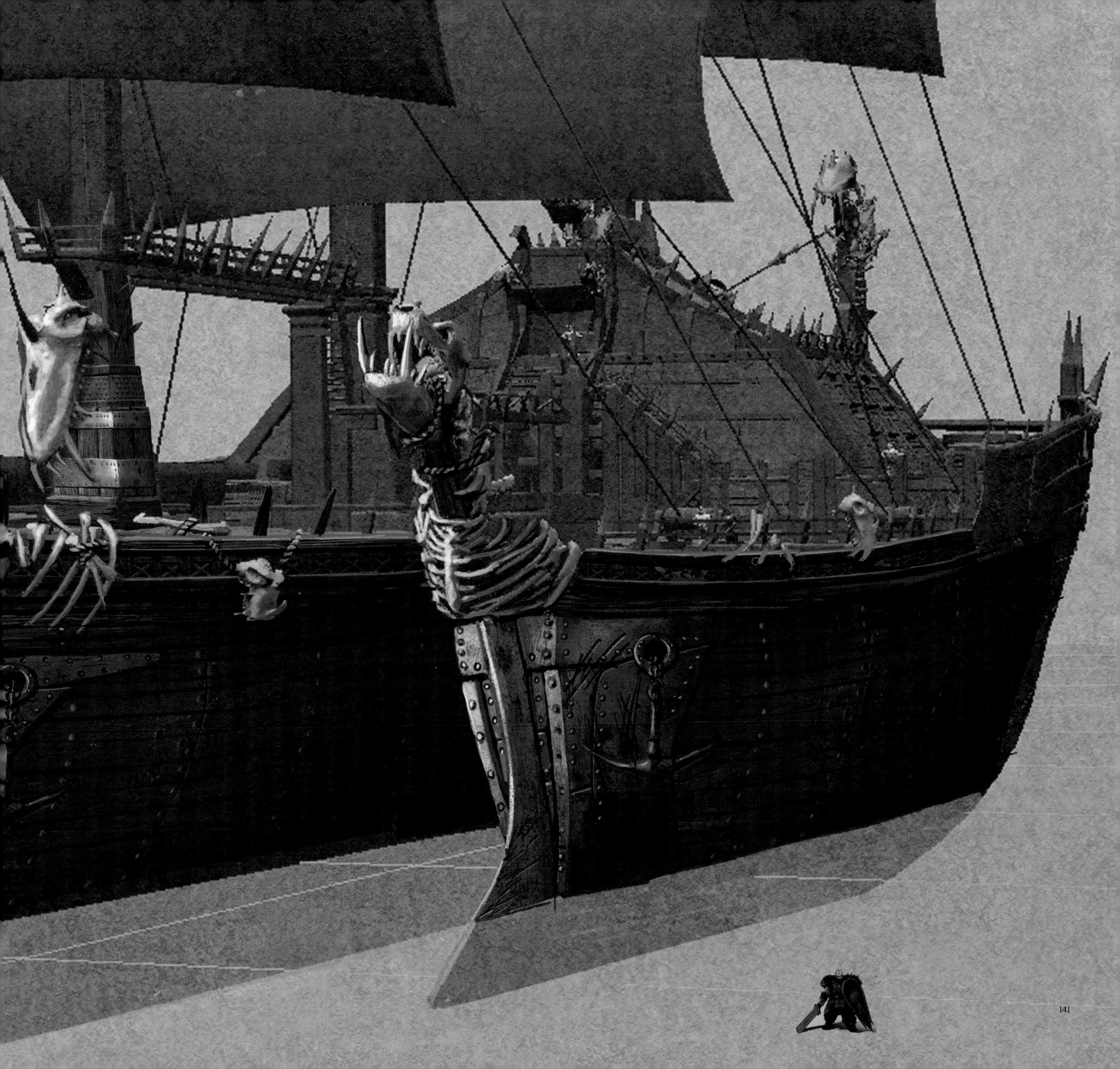

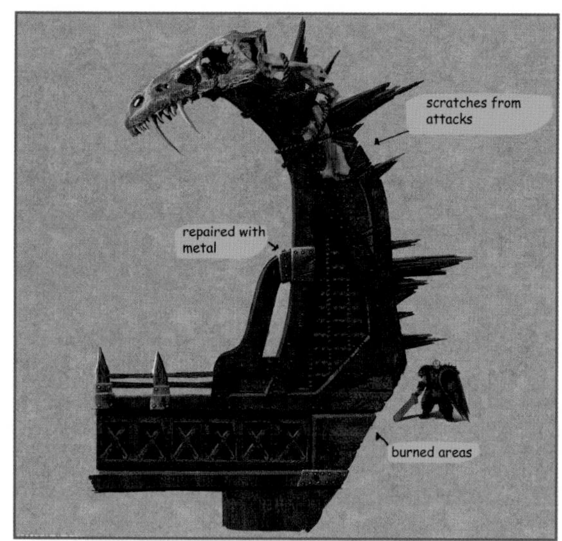


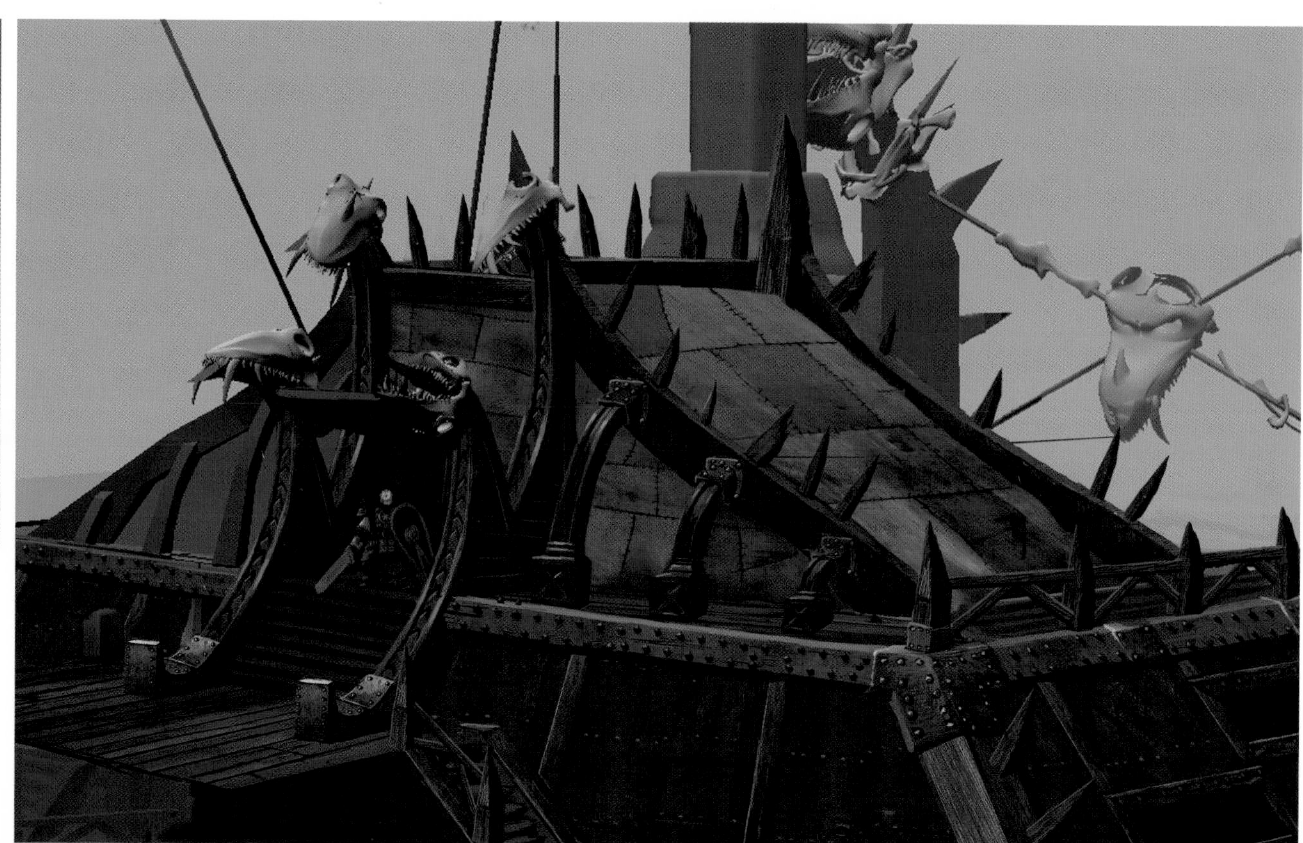

Drago is not a Viking. He comes from an entirely different part of the world so he has his own style, which we define as dark, brutal, and totally efficient. He has one purpose—to capture dragons. The simple parallel is that Hiccup is defending the natural world while trying to make peace and live in harmony with animals. Drago represents the mechanical world where everything is meant to look threatening, aggressive, and unnatural.

*—Pierre-Olivier Vincent, production designer*

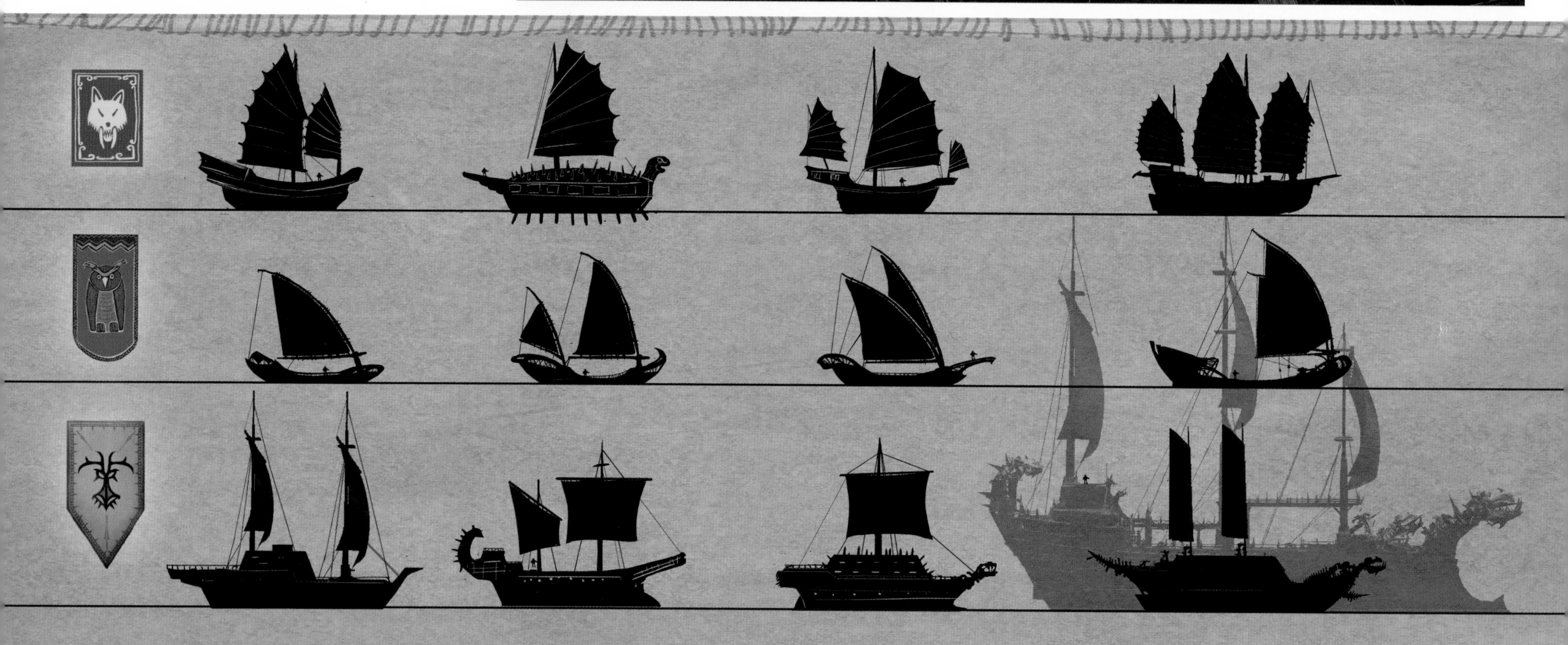

# Drago's War Machines

Drago wants to build a dragon army, so his war machines are designed to capture dragons, not kill them. The machine on this page is a throwing device designed to toss out nets to capture the dragon and perhaps knock him out. The machine on page 145 is called the Scrambler and its purpose is to make this horrible, deafening, screeching noise—like nails on a chalkboard, only louder—that will paralyze a dragon into submission. Then Drago can bend the animal to his will. (These ideas, by the way, come from our very gentle-looking director.) The Scrambler is a machine that is being built on *Dragon 2* and may be used on *Dragon 3*.

*—ZhaoPing Wei, art director*

OPPOSITE TOP LEFT & RIGHT: Drago's Ship Details
✦ *Kirsten Kawamura*
OPPOSITE FAR LEFT: Army Insignias
✦ *Kirsten Kawamura, Peter Chan, & Iuri Lioi*
OPPOSITE BOTTOM: Boat Silhouettes
✦ *Kirsten Kawamura*

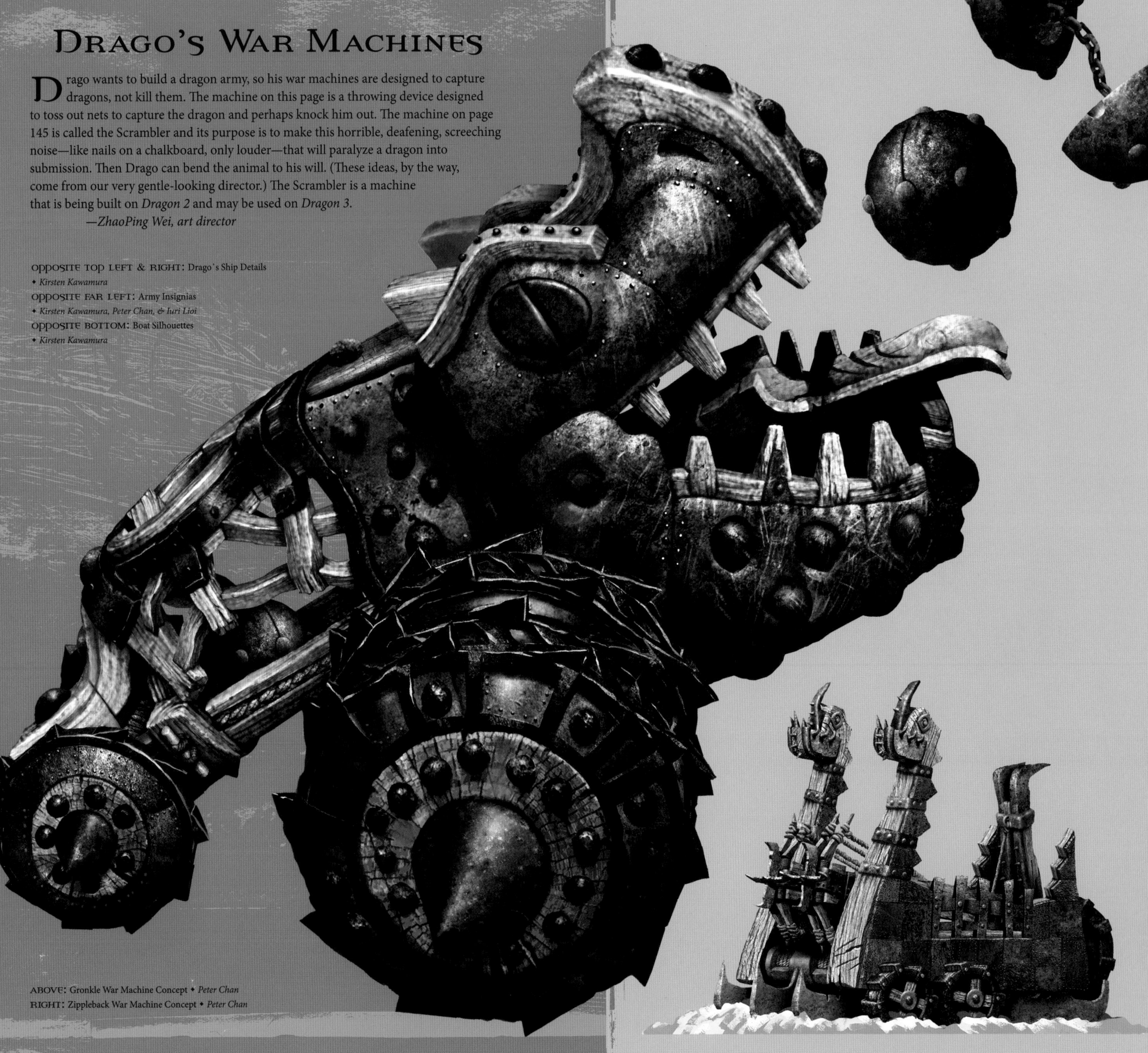

ABOVE: Gronkle War Machine Concept ✦ *Peter Chan*
RIGHT: Zippleback War Machine Concept ✦ *Peter Chan*

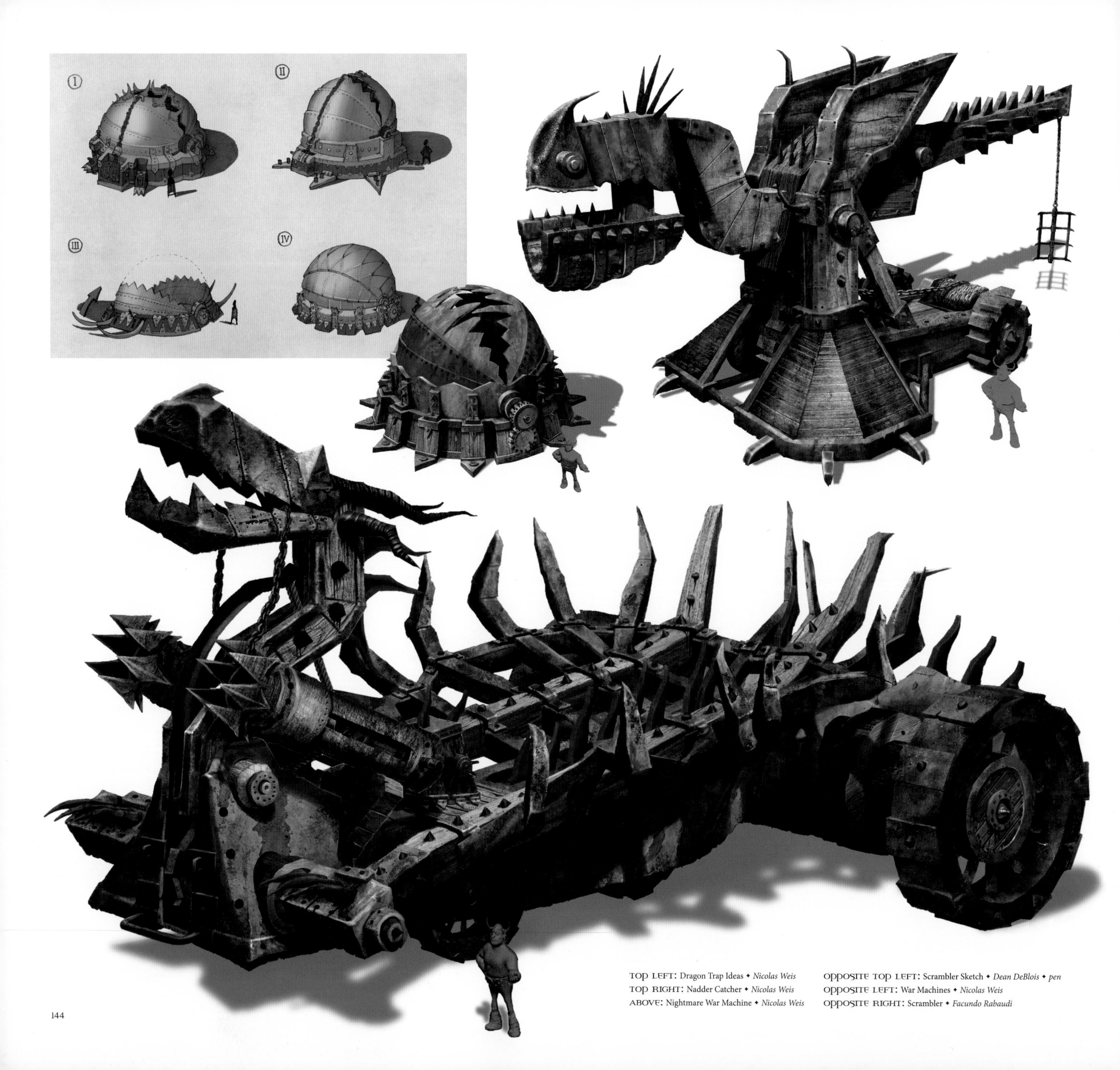


TOP LEFT: Dragon Trap Ideas ✦ *Nicolas Weis*
TOP RIGHT: Nadder Catcher ✦ *Nicolas Weis*
ABOVE: Nightmare War Machine ✦ *Nicolas Weis*

OPPOSITE TOP LEFT: Scrambler Sketch ✦ *Dean DeBlois* ✦ *pen*
OPPOSITE LEFT: War Machines ✦ *Nicolas Weis*
OPPOSITE RIGHT: Scrambler ✦ *Facundo Rabaudi*

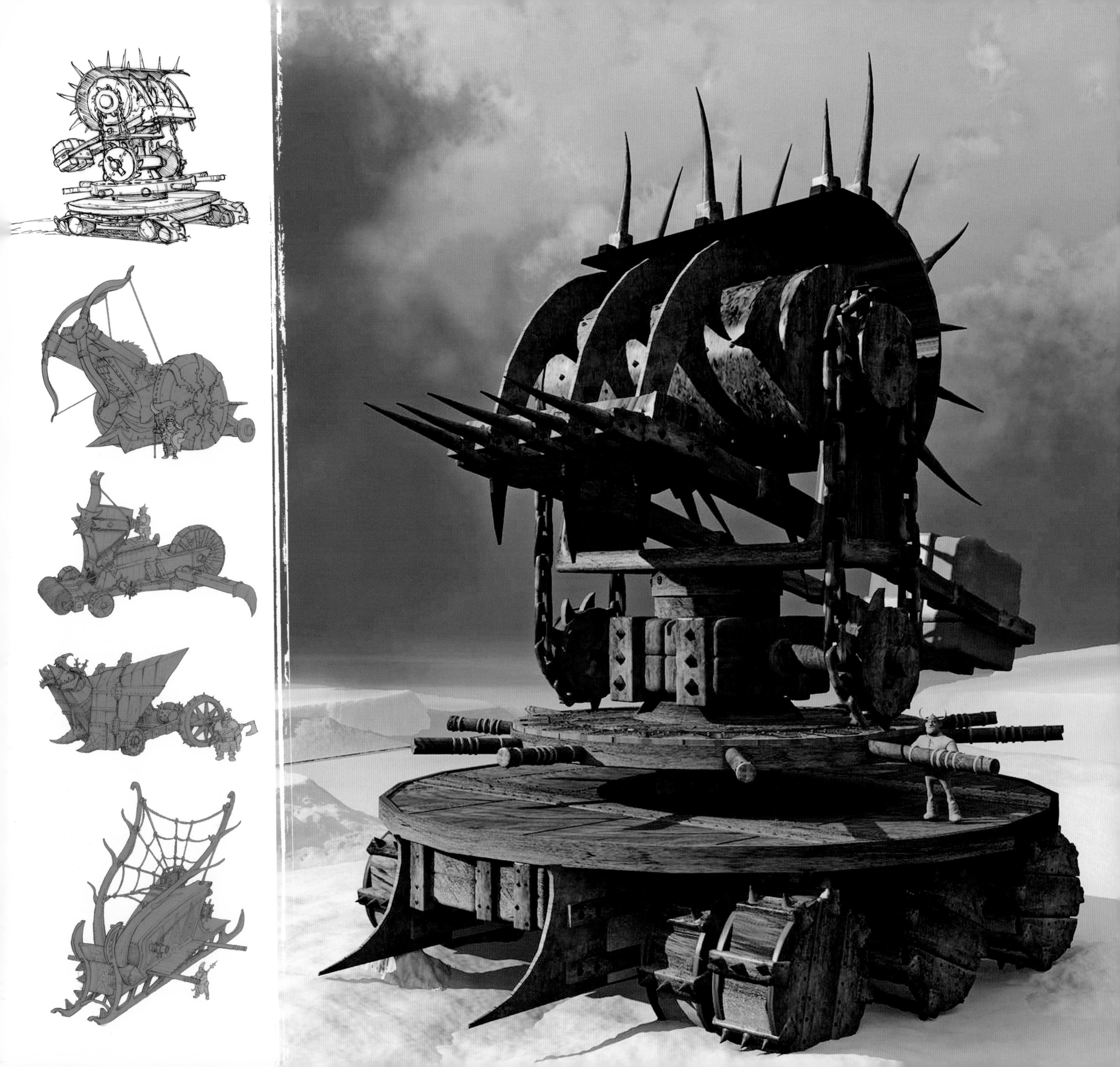

# PART VI
# WORLD WAR OF DRAGONS

"He who controls the Alpha, controls them all."

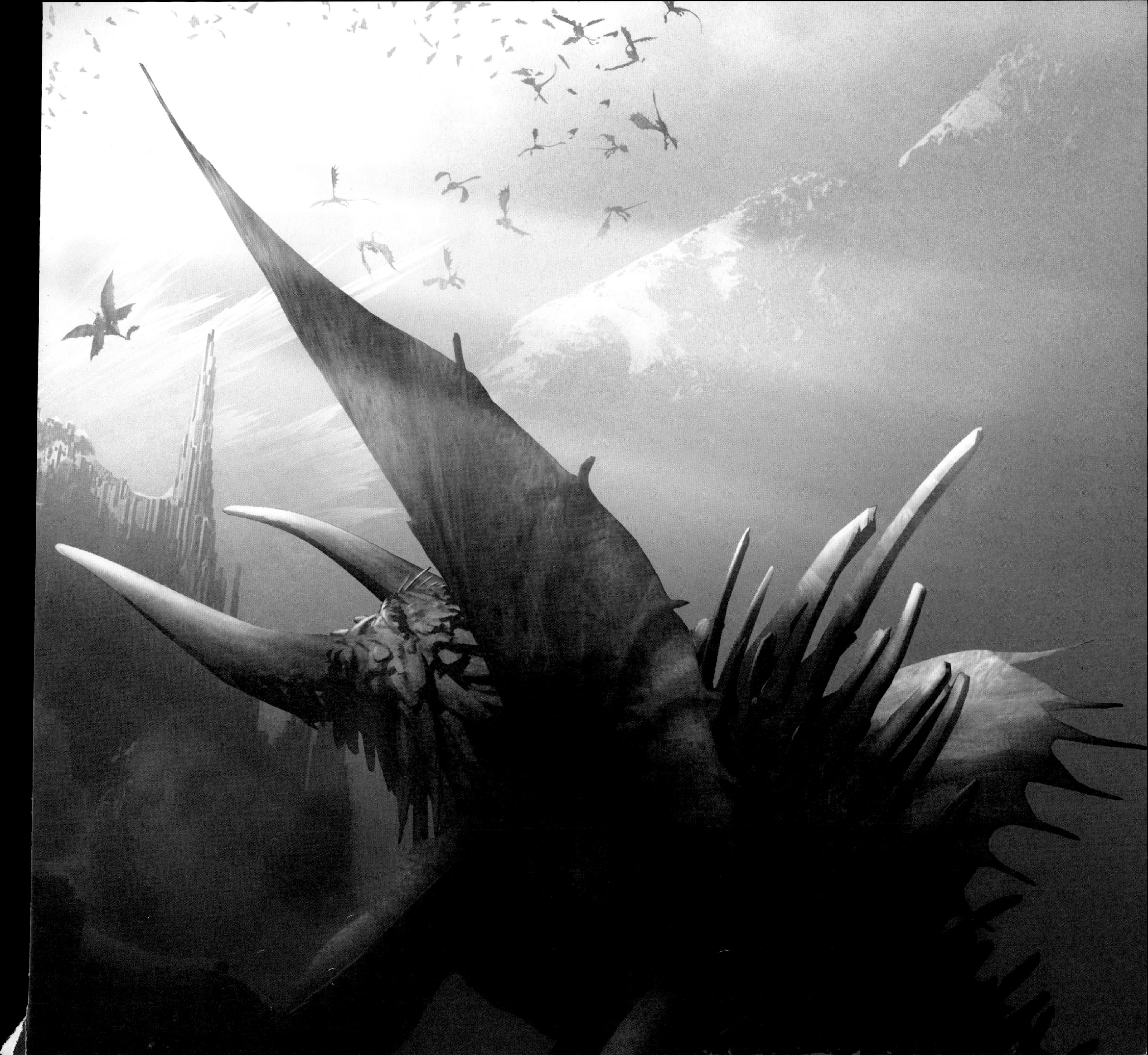

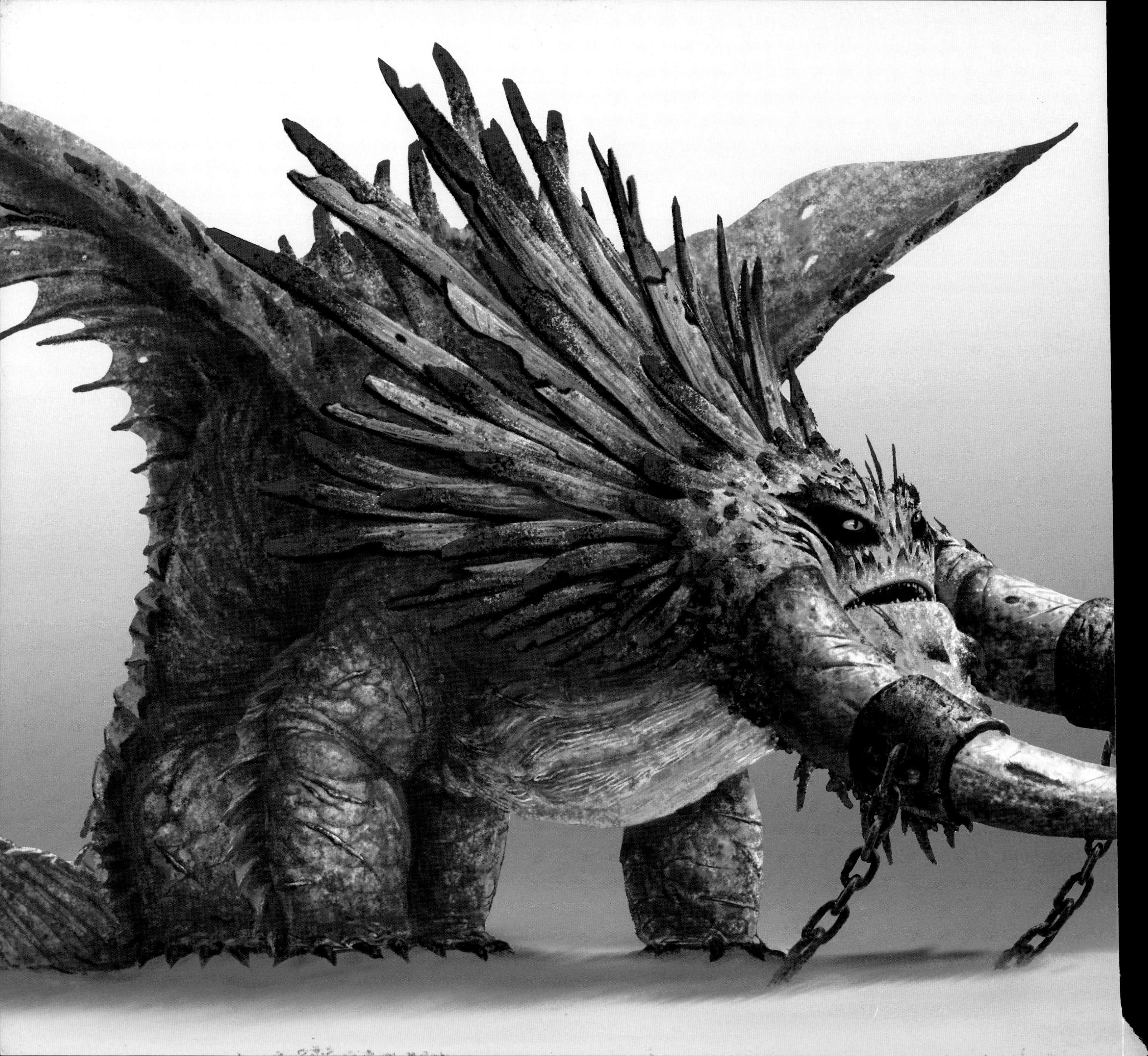

# Drago's Bewilderbeast

For a long time, we just had one Bewilderbeast and then it was decided that Drago should have his own but it should be quite different from Valka's in both design and temperament.

Valka's Bewilderbeast is pure and beautiful, like a polar bear. He is a kind and loving animal. He lives with the dragons and wants to protect them.

Drago's Bewilderbeast is just the opposite. He has probably been abused by Drago to turn him into an evil creature. He is like those zoo animals that are tortured and forced to perform. He has a different skin color and lots of scars almost as if he has seen a lot of battle. We wanted to give the impression that he has been poorly cared for and controlled for evil purposes.

By creating two such different looks, it was easy to separate the two beasts, especially during the climactic battle scene.

*—Pierre-Olivier Vincent, production designer*

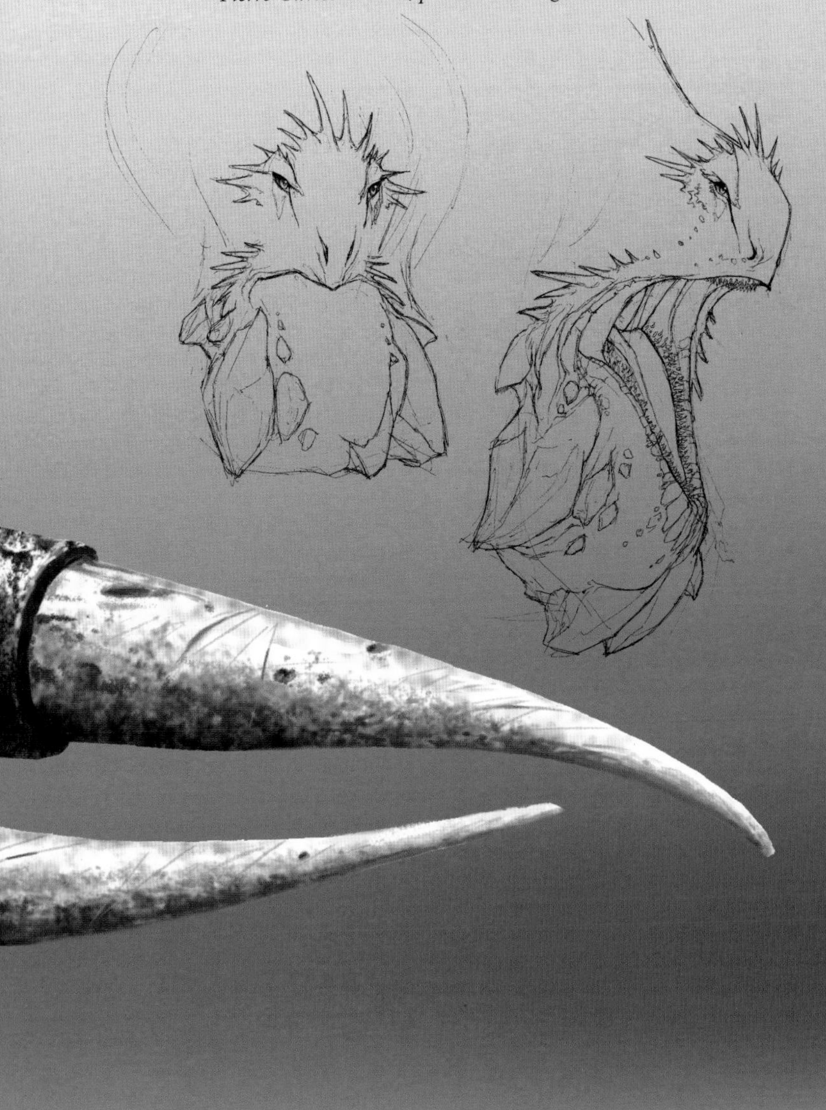

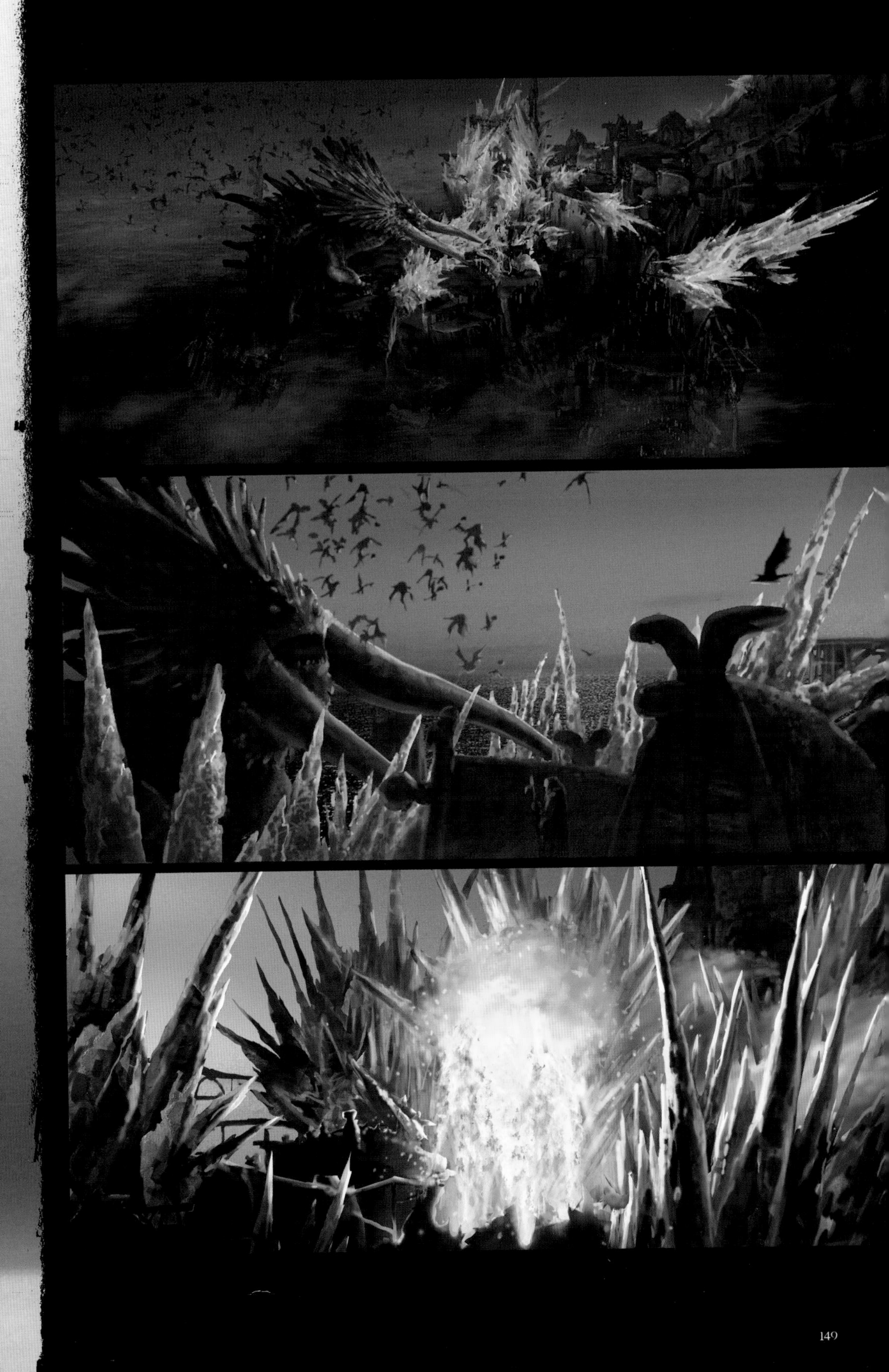

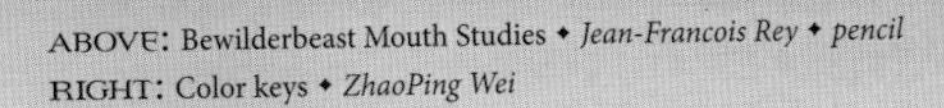

ABOVE: Bewilderbeast Mouth Studies ✦ *Jean-Francois Rey* ✦ *pencil*
RIGHT: Color keys ✦ *ZhaoPing Wei*
OPPOSITE: Drago's Bewilderbeast Painting ✦ *ZhaoPing Wei* ✦ Model ✦ *Seungyoung "Sean" Choi*
PREVIOUS PAGES: Battle ✦ *Pierre-Olivier Vincent*

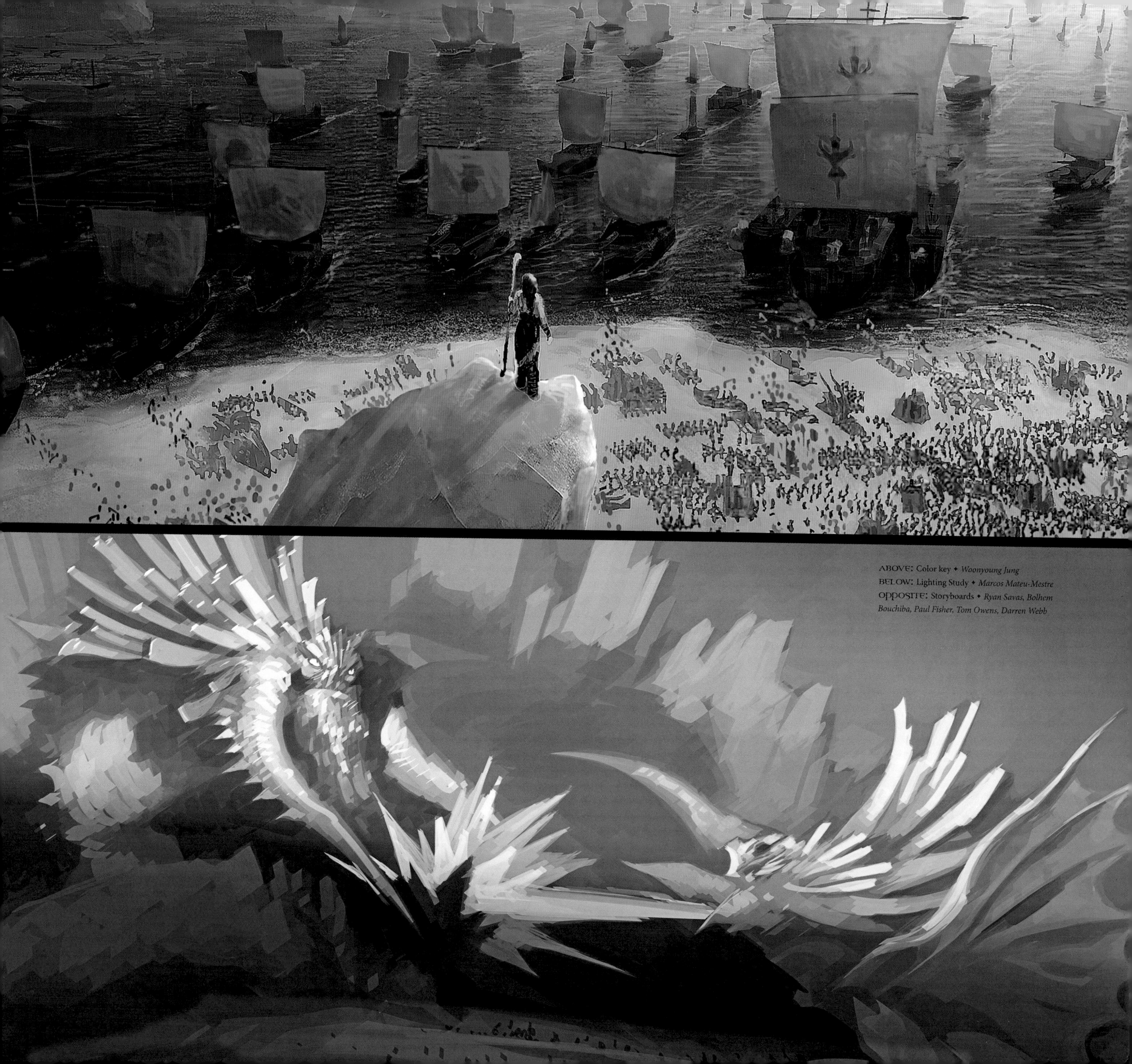

ABOVE: Color key ✦ *Woonyoung Jung*
BELOW: Lighting Study ✦ *Marcos Mateu-Mestre*
OPPOSITE: Storyboards ✦ *Ryan Savas, Bolhem Bouchiba, Paul Fisher, Tom Owens, Darren Webb*

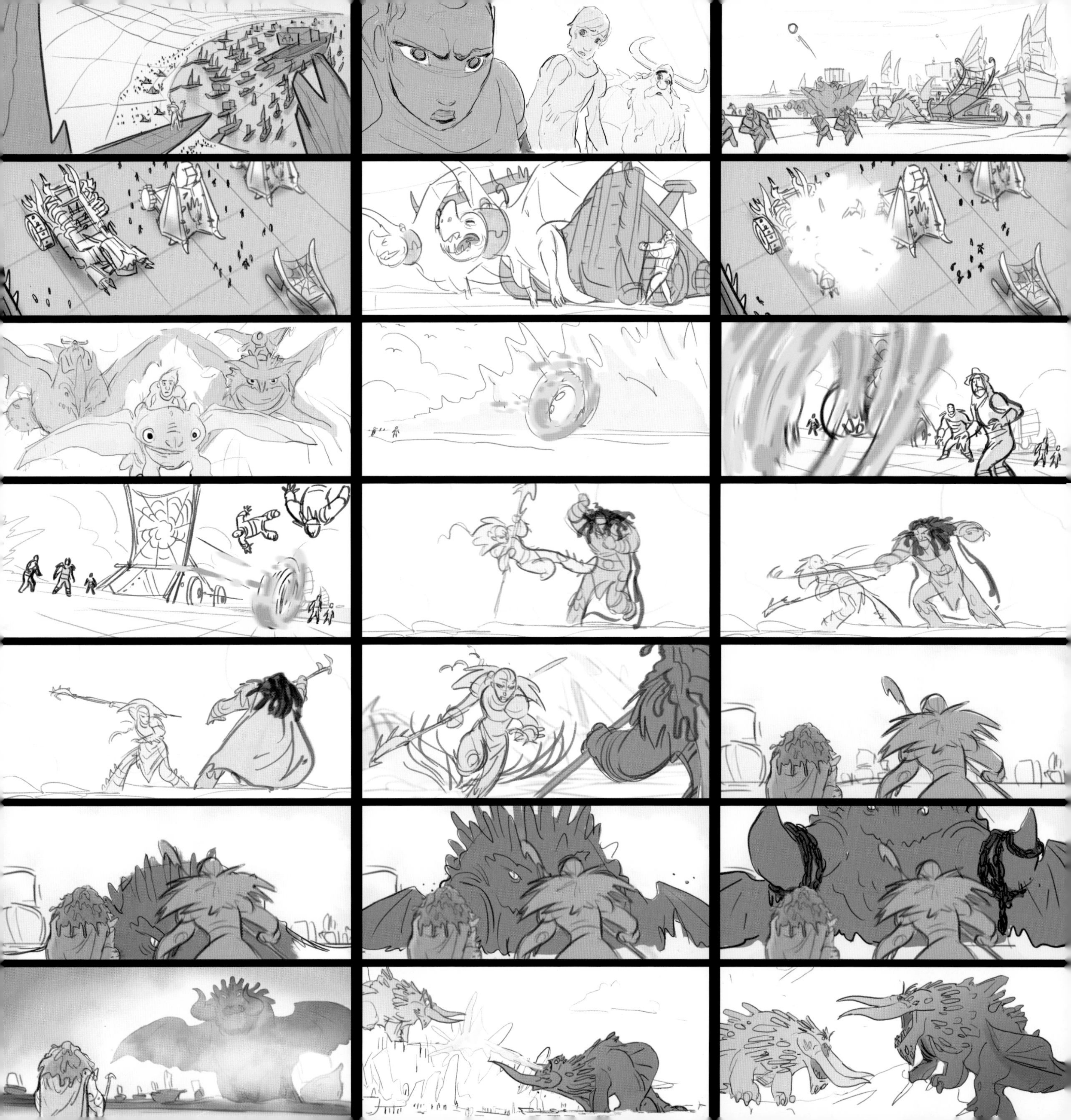

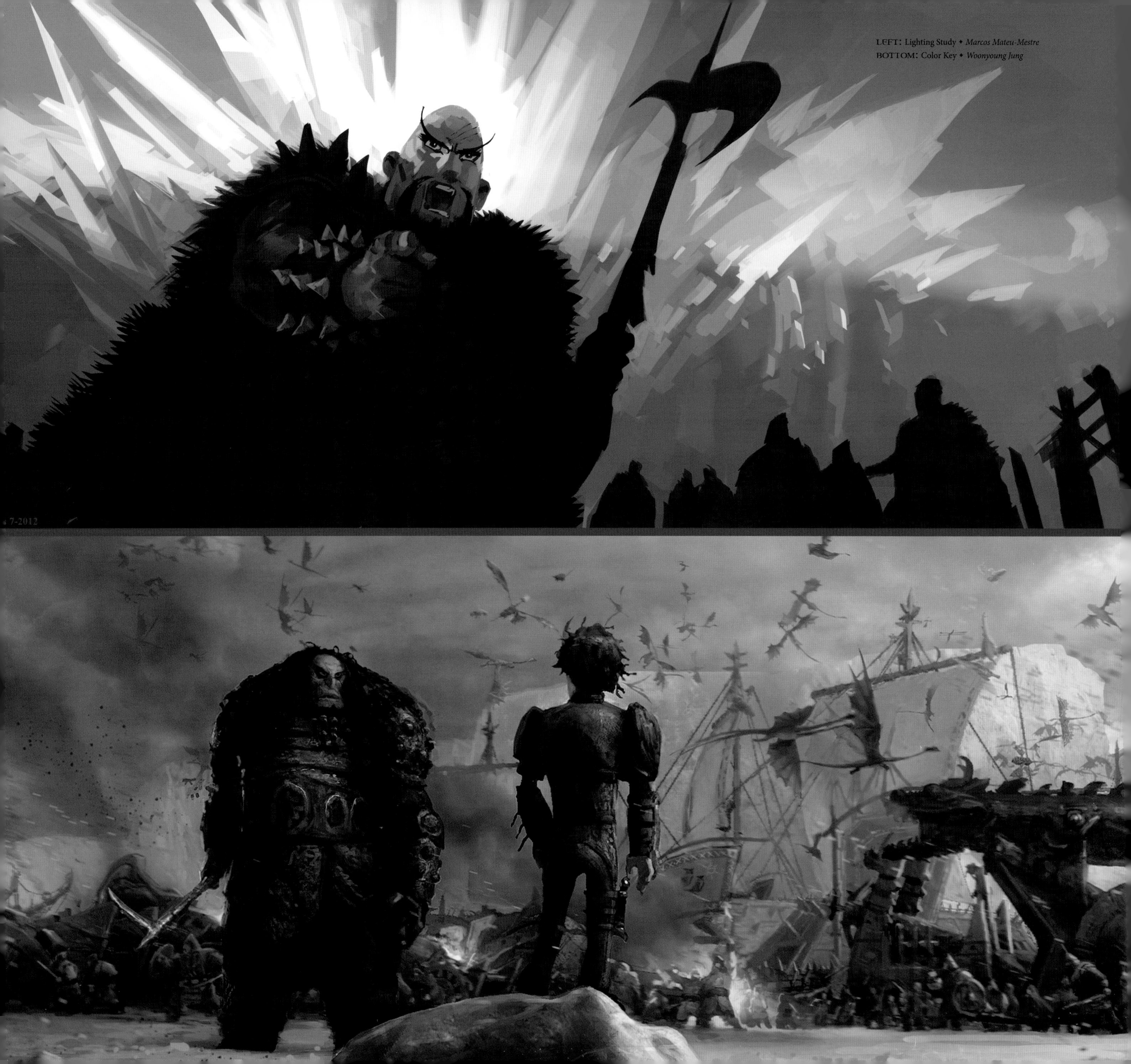


LEFT: Lighting Study ✦ *Marcos Mateu-Mestre*
BOTTOM: Color Key ✦ *Woonyoung Jung*

# War

When Dean first talked about the battle scene, he described it as the start of the World War of Dragons. I pitched the idea of opening with this one big *Lord of the Rings* type shot—one shot that said it all, I thought the scene needed the spectacle of a huge battle about to happen. Of course, it was expensive to do such a huge shot but I felt it would sell everything that is happening in the battle: the war machines, the shooting, taking down the dragons, attacking the mountain, soldiers coming in off the beach, and all the rest. After that establishing shot, we are tracking character moments with the battle raging on around them.

This battle was the biggest visual challenge for me because it is deceptively difficult from a storytelling standpoint. It's the next-to-last scene at the end of the second act and many story lines are meeting up in the midst of an action scene. We see what Valka is capable of doing as a warrior, it's Hiccup's final promise that he will confront Drago, it's Stoick trying to protect everyone from Drago, it's a big payoff to everything that has been set up previously. On top of this, there is the gigantic Bewilderbeast battle.

We had to approach this in a very different way, with the entire department working in tandem on this battle. We had to block the action scenes and create the crowd and then break it down into sections for the artists. It was a technical challenge, but for me it was the place where we completely shifted to be an extension of story for Dean.

These complex scenes are rarely done in story because too many things are happening at the same time. Often, when you are trying to tie up all these loose ends, they keep changing, even after storyboard is done with the scene. Still, we were able to incorporate all the notes and create a basic story line. In the end, this will span at least five sequences and last about 11 minutes on the screen, which is about 10 to 15 percent of the entire movie. It was a great challenge but a satisfying one.

*—Gil Zimmerman, head of layout*

# In the Red Zone

In this scene, we had to show that Drago's Bewilderbeast is controlling a dragon and forcing him to do things he'd never do on his own. The challenge wasn't so much in the acting but it was a difficult scene to stage. We needed to show that the dragon is seeing the world through a filter he can't control.

Here is a lovable character under the Bewilderbeast's control; we had to make him be threatening and scary. How do you tell the puppy to be fierce and dangerous?

*—Pierre-Olivier Vincent, production designer*

ABOVE LEFT: Rune ✦ *Kirsten Kawamura*
ABOVE RIGHT: Storyboards ✦ *Bolhem Bouchiba*
BELOW: Storyboards ✦ *Ryan Savas*
BOTTOM: Storyboards ✦ *Radford Sechrist*

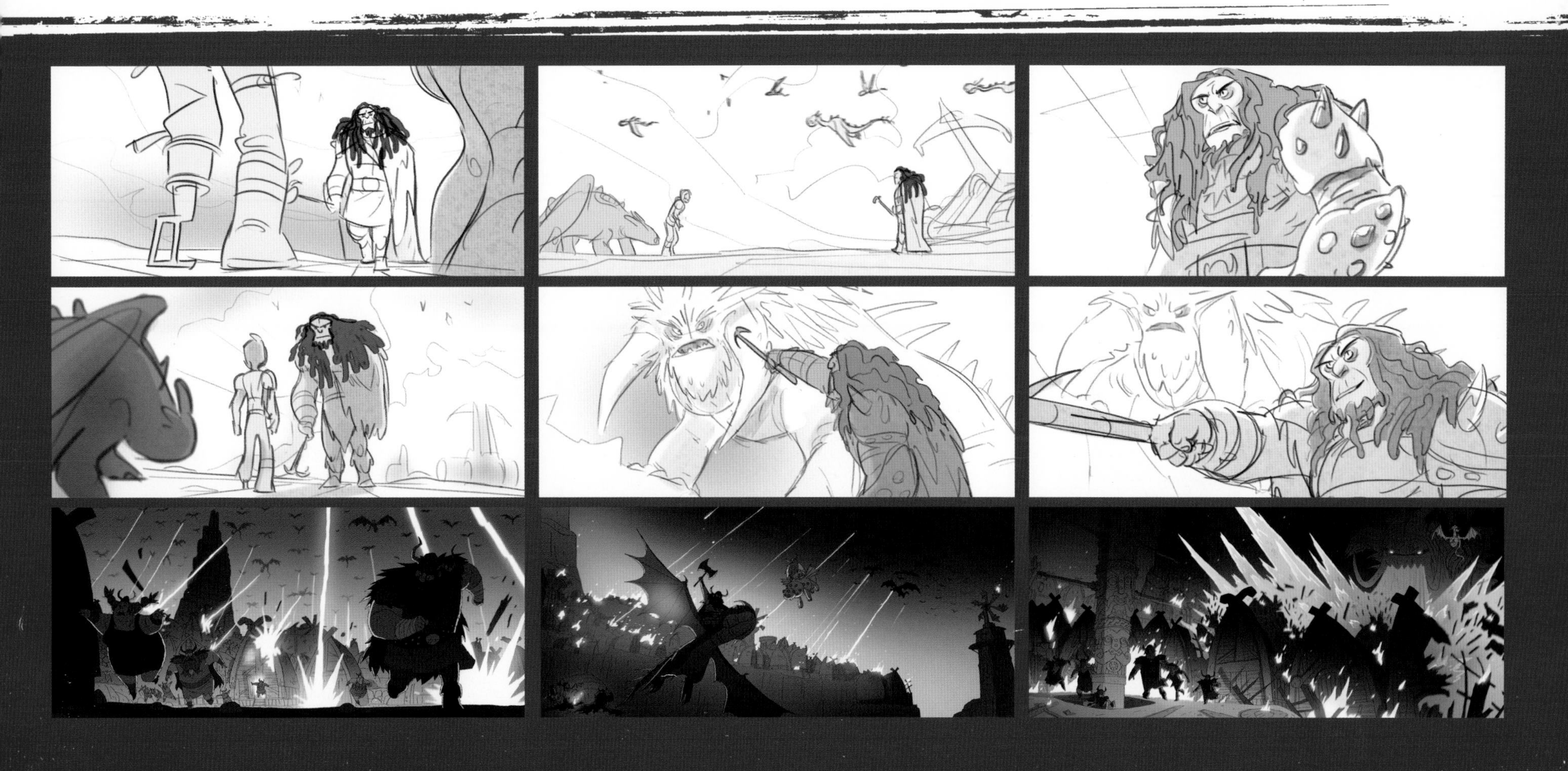

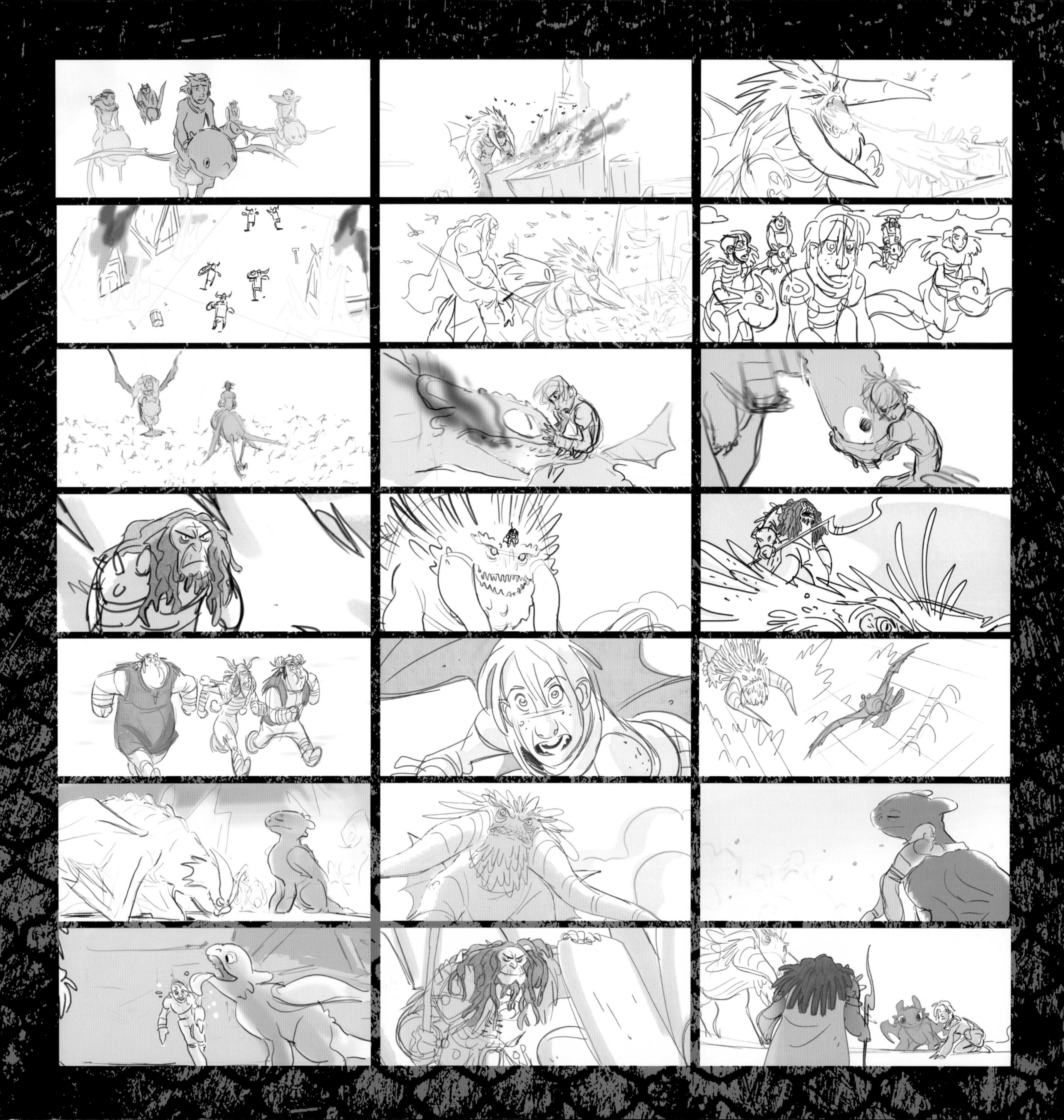

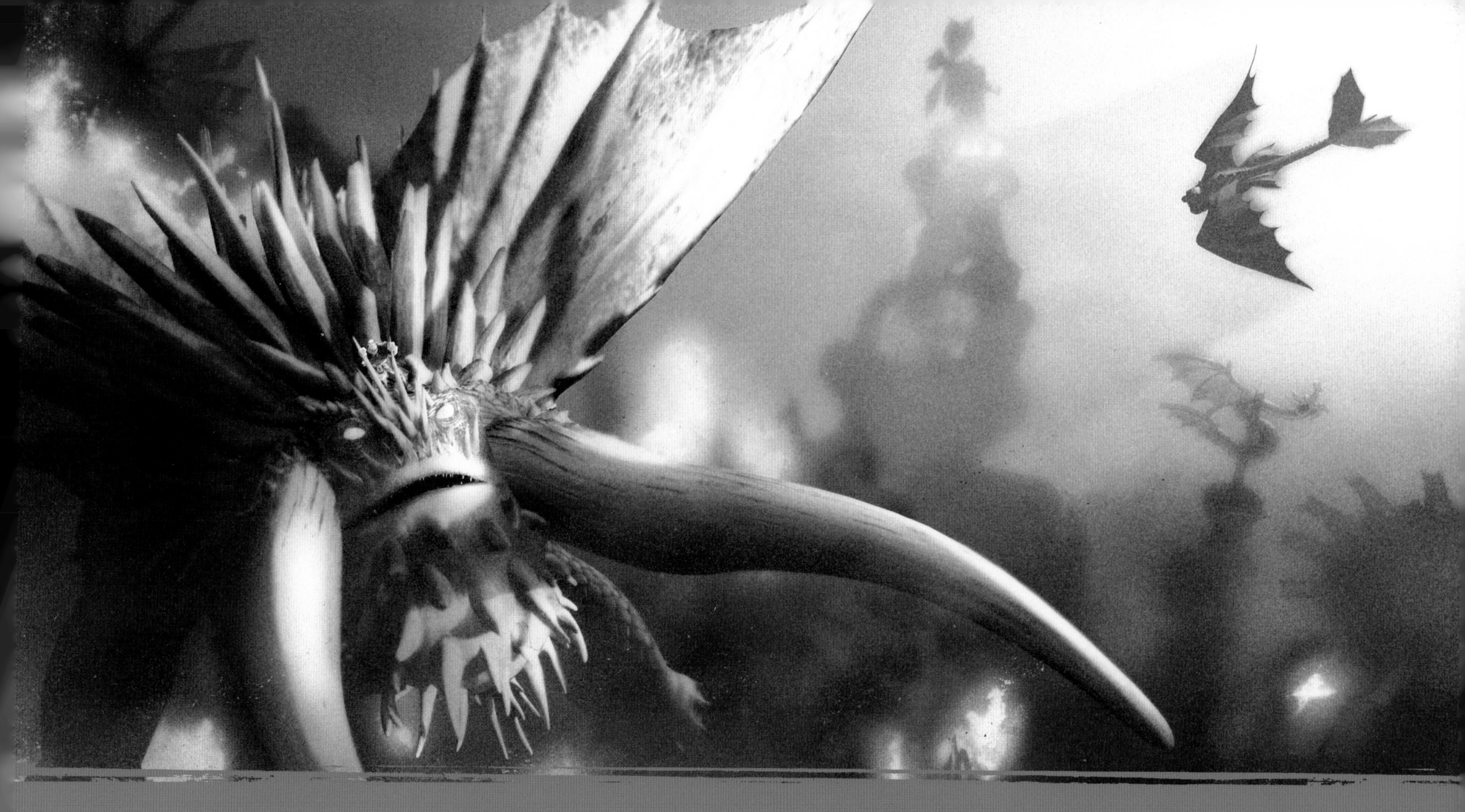

# Toothless vs. the Alpha

The core relationship of the trilogy lies in Hiccup and Toothless, but it does no good to just let them be pals without challenging their relationship. We all know story is conflict, so it was clear from the get-go that we would have to rattle their friendship to its foundation. By the end of the first movie, these former enemies had taken a chance on each other, become fast friends, and together managed to change the way dragons and Vikings get along, for good. By the time we pick up, five years later, Hiccup and Toothless are inseparable best buds and ace fliers. Their symbiotic relationship is bulletproof—or so we lead the audience to believe. To give it an emotional and satisfying arc, their relationship is put to the ultimate test, tearing them apart and turning them into enemies again. But through the power of their bond, they manage to rise above and reunite, making them stronger than ever.

*—Dean DeBlois, director*

This is an epic-scale movie, bigger than the first. There are more story lines, characters, dragons, and maybe the biggest battle scenes I've ever seen in an animated picture. While the first movie focused primarily on a boy and his dragon, the second film is a more complex story that is enriched with a cast of characters with different views of how people should cope with dragons in their daily lives.

*—John Carr, editor*

Our plan was to create and emphasize chaos. We have our traditional battle sequence, which has been done before, but here we also have the ginormous Bewilderbeasts and the ice being thrown. We have fire from the dragons, water from the ocean, and air because they are flying which creates a unique environment combining every element of nature into one big battle. We can't go any bigger because everybody and everything is thrown in there.

The challenge for the lighting department is to convey the scale and make sure all the madness is passed on but also that the key elements of the story are understood. We need to feel that Hiccup and Toothless are in this together. In the midst of all the smoke and chaos, we have to give Hiccup and Toothless a little stage to communicate and link.

*—Pablo Valle, head of lighting*

The last battle scene is really a data management problem. You've got tons of assets—8,000 guys and a hundred boats—and you have to push them all through a computer to make a picture.

*—Dave Walvoord, visual effects supervisor*

ABOVE: Toothless Fights the Bewilderbeast ✦ *Pierre-Olivier Vincent*
OPPOSITE: Storyboards ✦ *Megan Nicole Dong, John Puglisi, Ryan Savas, Tom Owens, Tron Mai, Bolhem Bouchiba, Paul Fisher*

"With Vikings on the backs of dragons, the world just got a whole lot bigger."

—Hiccup

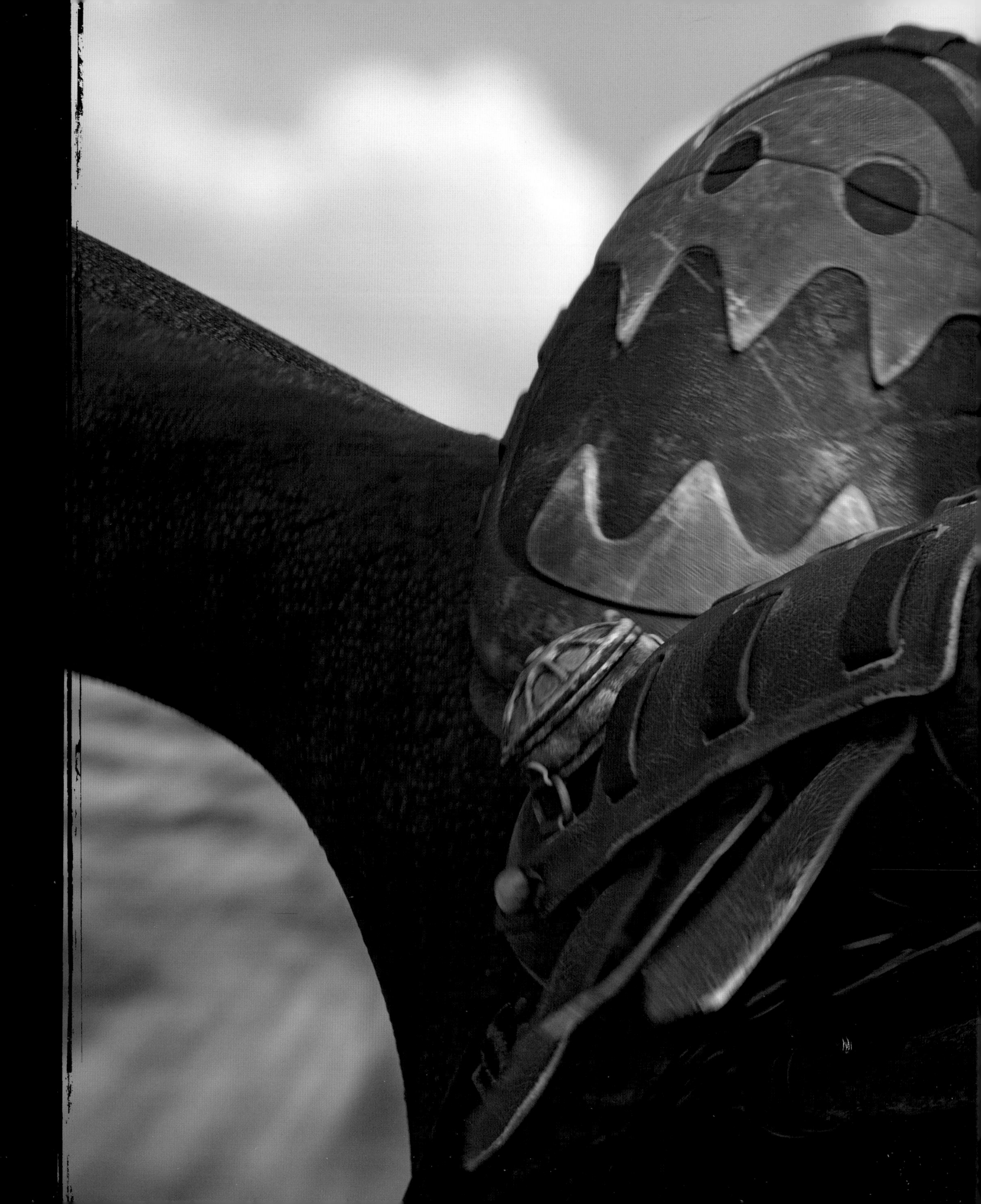

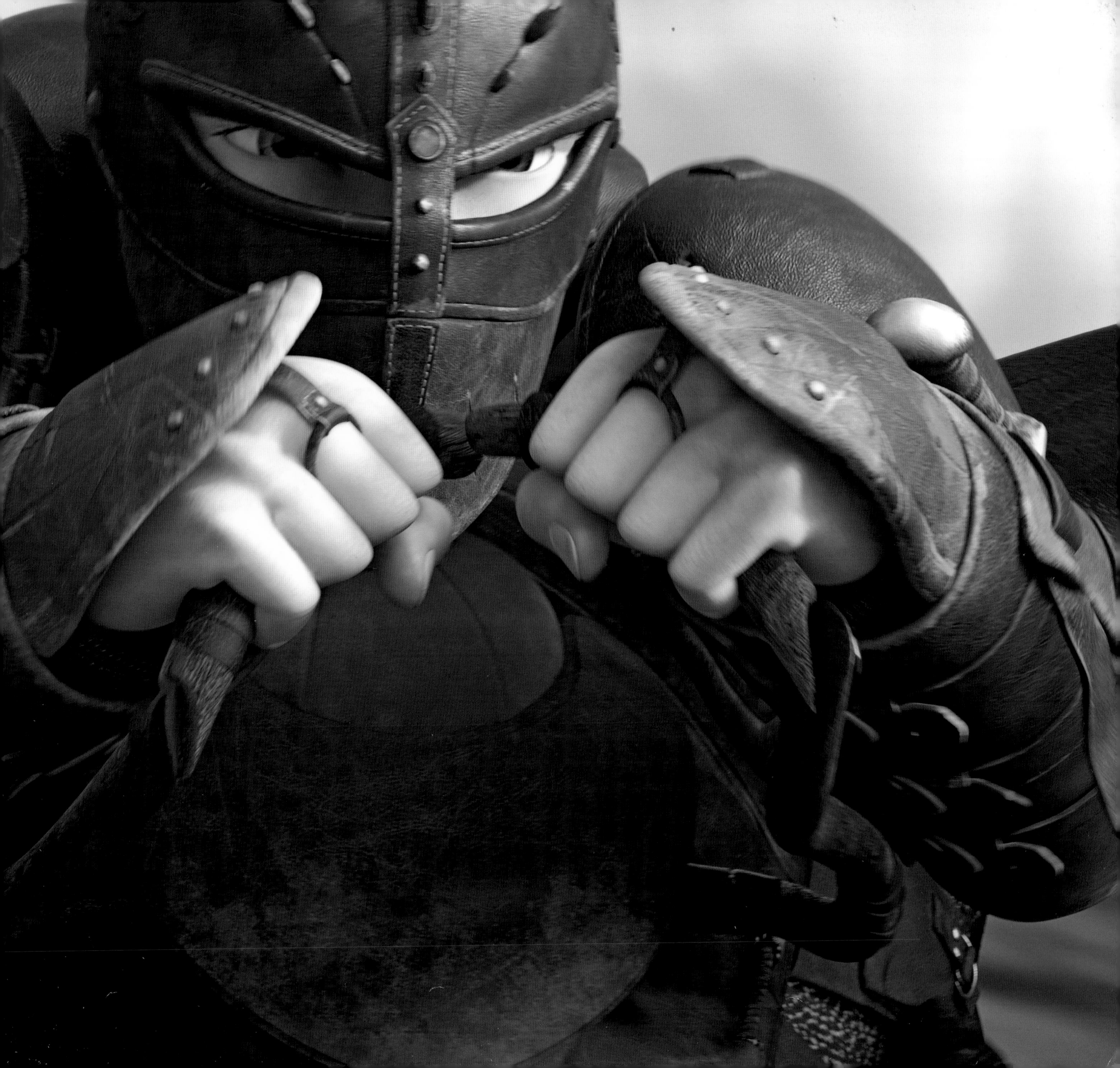

# Afterword

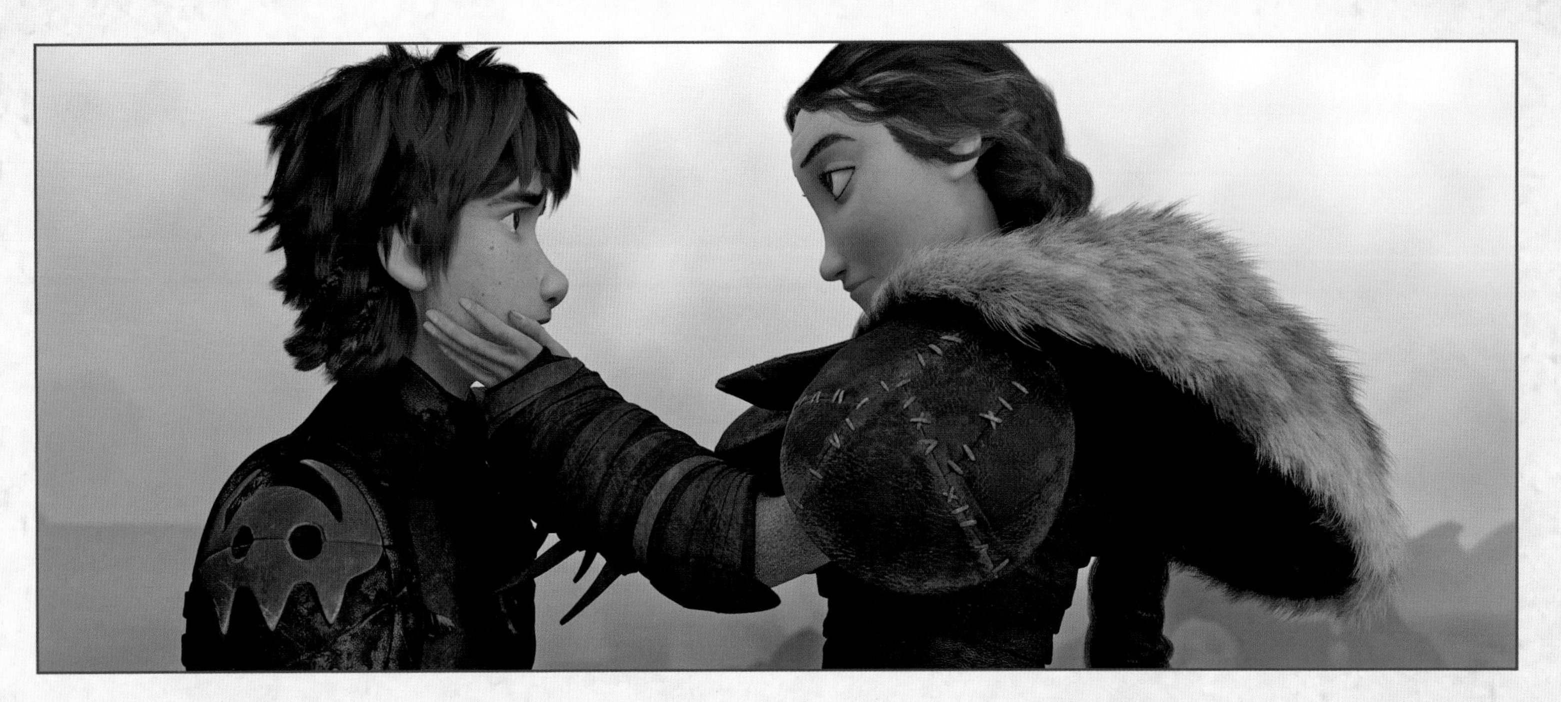

Movie making is about making magic, and perhaps this is truer for animated movies than for any other kind of film. This is an art form that begins and ends with imagination, which is why it appeals to the kind of artists whose eyes light up at the mention of Vikings and dragons.

The production of *How to Train Your Dragon 2* began in the frozen fjords of Norway where a dozen people gathered to discuss how to focus, shoot, light, and, in general, tell the story of Hiccup and Toothless. On its journey toward completion, that small team expanded and then contracted over the course of the next three years. At full production, more than 500 people worked on the film. What looks so easy and even simple on the screen is actually an extremely intense and complicated process that involves a mind-boggling amount of work.

My job was to pull together a book celebrating the art of this film and the people behind the computers and drafting boards. Along with presenting hundreds of pieces of art, Iain Morris, the book designer, and I wanted to give the reader a sense of the passion and dedication that went into making this film. The text, therefore, is presented as quotes from the principle filmmakers because their words best express how they came to create this movie. These quotes were culled from many hours of interviews, which were utterly fascinating, even when I couldn't quite keep up with the talk of geometry and algorithms. But what touched me the most was the emotion that resonated from everyone. From my first hour at the DreamWorks Animation studio in Glendale, California, I sensed that this movie was something very special and unique to this talented team. These filmmakers were so invested in their work that their eyes would tear up or they'd choke back emotion when talking about the characters. Many of them had worked on the first movie and will go on to the next installment, so by the time the third film is released, some of them will have spent a decade or more devoted to Hiccup and Toothless and all the other marvelous creations from Berk.

Ironically, most of us are barely aware of the concerns that these folks spend so much time and effort to perfect. How a frame is lit or how the camera moves from one character to another is probably not what the audience remembers. "If we do our job right, no one will notice," is a common refrain from the filmmakers.

And what a complicated job it is! Animated films are constantly changing with advances in technology and software that allow filmmakers to complete ever more sophisticated tasks and bring heightened images and action to the screen. We are heading toward a point in time when it will be difficult to distinguish between live action and 3-D animation, which means that almost anything will be possible. And with *How to Train Your Dragon 2*, it feels like we are at the apex of that place where animation feels like real life—only more exciting—because this is real life lived on the backs of flying fire-breathers.

*How to Train Your Dragon 2* is now almost completed and director Dean DeBlois is writing the screenplay for the third and final installment. There are a lot of ideas floating around the campus at DreamWorks Animation and, at this point, it is far too early to know exactly how the story of Hiccup and Toothless will pan out though we know for sure there'll be thrills, aerial spills, drama, laughs, and lots of surprises. So, along with the millions of devoted fans who made the first *How to Train Your Dragon* such a huge success—and with my Flight Suit cleaned and pressed and my Dragon Blade locked and loaded—we are eagerly waiting for the adventure to continue.

*—Linda Sunshine*

# Acknowledgments

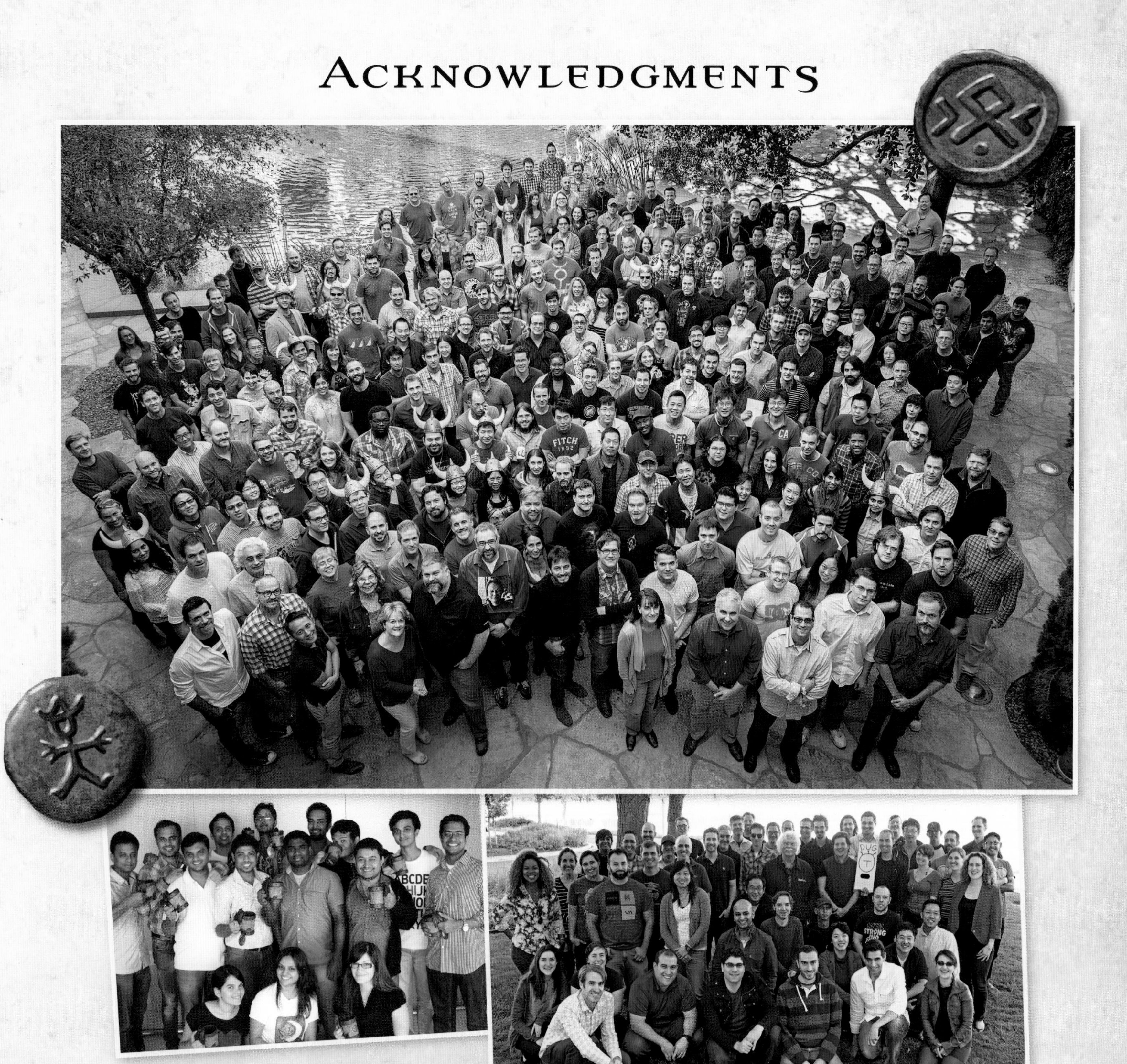

ABOVE: DreamWorks Animation India Crew ✦ *Photo by Nitin Krishan Garg*
TOP: DreamWorks Animation Glendale Crew ✦ *Photo by Michael Murphree*
RIGHT: DreamWorks Animation PDI Crew ✦ *Photo by Krzysztof Rost*
LEFT & RIGHT: Runes ✦ *Kirsten Kawamura*

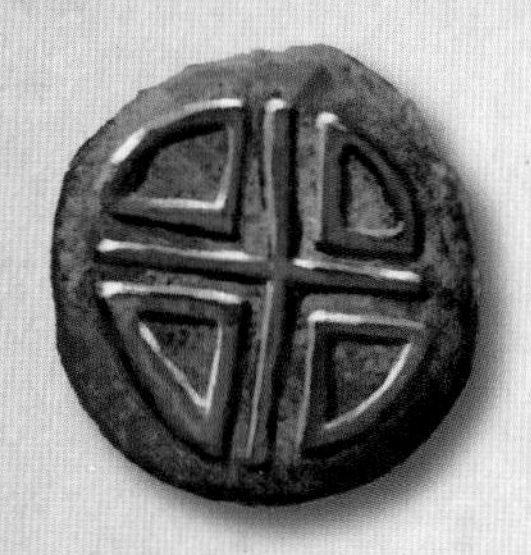

# Colophon

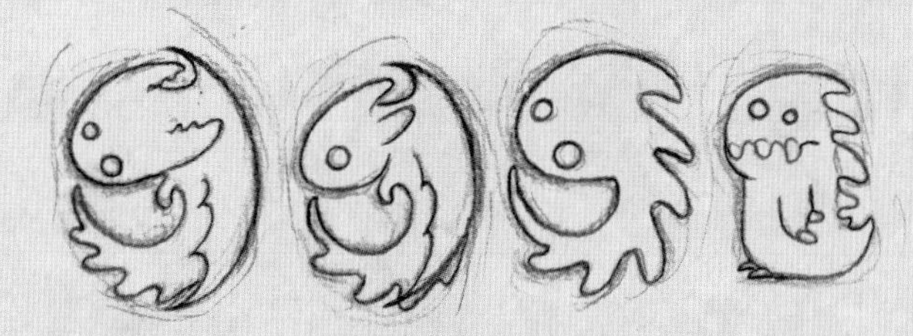

DreamWorks Animation would like to thank the following for their special contributions to the book: Pierre-Olivier Vincent, Bill Damaschke, Bonnie Arnold, Dean DeBlois, Kate Spencer Lachance, Debbie Luner, Kendra Haaland, Liz Camp, Lillian Ritchie, Jennifer Frey, Richard Hamilton, Michael Francis, Dawn Taubin, and our amazingly talented and tireless crew!

Linda Sunshine would like to thank everyone at DreamWorks Animation who were so fascinating to interview and generous with their time. Thank you Bonnie Arnold for bringing me into your amazing team and Jennifer Frey for being the most efficient person on the planet. Special thanks to Pierre-Olivier Vincent, Simon Otto, Kate Spencer Lachance, Debbie Luner, Liz Camp and Ryan Behnke for their problem-solving skills, attention to detail and helpful contributions to the making of this book. And Iain Morris, hardworking book designer extraordinaire, you rock!

On behalf of HarperCollins and Newmarket Press for It Books, executive editor Esther Margolis wishes to thank the wonderful DreamWorks Animation artists, writers, producers, and whole creative team whose work we are so pleased to celebrate in this spectacular book; Gerard Butler and Dean DeBlois for their special introductions; the super-talented book writer and designer Linda Sunshine and Iain Morris; and the many HarperCollins publishing, editorial, production, legal, and marketing colleagues whose expertise and patience helped marshal the book to the finish line and, ultimately, make it available for readers of all ages to view and read all over the world.

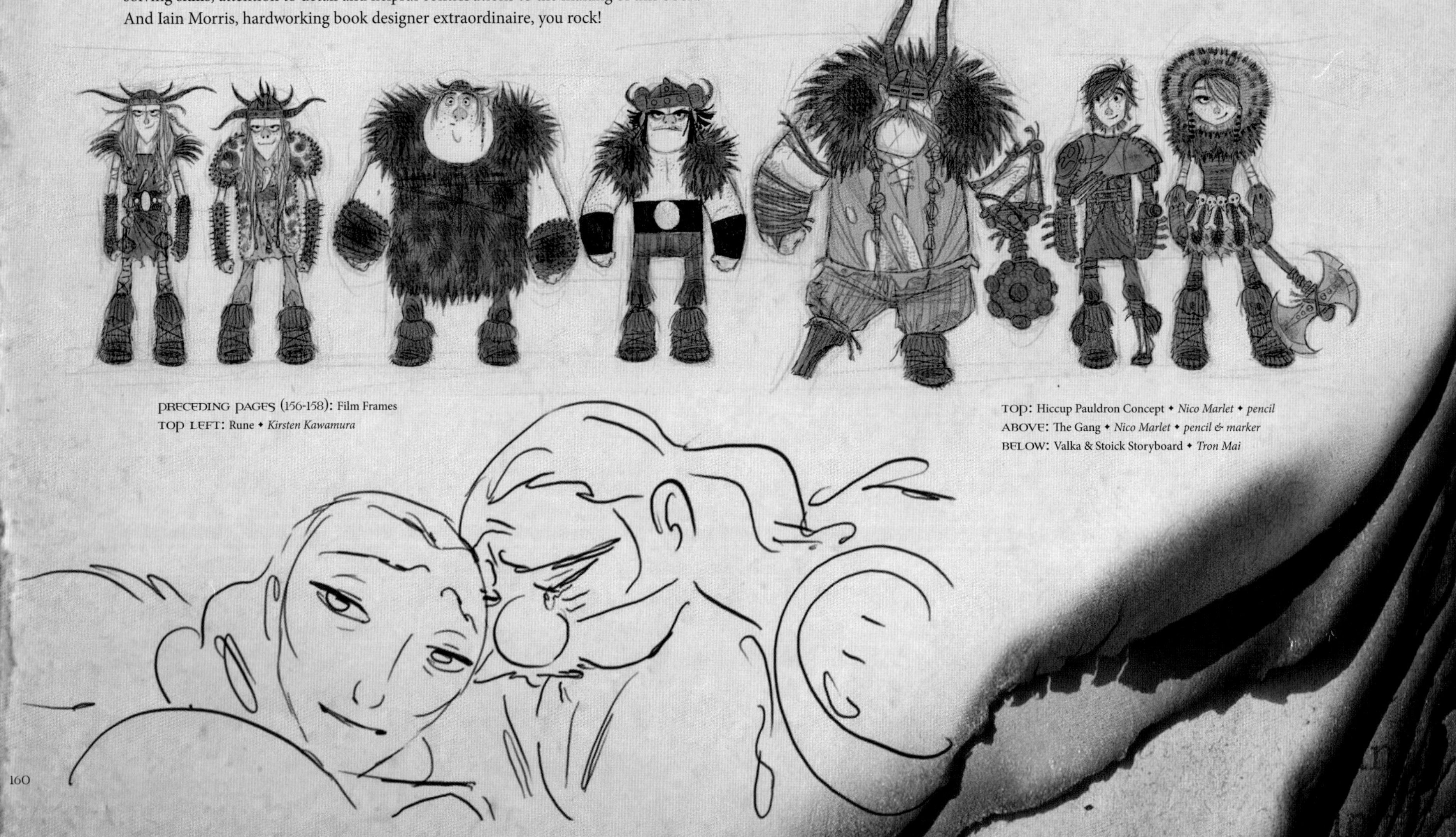

PRECEDING PAGES (156-158): Film Frames
TOP LEFT: Rune ✦ *Kirsten Kawamura*

TOP: Hiccup Pauldron Concept ✦ *Nico Marlet* ✦ *pencil*
ABOVE: The Gang ✦ *Nico Marlet* ✦ *pencil & marker*
BELOW: Valka & Stoick Storyboard ✦ *Tron Mai*